Governing, Protecting, and Regulating the Future of Genome Editing

Governing, Protecting, and Regulating the Future of Genome Editing

The Significance of ELSPI *Perspectives*

Edited by

Santa Slokenberga
Timo Minssen
Ana Nordberg

BRILL
NIJHOFF

LEIDEN | BOSTON

Originally published, in part, as Volume 29, Issue 3–5 (2022) of Brill's journal *European Journal of Health Law*.

Open Access funding supplied by the Lund University Library Book Fund.

Timo Minssen's research for this contribution was supported by a Novo Nordisk Foundation for a scientifically independent Collaborative Research Programme in Biomedical Innovation Law (Grant agreement number NNF17SA0027784).

The Library of Congress Cataloging-in-Publication Data is available online at https://catalog.loc.gov
LC record available at https://lccn.loc.gov/2022054000

Typeface for the Latin, Greek, and Cyrillic scripts: "Brill". See and download: brill.com/brill-typeface.

ISBN 978-90-04-52608-2 (paperback)
ISBN 978-90-04-52613-6 (e-book)

This book is printed on acid-free paper and produced in a sustainable manner.

Contents

PART 2
Bringing Genome Editing to the Market and Making It Available to Patients

Acknowledgements

We wish to thank Dr. Emilia Niemiec, Dr. Andelka Phillips, and Professor Jessica Almqvist for discussions on earlier drafts of the chapters at the Nordic Permed Law Symposium Genome Editing, Health innovation, and Responsible Regulation on November 3–4, 2021. Moreover, we are grateful to Dr. Emilia Niemiec for her insightful comments on the scientific aspects of genome editing.

Timo Minssen's research for this contribution was supported by a Novo Nordisk Foundation for a scientifically independent Collaborative Research Programme in Biomedical Innovation Law (Grant agreement number NNF17SA0027784).

Introduction: The Significance of ELSPI Perspectives in Governing, Protecting, and Regulating the Future of Genome Editing

Santa Slokenberga, Timo Minssen and Ana Nordberg

1 Genome Editing Technology and Its Significance

With the recent breakthroughs in genomics and advances in genome-editing techniques, most notably the discovery of the clustered regularly interspaced short palindromic repeats (CRISPR)-associated protein 9 (Cas9),[1] the matter of genome editing and health innovation has become of particular importance in society. New genome-editing techniques hold considerable potential to enhance personalized medicine and deliver cures to conditions and diseases that currently cannot be tackled. However, considerable work remains to be done in order to realize this potential.

Means to modify the human genome have been of interest to scientists for a considerable time and significant milestones were achieved during the second half of the last century.[2] Several tools have existed prior to the discovery of Cas9, such as meganucleases, zinc-finger nucleases (ZFNs), and transcription activator-like effector nucleases (TALENS).[3] Already in 2003, the first commercial gene-editing therapy – *Gendicine* – was registered in China.[4] Almost a decade later, in 2012, the first gene therapy medicinal product – *Glybera*

1 The discovery of Cas9 dates back to 2012, whereas the CRISPR system was discovered in 1987. *See* Y. Ishino and others, 'Nucleotide Sequence of the Iap Gene, Responsible for Alkaline Phosphatase Isozyme Conversion in Escherichia Coli, and Identification of the Gene Product', *Journal of bacteriology* 5429 (169) (1987) and Y. Ishino, M. Krupovic and P. Forterre, 'History of CRISPR-Cas from Encounter with a Mysterious Repeated Sequence to Genome Editing Technology', *Journal of Bacteriology* (2018). https://journals.asm.org/doi/abs/10.1128/JB.00580-17 (accessed 31 January 2022).

The bacterial CRISPR locus was first described by F.J. Mojica, G. Juez and F. Rodriguez-Valera, 'Transcription at different salinities of Haloferax mediterranei sequences adjacent to partially modified PstI sites.', *Molecular* microbiology 9 (3) (1993) 613–621.

2 T. Friedmann, 'A Brief History of Gene Therapy', *Nature Genetics* 93 (2) (1992).

3 G. Silva and others, 'Meganucleases and Other Tools for Targeted Genome Engineering: Perspectives and Challenges for Gene Therapy', *Current Gene Therapy* 11 (11) (2011).

4 S. Pearson, H. Jia and K. Kandachi, 'China Approves First Gene Therapy', *Nature Biotechnology* 3 (22) (2004).

DOI:10.1163/9789004526136_002

(alipogene tiparvovec) – was approved by the European Medicines Agency for marketing within the EU.[5]

Numerous studies are being conducted to develop novel applications and therapies, as well as to improve the techniques. Although different techniques have different strengths,[6] one of the newest additions – CRISPR[7] – has several important advantages and is therefore transforming the field. It is a relatively simple and efficient technique for site-specific gene editing and obliviates several important concerns connected to more traditional methods.[8] Strengths such as these position the technique as a paradigm shifter in the field.[9]

Despite the promising potential that genome editing holds, it also has limitations. For example, CRISPR-Cas9 and its follow-on techniques, like CRISPR-Cas12a, create safety concerns due to risks associated with off-target effects, impacting on any therapeutic and clinical applications of the technique.[10] There are different other techniques under development, with the aspiration to overcome such shortcomings as the CRISPR techniques demonstrate, such as prime editing and base editing. They too, have the challenge related to off-target effects but offer other advantages, such as facilitated alterations without the risk of breaking both DNA strands or using DNA templates.[11]

While there is hope that a newcomer in the field – Retron Library Recombineering – could overcome challenges related to off-target effects, that

5 European Medicines Agency, 2012, 'European Medicines Agency recommends first gene therapy for approval'. https://www.ema.europa.eu/en/news/european-medicines-agency-recommends-first-gene-therapy-approval (accessed 31 January 2022).

6 T. Gaj, C.A. Gersbach and C.F. Barbas, 'ZFN, TALEN and CRISPR/Cas-Based Methods for Genome Engineering', *Trends in Biotechnology* 397 (31) (2013).

7 For an overview, see K.S. Makarova and E.V. Koonin, 'Annotation and Classification of CRISPR-Cas Systems' in *Methods in Molecular Biology* (Clifton, N.J.,2015) 47–75., and for the developments see A. Pickar-Oliver and C.A. Gersbach, 'The Next Generation of CRISPR – Cas Technologies and Applications', Nature *Reviews Molecular Cell Biology* 490 (20) (2019).

8 F. Uddin, C.M. Rudin and T. Sen, 'CRISPR Gene Therapy: Applications, Limitations, and Implications for the Future', *Frontiers in Oncology* (10) (2020).

9 *Ibid.*

10 X.H. Zhang and others, 'Off-Target Effects in CRISPR/Cas9-Mediated Genome Engineering', *Molecular Therapy. Nucleic Acids* 264 (4) (2015). K. Murugan and others, 'CRISPR-Cas12a Has Widespread off-Target and DsDNA-Nicking Effects', *The Journal of Biological Chemistry* 5538 (295) (2020).

11 A.V. Anzalone, P.B. Randolph, J.R. Davis, et al. 'Search-and-replace genome editing without double-strand breaks or donor DNA', *Nature* 576, (2019), 149–157. K. Saha, E.J. Sontheimer, P.J. Brooks, et al., 'The NIH Somatic Cell Genome Editing program', *Nature* 592, (2021), 195–204.

remains to be established, along with other safety aspects.[12] Other cited limitations include a protospacer-adjacent motif requirement near the target site (which limits the regions in the genome that can be edited), as well as DNA damage toxicity and immunological response to the genome editing system.[13] Overcoming these limitations is central to ensuring precise, safe and effective genome editing and realizing the potential that the technique holds.[14] These practical limitations would suggest that genome editing is still in its infancy.[15]

2 Genome Editing, Health Innovation, and Responsible Regulation

The potential of genome editing in transforming personalized medicine is only one side of the coin. In principle, the techniques may be used to target virtually any part of the human genome, and thus their potential application is not limited to strictly health-related interventions, such as repairing, modulating, replacing, or adding gene(s) in order to prevent or cure genetic diseases. Acknowledging that there could be cases where the line between health-related and non-health-related interventions is thin, there could also be cases where concerns emerge over improving skills or performances (enhancement). Moreover, genome editing can be used on germline cells, not only somatic ones – thus, in the latter instance, irreversibly altering the genome of future descendants and raising concerns on the protection of the human genome as the common cultural heritage of humanity.[16]

The power of shaping the future of humanity that genome editing holds and the potential to do that at an unprecedented level and scale creates several considerable questions and concerns. The misuse of technology has been a significant concern in biology and medicine since the horrific Nazi experiments and equally abhorrent underlining eugenics ideology came to light. Humanity's need to ensure that such atrocities would never be possible again has informed the European legal standards in the field. Without denying the

12 Wyss institute, 2021, 'Move over CRISPR, the retrons are coming', 30 April. https://wyss.harvard.edu/news/move-over-crispr-the-retrons-are-coming/ (accessed 31 January 2022).

13 Uddin, Rudin and Sen *supra* note 8.

14 *Ibid.*

15 H. Li and others, 'Applications of Genome Editing Technology in the Targeted Therapy of Human Diseases: Mechanisms, Advances and Prospects', *Signal Transduction and Targeted Therapy* 1 (5) (2020).

16 UNESCO, 1997, 'Universal Declaration on the Human Genome and Human Rights' Art. 1, 11 November. http://portal.unesco.org/en/ev.php-URL_ID=13177&URL_DO=DO_TOPIC&URL_SECTION=201.html (accessed 31 January 2022).

need to develop solutions to effectively prevent misuse of the technology, it is now clear that a blanket ban on germline interventions as such could deprive patients and future children of a possibility to benefit from scientific advances in the field of preventive and curative medicine.

The design of the European regional legal standards pertaining to genome editing dates back to 1997, when the Council of Europe Biomedicine Convention was adopted,[17] and 2001, when the EU Clinical Trials Directive was adopted.[18] Both these dates fall before the registration of the first gene therapy medicinal product. The Biomedicine Convention prohibits deliberate heritable changes to the human genome, as well as non-health-related applications.[19] The EU clinical trials framework contains a similar norm vis-à-vis clinical trials.[20]

Since then, the European legal framework has become slightly more nuanced, covering the requirements for bringing gene therapy products on the market within the EU,[21] as well as preventing certain biotechnology applications from being patentable due to incompatibility with morality under the EU Biotechnology Directive.[22] Common to these legal frameworks is the fact that they were crafted and adopted prior to the discovery of the newcomers in the genome-editing toolbox, prior to the successful attempt to apply genome-editing techniques to human embryos in 2015,[23] and prior to the attempt to introduce heritable changes during the course of an *in vitro*

17 Council of Europe, 1997, 'The Convention for the Protection of Human Rights and Dignity of the Human Being with regard to the Application of Biology and Medicine: Convention on Human Rights and Biomedicine (ETS No 164)' Article 13, 4 April.

18 Directive 2001/20/EC of the European Parliament and of the Council of 4 April 2001 on the approximation of the laws, regulations and administrative provisions of the Member States relating to the implementation of good clinical practice in the conduct of clinical trials on medicinal products for human use, OJ L 121, 1.5.2001, p. 34–44, Article 9.6.

19 Article 13, Biomedicine Convention *supra* note 17.

20 Regulation (EU) No 536/2014 of the European Parliament and of the Council of 16 April 2014 on clinical trials on medicinal products for human use, and repealing Directive 2001/20/EC Text with EEA relevance OJ L 158, 27.5.2014, p. 1–76, Article 90.

21 Advanced therapy medicinal products merited a special legal framework in 2007, Regulation (EC) No 1394/2007 of the European Parliament and of the Council of 13 November 2007 on advanced therapy medicinal products and amending Directive 2001/83/EC and Regulation (EC) No 726/2004 (Text with EEA relevance) OJ L 324, 10.12.2007, p. 121–137.

22 Directive 98/44/EC of the European Parliament and of the Council of 6 July 1998 on the legal protection of biotechnological inventions OJ L 213, 30.7.1998, p. 13–21, Article 6.2.b.

23 P. Liang and others, 'CRISPR/Cas9-Mediated Gene Editing in Human Tripronuclear Zygotes' *Protein & Cell* 363 (6) (2015).

fertilization procedure in 2018.[24] Thus, the European legal responses were largely shaped for the future, against the background of a picture, painted in broad strokes, of what potential the technology held, the challenges it might bring, and how they should be balanced against each other.

Already in 1998, soon after the Biomedicine Convention was adopted, some critical remarks were made on the limitations to scientific advances that Article 13 prescribed. For example, Abbing noted that "[i]n as far as this [Article 13] is inspired by moral conservatism only, it stands in the way of an appropriate dynamic approach to human rights and health."[25] Since then, the criticism has been piling up. Some have called for removing obstacles to realize the full potential that the technology offers, arguing that harms could be tackled through remedies to victims of violations in specific cases.[26] Others have suggested such an approach would be morally reckless, calling for the establishment of clear avenues for further work from ethical, legal, social, and technical perspectives to prepare foundations for revisiting the current regulatory approach.[27]

Recent advances and occurrences have triggered intense debates on interventions in the human genome among scientists, lawmakers, and policymakers at multiple levels. To illustrate, the American National Academy of Sciences, the American National Academy of Medicine, the Chinese Academy of Sciences, and the Royal Society of the UK organized an International Summit in Washington, D.C. in December 2015. They released an International Summit Statement emphasizing that "it would be irresponsible to proceed with any clinical use of germline editing unless and until (i) the relevant safety and efficacy issues have been resolved, based on appropriate understanding and balancing of risks, potential benefits, and alternatives, and (ii) there is broad

24 S. Krimsky, 'Ten ways in which He Jiankui violated ethics', *Nature Biotechnol* 37 (2019). 19–20.

25 H. DC Roscam Abbing, 'The Convention on Human Rights and Biomedicine: An Appraisal of the Council of Europe Convention', *European Journal of Health Law* 377 (5) (1998).

26 A. Boggio and C. PR Romano, 'Freedom of Research and the Right to Science: From Theory to Advocacy' in S. Giordano, J. Harris and L. Piccirillo (eds), *The Freedom of Scientific Research: Bridging the Gap between Science and Society* (Manchester University Press 2018).

27 In regard to the Swedish national context, see S. Slokenberga and H.C. Howard, 'The Right to Science and Human Germline Gene Editing. Sweden, Its External Commitments and the Ambiguous National Responses under the Genetic Integrity Act', *Förvaltningsrättslig Tidskrift* 199 (2) (2019).

societal consensus about the appropriateness of the proposed application."[28] Similarly, in 2018, the International Bioethics Committee under the Universal Declaration on the Human Genome and Human Rights (1997) called for a "moratorium on genome engineering of the human germline, at least as long as the safety and efficacy of the procedures are not adequately proven as treatments."[29]

In 2021, the WHO issued Recommendations on Human Genome Editing for the Advancement of Public Health (2021) with the aspiration to set global standards for governance and oversight of human genome editing,[30] as well as recommendations on the issues related to genome editing.[31] Both these documents provide advice and recommendations on governance mechanisms for human genome editing at various regulatory levels.[32] The matter has also received attention from the Council of Europe and the EU, triggering a report on the Ethics of Human Genome Editing in 2021.[33] It has been on the agenda since at least 2015, but only modest action has followed thus far. In 2015, the HD BIO stated that it "agrees, as part of its mandate, to examine the ethical and legal challenges raised by these emerging genome editing technologies, in the light of the principles laid down in the Oviedo Convention."[34] In 2018, it emphasized that "ethics and human rights must guide any use of genome

28 The National Academies of Sciences, Engineering, and Medicine, 2015, 'On Human Gene Editing: International Summit Statement', 3 December. https://www.nationalacademies.org/news/2015/12/on-human-gene-editing-international-summit-statement (accessed 31 January 2022).

29 UNESCO, 2015, 'Report of the IBC on updating its reflection on the Human Genome and Human Rights', 2 October. https://unesdoc.unesco.org/ark:/48223/pf0000233258 p. 3 (accessed 31 January 2022).

30 World Health Organization, 2021, 'Human genome editing: recommendations', 12 July. https://www.who.int/publications/i/item/9789240030381 (accessed 31 January 2022).

31 *Ibid.*

32 A summary is available in the position paper, World Health Organization, 2021, 'Human genome editing: position paper, 12 July. https://www.who.int/publications/i/item/9789240030404 (accessed 31 January 2022).

33 European Group on Ethics in Science and New Technologies', 2021, 'Ethics of Genome Editing', March. https://ec.europa.eu/info/sites/default/files/research_and_innovation/ege/ege_ethics_of_genome_editing-opinion_publication.pdf (accessed 31 January 2022).

34 "Ethics and Human Rights must guide any use of genome editing technologies in human beings," Statement by the Council of Europe Committee on Bioethics. https://www.coe.int/en/web/bioethics/-/genome-editing-technologies-final-conclusions-of-the-re-examination-of-article-13-of-the-oviedo-convention (accessed 13 November 2022). See also Steering Committee for Human Rights in the fields of Biomedicine and Health (CDBIO), Intervention on the human genome, Re-examination process of Article 13 of the Oviedo Convention, Conclusions and Clarifications. https://rm.coe.int/cdbio-2022-7-final-clarifications-er-art-13-e-2777-5174-4006-1/1680a87953 (accessed 13 November 2022).

editing technologies in human beings,"[35] and included in its action plan for 2020–2025 the ambition to either clarify or revise the Biomedicine Convention. In 2021, a communiqué was released noting that some clarifications are to be expected, but no revision of the Biomedicine Convention is currently on the agenda of the HD BIO.[36]

3 Genome Editing a Stress Test for Biomedical Regulation

It is clear that the advances and the potential that genome-editing techniques holds for a myriad of possible applications present a stress test to the existing legal frameworks, going beyond the question of germline interventions. They require scrutiny and revisiting of the foundations that the current legal frameworks rest upon and possible ways forward, accounting for not only the legal concerns, but also the ethical, social and policy concerns that emerge. In tackling the multi-faceted problems related to human genome editing, the human rights pillars that the European legal frameworks in biomedicine and governance of medicinal products rest upon are of importance, as are market-related and property rights-related aspects. Several scholars have highlighted the rapidly developing intellectual property (IP) landscape, and the significant role that not only the IP and patent systems, but also competition law, may play for the governance of genome editing.[37] These legal areas play a central role not only in promoting research and development, but also in in enabling and governing the realization of rights such as the availability and accessibility of gene editing therapies in healthcare.[38]

---

35 Statement by the Council of Europe Committee on Bioethics, *Ethics and Human Rights must guide any use of genome editing technologies in human beings*, available online at https://www.coe.int/en/web/portal/-/-ethics-and-human-rights-must-guide-any-use-of-genome-editing-technologies-in-human-beings (accessed 31 January 2022).

36 Genome editing technologies: some clarifications but no revision of the Oviedo Convention. https://www.coe.int/en/web/bioethics/-/genome-editing-technologies-some-clarifications-but-no-revision-of-the-provisions-of-the-oviedo-convention (accessed 19 March 2022).

37 S. Parthasarathy, 'Use the Patent System to Regulate Gene Editing', Nature 486 (562) (2018); A. Shukla-Jones, S. Friedrichs and D.E. Winickoff, 'Gene Editing in an International Context: Scientific, Economic and Social Issues across Sectors', *OECD Science, Technology and Industry Working Papers* (2018).

38 Cf. Matthews, Duncan and Brown, Abbe and Gambini, Emanuela and Minssen, Timo and Nordberg, Ana and Sherkow, Jacob S. and Wested, Jakob and van Zimmeren, Esther and McMahon, Aisling, The Role of Patents and Licensing in the Governance of Human Genome Editing: A White Paper (July 30, 2021). Queen Mary Law Research Paper No. 364/2021, Available at SSRN: https://ssrn.com/abstract=3896308.

On 3–4 November 2021, the Nordic Permed Law network held a symposium on "Genome Editing, Health innovation, and Responsible Regulation", speakers, respondents and participants gathered to examine in greater detail the regulation of health innovation in the area of genome editing, illustrate the challenges and illuminate the possible policy avenues forward. This edited collection of contributions, that initially was a special issue of European Journal of Health law, is prepared in connection to the Symposium and with the extensive support of the journal's team, in particular, Professor Emeritus of Health Law, KU Leuven Herman Nys, journal's editor-in-chief. The goal of this issue is to shed light on the evolving debates, with a specific focus on interdisciplinary and legal perspectives and with a keen eye on elucidating the challenges of and opportunities for appropriate technology governance.

4 On the Structure of the Book

Key questions that shape this contribution are how the scientific advances challenge the existing legal solutions and values underpinning them, and how the law could and should respond to genome editing and health innovation in order to adequately reconcile the different competing interests at stake and enhance personalized medicine.

Contributions are organized in two parts. Part I explores general ethical, legal, social and policy implications of genome editing technologies. Part II continues this analysis now focusing on bringing genome editing to the market and making it available to patients and addressing genome editing technology regulation through procedures for regulatory approval, patent law and competition law.

4.1 *Part I: A Roadmap of ELSPI Perspectives*

Judit Sándor, with the contribution "Genome editing: Learning from its past and envisioning its future" offers a sophisticated scholarly insight into the fundamental milestones that are of key importance to the present technology and applications in the field of genome editing, with a particular focus on ethical and legal distinctions between somatic and germline interventions. Sándor examines ethical violations, such as the case of Dr. He Jankui, and describes the profound legal and ethical questions that such interventions raise and challenges to the fundamental concepts of medical law ethics and law and the existing legal frameworks in the field. Sándor highlights the need to "learn from the past episodes of eugenics and the instances of fraud and failure that have been the result of merciless scientific competition, unfettered commercial interest, or simply individual pride" and underscores human rights lawyers' responsibility to engage in discussions regarding the societal concerns that biotechnology creates.

New genome-editing techniques, such as CRISPR, can be of tremendous value for advancing and transforming medical care. Anne Kjersti Befring, in her contribution "Transformation of medical care through gene therapy and human rights to life and health – Balancing risks and benefits," examines how the right to health and life could shape regulations relating to access to gene therapy. Befring alerts readers to the need for common standards in international regulations, cooperation between countries and between public health services and commercial entities, in order to continue scientific development in the field and ensure fair access to therapies.

Artificial intelligence has been presented as a powerful tool in the field of genome therapy. While these two fields have several commonalities, such as their cutting-edge nature and capacity to transform society, they trigger different legal frameworks that are not sufficiently linked for regulating use of the technologies together. Anastasiya Kiseleva, in "Somatic genome editing with the use of AI: Big promises but doubled legal issues," examines the legal issues related to the use of AI in somatic genome editing and suggests some possible solutions. Kiseleva sheds light on the requirements and interplay of these frameworks, and argues that management of common risks is only possible through common procedures. Concrete measures need to be taken in order for effective procedures to be established.

Genome editing can be perceived not only as a tool to further the right to health and life, but also as a means that contributes to the realization of the right to habilitation under Article 26 of the Convention of the Rights of Persons with Disabilities. Pin Lean Lau, in "Addressing cognitive vulnerabilities through genome & epigenome editing: Techno-legal adaptations for persons with intellectual disabilities" examines how persons with disabilities may access the benefits that genome editing may offer, without compromising other rights and principles. Lau argues for the need for a paradigm shift in disability studies discourse, so that persons with disabilities are not excluded from the scientific advances that genome editing technology could offer.

Human rights have played a tremendous role in shaping the regulation of new health technologies.[39] In European legal fora, the interpretations provided by the European Court of Human Rights, which shape national laws and practices, have been of particular importance. Human germline genome editing is not an exception. While the Court has not had a chance to adjudicate on the question of genome editing yet, when the occasion comes, the point

39 See M.L. Flear and others (eds), *European Law and New Health Technologies* (Oxford University Press 2013).

of departure will be the ECHR, the European human rights catalogue – and the interpretation of these norms given by the Court on different occasions. Merel M. Spaander, in her contribution "The European Court of Human Rights and the emergence of human germline genome editing – 'The right to life' and 'The right to (artificial) procreation'," examines how the existing human rights interpretations could shape legal responses to human germline gene editing. Spaander shows that there is a tendency for the Court to extend the reproductive rights involving various reproductive technologies, but at the same time leave scope for member states to prescribe limitations. While germline gene editing could logically fall within the scope of protection of private life, the Court's openness to granting a wide margin of appreciation on matters pertaining to human dignity could be debated.

Currently, the European legal fora in the area of human germline gene editing are characterized by bans set forth in regional and national legal instruments. The creation of a possibility to enhance the reproductive rights of persons suffering from some genetic conditions would argue for removing the bans. Consequently, under this argument, the permissible applications would be rather limited. This has led to some questioning on whether limited application justifies the investment of public resources in order that the technology can be developed. Noemi Conditi agrees that when safety is no longer a concern, regulation may become a necessity. In her contribution "Regulating heritable human genome editing: Drawing the line between legitimate and controversial use," Conditi argues for introduction of a new threshold – accessibility to germline gene-editing technology for genetic conditions for which preimplantation genetic diagnosis is available. This threshold, in the author's opinion, avoids the controversies surrounding the concepts of health and disease and offers a possibility to shape harmonious national frameworks on technology governance.

4.2 *Part 2: Bringing Genome Editing to the Market and Making It Available to Patients*

The EU regulation on advanced therapy medicinal products is a key legal act shaping the detailed requirements for bringing gene therapy products to the market. However, under certain circumstances, gene therapy interventions can be lawfully applied in healthcare without having received the necessary approvals. Vera Lúcia Raposo in "A room with a view (and with a gene therapy drug): Gene therapy medicinal products and genetic tourism in Europe" examines the existing flexibilities for early access to medicinal products in the EU legal framework, and points at legal weaknesses in these mechanisms that risk compromising patient safety. Thus, Raposo indicates a need for better information management and controls, as means to enable responsible governance of the early use of somatic gene therapy for patients in need.

An additional challenge is that the regulatory framework in EU member states is fragmented between norms of international law, secondary EU law, and national legislation. Focusing on the "precautionary principle," which has often provided the basis for legislation, the contribution by Michal Koščík and Eliška Vladíková explores this challenge and analyzes the "The object-based and process-based regulation of genome editing." The authors ask "whether the wider regulatory framework applicable to the member states of the EU contains suitable tools to react to the rapid advances in science, especially as to the question of germline editing technologies." They arrive at the conclusion "that the EU framework for advanced treatments and medicinal products is in a state where it can, in principle, address the questions associated with the safety and efficacy of germline editing technologies." However, the authors also argue that the expanding knowledge in the field creates the need to replace current regulations, which are based on the lack of knowledge (such as precautionary moratoria), with regulations that are based on actual knowledge (such as risk-based regulation).

Eventually, when germline gene editing is considered relatively safe (shows a positive risk-benefit ratio), safety-related concerns will cease to function as arguments to uphold bans. Morality-based arguments will remain, which would allow countries and regional legal orders freedom in rethinking the bans. Putting aside the difficult question of whether to allow human germline gene editing, Santa Slokenberga, in her contribution "What would it take to enable germline editing in Europe for medical purposes?," examines the possibility of lifting the two bans shaping the European legal environment. Slokenberga argues that while neither ban is set in stone, a considerable level of agreement between stakeholders representing diverse groups will be needed. Moreover, she shows that willingness *per se* will not be sufficient; the substantive preconditions prescribed by each of the respective legal orders will need to be satisfied. This points at the need for a more sophisticated legal debate, focusing on key principles underpinning existing legal frameworks and shaping the practice of medicine.

Lastly, the full realization of the benefits that human genome editing technology promises society also requires that rules that directly or indirectly regulate the ownership and dissemination of the technology are adequate to promote its further innovation, development, and dissemination. In particular, patent law plays an important role, by balancing the rewards granted to those who have researched and developed key patent-protected human genome editing technology against the interest of securing access to the technology for those who may engage in further research and follow-on innovation. Rules regarding, e.g., research exemptions to the exclusivity of patent rights are crucial in protecting further research and development, while such exemptions cannot be made so broad as to discourage investments into pioneer technology and to encourage free-riding upon other market actors' investments into innovation.

Oliver Feeney, contributes to this discussion with a legal sociological perspective in "Genetics and Justice, Non-ideal theory and the role of Patents: the case of CRISPR-Cas9". The starting point of this piece is that there are ongoing concerns of social justice regarding inequalities in the distribution of access to potential genome editing technologies, and the prior work by Colin Farrelly within non-ideal theory, which advances a justification for the use of patents to speed up the arrival of safe and effective interventions for all, including the socially disadvantaged. Feeney argues that such success is less assured when one considers the actual functioning of patents and the practical implications of the patent system in the context of biotechnological innovations. Arguing also that non-ideal theoretical approaches risk reverting back to a form of ideal theory if they simply refer to such real-world constraints – e.g. patents – but do not critically assess and fully examine how such constraints manifest themselves in practice. The author highlights important considerations to develop and foster a more robust non-ideal approach to justice in biotechnological developments.

Continuing the discussion on Patents rights, Duncan Matthews, Timo Minssen and Ana Nordberg analyse the role that 'ordre public' and morality exceptions can play in the granting of patents on inventions in the field of human germline editing and the consequences of such policy option. This piece offers a contextual overview of the current patent landscape and related patent disputes and, proceeds with a brief analysis of 'ordre public' and morality exceptions under patent law in international, national and regional law, and their implications for innovation and access to novel treatments. The authors argue that patent exceptions should not be used as a blunt policy instrument, nor interpreted in a way that is contrary to the patent system's overall objectives. Consequentially, in the context of human germline editing, 'ordre public' and morality based exceptions should be interpreted and applied in a way which allows balancing providing incentive to health innovation with the protection of societal higher normative values. The authors further emphasise the need to base regulatory decisions on a sound understanding of both the underlying science as well as the broader ethical, social and legal implications. Thinking about the future, the authors propose and outline further analysis and debate as to the role that such patent law can play in the context of genome editing technologies.

Dissemination of human genome editing technology is also essential in order for the technology to be developed into commercial applications that will reach and benefit end consumers, such as specific disease treatments. In this endeavor, collaborations between the technology holder and other market actors are crucial. In this context, competition law may limit the methods for collaboration, as certain types of collaborations which involve the licensing of patent rights may restrict competition. Vladimir Bastidas Venegas argues, in his contribution "The application of EU competition law to the exploitation of human genome editing technology," that there are a number of uncertainties in the competition law regime regarding the assessment of patent pools as well as surrogate, exclusive, and ethical licensing arrangements, which are important methods for disseminating key technologies in the sector. Such uncertainties may have the effect of discouraging market actors from applying methods of collaboration that may be illegal under competition law, while promoting other types of collaborations that are less adapted to the needs of technology holders and potential users. All in all, this may have a negative effect on the dissemination of human genome editing technology. While competition law has the important role to protect a minimum level of competition in innovation and in markets for the commercial application of human genome editing technology, there is also a risk that the obstruction of effective dissemination may reduce or delay some of the benefits to society provided by this cutting-edge technology.

Combined, the contributions of this volume demonstrate how genome editing technologies bring along both, challenges and opportunities that are unique and exclusive to these technologies, as well as general implications also observed and attributable to many of the advances in the field of biomedicine. The former category captures the unprecedented power to impact the genetic makeup of individuals and the heritage of humanity. The latter category captures the indicated balance between potential benefits of the technology, possible solutions to humanities greater challenges coupled with the risks associated with dual-use and harm, equitable access to the scientific advances and their applications, as well as group empowerment and geopolitical power imbalances. Scientific advances in biomedicine have also more generally in common that they are impacted by the vagueness of the existing legal norms and regulatory approaches, a difficult to navigate multilayered and intersecting applicable legal frameworks, as well as frail enforcement mechanisms. This makes it often also a delicate task to reconcile the applicable rules when different technologies interact.

Responding to genome editing and health innovation, by developing or refining legal frameworks that support beneficial uses, manage risks and prevent misuses, is not a straightforward task. The patchwork of interacting legal frameworks and competencies of different lawmaking actors, adjudicators and enforcing entities, plays a significant role also here. While some challenges can be caught through the existing legal mechanisms, responses to other challenges may involve a more significant regulatory change. The same can be said to the tremendous opportunities provided by the technology, these can to some extent be nurtured by existing legal mechanisms and structures, but more needs to be done to carefully ensure that these are steered in the most fruitful direction.

PART 1

A Roadmap of ELSPI *Perspectives*

Genome Editing: Learning from Its Past and Envisioning Its Future

Judit Sandor | ORCID: 0000-0003-0134-4414
Department of Legal Studies and Political Science, Central European University, Quellenstrasse 51, 1100 Vienna, Austria
sandorj@ceu.edu

Abstract

With the technical possibility of genome editing, we have reached a new phase of transforming human beings and even altering our genetic legacy. Genome editing constitutes new responsibilities in many fields. Science and society have never been as dependent on each other as they are today. We must also learn from the past episodes of eugenics and we need to investigate fraudulent practices and cases of failure in scientific research that have often occurred due to merciless scientific competition, profit-seeking commercial interests, or individual pride. Genome editing raises numerous legal questions, such as: Would it be possible to make a legal difference between specific versions of gene editing? Who decides on what is considered a disease or an anomaly, a condition, or a variation? Which diseases are worth being corrected or treated and which ones are not? What kinds of social implications will gene editing bring about when it becomes widely available? Some normative distinctions have already been made in the case of gene therapy: separating somatic from germline interventions. But this distinction has not yet been analyzed in the light of the most recent editing practices. Genome editing also realigns the structure of ethical debates. It makes us rethink the concept of discrimination and scrutinize its cases in the field of assisted reproductive procedures. It revolutionizes the concept of medical treatment. It may increase or reduce inequalities based on health conditions. It may lead to numerous new rights in the field of genetics. Good genome editing practice can only be achieved through the close cooperation between the natural and social sciences. The present paper will endeavor to examine this new form of dialogue.

Keywords

genome editing – eugenics – research ethics – governance – genetic interventions

 | DOI:10.1163/9789004526136_003

1 Introduction: What Can We Learn from the Past?

The first draft sequence of the human genome was reported 20 years ago in the scientific journals *Nature*[1] and *Science*.[2] Back then, in 2001, the 21st century was already being heralded by many, optimistically, as the century of biology. Nevertheless, unlocking the secrets of the human genome has brought not only scientific success but also numerous ethical issues. In other words we reached a new phase of the textuality of genetics, as we use letters to describe gene sequences, and scientists refer to the codes obtained this way and eventual mutations using letter codes. This marks the beginning of genetic literacy as well.

In ethics debate on genetic interventions, reference to *eugenics* still play a crucial role even though this term has been used in many different contexts. The term *eugenics* was used by Francis Galton as early as in 1883.[3] It has gained several connotations over time and has been misused in ways that led to great human tragedies, but it was also seen by many as a progressive approach. Since the beginning of the 20th century, though in different waves, sometimes wandering astray and with numerous detours, human genetics has been growing vigorously and, thanks to the Human Genome Project, it has influenced almost all areas of medicine.

In human imagination, fantasy and literature, artworks related to this topic, and which still shape our thinking, had appeared long before modern genetics started to flourish. The first example to mention can be Mary Shelley's *Frankenstein*, written in 1818, which still serves as a reference in ethical debates. Since then, all irresponsible experiments on human subjects have been associated with the term 'Frankensteinian'.

Huxley's *Brave New World*, his modern classic that has been translated into many languages, was published in 1932. The list may be continued with the "Geneticists' Manifesto," an influential proclamation written in 1939.[4] Eugenics, experiencing a revival before the war, covered almost all areas of life, including psychiatry, child education, reproduction, sterilization and selective

1 International Human Genome Consortium, 'Initial Sequencing and Analysis of the Human Genome', *Nature* 409 (6822) (2001) 860–921.

2 C.J. Venter, M.D. Adams, E.W. Myers, P.W. Li, R.J. Mural, G.G. Sutton, H.O. Smith, M. Yandell, C.A. Evans, R.A. Holt, et al., 'The Sequence of the Human Genome', *Science* 291 (5507) (2001) 1304–1351.

3 N.W. Gillham, 'Sir Francis Galton and the Birth of Eugenics', *Annual Review of Genetics* 35 (2001) 83–101.

4 L. Darwin, The Geneticist's Manifesto, *The Eugenics Review* 31 (4) (1940) 229–230, available online at https://www.ncbi.nlm.nih.gov/pmc/articles/PMC2962351/pdf/eugenrev00238-0033.pdf (accessed 30 March 2021).

murder of people under the name of euthanasia. Selective murder and interventions committed in the name of eugenics cast dark shadows over genetics and still urge caution. However, the discovery of the double-helix structure of DNA by James Watson, Francis Crick and Rosalind Franklin in 1953 brought new momentum to the development of genetics.

Gene editing and embryo research would have not been possible without the development of the in vitro fertilization. Louise Brown in 1978,[5] the first human to have been born after conception by in vitro fertilization and embryo implantation. Following the first in vitro interventions, the Human Genome Project[6] and the first cloned mammal, Dolly the Sheep,[7] was born the same year, although her birth was officially announced only in 1997. Cloning made biotechnology's achievements tangible and, as a result, 1997 became the golden age of setting standards for bioethics. The Oviedo Convention,[8] UNESCO's Universal Declaration on the Human Genome and Human Rights,[9] was adopted. The movie *Gattaca*,[10] which foresaw a caste system of society based on genetic traits, was also released that year. From then on, news stories on genetics have been published on an almost daily basis and ranged from the announcement of the first draft of the human genome to the *en masse* emergence of biobanks.

Naturally, there have always been periods of setbacks, failures, and ethical fiascos. After Jesse Gelsinger, a young participant in the first gene transfer trial, died in 1999,[11] at least for a decade gene therapy had become a black label. Researchers failed to inform Jesse about the earlier patients' side effects or

---

5 L. Brown, 'Louise Brown on 40 Years of IVF: "I Was the World's First IVF Baby, This is My Story"', The Independent (2018), available online at https://www.independent.co.uk/life-style/health-and-families/ivf-baby-louise-brown-story-test-tube-world-first-40th-anniversary-a8455956.html (accessed 18 March 2021).

6 Starting on 1 October 1990 and completed in April 2003, the HGP gave the possibility for the first time, to read nature's complete genetic blueprint for building a human being.

7 The birth of Dolly was important because she was the first mammal to be cloned from an adult cell. Her birth proved that specialized cells could be used to create an exact copy of the animal they came from.

8 Convention for the protection of Human Rights and Dignity of the Human Being with regard to the Application of Biology and Medicine: Convention on Human Rights and Biomedicine, *ETS No. 164*.

9 UNESCO, Universal Declaration on the Human Genome and Human Rights, available online at https://unesdoc.unesco.org/ark:/48223/pf0000110220.page=47 (accessed 30 March 2021).

10 *Gattaca* is an American dystopian science fiction film written and directed by Andrew Niccol.

11 M. Rinde, 'The Death of Jesse Gelsinger, 20 Years Later', *Distillations* (4 June 2019), available online at https://www.sciencehistory.org/distillations/the-death-of-jesse-gelsinger-20-years-later (accessed 28 March 2021).

about the fact that two lab monkeys were killed by the high doses of adenoviruses. For a long time, his case has been an alarming reminder for supporters of gene therapy. In the field of another promising therapy, the embryonic stem cell research by the Korean Hwang Woo-Suk turned out to be fraudulent.[12] There was a tremendous pressure on him to make Korea the first country where embryonic stem cell therapy became possible. All these cases raised numerous ethical concerns. Hwang recruited his assistants to be egg donors; his lawyer was a member of the ethics committee that reviewed his research, and he was under great social pressure to make South Korea the world's leader in embryonic stem cell research.

In 2016 Karolinska Institutet had to face also serious consequences when it turned out that their employee, Paolo Macchiarini conducted a series of fatal trachea surgeries combining it with some stem cell technologies.[13] These scandals are cautionary tales about how cutting-edge technologies combined with fame can distort ethical principles not only on an individual but also on institutional and national level.

2 Gene Therapy and Gene Editing

In the field of genetic based therapy, we reached the latest stage of progress a few years ago, but this might be one of the most significant milestones so far. In fact, having a vast knowledge of the genetic background of certain human diseases, of stem cell research and of cell reprogramming is not enough if we cannot apply these technologies to cure people or eliminate certain biological threats. Without clinical application, these remain only interesting scientific achievements to be published; however, clinical applicability is crucial for mankind.

This is the area in which gene editing provides opportunities, by correcting the gene segments responsible for a predisposition to diseases. Although it is similar in many ways to gene therapy, gene editing opens new horizons. The most well-known gene editing technique is CRISPR.[14] The term CRISPR

---

12 D.B. Resnik, A. Shamoo and S. Krimsky, 'Fraudulent Human Embryonic Stem Cell Research in South Korea: Lessons Learned', *Accountability in Research* 13 (1) (2006) 101–109, doi: 10.1080/08989620600634193.

13 Available online at https://www.theguardian.com/science/2016/sep/06/two-nobel-prize-medicine-judges-fired-stem-cell-doctor-scandal-paolo-macchiarini.

14 CRISPR is the abbreviation of the term Clustered Regularly Interspaced Short Palindromic Repeats The discovery of the type II prokaryotic CRISPR "immune system" has allowed for the development for an RNA-guided genome editing tool that is simple to use.

was first used by the Spaniard Francisco Mojica in 2000 and it is an acronym that refers to the organization of short, repeated DNA sequences found in the genomes of bacteria. Although several journals rejected his publication as not interesting or required more laboratory proof, finally in 2005, he and his colleagues managed to publish his paper.[15] CRISPR is based on the molecular defense system in bacteria. It was known that the CRISPR defense system is found in many bacteria, but only much later was it discovered that it can be used as genetic scissors.

To use a more illustrative metaphor, gene editing works a bit like Microsoft's "replace text" feature. After writing a long text, it is not uncommon that we change our minds and decide to replace an expression with another that fits better. The replace text feature can be very useful in these cases. It searches through the text for the words to replace and it replaces them with one click. In any case gene editing unlikely "gene manipulation," or "gene engineering" is a friendly term that is followed by international curiosity and hope rather than fear.

The *enfants terribles* of DNA research, James Watson and Francis Crick, were famous for their cheekiness and vast self-confidence, which made it easy for them to overcome obstacles and failures. Their colleague, Rosalind Franklin, who did not receive the Nobel Prize, was much more reserved, just like Doudna. These women were aware of their knowledge and capabilities, but they always had to protect these values from others.

Studying RNA did not seem to be a good avenue for success in comparison with the fashionable DNA. But studying RNA led to the revolutionary technique of gene editing.

In 2020 Jennifer Doudna received the Nobel Prize in Chemistry for inventing the CRISPR gene editing technology together with Emmanuelle Charpentier. While most researchers were busy studying the DNA after the Human Genome Project was completed, Doudna chose to turn her attention to the relatively neglected RNA, and now we know that this decision brought her high returns. The groundbreaking article on the structure of RNA she coauthored was published in *Science* in 1996.[16]

The other key figure in the development of gene editing technologies, Emmanuelle Charpentier, was also an outsider at the beginning. Doudna and

15 F.J.M. Mojica, C. Díez-Villaseñor, J. García-Martínez and E. Soria, 'Intervening Sequences of Regularly Spaced Prokaryotic Repeats Derive from Foreign Genetic Elements', *Journal of Molecular Evolution* 60 (2) (2005) 174–182, doi: 10.1007/s00239-004-0046-3.

16 J.H. Cate, A.R. Gooding, E. Podell, K. Zhou, B.L. Golden, C.E. Kundrot, T.R. Cech and J.A. Doudna, 'Crystal Structure of a Group I Ribozyme Domain: Principles of RNA Packing', *Science* 273 (5282) (1996) 1678–1685.

Charpentier were famous and respected researchers on their own, and they did not meet until 2011, when they realized their common interests at a microbiology conference in Puerto Rico.[17]

In the field of RNA research, the Hungarian Katalin Karikó played a pioneering role in developing the Messenger RNA based vaccine technology. Karikó was also an outsider most of her life, and her research interests have also frequently departed from the mainstream.[18]

3 Application of the Technology

Even the most talented researchers and inventors cannot implement their technology without proper translation into innovation. This process of innovation requires both ethical and business skills. In the United States it was the engineer and public intellectual, Vannevar Bush, who first promoted the idea that centers of innovation should be located at universities and their scientific laboratories, as well as in a number of smaller for-profit research labs, as opposed to the mega-laboratories created by the state (as it had been in the case of developing the nuclear bomb). Basic science, as opposed to applied science, needs to be supported by the state, as it is the ultimate source of innovation. This model of financing scientific laboratories by the state proved to be very successful in the United States. This is especially salient in the world of biotechnology, where it is essential to have a sharp sense of business, good timing, and preparedness to file patent claims — it is not enough to be a good scientist, one has to be able to protect scientific knowledge.

In July 2019 an Afro-American woman suffering from sickle-cell anemia volunteered to undergo gene therapy made possible by the CRISPR-Cas-9 technology.[19] At first stem cells were extracted from her blood, then these cells were treated by gene editing, and finally the blood was infused back to her body. Emmanuelle Charpentier's CRISPR Therapeutics company conducted

17 K. Krämer, 'How CRISPR Went from Niche to Nobel', *Chemistry World* (15 October 2020), available online at www.chemistryworld.com/features/how-crispr-went-from-niche-to-nobel/4012604.article (accessed 20 September 2021).

18 In 1995 she even lost her research job at the University of Pennsylvania, but she never gave up and never slowed down. Many years later she became the vice president of BioNTech, the company located in Mainz, Germany, that has become famous for developing the first mRNA-based vaccine against the SARS-Cov-2 coronavirus.

19 R. Stein, 'CRISPR Revolution: In a First, Doctors in U.S. Use CRISPR Tool to Treat Patient with Genetic Disorder', *NPR* (29 July 2019), available online at www.npr.org/sections/health-shots/2019/07/29/744826505/sickle-cell-patient-reveals-why-she-is-volunteering-for-landmark-gene-editing-st (accessed 20 September 2021).

the clinical trial with great caution. The patient's first reaction to the CRISPR injection was a shock, she could not catch her breath and even her heart stopped temporarily, but soon after that she got better and recovered. The CRISPR technology proved to be successful. But CRISPR is not the only technology applied for gene editing.[20] The discovery of zinc finger nucleases (ZFN) in the 1980s[21] has already raised hope for gene editing. A similar technology was called *transcription activator-like effector nucleases* (TALENS). TALENS as a gene editing tool was still time and cost intensive and there were some limitations in its use.[22]

Today we can also think about the use of RNA editing technologies.[23] In 2018 the US Food and Drug Administration approved the first therapy using RNA interference technique in which a small piece of RNA is inserted into a cell. Researchers at the Wyss Institute for Biologically Inspired Engineering at Harvard University and Harvard Medical School (HMS) have created a new gene editing tool called *Retron Library Recombineering* (RLR) that makes editing task easier as RLR generates up to millions of mutations simultaneously.[24]

Time to time not only scientists but artists would like to go ahead with the application of a new technology. There have been people who tried CRISPR themselves; for example, Josiah Zayner, who injected himself with CRISPR at the SynBioBeta conference in 2017, trying to disable his myostatin gene to boost muscle growth in his arm. The idea of genetic modification has also become part of art is shown by numerous artists who use genetic interventions as inspiration or for further reflection. Nontraditional gene editing may pose future challenges to governance.[25]

---

20 See https://www.synthego.com/blog/genome-editing-techniques#4-gene-editing-techniques-tools-to-change-the-genome.

21 A. Klug, 'The discovery of zinc fingers and their development for practical applications in gene regulation and genome manipulation', *Quarterly Reviews of Biophysics* 43 (1) (2010) 1–21, available online at https://www.cambridge.org/core/journals/quarterly-reviews-of-biophysics/article/discovery-of-zinc-fingers-and-their-development-for-practical-applications-in-gene-regulation-and-genome-manipulation/D25ADFAFC0F47D14E52E36BF5A27FCDE.

22 A. Mah, *Genome Editing Techniques: The Tools That Enable Scientists to Alter the Genetic Code* (2019), available online at https://www.synthego.com/blog/genome-editing-techniques#4-gene-editing-techniques-tools-to-change-the-genome.

23 S. Reardon, 'Step aside CRIPR, RNA editing is taking off', *Nature* 578 (2020) 24–27.

24 L. Brownell, *New gene editing technique enables millions of genetic experiments to be performed simultaneously* (2021), available online at https://wyss.harvard.edu/news/move-over-crispr-the-retrons-are-coming/.

25 M.J. Mehlman and R.A. Conlon, 'Governing Nontraditional Gene Editing', in: I.G. Cohen, N.A. Farahany, H.T. Greely and C. Shachar (eds.), *Consumer Genetic Technologies* (Cambridge: Cambridge University Press, 2021), pp. 145–156.

4 The Role of Research Ethics in Developing Gene Editing Techniques

While innovation is competitive in case of life sciences human applications requires additional ethical assessment that is of course might be frustration and time consuming, but still cannot be ignored. In November 2018, a Chinese researcher, He Jiankui, revealed the birth of the first gene-edited babies, Nana and Lulu.[26] The babies' names, of course, are pseudonyms; the twins' birthplace and their real names are unknown. He Jiankui's glory did not last long, as even the Chinese authorities have since distanced themselves from experimental interventions in human subjects. It seems that the first announcement of a new biotechnological method is often scandalous, and the research results are surprising. Racing to be the first always involves keeping secrets from competitors. However, He Jiankui was not in a competitive position, as scientific consensus at the moment is against this kind of intervention; besides, the intervention was not even justified.

He Jiankui announced his work on gene editing at the Second International Summit on Human Genome Editing, in Hong Kong, on November 25, 2018. He expected a huge scientific success, but not long after the announcement several experts on bioethics suggested that such a surprising transformation could only occur if ethical approval procedures were ignored. It turned out that transparent ethical procedures indeed did not take place. Human gene editing, like many other biotechnological innovations, involves terminological novelties, too. In this case, changing the previous terms *genetic manipulation* or *genetic modification* to *gene editing*, also changed the connotation and suggested a much smaller intervention or correction with a better result.

In all, 22 embryos were gene-edited, and 11 embryos were used in six implantation attempts before Nana and Lulu were born. The procedure can raise many kinds of ethical concerns. One of them was the result they wanted to achieve by gene editing. The intervention's goal was to confer genetic resistance to HIV.

Dr He claimed that he received approval from Shenzhen Women and Children's Hospital, but he failed to obtain authorization from his university or the four other hospitals from which some of the gene-edited embryos came. Even though the couples participating in the experiment were informed, the focus of their consent was much more on the copyright of photographs of the unborn babies than highlighting the novelty of the procedure. Is it appropriate

26 BBC News, 'He Jiankui Defends "World's First Gene-Edited Babies"', *BBC News* (28 November 2018), available online at https://www.bbc.com/news/world-asia-china-46368731 (accessed 30 March 2021).

to ask for the public's help in the acceptance of a scientific announcement instead of going through prior professional challenges? He made an attempt to publish his results in a scientific journal a few days before the Hong Kong Summit.

The public knows relatively little about the birth of Nana and Lulu. The mother gave birth by emergency cesarean section. The twins' birthplace was not made public; all we know is that He Jian-kui left by plane to be there at the time of their birth. The goal of the procedure was to make the babies resistant to HIV. Therefore, on one of the babies' genes, the so-called CCR5 located on chromosome 3, He artificially created a CCR5Δ32 allele, with the help of the CRISPR "scissors."[27] In order to contract HIV, it is necessary to have a functioning CCR5 gene. Therefore, the aim of the experiment was to alter the function of this gene.

As a result of the international outrage following the incident, the case was also subject to court proceedings. That is how it emerged that a third child was also born. A court in Shenzhen found that He and two collaborators forged ethical review documents and misled doctors into unknowingly implanting gene-edited embryos in two women. The twins were born in November 2018, but it has not been made clear when the third baby was born; in fact, no information at all has been provided about the third child. He was sentenced to imprisonment and fined 3 million yuan (350,000 £). The Chinese government tightened its regulations on genome editing in humans. Experts from all over the world agreed that there are safer and more effective ways to prevent HIV infections. The experiment was deemed irresponsible, premature and unjustified, because it exposed the babies to risks associated with gene editing without any benefit.[28]

Responsible research requires risk assessment that takes into account the expected benefits, as well as the short- and long-term risks. In the case of a genetic intervention this assessment needs to consider some ripple effects, including epigenetic consequences. Modifying the genetic make-up of minors may also have a broader social impact, such as the commodification of human beings. A pre-implantation alteration of traits that do not serve any lifesaving

27 Myles W. Jackson published a rather interesting book on the history of CCR5 gene and Delta 32 allele, which is of great importance for both understanding how HIV infections develop and curing them. See M.W. Jackson, *The Genealogy of a Gene* (Cambridge, MA: The MIT Press, 2015).

28 K. Musunuru, 'Opinion: We Need to Know What Happened to CRISPR Twins Lulu and Nana', *MIT Technology Review* (3 December 2019), available online at https://www.technologyreview.com/2019/12/03/65024/crispr-baby-twins-lulu-and-nana-what-happened/ (accessed 30 March 2021).

or compelling medical purpose ultimately instrumentalizes the human being to serve the researchers' ambition or the parents' desire, or both.

5 Professional and Ethical Responses

Jian-kui He's announcement was so unexpected that the Nuffield Council's report titled Genome Editing and Human Reproduction: Social and Ethical Issues,[29] published in 2018, discussed the application of genome editing to the field of human reproduction only theoretically and in a futuristic way. It analyzed the, as yet, hypothetical situation when genome editing becomes routine and safe, and can be used among the assisted reproductive technologies available to women and men. This would mean that certain disadvantageous human characteristics, mutations, or susceptibility factors can be knocked out before the embryo is inserted into the womb. As a result, even those fetuses can be brought to life that previously did not have a chance to survive or to develop into a healthy child. In certain cases, even infertility, or other obstacles that make reproduction impossible, can be treated through genome editing. If genome editing works safely, it might lead to the possibility of altering or modifying genes in the gametes or embryos in order to ensure that a healthy child or one with specifically tailored characteristics can be born.

China's first reaction stressed He's success and its pride in the great accomplishment of Chinese science, but the general climate had changed by 26 November, as a group of 122 Chinese scientists and ethicists published a joint statement through a Chinese application, calling the experiment 'crazy' and asking for serious penalties to be applied against him.

They also emphasized that it is forbidden to conduct such an experiment on human beings. Subsequently, many other Chinese scientists condemned the experiment. On 26 November, the Chinese government opened an investigation and referred to the violation of several regulations, but it has not been made at all clear which laws were broken by He's work. On 29 November, the Vice-Minister of Science and Technology issued an order to suspend any work at He's laboratory. After He left the summit on gene editing, he went to an unknown destination and all kinds of rumors spread about his whereabouts.

Previously, He worked as a researcher both at Rice University and Stanford University, so he maintained extensive international scientific relationships.

29 Nuffield Council on Bioethics, *Genome Editing and Human Reproduction: Social and Ethical Issues* (17 July 2018), available online at: https://www.nuffieldbioethics.org/publications/genome-editing-and-human-reproduction (accessed 30 March 2021).

That is why, after announcing the birth of the gene-edited babies, investigations were also carried out at Stanford, during which they found that three of their academic staff were involved. It is interesting that the study report on gene editing was credited to several authors. Among other issues, the responsibility of Michael Deems, who is a researcher at Rice in genetic engineering as well as synthetic biology and one of the authors of the original study on editing CCR5, also arises. The paper was written by several co-authors who may also be held accountable.

There are a number of professional and ethical concerns regarding the intervention. For example, He disabled a completely healthy gene in order to reduce the risk of a disease that the children did not even have and that could have been prevented by antiviral drugs and safe sex. Even if the experiment was successful, disabling CCR5 does not guarantee full immunity to HIV infection, because some strains may enter healthy cells through another protein.

According to Kiran Musunuru, many scientific objections may be raised against He's experiment.[30] The most pervasive one is the mosaicism in the twins, which means that the gene editing did not lead to consistent outcomes in the cells and the interventions carried out influence the various cells of the children. in different ways. Moreover, only half of Lulu's CCR5 genes were edited; it appears that the other cells are all intact.

The Chinese gene-edited baby case was in front of the People's Court of Nanshan District, Shenzhen, Guangdong Province and the judgement was held on 30 December 2019.

The court found that Jian-kui He and others committed a crime of "illegal medical practice," sentenced to a fixed-term imprisonment of 3 years to probation, and a fine of RMB 3 million. Although the reference to *illegal practice* usually means that medical activity was conducted without license, it is not entirely clear what was the basis of the criminal proceeding in the Chinese law. Nevertheless, in December 2020 China modified its criminal code to include a ban on *changing the human genome*. In the new amendment[31] "Illegal medical practices" were added to Article 336, which includes "the implantation of genetically edited or cloned human embryos into human or animal bodies, or

30 The view from inside the 'medical scandal' of China's gene-edited babies. In a Q&A, geneticist Kiran Musunuru describes his unintentional connection to the scientist behind the scandal and the book that came out of the experience, see https://penntoday.upenn.edu/news/Penn-geneticist-offers-perspective-from-inside-medical-scandal-chinas-gene-edited-babies (accessed 30 March 2021).

31 Amendments to the Criminal Law of the People's Republic of China (11) (Adopted at the 24th meeting of the Standing Committee of the 13th National People's Congress on 26 December 2020), in this revision Act (article 39), a new article 336-1 were added.

the implantation of genetically edited or cloned animal embryos into human bodies." This amendment entered into force on 1 March 2021. This new law has no retroactive effect but clearly indicates that China would like include international standards of genome ethics in the future.[32]

6 What Are the Legal Aspects of Gene Editing?

Legal and ethical reactions to the latest transformation technologies have changed since the foundation of the Human Genome Project. First of all, reactions are no longer delayed, but mostly happen in parallel or, in the case of cloning, even anticipating the scientific possibilities. This is necessary because cloning or gene editing has created opportunities that cannot be corrected if implemented prematurely. The possibility of human cloning, for example, impelled legislators to introduce regulations banning cloning as early as in 1997, although the technology and successful implementation were far from being available then. The second important difference is that society today participates much more actively in shaping expectations, hopes and rejections of biotechnology, and several works of art, movies and literary pieces provided utopian or dystopian visions and predictions, some of which have already become reality. As all of this affects our thinking, law and ethics try to provide answers, and in many cases, they anticipate the changes in biotechnology. In the case of gene editing, it was Jennifer Doudna who drew the public's attention to the widespread social implications of gene editing.[33] Therefore, one can say she is a good example for a responsible scientist of the 21st Century. Earlier, it was not appropriate for scientists to share their doubts with the public. Instead, they were expected to behave as if they were successful and infallible.

Gene editing raises numerous legal questions, such as: would it be possible to make a legal difference between specific versions of gene editing? Who decides on what is considered a disease or an anomaly, which diseases are worth being corrected, treated and improved and which ones can be? What kind of social implications will gene editing have when it becomes widely available?

32 I am very grateful to Yao-Ming Hsu for his kind help with the clarification of the relevant Chinese law.

33 R. Sanders, 'CRISPR Inventor Calls for Pause in Editing Heritable Genes', *Berkeley News* (1 December 2015), available online at https://news.berkeley.edu/2015/12/01/crispr-inventor-calls-for-pause-in-editing-heritable-genes/ (accessed 30 March 2021).

Some normative distinctions have been made already in the case of gene therapies, separating somatic and germline interventions. Somatic gene therapies involve modifying a patient's DNA to treat or cure a disease caused by a genetic mutation.

While somatic gene editing affects only the patient who is being treated (and only a part of his/her cells), germline editing affects every cell of the organism, including eggs and sperm, and this way the edited characteristics are passed on to the future generations. At the moment, it is difficult to foresee its possible consequences.

Human germline genome editing means deliberately changing the human genome (not only a single cell) that will become a characteristic of the child to be born. Human germline editing modifies the genome of a human embryo and it may affect every cell, which means it may have an impact not only on the person to be born, but also on his/her future descendants. Because of this, the clinical application of germline editing is banned in the United States, Europe, the United Kingdom, China and many other countries.

Somatic gene therapies are often used for treating patients who suffer from genetic diseases. Somatic gene therapies involve the placement of genetic material into a targeted part of the patient's existing cells. Somatic gene therapies are often used for treating patients who suffer from genetic diseases. Somatic gene therapies involve the placement of genetic material into a targeted part of the patient's existing cells.

Although Article 13 of the Oviedo Convention (1997) was not drafted to respond to the issues of gene editing — at that time nobody knew of this procedure — nevertheless, the distinction it makes is also applicable for gene editing.

According to the Article, "an intervention seeking to modify the human genome may only be undertaken for preventive, diagnostic or therapeutic purposes and only if its aim is not to introduce any modification in the genome of any descendants."

The Committee on Bioethics of the Council of Europe reaffirmed this important distinction;[34] however, in the further future, it is questionable whether it is right to maintain the ban on germline gene editing, even when it will become completely accurate and safe. Must a serious genetic disease be treated generation by generation if it could be cured once and for all?

34 "Ethics and Human Rights must guide any use of genome editing technologies in human beings," Statement by the Council of Europe Committee on Bioethics, available online at https://rm.coe.int/168049034a (accessed 30 March 2021).

Among bans on interventions, it is important to mention Article 14 of the Oviedo Convention, which bans sex selection: "The use of techniques of medically assisted procreation shall not be allowed for the purpose of choosing a future child's sex, except where serious hereditary sex-related disease is to be avoided."

The other normative anchor is to examine that for what purpose could such an intervention serve. Although it is difficult to establish it legally, it is important to define the difference between a disease to cure and an anomaly. Who decides about what is considered a disease or an anomaly, and which conditions are worth correcting, treating and improving?

In the EU legal framework different aspects of the human gene editing are addressed in different legal instruments.[35] The EU frameworks clearly distinguishes between human and non-human application of biotechnology, between in vitro and in vivo applications, and between somatic and germline interventions. These normative anchors are based on safety or reversibility and irreversibility and overall, they aim to control the ethical boundaries of new inventions.

Furthermore, in general, patents can be considered as additional regulatory instruments beyond their commercial significance. Therefore, the Biotechnology Directive[36] provides limited scope for patentability, by allowing patents on products rather than methods in the medical field. This in turn facilitates the wide use of gene-editing methods of therapeutic, diagnostic, and surgical treatment on the human or animal body.

The ATMP Regulation[37] provides various incentives for the marketing of such products, not least the centralized marketing authorization procedure.

As we have seen the distinction between the therapy and enhancement is not so relevant for the law as for instance the distinction between somatic and germ line interventions. Furthermore, enhancement and performance enhancing have become accepted in many fields; it is enough to think about the improvement of vision through eye surgery, or the numerous — legal and illegal — means of performance improvement in sport.

---

35 A. Mahalatchimy, 'Genome Editing and the European Union', in: J. Sandor (ed.), *Genome Editing and the Law Around the World*, World Association of Medical Law: Newsletter (January–March 2019) 1–5, available online at http://wafml.memberlodge.org/resources/Documents/2019%20WAML%20Newsletters.pdf.

36 Directive 98/44/EC on the Legal Protection of Biotechnological Inventions, OJ 1998 L 213/13.

37 Regulation (EC) 1394/2007 on Advanced Therapy Medicinal Products of 13 November 2007 and amending Directive 2001/83/EC and Regulation (EC) No 726/2004, OJ 2007 L 324/121.

Julian Savulescu and his colleagues believe that most of the leading athletes are born with a genetic advantage; consequently, they claim that genetically enhancing athletic performance is completely legitimate, as elite and competitive sport above a certain level is all about competition between genetic advantages anyway.[38] Obviously, diligence and a lot of training are essential but, according to Savulescu, in this case, genetic intervention in order to enhance performance can be justified.

7 Therapy or Enhancement?

During the application of new procedures, one of the most controversial topics is how to set the boundaries between therapy and enhancement. Russian biologist Denis Rebrikov, for example, offered his help in gene editing to allow deaf couples to give birth to children without a genetic mutation that impairs hearing. Rebrikov emphasized that he will implant gene-edited embryos only if he receives regulatory approval. The community with hearing disability, nevertheless, may regard this offer as an indication that their identity needs to be gene-edited. For them gene editing may be regarded not as a desirable therapy but rather a form of intervention that indicates their disability. On the other hand, those who advocate for enhancement of different capabilities in sport and other fields of life may welcome gene editing as a form of enhancement.

According to a survey on gene editing, conducted by the Pew Research Center in 2018, 54% of respondents thought that people will use gene editing in morally unacceptable ways. Furthermore, about seven-in-ten Americans (72%) were on the opinion that changing an unborn baby's genetic characteristics to treat a serious disease or condition that the baby would have at birth is an appropriate use of medical technology, while 27% of the respondents say this would be taking technology too far.[39]

It is even a more complex moral question what constitutes an editable genetic anomaly. For instance, there are autistic individuals in the upper spectrum with exceptional mathematical creativity. An artist might suffer from several mood disorders, but in some ways, this is what feeds their artistic creativity. It can be concluded that neurodiversity is also an important value.

38 F. Baylis, *Altered Inheritance* Cambridge (Cambiurdge, MA: Harvard University Press, 2019), p. 58.

39 C. Funk and M. Hefferon, 'Public Views of Gene Editing for Babies Depend on How It Would Be Used', *Pew Research Center* (26 July 2018), available online at https://www.pewresearch.org/science/2018/07/26/public-views-of-gene-editing-for-babies-depend-on-how-it-would-be-used/ (accessed 30 March 2021).

Genome research and gene editing raise numerous ethical, legal and social questions, many of which — including privacy issues, informed consent and the equitable representation of participants — are still unsolved. Furthermore, the availability and open distribution of genomic data is still uneven.

The World Medical Association developed the main ethical principles of medical research in 1961, which are known today as the Helsinki Declaration and which has been amended several times since then. Besides containing the most important principles of research, this document also includes a section on the comparison of risks, disadvantages and advantages, and expresses that the potential risks of a medical research project cannot outweigh the potential benefits.

In 2018 The Nuffield Council's 205-page-long report reflected on the social and ethical issues related to genome editing in a more venturous way than any previously published ethical or legal statements.[40] To understand the novelty and ethical significance of this Report, it is important to state the ethical consensus that has defined the legal and ethical framework for interventions into human genes over the past two decades. For a long time, modification of the human gene was considered 'manipulation' and faced strong ethical and moral reservations. Although the relatively new technique of genome editing raises similar concerns as 'gene therapy', it modifies the human genome in a different way than the earlier 'gene therapy' or genetic modification procedures. Genetic modification inserts new, foreign genes or knocks out existing ones in the DNA artificially and as a result, the genetic material changes in a way that would not be possible through natural recombination or fertilization. Gene editing (or genome editing when more than one gene is edited), on the other hand, treats genes by repairing sections in the genetic structure of the DNA with the help of molecular scissors — and the outcome is 'natural' or naturally healthy without the disease.

By 2019 almost all relevant international organizations and professional societies issued a statement or a declaration on genome editing. In 2019, UNESCO's International Bioethics Committee organized a round table discussion with the aim to deal with the subject of gene editing as well.[41]

In September 2020, the American National Academy of Medicine and the Royal Society of Great Britain published a report entitled *Heritable Human Genome Editing* (HHGE).[42]

---

40 Nuffield Council on Bioethics *supra* note 29.

41 UNESCO, *Roundtable on the Impact of Genome Editing on Our Health and Environment* (2 December 2019), available online at https://en.unesco.org/events/roundtable-impact-genome-editing-our-health-and-environment (accessed 30 March 2021).

42 National Academy of Medicine, National Academy of Sciences, and the Royal Society, *Heritable Human Genome Editing* (Washington, DC: The National Academies Press,

The HHGE Report does not recommend a moratorium on research. Instead, it clearly delineates six categories of potential clinical applications of HHGE and indicates that only two of those could be considered today. HHGE may be applied initially for only the most severe monogenic diseases and in a limited number of situations. I think in the future, the sharp distinction between the somatic and germ line editing should be revisited.

In 2021 WHO published a useful guidance on the regulation of genome editing technology published.[43] This document applies a very clear structure and language, and it recognizes the broader social consequences of this technology, its impact on human rights, and on the sustainable development. It differentiates between somatic and germline technologies.

While gene editing is often discussed in its potential use for enhancement the therapeutic applications are much closer to the realization. For instance, Zolgensma, a recent gene therapy medicinal product that has obtained a marketing authorization valid throughout the EU from 18 May 2020, is a genetically modified vector infused into a vein to treat spinal muscular atrophy for patients with inherited mutations affecting specific genes.[44]

8 How Does Gene Editing Rewrite the Structure of Ethical Debates?

Gene editing changes not only the legal reactions but also significantly alter the usual camps in ethical debates. To put it simply, there are two very contrasting perspectives in ethical debates: there are those who argue for the sanctity of life, which cannot be altered, and the others who support the individual's decision and autonomy.

The fact that, through gene editing, those embryos that would not otherwise have gained a chance of life can also be implanted encourages pro-life advocates to support gene editing, because this way may give a chance of life to embryos and fetuses with serious diseases. However, this goes against the usual combination of protecting life and refusing interventions. A challenging intervention might save potential lives.

2020), available online at: https://www.nap.edu/catalog/25665/heritable-human-genome-editing (accessed 30 March 2021).

43 WHO, *Expert Advisory Committee on Developing Global Standards for Governance and Oversight of Human Genome Editing* (14 July 2021), available online at https://www.who.int/news/item/12-07-2021-who-issues-new-recommendations-on-human-genome-editing-for-the-advancement-of-public-health.

44 Spinal muscular atrophy is a serious condition of the nerves that causes muscle wasting and weakness. EMA, Zolgensma, European Public Assessment Report (2020), EMA/200482/2020.

The concept of autonomy is also difficult to define in the context of gene editing procedures. Whose autonomy are we talking about? The autonomy of the pregnant woman, the unborn child, the parents? It is important to highlight that one's genes are not one's fate, and personality is not determined by any single gene. The interests and viewpoints of families affected by genetic diseases have to be respected. Extreme interventions like germline gene editing may be justified only in exceptional and justified cases to fight serious diseases.

Consequently, gene editing also rewrites the structure of ethical debates. It affects the concept and cases of discrimination and the field of assisted reproductive procedures. It revolutionizes the concept of medical treatment. It may raise or reduce those inequalities based on health conditions. It may lead to numerous new rights in the field of genetics. Good gene editing practice can only be achieved through the close cooperation of natural and social sciences.

9 Conclusions

With the technical possibility of genome editing, we have reached a new era of altering human beings and even altering human inheritance. Genome editing constitutes new responsibilities in many fields. Science and society have never been so much dependent on each other. We may look optimistically into our future with mRNA-based vaccines in our arms and may rightly hope to tackle other dreadful diseases by using genetic knowledge. But we must also learn from the past episodes of eugenics and the instances of fraud and failure that have been the result of merciless scientific competition, unfettered commercial interest, or simply individual pride. As human rights lawyers we need to engage in regular communication with scientists in the field of biotechnology, as these emerging technologies are going to shape humanness in the future, and they may influence the rights of children and adults, and affect our perceptions of disability, discrimination and privacy.

Acknowledgements

I would like to extend my sincere thanks to Timo Minssen for his useful comments on my first manuscript and for the Nordic Permed Law for organizing a unique symposium on this topic.

Transformation of Medical Care through Gene Therapy and Human Rights to Life and Health – Balancing Risks and Benefits

Anne Kjersti Befring | ORCID: 0000-0003-3327-4692
Legal Department, University of Oslo, Kristian Augusts gate 17, 0164 Oslo, Norway
a.k.befring@jus.uio.no

Abstract

This chapter is about how somatic gene therapy can be legally regulated and risk assessed as medical treatment when taking the following international human rights conventions into consideration: the right to life in Article 2 of the ECHR and the right to health in Article 12 of ICESCR. The right to life can involve both protection against risky genetic methods and access to necessary health care. In this context, human rights can be a basis for identifying interests that must be considered in a rapid technological development. Focusing mainly on human rights to life and to health, it is argued (1) against a total ban or general moratoriums on gene editing; (2) that regulations should be based on international cooperation and consensus; and that (3) rights to health may involve obligations to provide access to genetic methods.

Keywords

personalized medicine – gene therapy – right to life – right to health – medical care – research

1 Introduction

The significant changes in medicine from the last century can be illustrated with a quote from 1892:

> if it were not for the great variability among individuals, medicine might as well be a science and not an art.
>
> SIR WILLIAM OSLER, John Hopkins School of Medicine, Baltimore, MD, USA, 1892

DOI:10.1163/9789004526136_004

The development has been even faster in the last decade. Genetic factors play a role in most human diseases, with gene variations contributing to their incidence or course.

Today, it is the knowledge of the significance of the variations that leads to a paradigm shift in medical treatment and science. The mapping of the Genome was a scientific breakthrough at the beginning of our millennium. Gene therapy by CRISPR technology was a similar breakthrough and developed since 2012.[1] The CRISPR method has been a controversial method. One of the scientists who had developed it, Jennifer Doudna, warned against the method.[2] The method can today be used in different contexts with different definitions.[3] CRISPR technology, and in particular the system called CRISPR-Cas9 has revolutionized the possibilities of medicine and can increasingly become an important part of personalized medicine.[4] "Personal medicine" refers to an emerging approach to medicine that uses scientific insights or methods in the genetic and molecular basis of health and disease. While knowledge of genetics can be used to predict, prevent and treat disease, gene therapy can be used as tailored medical treatment.[5]

The use of genetic methods has transformed medical treatment in recent years and is regulated in a fragmented legal landscape. The term "genetic methods" is used as a common term for genome sequencing, gene therapy

---

1 M. Angrist, R. Barrangou, F. Baylis, C. Brokowski, G. Burgio, A. Caplan, C. Riley Chapman, G.M. Church, R. Cook-Deegan, B. Cwik, J.A. Doudna, J.H. Evans, H.T. Greely, L. Hercher, J. Benjamin Hurlbut, R.O. Hynes, T. Ishii, S. Kiani, L. Hoskins Lee, G. Levrier, D.R. Liu, J.E. Lunshof, K.L. Macintosh, D.J.H. Mathews, E.M. Meslin, P.H.R. Mills, L. Montoliu, K. Musunuru, D. Nicol, H. O'Neill, R. Qiu, R. Ranisch, J.S. Sherkow, S. Soni, S. Terry, E. Topol, R. Williamson, F. Zhang and K. Davies, 'Reactions to the National Academies/Royal Society Report on *Heritable Human Genome Editing*', *The CRISPR Journal* 3 (2020) 332–349, doi: 10.1089/crispr.2020.29106.man.

2 H. Devlin and J. Doudna, 'I have to be true to who I am as a scientist.' *The Guardian* (2 July 2017); J. Doudna and E. Charpentier, 'Genome Editing. The new frontier of genome engineering with CRISPR-Cas9', *Science* 346 (6213) (2014) 1258096, p. 28. When the first Chinese experiment was published, Doudna and a group of scientists and philosophers asked that scientists for the time being refrain from using CRISPR to modify human fetuses.

3 N. Bostrom, 'A history of transhumanist thought', *Journal of Evolution and Technology* 14 (2005), 1–25, p. 18, available online at http://jetpress.org/volume14/bostrom.html. A. Nordberg, 'Patentability of human enhancement: from ethical dilemmas to legal (un)certainty', In: T. Pistorius (ed.), *Intellectual Property Perspectives on the Regulation of New Technologies* (Cheltenham: Edward Elgar, 2018), 54–92. p. 55, doi: 10.4337/9781786436382.00009.

4 K. Maxson Jones, R.A. Ankeny and R. Cook Deegan. 'The Bermuda Triangle: The Pragmatics, Policies, and Principles for Data Sharing in the History of the Human Genome Project', *Journal of the History of Biology* 51 (2018) 693–805, doi: 10.1007/s10739-018-9538-7.

5 N. Scholz, Personalised medicine, 'The right treatment for the right person at the right time', *European Parliament Briefing* (2015). A.K. Befring, *Persontilpasset medisin. Rettslige perspektiver* (Gyldendal, Oslo, 2019), Chapters 1 and 3.

and gene editing, although the legal considerations may vary with the method used. Gene editing is a collective term for methods that change the genetic material and is understood as the ability of genetic improvement through the correction of altered (mutated) genes or site-specific modifications that target therapeutic treatment.[6] Legally, there is a distinction between gene therapy that modifies a person's genes to treat or cure a disease and when this therapy leads to changes in the human germ line, and which involves "rewriting the gene pool for future generations."[7]

This chapter examines, if – and if so to what extent – states might be obliged to implement and use gene therapy and what these obligations may entail, on the basis of the right to life in Article 2 of the ECHR[8] and the right to health in Article 12 of the ICESCR.[9] The article analyses the content of these provisions and the collisions and ambiguities that arise between these human rights in a situation when further regulations of gene therapy in national law or as international standards are to be further developed, for example in the Biomedicine Convention.[10] Somatic gene editing can affect the genes in the targeted cells of existing patients without effecting future generations. To modify the human germline is in most legal orders, either prohibited or severely restricted. A brief analysis is given of the ban on gene therapy that affects the legacy of the next generation in Article 13 of the Biomedicine Convention and how the ban may have implications for the ECHR, Norwegian legislation and EU law. Challenges arise with how international regulations are to be applied, and how the clear distinction in regulations of health research and medical treatment is to be understood. The chapter derives and points out what will be relevant assessment themes and factors when the two mentioned human rights are to be applied in connection with gene therapy. This is particularly relevant when gene therapy is of great importance in order to provide medical treatment at the same time as it can lead to changes in the human germ line and heredity.

---

6 G.A. Rangel Gonçalves and R.de Melo Alves Paiva. 'Gene therapy: advances, challenges and perspectives Advances, challenges and perspectives.' *Einstein* 15 (3) (2017) 369–375, doi: 10.1590/S1679-45082017RB4024.

7 D. Cyranoski, 'The CRISPR-Baby Scandal: What's Next for Human Gene-Editing'. *Nature* 566 (7745) (2019) 440–442.

8 Convention for the Protection of Human Rights and Fundamental Freedoms, 1950, ETS 005.

9 The International Covenant of 16 December 1966 on Economic, Social and Cultural Rights. The right to health as a universal human right was first declared by the World Health Organization (WHO) in the preamble to WHO's constitution in 1946.

10 Convention for the Protection of Human Rights and Dignity of the Human Being with regard to the Application of Biology and Medicine, 1997, ETS No. 164 (hereinafter referred to as the Biomedicine Convention).

2 The Right to Life and Health as a Basis for Balancing Risk and Opportunity

2.1 *The Right to Life and Health as a Positive and Negative Commitment*

Analysis of whether the basic human rights are complied with in the regulation of gene therapy presupposes factual descriptions of gene therapy, opportunities, risks, and scenarios. The fundamental human right to life in Article 2 of the ECHR and rulings of the European Court of Human Rights (ECtHR) are relevant in order to identify and consider fundamental considerations and perspectives on when genetic methods can be used. The Court has also found the allegations from persons suffering from serious illnesses when not receiving sufficient health treatment to fall under Article 2 of the Convention when the circumstances potentially engaged the responsibility of the State.[11]

The right to life is called *the supreme value in the hierarchy of human rights*.[12] The obligation for states to fulfil this right can be divided into a negative obligation, which means that interventions must not be made that can take lives, as well as protection against interference from others that involves a similar risk, and a positive obligation to meet the necessary needs to sustain life. The state shall actively protect life and shall refrain from taking life, with some exceptions set forth in the provision.

Article 12 of the International Covenant on Economic, Social and Cultural Rights (ICESCR), formulates the right to 'the highest attainable standard of health'.[13] The right to health is a fundamental part of the right to life in article 2 of the Convention for the Protection of Human Rights and Fundamental Freedoms. The human right to health has the greatest significance in that it obliges the states to offer a medical treatment of sufficient quality. The right to a high standard entails an obligation to develop the health service in line with medical developments. Legal standards are dynamic and must be complemented in the light of medical technological developments and must therefore be elaborated in the context of genetic methods and the corona pandemic. The right to health is described *as a universal standard and as a minimum standard*

11 ECtHR 9 June 1998, no. 23413/94 (L.C.B. v. the United Kingdom), paras 36–41, concerning an applicant suffering from leukaemia. See also ECtHR 1 December 2009, no. 43134/05 (G.N. and Others v. Italy) (concerning applicants suffering from a potentially life-threatening disease) and ECtHR 9 July 2011, nos. 47039/11 and 358/1 (Hristozov and others v. Bulgaria). Bulgaria's refusal to allow terminally-ill cancer patients to use experimental medicine did not violate their rights to life etc. See also ECtHR 23 March 2010, no. 4864/05 (Oyal v. Turkey).

12 Streletz, Kessler and Krenz v. Germany (2001), no. 34044/96, 35532/97 and 44801/98, para. 94.

13 The Covenant was adopted by the United Nations General Assembly in its resolution 2200A (XXI) of 16 December 1966. It entered into force in 1976.

that must be seen in the context of the state's wealth.[14] Assessments of proportionality, benefit and risk must be based on individual and collective aspects.

In recent years, increasing attention has been paid to the contents of "the highest attainable standard of health." Article 14 of the UNESCO Universal Declaration on Bioethics and Human Rights (2005) states that "the highest attainable standard of health" is a fundamental right of every human being, which means in the present context access to the highest available healthcare.

The content of this standard and the requirements for quality can provide a basis for deriving an expectation that medical methods will be used. On this basis, the standard can be considered to contain a right to benefit from new methods when these are crucial to be able to provide effective medical treatment with the necessary quality. In this context, the standard is assessed in the light of new genetic methods and implementing new and effective medical methods.[15]

> The concept of human dignity, which is also highlighted, constitutes the essential value to be upheld. It is at the basis of most of the values emphasised in the Convention.[16]

The right to health must be seen in the context with article 15 in ICESCR and of the Universal Declaration of Human Rights which formulates a right to health and to enjoy scientific progress (article 25 and 27). What can be expected is elaborated in a General comment from the Committee on Economic, Social and Cultural Rights:

> scientific progress creates medical applications that prevent diseases, such as vaccinations, or that enable them to be more effectively treated. The right to participate in and to enjoy the benefits of scientific progress and its applications is therefore instrumental in realizing the right to health.[17]

14 K.H. Søvig, 'Minstestandarder og universalitet i norsk helse-og sosialrett, sett i lys av FNs konvensjon om økonomiske, sosiale og kulturelle rettigheter', *Jussens Venner* 41 (1) (2006) 36–56.

15 Committee on Economic Social and Cultural Rights (CESCR), General Comment No. 25 (2020) on science and economic, social and cultural rights (article 15 (1) (b) (2) (3) and (4) of the Covenant), para. 70.

16 Explanatory Report, Biomedicine Convention, ETS. No 164 (1997), p. 3.

17 Para. 67 in General Comment No. 25 (2020) on science and economic, social and cultural rights (article 15 (1) (b) (2) (3) and (4) of the Covenant), Committee on Economic Social and Cultural Rights (CESCR).

It is stated in the same section that the states shall take an active role in promoting "scientific research, through financial support or other incentives, to create new medical applications and make them accessible and affordable to everyone."

Article 12 and Article 15 must be seen in context, cf. also a general comment from the committee. Quality in terms of including research will be a common criterion for how life and health can be safeguarded. The content of the rights to necessary health care based on a universal standard and gene editing means that the obligation for states to develop high-quality medical treatment regimens may include medical treatments with elements of research. The content of the right to health can, with genetic methods, be based on presumed evidence which replaces evidence-based medicine. There is no doubt that access to new genetic methods can be crucial for public health and for the individual health situation and crucial to sustaining life. Increased use of gene therapy could have been an effective tool. Furthermore, parties of the State should "prioritize the promotion of scientific progress to facilitate better and more accessible means for the prevention, control and treatment of *epidemic*, endemic, occupational and other diseases (Article 12 (2) c)."

The obligation for states includes to safeguard positive and negative rights. The state shall both fulfil the rights to have basic needs and services covered, and to refrain from using methods that may harm, or to intervene unnecessarily in people's lives. The use of gene therapy can be crucial in saving lives and can lead to injuries and it must be assessed whether it is part of the necessary and the standard health care we should require. This may be an argument that it is forbidden to use medical methods that can harm people or that can have unintended effects as a result of changes in genetics.

2.2 *Balancing Risks and Benefits and Assessment Topics*

Compliance with fundamental rights to life and health are part of the considerations which must be included when risk and opportunities are to be balanced in connection with the regulation of gene therapy.

First, the authorities must have a "regulatory framework" in place and implement preventive operational measures that are "necessary and sufficient" to avert the danger.[18]

The obligation to take measures to avert external risk may arise when the state knew or should have known about it (Osman v. The United Kingdom (para. 116)). Accordingly, not every claimed risk to life can entail for the authorities a Convention requirement to take operational measures to prevent that

18 ECtHR 30 November 2004, 48939/99 (Öneryildiz v. Turkey), para. 101.

risk from materializing. This positive obligation means that the state should take appropriate steps to safeguard the lives of those within its jurisdiction, (a) to provide a regulatory framework; and (b) to take preventive operational measures.[19] The obligation also applies in the context of health care.[20]

When assessing whether a method should be permitted, several considerations must be considered, including the benefit that others may have from the research. The precondition for such medical experiments to be carried out is nevertheless that the risk and strain on the subject is minimal, cf. Article 17(2)(i) of the Biomedical Convention and Article 6(2) of the Additional Protocol CETS 196. By minimal risk and strain is meant research that in the worst-case results in a very small and transient negative impact on the health status of the subject. See also article 5(2) of the 1997 UNESCO Declaration and Article 28 of the Helsinki Declaration. The obligation for the authority will include legal regulations, clarity in the placement of responsibilities and legal liability. The state has the burden of proving that it has provided "effective protection."[21] The closer choice of measures belongs to the state's margin of discretion.[22]

Secondly, the legislation must allow for the rapid development of genetic methods, but with time to assess the developments. Human rights have historically been about protecting the individual also in such situations. The principle is that in such situations Article 2 applies either if (a) the activity at issue was dangerous by its very nature and put the life of the people concerned at real and imminent risk, or if (b) the injuries suffered by them were seriously life-threatening. In germline-based gene therapy, precautionary considerations are important, as well as that the burden of justifying restrictive regulation must lie with the state in the event of uncertainty. Risk assessments are used both in order to prevent hazards and to contribute to the balancing between the material goals to be achieved and risks to be avoided. In germline-based gene therapy, precautionary considerations are important, as well as that the burden of justifying restrictive regulation must lie with the state in the event of uncertainty, but with the reservation that it takes time to assess new forms

19 Centre for Legal Resources on behalf of Valentin Câmpeanu v. Romania [GC] (2014) no. 47848/08, para. 130.

20 ECtHR 17 January 2002, no.32967/96 (Calvelli and Ciglio v. Italy); ECtHR 8 July 2004, no. 53924/00 (Vo v. France).

21 Öneryildiz v. Turkey, *supra* note 18, para. 89, ECtHR 20 March 2008, nos. 15339/02, 21166/02, 20058/02, 11673/02 and 15343/02 (Budayeva and Others v. Russia), para. 132, ECtHR 24 October 2014, nos. 60908/11, 62110/11, 62129/11, 62312/11 and 62338/11) (Brincat and Others v. Malta), para. 110.

22 *Ibid.*, para 101.

of treatment and a limitation for the costs.[23] The principle of proportionality is used to balance different interests, even when human rights collide and some obligations can be deduced in connection with the application of gene therapy when such therapies are sufficiently safely developed in order to be part of the health care.

Assessments of the risk with the method must be based on actual descriptions of how the method works and legal factors.[24] The margin of discretion seems to be narrower where the risk is of "man-made origin" such as gene therapy, compared to life-threatening situations that are "beyond human control."[25] The expectations of the state must be reasonable. This means that they will vary according to the possibilities for averting risk, the seriousness of the situation, investment needs and the possibilities for a fair distribution of health benefits.

Third, the risk must be seen in connection with the right to health and in the context of the possibilities for medical treatment that the genetic method can provide. In gene therapy in medical treatment, several aspects must be considered, the consequences for those who have a disease and where there are no other effective methods, and consequences for others. It must be considered whether a higher risk may be acceptable and necessary to meet the need for medical treatment for patients with life-threatening conditions. The state's obligations to further develop medical treatment regimens in line with genetic development, and quality requirements, may be an argument that certain genetic methods must be made available. This means that the proportionality assessment must include the risk of using the method, the possible benefits of the method and the consequences of not using the genetic method.

In connection with gene therapy, both the benefits and risk to the individual and the risk to humanity must be considered. On the one hand, the state's has the burden of proving that "effective protection" has been provided.[26] The system must actively consider new genetic methods, for the purpose of making methods available or to prevent methods that do harm. New opportunities with gene editing, and risk-reducing measures, at the same time increase the state's responsibility to ensure access to gene methods and that it takes place step by step in accordance with what is justifiable.

It is unclear what significance this human right has in terms of the states' obligation to offer methods that involve elements of research to reduce the

---

23 R. Yotova. 'Regulating genome editing under international human rights law', *International & Comparative Law Quarterly* 69 (3) (2020) 653–684, p. 666, doi: 10.1017/S0020589320000184.

24 ECtHR 25 June 2019, no. 41720/13 (Nicolae Virgiliu Tanase v. Romania), para. 139–145.

25 Budayeva and Others v. Russia, *supra* note 21, paras 134, 135 and 137.

26 *Supra* note 21.

risk of loss of life, and to what extent costs of the method should be taken into account. The right entails on the one hand a duty to protect lives through access to medical research such as to new genetic methods, and on the other hand a protection against gene editing that can harm man and humanity. A reservation must be made that the right can be limited in this context, among other things in order to be able to distribute access to medical treatment methods in a fair way.

3 Gene Therapies as Medical Treatment and Research

3.1 *Rights to Access Genetic Therapy in Clinical Trials*

A characteristic of the use of genetic methods is that medical treatment will include clinical trials with a primary purpose of providing effective medical treatment and a secondary goal of gaining knowledge that may be of general interest.[27] There are clear distinctions in how medical treatment and research are regulated. Declaration of Helsinki and CETS 196. Many countries, including Norway, have their own law on health research.

Such a distinction between regulations of health research and medical treatment cannot be inferred from the right to life in Article 2 of the ECHR and Article 13 of the Biomedical Convention, and the ban on using germline-based gene therapy. Genetic methods can be crucial in securing life and can lead to damage that can affect several generations and unintended effects.

The right to health is *traditionally* understood as the right to methods based on medical knowledge and science, and not a right to take part in clinical trials as part of medical treatment. The genetic methods challenge the distinction between medical care and health research and provides new assessment topics about the content of the universal standard in ICESCR Article 12. On the one hand, the offer of medical treatment must be distributed in a fair way. The distribution of health must consider that suffering from an illness can be an injustice and that a rare illness can limit the treatment options. On the other hand, there is no medical treatment for all diseases, and there may be other forms of restrictions, for example that the person will not tolerate such treatment or that it is too expensive in connection with the effect. In determining

---

27 Summary of the Norwegian Strategy for Personalised Medicine in Health Care, available online at https://www.helsedirektoratet.no/rapporter/strategi-for-persontilpasset-medisin-i-helsetjenesten/Summary%20of%20the%20Norwegian%20Strategy%20for%20Personalised%20Medicine%20in%20Health%20Care.pdf/_/attachment/inline/5a6c511c-b245-4546-8dfa-daa057f275dc:f0a88b9e56dddd83901639bea4de5c04919bf407/Summary%20of%20the%20Norwegian%20Strategy%20for%20Personalised%20Medicine%20in%20Health%20Care.pdf.

the content of the right to health, a distinction must be made between pure improvements of human beings and medical treatment of illness. Risk assessments and access to gene therapy must be seen in relation to the disease's severity, rarity, and consequences of not having access to gene therapy. Otherwise, risk assessments may limit the possibilities for medical treatment for some groups of diseases, such as rare diseases. There may be an argument that the right to health will apply to methods that include research when this is the only method that provides an effective health service developed in line with medical knowledge. Overall, these may be arguments that there may be a right to certain methods when these methods are crucial to fulfil the right to health.[28] When more of the medical treatment is offered through clinical trials, the question arises of a fair distribution of who should be offered to participate in such trials.

The patient is at the same time a research subject for whom consent and the conditions for research and medical treatment will be linked. At the same time, rights as a patient will be important during research. When using gene therapy can risk assessments that do not take sufficient account of the need for *medical treatment* may limit the possibilities for safeguarding life and health in accordance with Article 2 of the ECHR and Article 12 of the ICESCR. The accumulation of new knowledge nevertheless becomes an *outcome and a secondary purpose.*

The necessity of defining the consideration for the patient as the primary purpose can be deduced from the restrictions that currently exist in the Biomedicine Convention. Article 1 emphasizes the consideration for human dignity and that human beings have an intrinsic value that is important for the legality of using biomedical methods in research and health care.

These considerations take precedence over the consideration of gaining knowledge using gene therapy, see Article 2 of the Convention. Humans should not be made a means of biomedical treatment, but it can be discussed how far it is legal to go by using humans in research. Corresponding regulations are found in Article 8 of the Helsinki Declaration.[29]

In assessing whether gene therapy should be offered, consideration must be given to others, for example if the method leads to lasting changes in the significance for humanity and whether others benefit from the research. These considerations and the need to minimize risk must include the generation and verification of data from clinical trials, treatment measures and how the effect of treatment is controlled.

---

28 Befring, *supra* note 5, pp. 374–377.

29 Article 10 of the UNESCO Declaration (1997) and Article 3 (2) of the UNESCO Declaration (2005).

This means at the same time that the patient must accept conditions for receiving the treatment offer, which may include the processing of data and examinations after the medical treatment has ended. Conditions must be set prior to the medical treatment, to meet requirements that apply in the research, and which will include the agreeing to examinations that can go over a longer period to get an overview of effects and side effects. Genetic methods will require new forms of participation as the changes will affect more than those who are patients. The opportunities to use these methods depend on more people contributing data and the data obtained can be crucial in satisfying other people's needs for medical treatment.

The implementation of genetic methods and the element of research will change the course of patient treatment, in the sense that it becomes more circular than the traditional linear approach with a clear start and end.[30] While a traditional course of treatment starts with a diagnosis, then medical treatment and the end of the treatment, i.e., a linear course, a course of treatment with clinical trials will be more circular. It may be necessary to maintain contact with the patient over time.

These changes in the medical care implies a different approach from that in ordinary research and will affect the content of obligations and patient rights. In any case, the purpose and method must be made clear in advance, and the rules must be applied based on these descriptions. It must be considered what is the state of art when there is only one method that can give the necessary effect and when it involves elements of clinical trials. If standard procedures are introduced that involve an alternation between documented medical treatment and clinical trials, a decision must also be made as to whether these standards are included as part of the right to health care.

3.2 *Possible Conflicts of Interest between Public and Commercial Actors*

Access to gene therapy and new methods can be hindered by the country's legislation, cf. Norwegian law in the next chapter, economy, and various forms of ownership. Common denominators in the basic principles include several aspects of the implementation of new genetic methods.[31] The distribution of new methods shall be safeguarded and be based on principles of equality, and the protection of the individual's integrity – in a broad sense – as well as voluntariness. International law can contribute to common practice and that can limit harmful methods that apply to humanity, i.e., methods that lead to lasting and harmful changes in the human genome. Ownership of methods

30 Befring, *supra* note 5, pp. 241–247.
31 *Ibid.*, Chapters 5 and 11.

that provide knowledge about genes were put at the forefront by American researchers (the American Civil Liberties Union (ACLU)) when they launched a lawsuit against Myriad Genetics. In the decision of the US Supreme Court in 2013 (Association for Molecular Pathology against Myriad Genetics) it was decided that it is not possible for the company to patent human genes.[32] The US Supreme Court ruled in 2013 and ruled that naturally occurring DNA sequences are not patentable. This decision has had ripple effects throughout the scientific community and the biotechnology industry.

Patients' access to genetic methods can be hindered by protected intellectual property protection. Jorge Contreras proposes that patent schemes must be developed for rapidly evolving genetic technologies that must be used in connection with medical treatment.[33] There is a close relationship between patient rights and patent rights. As stated in the World Trade Organization Doha Declaration, the intellectual property regime should be implemented in a manner supportive of the duty of States "to protect public health and, in particular, to promote access to medicines for all."[34] The right to participate in and to enjoy the benefits of scientific progress and its applications assists States in making sure that these property rights are not realized to the detriment of the right to health.[35] This right becomes a significant mediator between a human right – the right to health – and a property right.[36] Thus, State authorities should use, when necessary, all the flexibilities of the TRIPS Agreement, such as compulsory licences, to ensure access to essential medicines, especially for the most disadvantaged groups. State authorities should also refrain from granting disproportionately lengthy terms of patent protection for new medicines in order to allow, within a reasonable time, the production of safe and effective generic medicines for the same diseases. Models must be developed for collaboration between public health enterprises and commercial actors and ownership of methods.

32 Supreme Court Of The United States: *Association for Molecular Pathology et al. v. Myriad Genetics*. No. 12-398. Argued 15 April 2013. Decided 13 June 2013.

33 J. Contreras, 'Association for Molecular Pathology v. Myriad Genetics: A Critical Reassessment', *Michigan Technology Law Review* 27 (2020–2021) 1–54, doi: 10.36645/mtlr.27.1.association; J. Contreras, *The Genome Defense: Inside the Epic Legal Battle to Determine Who Owns Your DNA* (New York, NY: Algonquin Books, 2021), available online at https://www.booktopia.com.au/the-genome-defense-jorge-l-contreras/book/9781616209681.html.

34 WTO: Declaration on the TRIPS agreement and public health (DOHA), 20. November 2001.

35 O. Feeney, O.J. Cockbain and S. Sterckx, 'Ethics, Patents and Genome Editing: A Critical Assessment of Three Options of Technology Governance', *Frontiers in Political Science* 3 (2021) 731505, p. 3, doi: 10.3389/fpos.2021.731505.

36 Para. 69, General Comment No. 25 (2020) on science and economic, social and cultural rights Article 15(1)(b), and 15(2),(3) and (4) of the Covenant).

4 Biomedicine Convention, EU-Law, and Norwegian Laws

4.1 *Biomedicine Convention and EU Rules*

The content of the ban on gene therapy that can lead to hereditary changes must be considered further, in light of the fact that such changes may be necessary in medical treatment. Article 13 of the Biomedicine Convention limits the modification of the human genome for diagnostic, preventive, and therapeutic purposes, and prohibits germline-based gene therapy:

> An intervention seeking to modify the human genome may only be undertaken for preventive, diagnostic or therapeutic purposes and only if its aim is not to introduce any modification in the genome of any descendants.

The ban on interventions that are intended to alter the human genome in a way that inherited was justified during the preparatory work of the convention by the scientific uncertainty as presented, and the unpredictable effects such an intervention would have on future generations.[37] The restriction imposed by article 13 of the Biomedicin Convention entered into force on 1 December 1999. It is not clear how this ban will be applied. When changing the CRISPR technology so that it is possible to see the risk and achieve the benefit, it must be considered whether the prohibitions against germline-based gene therapy and human improvement will be maintained, and how rules are to be applied and developed.[38]

Nordberg et alia have emphasized that the wording of Article 13 is "only if its aim is not to introduce any modification," and that the Convention therefore does not prohibit any actual modification of the germ line, but only interventions that have such a modification intended.[39] This means that Article 13 can be understood as a general ban on interventions that can change the germ line, but with the exception cf. "modification" as an exception for therapeutic

---

37 Preparatory Work on the Convention on Human Rights and Biomedicine (2000) p. 63. Only 28 countries have ratified (out of 47 member states). Absences include, e.g., the EU as an institution, Germany, Ireland, Italy, The Netherlands, Poland, Sweden, UK, Israel, and the Russian Federation.

38 B.C. van Beers, 'Rewriting the human genome, rewriting human rights law? Human rights, human dignity, and human germline modification in the CRISPR era', *Journal of Law and the Biosciences* 7 (1) (2020), 1–36, p. 18, doi: 10.1093/jlb/lsaa006.

39 A. Nordberg, T. Minssen, S. Holm, M. Horst, K. Mortensen and B. Lindberg Møller. 'Cutting edges and weaving threads in the gene editing (Я)evolution: reconciling scientific progress with legal, ethical, and social concerns.' *Journal of Law and the Biosciences* 5 (1) (2018), 35–83, p. 54. https://doi.org/10.1093/jlb/lsx043.

methods.[40] Formulations of this ban can be interpreted so that somatic gene therapy that may have an effect on germ line as a side effect, is allowed.[41]

In connection with the legislative changes in Norway in 2020, the parliament (Stortinget) discussed whether mitochondrial donation is legal vis-à-vis the Biomedical Convention as there is no manipulation of genes as the genetic material in the egg nucleus does not change.[42] A proposal was made that the government amend the Biomedical Convention to ensure that mitochondrial donation can be allowed in Norway when the method is safe and professionally sound.

It must be added that it is assumed that the Convention must be amended in line with new scientific discoveries and developments.[43] The Biomedicine Convention can be interpreted dynamically in the light of the Convention preparatory work and subsequent practices and agreements between convention countries, cf. the Vienna Convention Articles 31 and 32.

Neither the directive on biotechnological inventions nor the regulation on clinical trials provides basis for a general regulation of germline-based gene therapy at EU level.

Article 2(5) of Regulation (EC) No. 1394/2007 specifies that gene therapy is both a gene therapy medicinal product and a 'somatic cell therapy medicinal product' or a 'medicinal product derived from engineered tissue'. Gene therapy can be carried out without gene editing, with the addition of genetic material where the patient's own genome is untouched. Such treatment will only have a temporary effect.

Clinical trials of gene therapy require approval in accordance with the rules in EU Regulation No. 536/2014 on clinical trials of medicinal products for human use. Pursuant to Article 90 of the Regulation, other paragraph is prohibited with clinical trials of gene therapy "which result in modifications to the subject's germ line genetic identity." Procedures for genetic modification of human germ cells are not patentable, cf. Article 6(2)(b) of the EU Directive 1998/44/EC on legal protection of biotechnological inventions. EU consensus on a ban on germ-based gene therapy is also reflected in point 40 of

40 A. Nordberg, 'Patentability of human enhancement: From ethical dilemmas to legal (un) certainty.' In T. Pistorius (eds.). *Intellectual Property Perspectives on the Regulation of New Technologies* (Edward Elgar Publishing, 2018), p. 77. https://doi.org/10.4337/9781786436382.00009.

41 Preparatory Work on the Convention on Human Rights and Biomedicine, *supra* note 37, p. 65.

42 Innst. 296 L (2019–2020) p. 18.

43 Preparatory Work on the Convention on Human Rights and Biomedicine, *supra* note 37, pp. 65, 124.

the preamble to the Directive: "[T]here is a consensus within the Community that interventions in the human germ line and the cloning of human beings offends against ordre public and morality [...]."

The EU Charter of Fundamental Rights has a scope that is limited to "the institutions, bodies, offices, and agencies of the Union" and to the Member States "only when they are implementing Union law," cf. Article 51. Article 3(2)(b) of the EU Charter sets out several bioethical requirements, including the ban on "eugenic practices". In the explanations of the Charter (2007/C 303/02) states that the principles set out in Article 3 are already enshrined in the Council of Europe's Biomedicine Convention, and that the Charter does not intend to depart from these principles. One conclusion is that EU rules do not contain a general ban on germline-based gene therapy, except when it is aimed at eugenics.[44] Such a ban must in any case have been formulated more clearly.[45]

The distinction between therapy and eugenics can be difficult to draw, for example, it is discussed whether the improvement of immunological systems is eugenics, and thus prohibited, or medical treatment that is legal.[46] In this context, the purpose of applying the method and effects will be factors that can determine whether it is legal.

4.2 *Norwegian Legislation: From Bans to Modifications, Pre-Approvals, and Legal Standards*

In Norway, several laws must be used to get an overview of how somatic gene therapy is regulated and patient rights. The Biotechnology Act of 1994 regulates which genetic methods can be used. The Patient and User Rights Act of 1999 regulates rights to medical treatment.[47] Clinical research and other health research are regulated by the Health Research Act of 2008.

The Biotechnology Act does not contain a ban on somatic gene therapy. Changes in the human germline have been prohibited in the Norwegian Biotechnology Act since it came into force in 1994, and in para. 7-1 (2) and later in para. 6-1 (2) of the current 2003 Act.[48] In Norway, increased opportunities were provided for gene editing through amendments to the Biotechnology Act

44 van Beers, *supra* note 38.

45 Yotova, *supra* note 23, pp. 670–671.

46 N. Bostrom and R. Roache, 'Ethical issues in human enhancement.' In J. Ryberg, T. Petersen, and C. Wolf (eds.) *New Waves in Applied Ethics*. (Basingstoke: Palgrave Macmillan, 2008), pp. 120–152.

47 Act of 2 July 1999 no. 63.

48 Act of 5 December 2003 no. 100.

in 2020.[49] Before the law was changed, gene therapy was only allowed for "serious" diseases.[50]

The reason is that Gene therapy can be crucial in preventing all genetic diseases. In the Biotechnology Act para. 6-2 (2) Gene therapy is prohibited except for the treatment of disease or to prevent disease from occurring. In the preparatory work, it is stated that gene therapy and other transmission of genetic material to human cells, fetuses and fertilized eggs that cause genetic changes that are inherited in gametes are prohibited.[51] There are still some ambiguities in the law, including whether the exception that applies to medical treatment applies to all forms of gene therapy. The preparatory work for an amendment law points out that there are several medical treatments that can lead to changes in gametes and emphasizes that the CRISPR method cannot be used to treat hereditary genetic defects in gametes, but that it can be used in treatment of somatic cells, for example in cancer treatment.[52] Amendments to the law have led to the ban being clarified to apply to "genetic changes that are inherited in germ cells," shall be understood as meaning that gene therapy shall be prohibited if it is "predominantly probable" that the treatment causes hereditary genetic changes.[53]

The ban has been elaborated in the previous preparatory work. Emphasis is placed on three considerations, that prudential considerations justify a ban on methods that influence future generations, and that the rules must be seen in the context of international cooperation and international consensus.[54] The technological development and the development of the international regulations will thus be factors when ambiguities in the law are to be interpreted.

The definition of gene therapy has been changed so that it is in line with relevant EU regulations to ensure simplification and harmonization with international regulations (para. 6-1) and the approval scheme for gene therapy was simultaneously removed.

4.3 *General and Individual Decisions*

In legal theory and in the public debate, it is discussed how far *general decisions* can limit fundamental individual rights to health care and the content of

49 Legislative change 19th of June 2020 no. 78.

50 Prop. 34 L (2019–2020).

51 Innst. 296 L (2019–2020) pp. 18 and 19.

52 Prop 34 L (2019–2020) p. 58.

53 Innst. 296 L (2019–2020) p. 18.

54 Ot.prp. nr. 37 (1993–1994) pp. 41–42. Ot.prp. nr. 64 (2002–2003) pp. 16 and 115. Halvorsen, M. Rettslig grunnlag for medisinsk behandling, 1998, p. 101.

the right.[55] Although the approval scheme for gene therapy has been removed, the Norwegian law includes a general requirement for approval of all medical methods used in hospitals, by the owner of the hospitals, the regional health authorities, cf. the Specialist Health Services Act para. 4-4. This provision does not apply to health research but will be a legal barrier to using non-research gene therapy. The approval scheme is justified by the need to prioritize methods based on cost and benefit, and not to protect the population from harmful methods. In regulations of the right to necessary health care, in the Patient and User Rights Act para. 2-1b, it is pointed out that the right is limited by the general decisions on new methods. This means that gene therapy must both be considered justifiable in accordance with the Specialist Health Services Act para. 2-2 and must be pre-approved by the owner of the hospitals.

Criticism of this system is strong mainly because ownership decisions are not without conflicts of interest and because it takes a long time to obtain prior approval. The national approval scheme reduces access to new genetic methods, which is particularly important for people with rare diseases. Norway is the only country in Europe that has such a scheme. Other countries, including England, have independent committees that make recommendations.

There is little doubt that this scheme may at the same time conflict with the human right to health and the duty to make individual assessments of benefit and risk.

In The Human Rights Act (Act relating to the strengthening of the status of human rights in Norwegian law) in section 2, the ECHR and the ICESCR are included among three other conventions.[56] It appears from section 3 of this Act that national laws give way if they conflict with a provision in one of the enumerated conventions.

The rapid development of gene therapy forms means that the laws are generally formulated with legal standards. The use of gene therapy that does not affect the next generation is mainly regulated by a general standard of soundness: "State of the art," cf. Health Personnel Act para. 4, the Specialist Health Services Act para. 2-2 and the Health Research Act para. 5.

55 PROBA, Evaluering av systemet for Nye metoder i spesialisthelsetjenesten, *Rapport 2021/16. Projekt nr. 20048.*

56 Act of 5 May 1999 no. 30. The other conventions are The International Covenant of 16 December 1966 on Civil and Political Rights, The Convention of 20 November 1989 on the Rights of the Child, The Convention of 18 December 1979 on the Elimination of All Forms of Discrimination against Women with Optional Protocol of 6 October 1999.

In the preparatory work for the laws, it is specified that soft law is important when the content of the standards is to be determined.[57] When this standard is to be interpreted, soft law, including recommendations from the WHO, will be of great importance in identifying and analysing the legal issues, and when the legislation is to be applied. The two publications from the WHO Expert Advisory Committee on Developing Global Standards for Governance and The Oversight of Human Genome Editing are the first framework that can contribute to common global standards and a common understanding of how the field should be governed.[58] The recommendations of the WHO Committee include both somatic and hereditary human genome editing and apply to the state's improvements to create capacity for the genetic methods.

In this perspective, human rights to life and health will be a barrier to replacing individual rights with general considerations. This follows both from the fact that Norway has ratified these conventions and from the fact that Norway has its own law that can be used when national laws conflict with human rights conventions.

5 Assessments of Fulfilment of Rights and Obstacles, Global Standards

Allowing genetic methods and giving the right to such methods can be described as different legal levels and where the law is based on the fact that it is allowed. *Prohibition* of the use of gene therapy may apply to the development and application of these methods, although there are different rules for health research and medical treatment. When the method *is allowed*, it can be offered either as clinical trials or medical treatment, or in combination. This raises the question of several rights, equal access to the method, regardless of ability to consent, assessments of the significance of the consent, and whether the right to medical treatment applies when gene therapy is used as research. The use of gene editing methods and measures must be based on more than the individual's voluntariness, as common interests must be considered. The individual will

57 Ot. prop. nr. 13 (1998–1999) comments to para. 4. Ot.prp.nr.74 (2006–2007) comments to para. 5.

58 WHO, 'Human Genome Editing: Recommendations', *World Health Organization* (2021), available online at https://apps.who.int/iris/handle/10665/342486 (accessed 10 January 2022); WHO, Human Genome Editing: A Framework for Governance, 2021. World Health Organization, 'Human Genome Editing: Position Paper', *World Health Organization* (2021), available online at https://apps.who.int/iris/handle/10665/342485 (accessed 10 January 2022).

have limited opportunities to gain insight into the method and its effects. This means that a clear distinction must be made between risk assessments of the method and the legal responsibility that is to safeguard an integrity protection, and the permission for it to be used.[59]

With new technology, it is necessary that the legal responsibility for the medical treatment is clearly placed and that errors that arise because of the method not being of sufficient quality are not to be explained with the patients' position. Volunteering for the individual, on the other hand, is of great importance in connection with medical treatment to maintain trust. It can be difficult to clearly distinguish between ethical and legal aspects when determining the content of fundamental human rights. In this context, the risk for the next generations and precautionary assessments must be considered.

Global perspectives on the right to life and health are about what expectations are justified towards countries, and about cooperation. UNESCO have provided guidelines for the processing of the genome or genetic data in three declarations.[60] In the Universal Declaration of Human Genome and Human Rights the human genome presented as a symbolic 'human heritage'.[61] IBC (UNESCOs International Bioethics Committee) to 'provide advice on the follow-up of this statement especially with regard to genetic methods of importance to the next generations.[62] This applies to the consequences of eugenic methods. At the same time, it is understood that a ban on access to therapeutic intervention may conflict with the right to health.' In 2017, the IBC published a report on the human genome and human rights that recommends a moratorium on genome editing of the human germ line.[63] IBC emphasizes, on the one hand, that there are crucial differences between medical and non-medical use of gene therapy and that there is a need for greater security. Then it is pointed out that the right to health should include precision and personalized medicine on the grounds that every human being should have the opportunity to have the highest possible standard of health. The importance of global responsibility and governance regarding scientific and technological advances in genomics was emphasized.[64] Different regulations will lead to the liberal

59 Befring, *supra* note 5, pp. 291–293.

60 UNESCO 1997/1998, 2003 and 2005.

61 Article 1 and 24 in The Universal Declaration on the Human Genome and Human Rights, adopted by the UNESCO General Conference, 1997/1998.

62 UNESCO, *Report of the IBC on Updating Its Reflection on the Human Genome and Human Rights*, SHS/YES/IBC-22/15/2REV.2 (Paris, Oct. 2, 2015), at pp. 127–128.

63 *Ibid.*

64 *Ibid.*, pp. 115–122.

countries being used for research and commercialization regarding genetic methods with potential for harm.

There will be differences in what can be expected of the states. In addition to safeguarding their own populations, the rich states can be expected to contribute to the global community and to poor countries, for example with CRISPR technology, medical knowledge, and logistics for a more equitable distribution of health benefits. When Article 2(1) of the ICESCR stipulates that the States Parties are obliged to implement these rights "individually and through international assistance and co-operation, especially economic and technical," it was made clear that the achievement of a reasonably good standard of health in poor countries demands development assistance and cooperation on the part of rich countries. WHO has pointed out that the justification for international health regulations lies in the fact that in today's globalized world, disease can spread swiftly and widely due to international travel and trade. Global perspectives on the right to life and health are about what expectations are justified towards countries, and about cooperation.

6 Conclusions and the Way Forward

In the next decades, gene editing technologies are expected to be used in the treatment and prevention of human diseases as personalized medicine.[65] Van Beers, raises the question of whether changes in the genome lead to changes in human rights.[66] Human rights are dynamic in the sense that legal issues and perspectives can be deduced when the actual possibilities for medical methods change. The European Court of Human Rights has on several occasions ruled that the European Convention on Human Rights is a "living instrument" that is subject to dynamic interpretation. The rapid changes and benefit of gene therapy are having an impact on how gene therapy can and should be regulated to comply with human rights.[67] Some conclusions on how the right to life and the right to health should be used in gene editing can be drawn:

First, the State's obligations to protect life in Article 2 (ECHR) and safeguard health in Article 12, are increasing with new genetic knowledge. The right to health is a fundamental part of the right to life, and the understanding of a

65 L.F. Moutinho Rocha, L.A. Maciel Braga and F. Batista Mota. 'Gene Editing for Treatment and Prevention of Human Diseases. A Global Survey of Gene Editing-Related Researchers', *Human Gene Therapy* 31 (15–16) (2020) 852–862, doi: 10.1089/hum.2020.136.

66 van Beers, *supra* note 38.

67 Nordberg, supra note 40, p. 60; F. Fukuyama, *Revolution* (New York, NY: Farrar, Straus and Giroux, 2002), pp. 6–10, 98, 100–102 and 173.

life in dignity. And vice versa, the right to life can be a central part of the right to health. The universal standard in Article 12 can be further defined by the requirement to allow the population to take part in scientific advances and methods, and which will include new genetic method. The right to life and health may provide a basis for states to have a system that can actively take a position on new genetic methods. Balancing the health benefits of genetic methods with basic human rights requires rethinking the way healthcare is organized and regulated. Further development of legislation and governance of new genetic knowledge should take place based on the basic concepts and principles. On the other side the expectations of the state must be reasonable and the choice of measures belongs to the state's margin of discretion.[68] Although it is unclear how far the obligations to fulfil the right to life extend in this context, an obligation to establish a transparent system of governance can be deduced.

Nordberg and several others have pointed out that a moratorium on germline-based gene therapy may make other forms of use of CRISPR technology seem legitimate and acceptable.[69] The World Health Organization has stated that over 10 000 monogenic diseases are caused by a defect in a single gene of DNA, which occurs in 1% of births.[70] The application of gene therapy must be based on balancing risk and benefits. Harmful diseases cannot be met with harmful genetic methods. Gene therapy can be of great importance to reduce serious and rare diseases. An example could be the ban of the treatment of a rare disease due to lack of sufficient risk assessment and as a consequence persons having the disease not receiving the necessary health care. New questions arise about equal access to medical treatment methods for people with rare diseases and disabilities, for example whether genetic mutations that cause disease can be reversed. The legislation must consider the rapid development of The CRISPR method. This argues for that the ban against germline-based gene therapy should be nuanced. Common standards can be to achieve a desired development of how gene therapy should be used. These must be developed continuously in line with the development in supplementary regulations in the form of soft law.

Secondly, gene editing will lead to changes in the State's obligations to further develop the health service also entail a further development of patient rights. Regulations of health research will cover a wide range of considerations, in which medical treatment of a patient may be a primary – and not a secondary

68 Brincat and Others v. Malta, *supra* note 21, para. 101.

69 Nordberg et al., *supra* note 39, p. 75.

70 WHO, http://www.who.int/genomics/public/geneticdiseases/en/index2.html.

purpose, as is usually the case in research. The clear distinction between medical treatment and health research is becoming less clear and the diversity of interests must be safeguarded, including health justice. Patient rights must be rewritten to include the consequences of medical treatment containing elements of research and changes in the course of treatment. Some argue that it should be left to the individual to assess how much risk one wants to take with regards to medical treatment – like an individual voluntary risk taking in sports and leisure activities. Such an approach could disrupt the possibilities for a clearly placed legal responsibility for the genetic method. If the patient is to take greater responsibility for risk assessments, and with an opportunity to take over responsibility, this will have consequences for trust in research and the health service. This approach will also lead to different offers of health services to people with and without consent competence, which can have unpredictable effects when the health service and health research are used towards people who lack consent. A clear distinction must be made between liability principles and formal requirements for consent.

Finally, Gene therapy represents a significant transformation of medical treatment that requires global regulation and standards for achieving common practice. International law provides guidance on both rights and assessment topics when gene therapy is to be used and when we are faced with technologies that can change mankind and affect the future of humanity. Models for cooperation between countries, and between public health services and commercial actors, must be further developed in order to achieve new genetic methods and fair access to these methods. For this reason, the distinction between gene therapy that is important for next generations and somatic gene therapy must be maintained and at the same time, it must be further developed. The rapid development of complex technologies requires both international exchange, cooperation and a dynamic development of rules in order to be sustainable.

Somatic Genome Editing with the Use of AI: Big Promises but Doubled Legal Issues

Anastasiya Kiseleva | ORCID: 0000-0003-4405-0272
Subgroup Health and Ageing Law Lab (HALL), Research Group Law, Science, Technology and Society (LSTS), Vrije Universiteit Brussel, Pleinlaan 2 1050 Brussels, Belgium
ETIS Research Lab, CY Cergy Paris University, 33 Boulevard du Port, 95000 Cergy, France
anastasiya.kiseleva@vub.be

Abstract

Both Artificial Intelligence ('AI') and genome editing are technologies that on their own promise to revolutionise healthcare. But their common application can facilitate progress in the field even more. Multiplied benefits go along with increased risks. In this chapter I identify and analyse legal challenges associated with applying AI facilities in medicinal products based on somatic genome editing. These challenges are caused by several factors. First, the two technologies share the characteristics that create and facilitate common risks. Second, each of the technologies is subject to very complex regulatory frameworks. These frameworks are not substantially connected to control the safety and quality of the common product. The main argument of this paper is that the management of common risks is only possible through common procedures. I discover the gaps in the current legislation that prevent from establishing these common procedures and provide recommendations to fill them in.

Keywords

artificial intelligence – genome editing – medical devices – advanced therapy medicinal products – clinical trials – marketing authorisation – post-market surveillance – pharmacovigilance

1 Introduction

'Artificial intelligence (AI)[1] is a discovery that is as delicate as it is powerful and the same can be said for genome editing.'[2] Combined application of the two technologies increases both the possibilities and risks. The power of AI to quickly operate on huge amounts of data accelerates the analysis of DNA data which otherwise is time-consuming and tedious.[3]

AI can be used at different stages of genome editing starting from the identification of the harmful genes that shall be edited[4] and finishing with the monitoring of the consequences of the editing. 'AI algorithms are used to identify the precise location for DNA alteration which is the fundamental aspect of gene editing.'[5] Another use of AI is the accurate delivery of new genetic code to a diseased cell. For example, Charles River developed a deep learning algorithm to assay digital microscopic images for the quality of genetic material.[6] 'AI also provides insights about how to ensure that the repair process of the DNA strand is successful, helping in reducing potential mistakes during the entire process.'[7] The combined use of the technologies has the potential to increase the accuracy of genome editing, predict and prevent relevant risks and to improve the safety and quality of the process.[8]

Used together, the technologies not only provide great benefits but also multiply the relevant legal issues. Each of the technologies and the associated

1 Artificial Intelligence is a broad term and includes different technologies. The use of the term 'AI' in this chapter refers to machine learning (characterised by autonomy, self-learning and opacity but at the same time by high efficiency).

2 A. Sankar, 'The Role of AI in Gene Technology', *Young Scientists Journal* (2020), available online at https://ysjournal.com/rosalind-franklin-day/the-role-of-ai-in-gene-technology/ (accessed 30 July 2021).

3 *Ibid.*

4 For example, AI is also used for the identification of genetic mutations within tumours with 3D imaging (see here: S. Dutta, 'Role of Artificial Intelligence & Machine Learning in Genomics', *SG Analytics, Healthcare* (18 October 2020), available online at https://us.sganalytics.com/blog/role-of-artificial-intelligence-machine-learning-in-genomics/ (accessed 16 September 2021)).

5 *Ibid.*

6 C. River, 'Somatic Gene Therapy: On the Cusp of Major Innovation. What Would a World Without Disease Look Like?', *Charles River, Featured Story* (20 May 2021), available online at https://www.criver.com/insights/somatic-gene-therapy-cusp-major-innovation (accessed 16 September 2021).

7 Dutta, *supra* note 4.

8 W. Johnson and E. Pauwels, 'How to Optimize Human Biology: Where Genome Editing and Artificial Intelligence Collide', *Wilson Briefs* (October 2017), available online at https://www.wilsoncenter.org/sites/default/files/media/documents/publication/how_to_optimize_human_biology.pdf (accessed 18 October 2021).

legal challenges are extensively explored by legal scholars and policymakers. Even discussed separately, AI and genome editing are both very complex and controversial topics, where the solutions to the identified challenges are yet to be developed and finalised in the legislation. To decrease the number of complexities, this chapter focuses on the least controversial type of genome editing — the somatic one. This type affects only the patient being treated (and only some of his or her cells), in contrast to the germline editing which affects all cells in an organism, including eggs and sperm, and so is passed on to future generations.[9] Due to that, somatic genome editing is considered as an acceptable technology[10] that constitutes medical progress and should be supported.[11] 'Such treatments should be considered as any other gene therapy.'[12] Classification of somatic genome editing as gene therapy (and more specifically as a medicinal product)[13] enables applying to them already existing legal frameworks which makes the analysis in this paper more practice-oriented.

Although somatic genome editing is less controversial technology, it is still rather novel and complex. Consequently, the discussion of it used together with AI is far from being simple and is not yet extensively covered in literature. Due to that, this chapter is two-fold: its primary goal is to identify the legal issues for the use of AI in somatic genome editing[14] and based on that to suggest some possible solutions.

I start with the analysis of the common features of AI and genome editing. This analysis (in Section 2) is necessary for seeing that the combination of the technologies is especially challenging (in comparison to their separate use) because of their shared characteristics. Opacity, lack of full predictability and control, high dependency on data are the features attributed to both AI and genome editing. When the technologies are used together, the risks resulting from these features are substantially amplified.

---

9 M.T. Bergman, 'Perspectives of Gene Editing', *The Harvard Gazette* (9 January 2019), available online at https://news.harvard.edu/gazette/story/2019/01/perspectives-on-gene-editing/ (accessed 16 September 2021). With the reference to the words of I. Glenn Cohen, faculty director of the Petrie-Flom Center for Health Law Policy, Biotechnology, and Bioethics at Harvard Law School.

10 S. Polcz and A. Lewis, 'CRISPR-Cas9 and the non-germline non-controversy', *Journal of Law and the Biosciences* 3 (2) (2016) 413–425, https://doi.org/10.1093/jlb/lsw016.

11 Comité Consultatif National d'Éthique pour les Sciences de la Vie et de la Santé 'Opinion 133 on Ethical Challenges of Gene Editing: Between Hope and Caution', CCNE, 2019, available online at https://www.ccne-ethique.fr/sites/default/files/2021-02/avis_133_-_ad_final.pdf (accessed 21 November 2022).

12 *Ibid.*

13 See the explanation of this argument in Section 3 of this chapter.

14 Further in this chapter the term 'genome editing' refers to the somatic one.

At the same time, both AI and genome editing are subject to very complex regulatory frameworks. To go through the complexities, I first outline the frameworks applicable separately to AI and therapeutic genome editing (Section 3). Then I identify how these frameworks establish classifications for the products where the two technologies are used together. Full understanding of when and how AI is implemented in the specific genome editing process is crucial because it will define the classification of the common product. Different classifications lead to different scenarios of the frameworks' correlations and thus to differences in verification procedures.

I demonstrate these differences in the overview (Section 4) of the correlations between the applicable frameworks for two classifications of the common products: when AI is combined with a medicinal product or when AI companions it. The roles of involved actors are also identified. To discover the relevant risks and to see how they are addressed I provide a more detailed view of the relevant procedures at every stage of the products' life cycles starting from clinical trials and finishing with post-market control (Section 5).

The main argument of this chapter is that the management of common risks is only possible through common procedures. Yet, the existing frameworks are rather separated which I prove in sections 4 and 5. Based on the common features of the two technologies and discovered legal issues, I develop common (for the two types of products) recommendations for making use of AI in genome editing more safe and more qualitative (section 6). I also further provide more concrete suggestions to be considered by policymakers in the relevant guidelines differentiated based on the type of the common product (section 7).

2 Common Features of AI and Genome Editing Technologies

2.1 *Code-Based Character*

AI and genome editing are far more similar than just being two cutting-edge technologies. Both of them are code-based. Genomic information is coded in our DNA. 'DNA contains the instructions for human development, survival, and physiologic functions, as well as ensuring that our biological information will be passed to our children and future generations.'[15] Similarly, any AI system includes computer code which sets the basic rules of turning an input to an output.

15 G. Annas and S. Elias, *Genomic Messages. How the Evolving Science of Genetics Affects our Health, Family and Future* (New York, NY: HarperCollins, 2016), p. 1.

The common code-based nature of the two scientific fields gave rise to the idea of technologically driven genomics[16] or even of biology as a machine.[17] Data belongs to computers[18] and sequenced DNA consists of huge amounts of data.[19] To turn this data to information and then to knowledge that can be scientifically and clinically applied, the power of computers is needed. Developing this idea, some authors argue that 'the digitised DNA will let us construct a "stairway to heaven" or even better life on Earth.'[20] 'Digitised genomic messages can change the way we think about life itself as data bring the material (DNA) and the virtual (digital) into new relationships.'[21] In the digitised word AI is the most sophisticated and powerful technology so far. The ability of AI to process very quickly huge amounts of data and find new correlations in it brings the possibilities of genomics, including genome editing, to a completely new level. This great symbiosis of the two technologies is possible due to their common code-based and data-based (as explained in Section 2.5) characters.

2.2 *Adaptations Based on External Influence*

The two technologies are also similar in how their functioning is influenced by external factors. The self-learning nature of AI results in algorithmics adaptations based on the new input data. It means that AI systems are never locked, and their functioning is greatly influenced by data. The same applies to the human genome. Although we are used to think that 'our DNA is stable and its functioning cannot be easily modified',[22] the recent scientific discoveries inform that our external and internal environments modify the functioning of genes.[23] This feature makes both AI and genetic systems constantly changing: 'to evolve, a successful system must be able to learn, and pass what it learns on

16 *Ibid.*, 4.

17 Johnson and Pauwels, *supra* note 8, p. 4.

18 Annas and Elias, *supra* note 15, p. 3. Reference to H. Stevens, *Life out of Sequence: a Data-Driven History of Bioinformatics* (Chicago, IL: University of Chicago Press, 2013), pp. 8, 69.

19 'Capable of storing 215 petabytes (215 million gigabytes) in a single gram of DNA, the DNA-based data storage system could, in principle, store every bit of datum ever recorded by humans'; R.F. Service, 'DNA Could Store All of the World's Data in One Room. New Algorithm Delivers the Highest-Ever Density for Large-Scale Data Storage', Science.org (2 March 2017), available online at https://www.science.org/content/article/dna-could-store-all-worlds-data-one-room (accessed 16 January 2022).

20 Annas and Elias, *supra* note 15, p. 4.

21 Annas and Elias, *supra* note 15, p. 3. Reference to Stevens, *supra* note 18, pp. 8, 69.

22 Annas and Elias, *supra* note 15, p. 6.

23 *Ibid.*, p. 7.

to its offspring.'[24] This learning feature enables the permanent progress of the technologies. At the same time, the changes can be unpredictable and opaque (explained further) which makes their control difficult. Fortunately, the scopes of adaptations in both technologies are not unlimited. As with AI where its self-learning adaptations do not change the whole code, environments do not completely change the genome. However, even the limited impact of environments influence on both AI and DNA and thus shall be taken into consideration during their use.

2.3 *Lack of Full Predictability*

The constant interactions of both AI and DNA with their external environments lead to their changes. The issue with these changes is that they are not fully predictable. Of course, AI is trained by its developers before its real-life usage. This training involves verification of the outcomes generated by AI, which means that some level of AI's accuracy is predicted (and promised). However, in real-life usage, AI receives more quantity and more variety of data which might lead to unpredictable changes in algorithmic outcomes. This affects the safety, accuracy, and quality of decisions made with the use of AI tools. But unpredictability also exists in genome editing which makes the use of the two technologies together even riskier. 'Most assays of germline transmission have low sensitivity, and thus a certain degree of uncertainty may have to be managed in considering clinical development and regulation.'[25] With the most recent but still quite novel advances in genome-editing technologies such as CRISPR, the risks of unpredictable consequences remain rather high.[26]

2.4 *Lack of Full Transparency*

Lack of full predictability is complicated by another issue common for both AI and genome editing — lack of full transparency. Due to the 'black-box' effect of AI, it is difficult to say how the input turned to the output or in other words, how AI made a specific decision and what were the factors that influenced it. Together with the lack of full predictability and algorithmic changes, this

24 M. Alemi, *The Amazing Journey of Reason: from DNA to Artificial Intelligence* (Berlin: SpringerOpen, 2020), p. 93, https://doi.org/10.1007/978-3-030-25962-4.

25 National Academies of Sciences, Engineering, and Medicine, *Human Genome Editing: Science, Ethics, and Governance* (Washington, DC: The National Academies Press, 2017), https://doi.org/10.17226/246235 (accessed 18 October 2021).

26 For example, research published in Nature discovered that off-target effects, or the possibility of altering unintended parts of the genome occur more often than previously thought; Johnson and Pauwels, *supra* note 9, referring to K.A. Schaefer, W.H. Wu, D.F. Colgan, S.H. Tsang, A.G. Bassuk and V.B. Mahajan, 'Unexpected Mutations after CRISPR-Cas9 Editing in Vivo', *Nature Methods* 14 (6) (2017) 547–548. https://www.nature.com/articles/nmeth.4293 (accessed 18 October 2021).

makes the control over AI's safety and quality even more challenging. At the same time, as mentioned before, the human genome, its functioning, and interaction with environments are not fully explored areas. Genomics and epigenetics are called the black boxes of biology.[27] Although genome editing is more transparent than AI's decision-making in the sense that it is easier to say how the editing was carried out, it still includes some unforeseeable risks due to the novelty of the technology. Of course, the combination of the two opaque technologies results in more opaqueness.

The common opaqueness is facilitated not just only by the cumulation of the opacities of the two technologies, but also by the obscurity of how the technologies work together. The sequenced genome has a huge amount of data,[28] and it is not always possible to say what kind of data AI considered for its analysis. It might be the type of data that developers of AI systems consider important (for example, the specific gene that causes the disease to be treated by its editing), but it can also be the other gene or even so-called 'junk' or 'non-functioning DNA.'[29] And how these 'junk' DNA affect the whole process is still unclear: scientists mention that 'gene expressions can be controlled by "switches" in the non-coding regions of the genome which can turn genes on and off.'[30] On top of that, 'it is extremely complicated to figure out which switches went with which genes.'[31] Generally, 'the complexities of genetic interactions are poorly understood'[32] which might affect genome editing process and its results. In these circumstances, it is difficult to filter what kind of data in the whole genome shall be used as input data in an AI system. Taking too much data would increase the chances of AI making unpredictable decisions and taking a small amount of data would decrease the efficacy and the chances of new discoveries. In addition, the evaluation of decisions made by AI is complicated not only by the algorithmic 'black-boxness',[33] but also by the existing lacunes in genomics. Fortunately, both AI and genomics, including gene editing, are

---

27 M. Morange, *The Black Box of Biology. A history of the Molecular Revolution*, 2nd edn. (London: Royal Society of Biology, 2013).

28 See *supra* note 19.

29 E. Margulies, *Non-coding DNA* (*National Human Genome Research Institute*), available online at https://www.genome.gov/genetics-glossary/Non-Coding-DNA (accessed 16 January 2022).

30 Annas and Elias, *supra* note 15, p. 5.

31 *Ibid.*, p. 7.

32 CEC Bioethics Thematic Reference Group, *Moral and Ethical Issues in Human Genome Editing* (May 2018), available online at https://www.ceceurope.org/wp-content/uploads/2019/01/Gene-editing-for-CEC-13.3.18-final-version_v2.pdf (accessed 16 January 2022).

33 The term is used by Z.C. Lipton, 'The Mythos of Model Interpretability', *2016 ICML Workshop on Human Interpretability in Machine Learning* (*WHI 2016*), *New York, NY, USA*, available online at https://arxiv.org/abs/1606.03490.

highly dependent on data and thus can be partly controlled through proper data governance and management. This argument is explained below.

2.5 *High Dependency on Data*

The relevance of the data defines the quality of the outcomes generated on the basis of this data. Proper data governance and management are the main available tools to decrease the amount of opacity and non-predictability of AI and genome editing, and especially of their combination.

In the genome editing context, the medical treatment is tailored to the unique characteristics of the treated person, including genes. In addition, for any medical research, product, and process full avoiding of any risks is not possible and there is always the need to accept some risks balanced with the possible benefits. Yet, the minimisation of risks is required, and this minimisation is only possible through collecting, generating and verification of data both from clinical trials and during the pharmacovigilance process. 'Moral decisions, especially in biomedicine, are empirically informed.'[34]

In the AI context, data is everything: algorithms learn from it at the development and real-life usage. If AI is trained and verified on the data that is not substantially relevant to the real-life usage, then the algorithms can change and produce the outcomes that are not predicted at the development stage and thus can be inaccurate (or at least their accuracy is not verified). It means that at the development stage the relevance and quality of data used to train and validate AI shall be highly controlled. At the same time, AI continues to learn from new data after it is placed on the market which means that it is crucial both to control the data to be added to AI system in real life and also to monitor the generated outcomes to see if the AI system changed substantially in a way that it affects safety and quality of the authorised product.

2.6 *Summary*

In this section, I explored the common features of AI and genomics, including genome editing, that constitute the great synergy between the two technologies (such as their code-based character and data dependency), but also facilitate the relevant issues (such as constant adaptations, lack of full predictability and transparency). To make the genome editing treatment with the use of AI safe and qualitative, these issues shall be addressed during the relevant clinical

34 C. Brokowski and M. Adli, 'CRISPR Ethics: Moral Considerations for Applications of a Powerful Tool', *Journal of Molecular Biology* 431 (2019), 88–101, https://doi.org/10.1016/j.jmb.2018.05.044.

trials, marketing authorisation, and post-market control. These procedures are established by different legal frameworks that are outlined in the next section.

3 Legislative Frameworks Applicable to the Use of AI in Somatic Genome Editing

To identify the legal and ethical challenges arising out of the use of AI in somatic genome editing, it is first necessary to define the frameworks applicable for these two technologies. This task is far from being trivial. Both medical AI medical applications and somatic genome editing medical products are subject to very complex and multi-layered frameworks. This section identifies these frameworks (separately for each of the technologies) and then based on that explores how the frameworks correlate when the technologies are used together.

3.1 *Frameworks for Somatic Genome Editing*

The main legislative act applicable to somatic genome editing is the Regulation No. 1394/2007 as of 13 November 2007 on advanced therapy medicinal products[35] ('The ATMP Regulation'). The Regulation defines that advanced therapy medicinal products ('ATMPs') include gene therapy medicinal products[36] that, in turn, cover genome editing technologies.[37] While the germline genome editing technologies are prohibited in the EU clinical trials and thus cannot be authorised,[38] it concerns the only one permitted type of genome editing — the somatic one. Thus, in this chapter ATMPs refer to gene therapy medicinal products based on somatic genome editing technologies.

The ATMP Regulation is the *lex specialis* to the general framework governed by the Directive 2001/83/EC as of 6 November 2001, on the Community code relating to medicinal products for human use and the Regulation 726/2004 of

35 Medicinal products — any substances or combinations of substances presented for treating or preventing disease in human beings (the Directive on Community Code Relating to Medicinal Products for Human Use, Article 1(2)).

36 Regulation (EC) No 1394/2007 of the European Parliament and of the Council of 13 November 2007 on advanced therapy medicinal products and amending Directive 2001/83/EC and Regulation (EC) No 726/2004, L 324/121 (ATMP Regulation), Article 2(1)(a).

37 Directive 2001/83/EC of the European Parliament and of the Council of 6 November 2001 on the Community code relating to medicinal products for human use, *OJ L* 31 (Directive on Community Code Relating to Medicinal Products for Human Use), Annex I, part IV, 2.1.

38 Regulation (EU) No 536/2014 of the European Parliament and of the Council of 16 April 2014 on clinical trials on medicinal products for human use, and repealing Directive 2001/20/EC, L 158/1 ('CTR'), recital 75 and Article 90(2).

31 March 2004 laying down Community procedures for the authorisation and supervision of medicinal products for human and veterinary use[39] (together 'Framework on Medicinal Products for Human Use'). This Framework together with the ATMP Regulation concerns the authorisation, supervision, and pharmacovigilance of ATMPs, including gene therapy products based on genome editing.

Any medicinal product that is authorised to be placed on the market has to be verified in clinical trials, which means the necessity to comply with the additional framework — Regulation 536/2014 as of 16 April 2014 on clinical trials on medicinal products for human use ('Clinical Trials Regulation' or 'CTR'). The CTR concerns the safety and efficacy of medicinal products and mostly covers scientific research and verification of the medicine in question with the inclusion of human participants. The main aims of the Regulation are to protect the rights, safety, dignity, and well-being of trials' subjects and to ensure that the data generated during trials is reliable and robust.[40]

The ATMP Regulation also covers combined medicinal products — one of the types of ATMPs that incorporate medical devices.[41] These devices shall meet the requirements of the Medical Devices Regulation[42] which means that they should be verified through the conformity assessment procedures established in this act. The ATMP Regulation states that the results of this conformity assessment shall be 'recognised by the European Medicine Agency ('EMA') in the evaluation of a combined advanced therapy medicinal product ('cATMP').'[43] This correlation between two frameworks established in the legislation is important in the context of this work because AI medical applications are covered by the Medical Devices Framework as explained below.

3.2 *Frameworks for Medical AI Applications*

The general framework to regulate AI is in its development process. In April 2021 the European Commission issued its Proposal for the AI Act ('EC Proposal

39 Regulation (EC) No 726/2004 of the European Parliament and of the Council of 31 March 2004 laying down Community procedures for the authorisation and supervision of medicinal products for human and veterinary use and establishing a European Medicines Agency (Text with EEA relevance) OJ L 136/1.

40 CTR, recital 1.

41 ATMP Regulation, recital 18.

42 Regulation (EU) 2017/745 of the European Parliament and of the Council of 5 April 2017 on medical devices, 1223/2009 and repealing Council Directives 90/385/EEC and 93/42/EEC, OJ L 117 (MDR).

43 ATMP Regulation, recital 18.

for the AI Act').[44] The proposed AI Act establishes the requirements for high-risk AI applications. AI applications used for medical purposes and covered by the Medical Devices Framework are considered to be high-risk and will have to conform with the requirements of the AI Act.[45] Thus, AI-based medical devices would have two frameworks to comply with: the general AI Act and the specific for AI devices for medical use — Medical Devices Framework. According to the proposal, AI Act will be integrated into the existing sectorial legislation: 'the safety risks specific to AI systems are meant to be covered by the requirements of the AI Act, and the sectorial legislation (the MDF) aims to ensure the overall safety of the final product.'[46]

While the AI Act is not yet adopted, the main framework currently applicable to medical AI applications is the Medical Devices Framework. It includes two acts — Medical Devices Regulation ('MDR')[47] and In-Vitro Diagnostic Medical Devices Regulation ('IVDR').[48] The main difference between the two Regulations is where and for what the device is used — in-vitro (outside the human body) and for diagnostic purposes — for the IVDR; and all other cases (including therapy) for the MDR.[49]

3.3 *Classifications of the Somatic Genome Editing Medicinal Products Used with AI-Tools*

'The correct classification of a product at an early stage of development is a critical point since it will determine the regulatory framework.'[50] When AI is used in somatic genome editing, different variations exist depending on how and where the tool is used. The IVDR covers the specific type of devices that are

44 European Commission, Proposal for a Regulation of the European Parliament and of the Council Laying Down Harmonized Rules on Artificial Intelligence (Artificial Intelligence Act) and Amending Certain Union Legislative Acts ((COM (2021) 206 final), 21 April 2021) (EC Proposal for the AI Act).

45 *Ibid.*, Article 6.

46 *Ibid.*, p. 4.

47 *Supra* note 42.

48 Regulation (EU) 2017/746 of the European Parliament and of the Council of 5 April 2017 on in vitro diagnostic medical devices and repealing Directive 98/79/EC and Commission Decision 2010/227/EU (OJ L 117 (the 'IVD Medical Devices Regulation' or the 'IVDR')).

49 The two acts included in the MDF are rather similar in their procedures and concerned subjects. For the simplicity of further analysis, the MDR will be used as a point of reference when the two acts do not substantially differ. When they do, both acts (IVDR and MDR) will be observed.

50 C. Iglesias-Lopez, A. Agustí, M. Obach and A. Vallano, 'Regulatory Framework for Advanced Therapy Medicinal Products in Europe and United States', *Frontiers in Pharmacology* 10 (2019) 921, https://www.frontiersin.org/articles/10.3389/fphar.2019.00921/full (accessed 20 October 2021.

relevant in the context of genome editing applications — companion diagnostic devices. This type of device is used together with a medicinal product for 'identification, before and/or during treatment, patients who are most likely to benefit from the corresponding medicinal product or patients likely to be at increased risk of serious adverse reactions.'[51] Thus, AI applications used for identification of harmful genomes that shall be edited or for predicting the consequences of genome editing for the specific patient, most probably will be covered by the IVDR as a companion diagnostic device. Genetic testing devices are also covered by the IVDR.[52] These two types of devices are classified as class C.

On the other side, when an AI application is used for the accurate delivery of a new genetic code to a deceased cell and is an integral part of the product, this type of usage is difficult to consider in vitro diagnosis and thus such device will fall under the scope of the MDR. In this case, the applications are classified as level III of risks because this class is attributed to the medical devices incorporating, as an integral part, medicinal product.[53]

As the result, there is no one-way-to-go framework for AI applications, and it will be defined on the basis of the type and stage of AI usage in the somatic genome editing process. The type of the AI-based medical device will also define how the frameworks shall work together and the necessary compliance procedures.

When an AI device is covered by the MDR and is used integrally with the medicinal product (for example, for the accurate delivery of new genetic code to a deceased cell), then the whole product is considered as the *combined* ATMP. It means that the product will be generally covered by the ATMP Regulation and the Framework on Medicinal Products for Human Use for receiving marketing authorisation.

When an AI device is covered by the IVDR and is used *in companion* with the relevant medicinal product (for identifying patients that are suitable or unsuitable for treatment,[54] for example), the single authorisation is not yet established and thus each of the elements will be authorised separately.[55] In this case, the medicinal product element will be still considered as the ATMP (but not the combined one) and will be separately covered by the ATMP Regulation and by the Framework on Medicinal Products for Human Use.

51 IVDR, Article 2(7).

52 IVDR, Article 4(1).

53 MDR, Annex VII, Chapter III, Article 7(1).

54 European Medicines Agency, Human Regulatory, Medical Devices https://www.ema.europa.eu/en/human-regulatory/overview/medical-devices (accessed 22 October 2021).

55 Yet with some cooperation as explained further in Section 4.

To sum up, the genome editing medicinal product with the use of AI might be classified differently resulting in different compliance scenarios. Although the relevant procedures are similar, their applicability differs due to varied correlations between the frameworks and the different roles of involved actors. These differences are outlined in the next section.

4 Overview of the Relevant Procedures and the Roles of Accountable Subjects

4.1 *Overview of the Roles of Accountable Subjects*

The list of subjects involved in genome editing with the use of AI tools is extensive and complex. For the part related to ATMPs (gene editing medicinal products) — holders of marketing authorisation ('MA holders') are the main subject responsible for placing a medicinal product on the market and its pharmacovigilance.[56] Sponsors and investigators are responsible for carrying out clinical trials preceding marketing authorisation.[57] For AI-based medical device — its manufacturer is the main figure responsible for clinical investigation, marketing authorisation and post-market surveillance of the device in question.[58]

Under the current frameworks, the listed subjects are only accountable for their fragments of the products where AI and genome editing technologies are mixed. This state of affairs makes the common control over safety and quality rather challenging. The things are also complicated with the differences in procedures depending on how an AI element is used — integrally combined with ATMPs or used in companion with them. The current legislation only partly defines the correlation between the frameworks and below I demonstrate it for the different types of products starting with the combined ATMPs.

4.2 *Correlation of the Frameworks and the Roles of Accountable Subjects for Combined ATMPs*

Combined ATMP in the context of this chapter is, for example, when AI-device is used to deliver new genetic code to a diseased cell. The ATMP Regulation sets that for this type of product 'the marketing authorisation application shall include the results of the assessment by a notified body of the medical

56 Regulation on Community procedures for the Authorisation and Supervision of Medicinal Products, Article 2.

57 CTR, Article 2(2)(14) and Article 2(2)(15).

58 MDR, Article 2(12).

device part.'[59] It means that the AI-based part of genome editing medicines shall be verified under the MDR before the combined product is submitted for marketing authorisation. This rule establishes the order of verification and of preparing of the relevant documents with respect to different parts of the combined product. The final combined product is to be evaluated by the EMA that decides on marketing authorisation. Based on this, it can be implied that the main subject accountable for the marketing of the whole product is the MA holder. Consequently, the MA holder is responsible for post-market control of the authorised combined product. Yet, a manufacturer of a medical device is separately responsible for post-market surveillance of the device part which makes the correlation between the procedures unclear. Uncertainties are also presented on the correlation between the procedures for clinical trials (for the ATMPs part) and clinical investigations (for the medical device part) and cooperation between the subjects responsible for different parts of the product. For this procedure, there is no main subject controlling the whole process for the combined product and cooperating with authorities in this regard. This situation is summarised in picture 1 below.

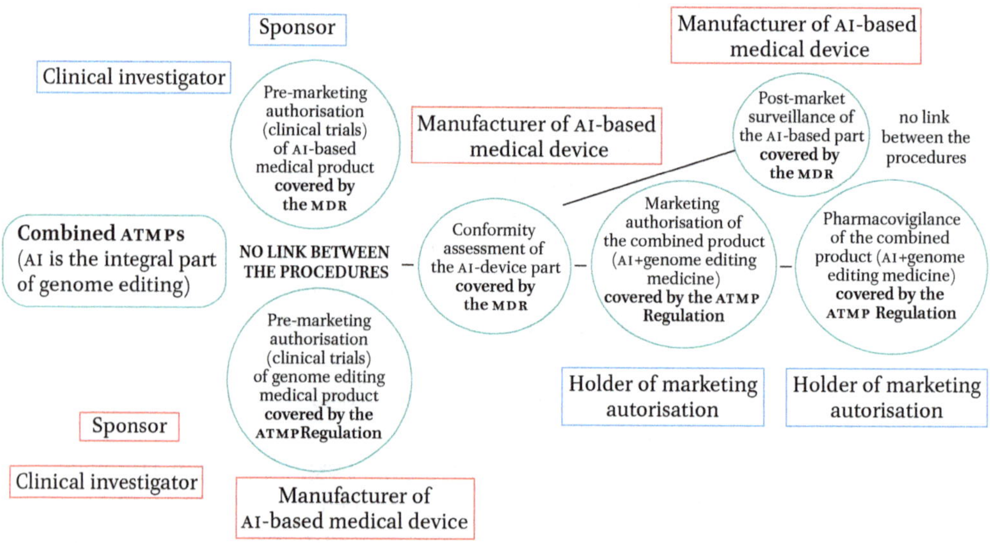

FIGURE 1 Correlation of the applicable frameworks and the roles of accountable subjects for combined ATMPS

59 ATMP Regulation, Article 9(3).

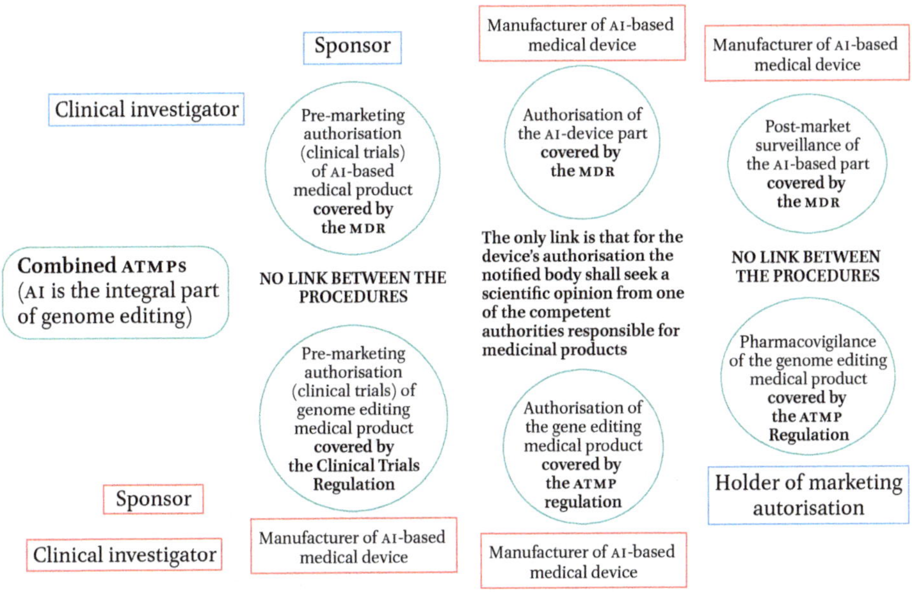

FIGURE 2 Correlation of the applicable frameworks and the roles of accountable subjects for companioned ATMPS

4.3 *Correlation of the Frameworks and the Roles of Accountable Subjects for Companioned* ATMPS

The whole picture becomes even more complicated when an AI-device is used for companion diagnosis (such as predicting the patients' risks and benefits from the medicinal product). In this case, the authorisations for different parts of the product are almost not linked. The only link established by the legislation is the requirement to seek a scientific opinion by the notified body for the device's authorisation from one of the competent authorities responsible for medicinal products (EMA or Member States' competent authorities).[60] This rule however does not establish the single marketing authorisation to verify the parts of the product in their combination and does not establish the common procedures for accountable subjects. The procedures preceding (clinical trials) and following (pharmacovigilance and post-market surveillance) marketing authorisation are not linked too (similar to the situation with combined ATMPS described above). Picture 2 demonstrates the lack of correlation between the frameworks.

60 IVDR, Annex IX, Chapter II, 5(2).

4.4 *Summary*

The pictures above demonstrate how the applicable frameworks correlate to each other and what kind of actors are involved at different stages of the products' life cycles. This first overview already shows that the frameworks are not fully linked, and that it is not substantially clear how the actors shall cooperate. The next section provides more details to this argument and explains the associated problems.

5 Compliance Procedures and Legal Challenges

To explore legal challenges arising out of complexities with different frameworks' correlation and cooperation between accountable subjects, I structure the analysis based on the phases of a product's life cycle. These phases are: (1) procedures before marketing authorisation (mostly concerning clinical trials of ATMPs (gene therapy medicinal products) and manufacture of the AI-device element); (2) marketing authorisation; and (3) procedures after marketing authorisation. The latter stage can be divided into two types: post-market control and continuous real-life usage of the product (in the best-case scenario) or causing damages by the product and applying the liability rules (in the worst-case scenario).

5.1 *Before Applying for Marketing Authorisation*

Although the procedures and correlations between the frameworks are different for two types of products (for ATMPs combined with the AI-device and ATMPs used in companion with them), the differences mostly concern the stage of marketing authorisation which is explored in the next subsection. At this stage is important to understand the procedures that precede applying for marketing authorisation — clinical trials of medicinal products and clinical investigations of medical devices. In this case, the procedures for the two types of products do not substantially differ (and thus the relevant issues) and are explored together.

The Clinical Trials Regulation establishes the procedures to involve human subjects for assessing the safety and quality of medicinal products. Similarly, the Medical Devices Framework requires to carry out clinical investigations for AI-based medical devices.[61] This procedure also 'involves one or more human subjects, undertaken to assess the safety or performance of a device.'[62]

61 The clinical investigation is required because both types of AI devices (companion and combined) used with medicinal products are classified with high risks (MDR, recital 63).

62 MDR, Article 2(45).

However, neither the Clinical Trials Regulation nor the Medical Devices Framework establishes how they shall work together in case of developing the product that involves the elements covered by the two frameworks. Each of the frameworks concerns the involvement of human subjects and generating of data to assess the safety and efficacy of the product in question. The idea to assess different product's elements (medicinal product and medical device) under the most relevant to these parts frameworks is deemed reasonable because it means applying the most relevant expertise. But the knowledge of how the elements work in combination is highly important due to the common risks of AI and genome editing described in Section 2.

Both AI-applications and genome editing tools are crucially dependent on data. AI learns from data that it receives from training, it is controlled based on verification data and it keeps learning from data it receives from patients during real-life usage. Genome editing tools are also greatly dependent on data, specifically, on genetic data of individuals and how somatic genome editing affects them. If the clinical investigations on these two parts are carried out separately and then only assessed together for the marketing authorisation or conformity assessment of a medical device (which does not cover clinical trials), then a substantial amount of crucial data might be missing. This, in turn, might affect the safety and quality of the whole product. It is important to establish the relevant common procedure — how the inclusion of an AI element into the genome editing therapy affects the safety of treated subjects and the quality of the product. And vice versa — how processing of complex and opaque real-world genetic data affects AI's functioning and accuracy of its outcomes.

If an AI-device and a gene editing medicinal product are to be clinically evaluated together, the open question is which framework shall regulate it. Another question is when the clinical evaluations are carried out together, would it still be necessary to perform separately clinical trials for medicinal product part and clinical investigations for an AI-based element.

One option would include carrying out of clinical trials and clinical investigations separately and then the common verification of the whole product in the end.[63] This option enables to ensure the sufficient amount of control for each of the elements separately and then in their combination and thus can guarantee safety and quality. It also suggests flexibility and due to this, is preferred for products where AI-device is used as companion to medicinal products. One downside of might be the extensive regulatory burden for developers

63 Either by means of clinical procedures with involvement of human subjects or by means of non-clinical evaluations (depending on how the risks and benefits change for the combined product).

of the product and more importantly, the extensive involvement of human participants for trials that partly coincide.

Another option would include only carrying out one clinical evaluation for the whole product. In this case, the common procedure can be governed by one of the applicable frameworks (subject to necessary adjustments) or by the policy guidelines specifically issued on this matter. While this option suggests the common procedure, it is deemed more applicable to products that are supposed to be used inseparable, such as combined ATMPs. This option does not put an extensive burden on products' developers and human participants but might decrease the amount of data about the safety and quality of the components of the product. Due to that, before the clinical part, the non-clinical research[64] on the safety and quality of the two elements and their combinations shall be made to minimise the risks of human participants of the common clinical evaluations.

5.2 *Applying for Marketing Authorisation*

At the stage of marketing authorisation, the relevancies between medicinal products' and medical devices' frameworks are established for both types of the products: the combined ATMPs and the ATMPs with companion AI-devices.

5.2.1 Marketing Authorisation for Combined ATMPs

For the combined ATMP, the procedure of marketing authorisation is rather clear and also supplemented by policy guidelines. The application is submitted by the MA holder to the EMA and shall include the results of the conformity assessment of the AI-device used in the combined product. The EMA guidelines on the evaluation of combined advanced therapy medicinal products ('EMA CATMP Guidelines')[65] establish how the verification bodies and relevant actors shall cooperate.

Specifically, the guidelines set that the EMA shall consult before and after the application submission to the notified body that verified the medical device, have access to all the relevant data about the device component necessary to assess the combined product. The MA applicant shall be involved

64 For example, the MDR enables a manufacturer of a medical device to apply alone non-clinical testing of the device for assessment of its quality and performance subject to reasonable justification where the demonstration of conformity with general safety and performance requirements based on clinical data is not deemed appropriate (MDR, Article 61(10)).

65 European Medicines Agency, 'Procedural advice on the evaluation of combined advanced therapy medicinal products and the consultation of Notified Bodies in accordance with Article 9 of Regulation (EC) No. 1394/2007', February 11, 2011, EMA/354785/2010.

in the interaction between the EMA and notification bodies.[66] At the same time, the applicant shall provide or ensure access to all the requested data about the device to the EMA. Interestingly, the guidelines admit that the inclusion of the medicinal product's component might influence the safety and quality of the already verified device — the issue similar to the one described in the previous subsection. 'Evaluation of combined ATMPs may require assessment of this effect on the characteristics of the device part. Potential interactions and the effect of the combination of the ATMP on the device part may require assessment. In such cases, the EMA may seek an opinion on the effect of the combination on the device part from a notified body.'[67]

Although the EMA guidelines provide important rules on the interaction between different actors in relation to marketing authorisation of combined devices, it does not define the role of the device's manufacturer. However, AI-powered medical devices can greatly influence the safety and quality of the combined product. In addition, the complexity, non-predictability, and opacity of the technology require special expertise and constant control over the process due to algorithmic self-learning. Thus, the rights and obligations of AI-device manufacturers within the submission of the marketing authorisation application shall be defined.

5.2.2 Marketing Authorisation for Companion ATMPs

For the AI-devices that companion medicinal products, the two elements of the products are authorised separately. The only link between the two procedures is that during the device's authorisation the notified body shall seek a scientific opinion from one of the competent authorities responsible for medicinal products.[68] However, the relevant obligations of the device's manufacturer and more importantly, of the MA holder for the companioned ATMP are not defined. For example, it is not established how the subjects shall exchange data about the safety and performance of their components and who shall accumulate the data for the common product, who shall provide it to the controlling bodies.

5.3 *Post-Market Surveillance and Pharmacovigilance*

While post-market control is an important phase of any medical product's life cycle, for the products where the two highly innovative but very complex and novel technologies are combined (genome editing and AI-tools), this phase is crucial. To explore the challenges that might arise at this stage, it is first necessary to identify the procedures applicable to each of the product's elements

66 *Ibid.*, 4.1.

67 *Ibid.*, 4.3.

68 IVDR, Annex IX, Chapter II, 5(2).

under the relevant frameworks. The procedures differ for the two types of products, and I start the observation with the combined ATMPs where the AI-device is used integrally with the genome editing medicinal product.

5.3.1 Post-Market Procedures for Combined ATMPs

Combined ATMPs receive marketing authorisation under the Framework on Medicinal Products for Human Use, and thus are controlled afterward also under this framework. The procedure is called pharmacovigilance and is established to monitor the risk-benefit balance of the authorised products. MA holder takes responsibility for that because he places the combined product in the market. With this regard, the MA holder has a substantial scope of obligations: ensure the receival of all the relevant information about adverse reactions and the provision of such information to the EMA;[69] ensure encouraging of patients to communicate any adverse reaction to healthcare professionals;[70] record and report to the EMA of all the adverse reactions brought to the attention of the holder by healthcare professionals;[71] submit periodic (every six months) safety update reports.[72] If the product presents the negative risk-benefit balance, it shall be rapidly withdrawn from the market.[73] The described procedure applies to the whole combined product and thus covers any adverse reactions, including the ones related to the use of its AI element. However, the Medical Devices Framework also establishes its own regime for controlling a device after it is placed on the market — post-market surveillance.

The post-market surveillance system for medical devices is similar to the pharmacovigilance of medicinal products. The differences mainly concern responsible subjects and controlling bodies. For a medical device, the main accountable subject is its manufacturer who 'shall plan, establish, document, implement, maintain and update a post-market surveillance system.'[74] 'The system shall enable the manufacturer to actively and systematically gather, record, and analyse relevant data on the quality, performance and safety of a device throughout its entire lifetime.'[75] Based on this surveillance system and collected data, the manufacturer shall inform the relevant notified bodies about any adverse events, incidents related to the use of devices and to take corrective actions.

69 *Ibid.*, Article 22.
70 *Ibid.*
71 *Ibid.*, Article 24(1).
72 *Ibid.*, Article 24(3).
73 *Ibid.*, recital 29.
74 MDR, Article 83(1).
75 MDR, Article 83(2).

Although pharmacovigilance is established as the main governing procedure applicable for the common product, post-market surveillance of an AI-based medical device still has to be carried out. It means that the two frameworks are applicable: one covers the whole combined product and the other one — only its medical device part. In this situation, the MA holder is responsible for the overall pharmacovigilance of the combined product and the device's manufacture — for the post-market surveillance of the device part of the product. However, it is not clear how the two frameworks shall work together and how the MA holder shall cooperate with the device's manufacturer (and vice versa). The cooperation issue especially concerns collecting of and access to data about the combined product and its elements. For example, the device's manufacture needs data about the device's use for post-market surveillance, but all data is collected during the pharmacovigilance by the MA holder, and it is not yet established how the device's manufacturer shall access the data.

5.3.2 Post-Market Procedures for Companion ATMPs

The described regulatory pathway relates to the situation of the single marketing authorisation issued by EMA and concerns the combined ATMPs. The relevant procedure is missing for the second type of product — when AI-device is used in companion with medicinal products. In this case, adverse reactions are monitored and reported under the two frameworks separately. This raises similar challenges as in the case of the combined ATMPs, but in this situation, it is even worse. It concerns not only integration of pharmacovigilance data into the post-market surveillance system of a medical device, but also the other way around — integration of device vigilance data into pharmacovigilance tools of the companioned medicinal product.[76] Crucially in the context of AI and genome editing, the current legislation does not establish the combined reporting of medicine and medical device adverse events.[77]

'Furthermore, the ability to adequately implement regulatory actions, such as recalls and safety alerts for a companion medical device must be considered. This can have a significant impact on the ability to administer and monitor the accompanying pharmaceutical, including the potential impact of delayed or interrupted therapy cycles. Appropriate systems to communicate and manage

76 A. Craig, 'Personalised Medicine with Companion Diagnostics: The Intercept Of Medicines And Medical Devices In The Regulatory Landscape', *EMJ Innovations* 1 (1) (2017) 47–53, https://www.emjreviews.com/innovations/article/personalised-medicine-with-companion-diagnostics-the-intercept-of-medicines-and-medical-devices-in-the-regulatory-landscape/ (accessed 15 October 2021).

77 *Ibid.*

the risk of post-market problems with either the medicine or medical device component must be considered and documented.'[78]

5.4 *Liability Rules*

Considering the amount of the involved subjects and difficulties in cooperation between them (demonstrated previously), the lack of links between the relevant frameworks does not enable to properly share obligations and responsibilities. In this situation, attribution of liability for the damages caused by the use of the product created and distributed by many stakeholders becomes a very challenging task.

The rules of civil and criminal liability of subjects involved in the development and distribution of medicinal products and medical devices are subject to local legislations.[79] It means that these rules are not unified and can vary for subjects from the different Member States. Together with the lack of a common framework that defines the roles of all the accountable subjects at all the stages of the product's life cycle, this state of affairs impacts legal certainty and predictability. Since the rules of criminal and civil liability are the competence of the Member States, defining the roles of accountable subjects is the most available tool to decrease legal uncertainty.

6 Recommendations

As the previous section demonstrates, the main legal challenge to regulate medicinal products that involve genome editing and AI power is to connect the dots between numerous and complex frameworks governing different parts of the product. In this section, I suggest what factors and why shall be taken into consideration during the adjustment of the existing legal frameworks to the challenges caused by the two innovative technologies.

6.1 *Common Data Governance and Management*

The quality of decisions made by AI is strongly based on the quality of data used to train, test, and validate it.[80] As data scientists stress out, 'garbage in —

78 *Ibid.*

79 See MDR, recital 66 and CTR, Article 71.

80 G. Cheung, 'A Deep Dive Into Data Quality', TowardsDataScience (3 January 2019), available online at https://towardsdatascience.com/a-deep-dive-into-data-quality-c1d1ee576046 (accessed 16 January 2022).

garbage out'.[81] If the training data is irrelevant or non-representative to its real-life usage, an AI model will generate inaccurate results. This consequence is negative itself, but in healthcare, and especially in its more high-risk area such as genome editing, it becomes dramatic.

Considering opacity and non-predictability of the technology, proper data management and governance is one of the main tools to verify and control decisions made by AI. The importance of data governance in the AI context is already recognised by the EU legislator because it is included in the proposed AI Act as one of the requirements for high-risk AI systems.[82] At the same time, genetics, and genomics, including genome editing, are also data fuelled. While the technology is rather novel, it is important to continuously collect and implement new data received through its clinical use and adjust the relevant risk-benefit analysis. Adding the AI element can substantially change the risk-benefit ratio (because it has its own risks). It can also find new correlations in data that might result in either new scientific insights or inaccurate decisions or both.

'In essence, data governance concerns the deployment of the right mixture of process, technology, and personnel to govern the input, storage and usage of data to achieve the objectives of the system where data is used.'[83] It includes data stewardship (promoting accountability by assigning stewards/custodians to relevant datasets), data accessibility (facilitating the availability of data for relevant stakeholders), data security, quality control and knowledge (preserving and improving data knowledge by ensuring documentation of data systems and related processes are kept up to date).[84]

I suggest that these elements shall be facilitated in the life cycle of genome editing medicinal products that involve AI facilities. To ensure the relevance and quality of the data at all stages, the data shall concern the combined product, not only its separate elements. Yet, the current legislation does not fully solve this task. As the previous section demonstrated, the procedures to govern the creation, clinical trials, marketing, and post-market surveillance of genome editing products involving AI facilities are fragmented and separated. This state of affairs does not enable to create the system that allows collection,

81 R. Schmelzer, 'The Achilles' Heel Of AI', *Forbes* (7 March 2019), available online at https://www.forbes.com/sites/cognitiveworld/2019/03/07/the-achilles-heel-of-ai/?sh=7ceb254d7be7 (accessed 15 January 2022).

82 EC Proposal for the AI Act, Article 10.

83 N. Sundararajah, 'Effective data governance: a key enabler for AI adoption', *AECOM*, available online at https://aecom.com/without-limits/article/effective-data-governance-a-key-enabler-for-artificial-intelligence-adoption/ (accessed 13 January 2021).

84 *Ibid.*

comparison, assessment, control, receival and management data commonly. It is because the roles of involved subjects and the applicable procedures generally and concerning data are not clearly defined. And for the product that combines two complex, unpredictable, and opaque technologies, the common procedures that allow to continuously gather data about the whole product are crucial. Besides being important itself, it would allow keeping positive the risk-benefit ratio which is explained next.

6.2 *Common Risk-Benefit Analysis*

The legal frameworks in healthcare recognise and promote the need to balance risks and benefits. The established procedures are aimed to discover and minimize risks posed to individuals due to their involvement in diagnosis and treatment procedures. For example, the Medical Devices Framework establishes that safety and quality requirements mean 'reduction of risks as far as possible without adversely affecting the benefit-risk ratio.'[85] Similarly, the ATMP Regulation requires the MA holder 'to put in place a suitable risk management system to address risks related to ATMPs.'[86] The management of risks is carried out during the whole life cycle of products, starting from creation and clinical validation finishing with pharmacovigilance (for medicinal products) and post-market surveillance (for medical devices). Similarly, the EC Proposal for the AI Act also requires implementing a risk-management system for high-risk AI applications.[87]

As explored in Section 2, both AI and genome editing pose substantial risks which are amplified when the technologies are used together. However, the procedures to commonly assess and manage the risks are not yet established. Although the elements of the combined products are covered by the relevant frameworks, the procedures for the final product in general are not fully established. In other words, the current frameworks enable to conduct and continuously monitor the risk-benefit analysis for the product's components, but not for the whole product. This state of affairs shall be changed to ensure the overall safety and quality of genome editing with the use of AI. One of the tools to facilitate the common risk-benefit analysis is to strengthen the accountability of all the involved actors. This argument is explained next.

---

85 Medical Devices Regulation, Annex I, Chapter 1, Article 2.

86 ATMP Regulation, recital 20.

87 EC Proposal for AI Regulation, Article 9.

6.3 *Establishing the Roles of All the Subjects Involved in the Product's Life Cycle*

Accountability is one of the tools to tackle the lack of transparency and predictability amplified by the common use of AI and genome editing. According to D. Brinkerhoff, 'being accountable means having the obligation to answer questions regarding decisions and/or actions.'[88] I would add that the proper accountability system shall refer to not only the obligation but also the capability to answer. For that, the involved actors shall have appropriate tools, including access to data, the ability to cooperate with other actors, and having the relevant rights towards them. These tools shall help the actors to carry out their obligations to justify their actions.

To facilitate accountability and mitigate the common risks, the roles and responsibilities of every subject involved in the product's life cycle shall be clearly defined and distinguished. As demonstrated, uncertainties about who shall do what start from the idea to create the product and carry out the relevant clinical trials and finish with the post-market control. It is not clear how involved actors shall cooperate with each other with respect to the whole product, how and with whom they shall exchange data they have for their part of the product, who shall generate and assess the common data, as well as who shall conduct the common risk-benefit analysis. These uncertainties can result in different negative consequences such as lack of motivation to develop products that are governed by the complex and non-predictable legal regimes, risks to safety and quality of the product due to lack of proper control, legal uncertainty in the attribution of the liability, and as the result lack of trust from patients and the society.

6.4 *Strengthening the Role of the AI-Based Device Manufacturer*

Among all the involved actors, special consideration shall be given to the role of manufacturers of AI-based medical devices. Because AI constantly conducts self-learning and its performance can substantially change based on new real-world data, the subject who has AI expertise shall have non-stop and easy access to data generated by AI. Otherwise, AI can start providing inaccurate decisions and thus endanger the safety of patients. In addition, the quality of AI decisions depends on the quality and relevance of the input data — for that, AI manufacturer has to provide instructions to AI users on how to apply the device and what kind of data can be added to the AI system in question.

88 D. Brinkerhoff, 'Accountability and health systems: toward conceptual clarity and policy relevance', *Health Policy and Planning* 19 (6) (2004) 371–379.

Fortunately, this type of requirement is included in the proposed AI Act[89] and therefore, it can be taken as an inspiration for the current frameworks.

6.5 *Implementing the Requirements of AI Conformity Assessment to the Overall Process*

Besides facilitating the role of an AI manufacturer, the proposed AI Act aims to minimise the risks associated with the lack of AI's transparency and predictability. Due to that, the requirements of the AI Act as soon as it is adopted shall be integrated into the existing legal frameworks applicable to the use of AI in genome editing processes. This might become another challenge because the currently proposed AI Act is mostly linked with conformity assessment procedures established under the MDF. The processes related to the verification, authorisation and pharmacovigilance of medicinal products (established under the different framework) are not yet correlated with the AI Act. Thus, to link all the relevant frameworks becomes even more difficult.[90]

7 Policy Suggestions

To implement all the recommendations developed in the previous section, the relevant policy guidelines shall be issued. To consider the differences between the genome editing products that are integrally combined with AI-devices and the ones that are used in companion with AI-tools, the guidelines can be differentiated too. Below I provide the policy suggestions for these two types of products.

7.1 *Suggestions for Policy Guidelines for Genome Editing Medicinal Products Combined with AI-Devices*

The policy guidelines that relate to the genome editing ATMPS combined with AI-devices can be issued by the EMA because it is responsible for the single marketing authorisation of this type of products. These guidelines shall clarify how the clinical trials and clinical investigations for the elements of the combined products shall be carried out together and how the roles of the involved subjects shall be defined. This would also enable the common data governance and management of risks. Although for this type of products marketing

89 EC Proposal for the AI Act, Article 13 (2) and (3).

90 For example, the AI Act establishes the obligations of the user of AI system and in the scenario when AI is part of a medicinal product, it is not sufficiently clear who shall be deemed as the user. In this case, it becomes challenging to continuously monitor the outcomes of AI decision-making because a patient can be the only subject having immediate access to such outcomes.

authorisation and post-market control are more linked (with the main procedure established by the ATMP Regulation), some clarifications shall be made too. The clarifications shall specifically concern the role of the AI medical device's manufacturer (as the subject whose role is currently less defined), his access to data at all the stages, and especially after the product is placed on the market. This would enable the manufacturer to assess the changes in AI algorithms (made as the result of the new input data received during real-life usage) and decide how these changes affect the safety and quality of the whole product. The proposed AI Act suggests the approach to take into considerations the possible algorithmic changes in AI device after it is placed on the market.[91] It is deemed reasonable to implement this approach to the relevant policy guidelines.

7.2 *Suggestions for Policy Guidelines for Genome Editing Medicinal Products Companioned by AI-Devices*

The guidelines on the genome editing ATMPs used in companion with an AI-device will require more clarifications. While there is no single procedure to authorise this type of products (each of its elements is authorised by different authorities), the cooperation between the regulatory bodies shall be facilitated. Besides the obligation to consult EMA during authorisation of a medical device, the overall process to verify the quality and safety of the whole product shall be established. Considering that the product's elements can be used separately (or at least the medicinal product part), the process to be developed shall be flexible enough to enable the verification of the product's elements separately, but at the same time to ensure safety and quality of the elements when they are used together. The verification process shall build the risk-management system by defining the roles of all the involved subjects and exchanging data between them at all the stages of the product's life cycle from clinical investigations through marketing authorisation and during post-market surveillance. Especially important is to define who is responsible for monitoring and reporting the adverse reactions and other data about the whole product (since now it is reporting on the separate elements of the product). How the relevant data shall be collected and exchanged shall be established too. A similar approach shall be taken with regards to clinical investigations and marketing authorisation — it is deemed reasonable to appoint the subject who is responsible to maintain the overall process and to coordinate with controlling bodies — the front-row accountable subject. At the second (lower) level the rights and obligations of the other involved subjects towards the front-row subject and to each other (at the horizontal level) shall be clarified.

91 EC Proposal for the AI Act, Article 13(3)(c).

8 Conclusion

The chapter identified and explored the legal frameworks applicable for medicinal products based on genome editing with the involvement of AI-devices. The analysis enabled the discovery of the possible classifications of the AI-devices used in different variations with genome editing medicinal products: in combination (classified as cATMPs) or in companion (classified as ATMPs companioned by AI-devices). This differentiation impacts the choice of the applicable frameworks, their correlation, compliance procedures and on responsibilities of accountable subjects.

The main difference between regulating the two types of products lies in marketing authorisation and post-market control. For cATMPs the current legislation establishes the main governing framework (related to medicinal products) with the main accountable subject — MA holder. The AI-device part of the product is also verified under the MDR (the results of the verification are included in the final authorisation). For ATMPs companioned with AI-devices the two elements of the whole product are authorised and monitored afterward separately. Despite the differences, both types of products confront similar legal issues resulting from the lack of guidelines on the procedures for the full life cycle of the common products, not only their elements individually.

The chapter justified the need for establishing the procedures that enable to conduct the risk-benefit analysis not only for the product's elements separately, but in their combination. Due to the complexity, opacity and non-predictability of both technologies, data about their usage in combination shall be gathered and reported at all the stages of the product's life cycle. The proper data governance and management shall be ensured to enable the accountable subjects and verification bodies to continuously monitor the risk-benefit ratio of the product and to react promptly. This would also increase the compatibility of the procedures with the future AI Act that focuses on collecting, storing, and reporting data around AI use.

Besides data governance and data management of the common products, the policy guidelines shall establish the procedures of cooperation between different subjects responsible for different parts of the products and involved at different phases. This shall include the appointment of the front-row subjects (acting as a contact point with verification bodies and managing the process), their vertical cooperation with other subjects and cooperation between the subjects at the horizontal level. In addition, the overall procedures on the products' development, authorisation and post-market surveillance shall be established. All these measures would increase legal certainty, improve the quality and safety of products, guarantee proper liability and in general ensure trust in the technologies from healthcare professionals, patients, and society.

Addressing Cognitive Vulnerabilities through Genome and Epigenome Editing: Techno-Legal Adaptations for Persons with Intellectual Disabilities

Pin Lean Lau | ORCID: 0000-0002-2447-9293
Brunel Law School, Brunel University London, Kingston Lane, Uxbridge, London, Middlesex UB8 3PH, UK
PinLean.Lau@brunel.ac.uk

Abstract

The key aim of this chapter is to highlight the oft-under-represented narrative of how persons with disabilities (specifically, those with intellectual disabilities) may access the benefits that genome editing may offer. Firstly, this chapter reflects on the critical need for a paradigm shift in how we view intellectual disabilities, and centering the rights of persons with disabilities to allow them to access the broad scope of their right to health under various international law instruments (including the complementary right to habilitation under Article 26 of the CRPD). Secondly, the chapter evaluates the legal provisions in the CRPD and other international instruments relating to the rights of persons with intellectual disabilities, and their access to genome editing technologies. This analysis intends to demonstrate that human rights in disability discourse be complemented with emancipatory, participatory, and transformative research. Finally, the chapter argues for a reinvigorated line of thinking that expands on the social model of disability: to align with inclusive, contemporary disability discourse that embodies greater responsibility and innovation in perpetuating better access to genome editing technologies for persons with intellectual disabilities.

Keywords

genome editing – intellectual disabilities – disability discourse – empathy – non-discrimination – right to health – right of habilitation – health innovation – techno-legal adaptations

DOI:10.1163/9789004526136_006

1 Introduction

Over the last several years, issues and concerns relating to genome editing have gained considerable traction on a global level. The gene editing tool, CRISPR/Cas9[1] has demonstrated successes and promises since its invention — but it particularly became more scrutinized due to the case of Dr. He Jian Kui.[2] Whilst there have been a variety of international instruments that deal with the use and governance of genome editing,[3] the WHO Expert Advisory Committee on Developing Global Standards for Governance and Oversight of Human Genome Editing (Committee) recently published two reports: Human Genome Editing: A Framework for Governance,[4] and Human Genome Editing: Recommendations.[5] These reports represented a new governance framework that builds on identifiable tools, organizations and situations that integrate the practical difficulties of regulating human genome editing.

One of the fields in which the potentiality of genome editing is still under-represented is in disability discourse. The key aim of this chapter therefore, is to highlight the oft-under-represented narrative of how persons with disabilities (specifically, those with intellectual disabilities) may access the benefits that genome editing may offer. For example, since CRISPR first made the headlines in 2012, it has remained the subject of fiery legal and ethical debates centered around human genome editing and possibilities of 'designer babies'[6] in our foreseeable future. In the meantime, disability discourse in the context of genome editing has been equally controversial. These include Peter Singer's controversial utilitarian philosophy, where he regards that "killing them

1 J.A. Doudna and E. Charpentier, 'The New Frontier of Genome Engineering with CRISPR-Cas9', *Science* 346 (2014) 1258096.

2 H.T. Greely, 'CRISPR'd Babies: Human Germline Genome Editing in the "He Jiankui Affair"', *Journal of Law and the Biosciences* 6 (2019) 111–183.

3 These include, amongst others, the European Convention on Human Rights; the Convention for the Protection of Human Rights and Dignity of the Human Being with regard to the Application of Biology and Medicine: Convention on Human Rights and Biomedicine (the Oviedo Convention); the UNESCO Universal Declaration on the Human Genome and Human Rights; and the UNESCO Universal Declaration on Bioethics and Human Rights.

4 World Health Organization, *Human Genome Editing: A Framework for Governance* (Geneva: World Health Organization, 2021), available online at https://apps.who.int/iris/handle/10665/342484 (accessed 4 October 2021).

5 World Health Organization, *Human Genome Editing: Recommendations* (Geneva: World Health Organization, 2021), available online at https://apps.who.int/iris/handle/10665/342486 (accessed 4 October 2021).

6 E. Yong, 'The Designer Baby Era Is Not Upon Us', *The Atlantic* (2017), available online at https://www.theatlantic.com/science/archive/2017/08/us-scientists-edit-human-embryos-with-crisprand-thats-okay/535668/ (accessed 19 September 2017).

[infants], therefore, cannot be equated with killing normal human beings, or any other self-conscious beings. No infant — disabled or not — has as strong a claim to life as beings capable of seeing themselves as distinct entities existing over time."[7] It may be observed that tackling disability discourse raises a much more complex ELSI (ethical, legal, and social implication) question that makes it uncomfortable to comprehend.

Viewed in context of rights of persons with intellectual disabilities (ID), primarily with reference to the United Nations Convention on the Rights of Persons with Disabilities (CRPD)[8] and other relevant international and/or regional instruments,[9] this chapter first highlights the alignment of a right to health (broadly)[10] for persons with ID. Specifically, the argument that is being made, is that persons with ID need equitable access to genome technologies, so that they can fully realize their right to health, which includes a right to habilitation (narrowly) under Article 26 of the CRPD.[11] Whilst the CRPD has been touted to be a landmark convention that addresses the human rights needs of persons with disabilities on a large scale, and appears to have been

7 P. Singer, *Practical Ethics*, 3rd edn. (Cambridge: Cambridge University Press, 2011).

8 United Nations, *Convention on the Rights of Persons with Disabilities and Optional Protocol* (2006), available online at https://www.un.org/disabilities/documents/convention/convoptprot-e.pdf (accessed 15 January 2022).

9 These include, amongst others, the European Convention on Human Rights; the Convention for the Protection of Human Rights and Dignity of the Human Being with regard to the Application of Biology and Medicine: Convention on Human Rights and Biomedicine (the Oviedo Convention); the UNESCO Universal Declaration on the Human Genome and Human Rights; and the UNESCO Universal Declaration on Bioethics and Human Rights.

10 OHCHR and WHO, 'The Right to Health' (New York, NY: Office of the United Nations High Commissioner for Human Rights), available online at https://www.ohchr.org/Documents/Publications/Factsheet31.pdf (accessed 10 March 2020).

11 Article 26 of the CRPD on Habilitation and Rehabilitation reads:

"1. States Parties shall take effective and appropriate measures, including through peer support, to enable persons with disabilities to attain and maintain maximum independence, full physical, mental, social and vocational ability, and full inclusion and participation in all aspects of life. To that end, States Parties shall organize, strengthen and extend comprehensive habilitation and rehabilitation services and programmes, particularly in the areas of health, employment, education and social services, in such a way that these services and programmes:

a) Begin at the earliest possible stage, and are based on the multidisciplinary assessment of individual needs and strengths;

b) Support participation and inclusion in the community and all aspects of society, are voluntary, and are available to persons with disabilities as close as possible to their own communities, including in rural areas.

2. States Parties shall promote the development of initial and continuing training for professionals and staff working in habilitation and rehabilitation services.

relatively successful in terms of protecting such rights[12] — there does appear to be a lack of concerted effort or will in addressing their human rights in the context of new and emerging technologies. Article 26, which deals with habilitation and rehabilitation of persons with disabilities, should, in theory, address such access to technologies (including genome editing technologies).

Thereafter, the chapter evaluates the legal provisions on non-discrimination and equality relating to genome editing technologies, contained in the CRPD and other international instruments, considered through the lens of persons with ID. The intention is to highlight any shortcomings that needs to be addressed to allow persons with ID to fully realize their right to health *vis-à-vis* existing legislation. This is especially telling in light of the fact that there are currently specific points of interest around the potential use of epigenome editing therapies for treating, or even reversing some genetic mutations that cause ID. Finally, the chapter suggests a reinvigorated line of thinking that expands on the social model of disability: to align with inclusive, contemporary disability discourse that embodies greater responsibility and innovation in perpetuating better access to genome editing technologies for persons with ID.

2 Addressing the Rights of Persons with Disabilities in Genome Editing

2.1 *Disability Discourse Models*

The focus put forward in this chapter is around somatic gene editing (and not human germline gene editing), attracting concerns such as safety, risks versus benefits considerations, and long-term patient care and monitoring mechanisms,[13] and therefore arguably attracts less of the ELSI debate. The crux of these considerations as a starting point, however, are inadequate when we encounter questions of inequalities and vulnerabilities in disability discourse. It is therefore imperative to reflect on the difficult questions that address the

---

3. States Parties shall promote the availability, knowledge and use of assistive devices and technologies, designed for persons with disabilities, as they relate to habilitation and rehabilitation."

12 A. Conti, 'Drawing the Line: Disability, Genetic Intervention and Bioethics', *Laws* 6 (2017) 9, p. 10.

13 H.C. Howard, C.G. van El, F. Forzano, D. Radojkovic, E. Rial-Sebbag, G. de Wert, P. Borry and M.C. Cornel on behalf of the Public and Professional Policy Committee of the European Society of Human Genetics, 'One Small Edit for Humans, One Giant Edit for Humankind? Points and Questions to Consider for a Responsible Way Forward for Gene Editing in Humans', *European Journal of Human Genetics* 26 (2018) 1–11.

experiential, intersectional, spatial practices of identities and spaces of persons with disabilities.

With the knowledge that genome editing therapies may possibly be successful in curing or treating ID — a crucial question which some may ask is whether we should, indeed, remove, or encourage that these disabilities be removed. This is, however, not an objective question. For some time, disabilities had always been viewed from the perspective of the medical model. The medical model of disability traditionally focuses on the impairment or disability of a person and has been instrumental in influencing the "development and structure of the legislation, and is reflected in people's attitudes and associated negative outcomes."[14] From the viewpoint of the medical model, disabilities are often seen as impairments that needed to be 'fixed', that persons with disabilities were a problem that had to be cured. Therefore, an incurable impairment, or disability that cannot be rehabilitated, invites unconscious bias and may imply a disabled person's 'lesser' value in society.[15] For example, in the UK, whilst the medical model has been central to the drafting of the Equality Act 2010, parts of the Act that relate to disability discrimination tend to "focus on what a person is unable to do."[16]

The medical model of disability has attracted criticism over the years due to its parochial approach; and disability activism and scholarship have now evolved to a more inclusive perspective, the social model of disability.[17] Disability rights scholar, Mike Oliver, raises three critical points about the social model of disability:[18]

> Firstly, it is an attempt to switch the focus away from the functional limitations of individuals with an impairment on to the problems caused by disabling environments, barriers and cultures. Secondly, it refuses to

14 The Parliamentary and Health Service Ombudsman, 'Introduction to the Social and Medical Models of Disability' (London: The Parliamentary and Health Service Ombudsman), available online at https://www.ombudsman.org.uk/sites/default/files/FDN-218144_Introduction_to_the_Social_and_Medical_Models_of_Disability.pdf.

15 S. Bunbury, 'Unconscious Bias and the Medical Model: How the Social Model May Hold the Key to Transformative Thinking about Disability Discrimination', *International Journal of Discrimination and the Law* 19 (2019) 26–47.

16 The Parliamentary and Health Service Ombudsman, *supra* note 14.

17 M. Oliver, 'The Social Model in Action: If I Had a Hammer', in: C. Barnes and G. Mercer (eds.), *Implementing the Social Model of Disability: Theory and Research* (Leeds: The Disability Press, 2004), available online at https://disability-studies.leeds.ac.uk/wp-content/uploads/sites/40/library/Barnes-implementing-the-social-model-chapter-2.pdf (accessed 13 January 2022).

18 *Ibid.*, 20.

> see specific problems in isolation from the totality of disabling environments: hence the problem of unemployment does not just entail intervention in the social organization of work and the operation of the labor market but also in areas such as transport, education and culture. Thirdly, endorsement of the social model does not mean that individually based interventions in the lives of disabled people, whether they be medically, rehabilitative, educational or employment based, are of no use or always counter-productive.

Because the social model of disability was created by persons with disabilities themselves, its main objectives anchor disabilities as experiences, instead of impairment or limitations.[19] In addition, the *leitmotif* of this model is forward-looking and prospective. With disabilities being viewed as experiences, the idea is that any kind of barriers (that would prevent persons with disabilities from fully participating in the vicissitudes of daily life) should be eradicated. This includes accessibility to public spaces such as work and education, independent living instead of institutionalization, and other unconsciously formed biases or challenges towards those with disabilities.[20] The social model of disability is now the preferred model for engaging in meaningful discussions about persons with disabilities, and has been endorsed by the Government Equalities Office in the UK in 2014.[21]

There are many non-profit or non-governmental organizations that have been devoted to the advancement of rights and interests, and awareness of persons with disabilities and their experiences. Inclusion and adaptability in society are seen as the key components for the integration of persons with disabilities, into daily life. Notwithstanding, persons with disabilities still continue to face discrimination and iniquity in their daily lives, including but not limited to fully exercising their right to health.[22] This was also highlighted by the UN Special Rapporteur in report number A/73/161 on the rights of persons with disabilities.[23]

---

19 The Parliamentary and Health Service Ombudsman, *supra* note 14.

20 *Ibid.*

21 *Ibid.*

22 World Health Organization, *Disability and Health* (24 November 2021), available online at https://www.who.int/news-room/fact-sheets/detail/disability-and-health (accessed 14 January 2022).

23 C. Devandas-Aguilar, *Report of the Special Rapporteur on the Rights of Persons with Disabilities: Right to Health of Persons with Disabilities* (New York, NY: United Nations General Assembly, 2018) A/73/161 8–15.

To answer the question earlier posed in this section, as to whether we should remove, or encourage that these disabilities be removed: the answer this chapter provides is "it depends on the person"; because the answer is strictly premised on the capacity, autonomy and integrity of such persons with the disability making that full and informed decision; absent prejudice, interference, interjections and influences of the social and economic order of things. Essentially, this is a question that can only be answered on a very personal level. Additionally, to enable such full and informed decision to be made, full, clinical and neutral information must be provided. What can also be done further is to bring emphasis to the voices of persons with disabilities as a way to continue targeting discrimination and inequality. Whilst the journey in fighting discrimination will always continue, the tools that are available on that journey can now be different, powerful and yet, transformative. Therefore, the author of this chapter views this question as no longer being about eradicating disabilities; but for the attainment of maximum independence and being able to access any kind of therapies that would allow persons with disabilities to attain this maximum independence, and to enjoy their right to health (even if this right to health is ultimately, on their own volition, to eradicate disability).[24] Besides this, it may also be that the presence of ID could also impede free choice and democratic decision-making — in which case, it becomes more urgent to switch the dialogue and truly incorporate solidarity and inclusion.[25]

2.2 *Realization of the Right to Health for Persons with Disabilities*

The right to health, now recognized as a universal and fundamental human right, is a central component of the argument made in this chapter which links to how persons with disabilities (specifically, ID) should access genome editing technologies to realize their right to health. In the 1946 Constitution of the WHO, the preamble provides an encompassing definition of health as "a state of complete physical, mental and social well-being and not merely the absence of disease or infirmity."[26] This also includes the understanding that "the enjoyment of the highest attainable standard of health is one of the fundamental rights of every human being without distinction of race, religion, political

24 *Ibid.*

25 C. Devandas-Aguilar, *Report of the Special Rapporteur on the Rights of Persons with Disabilities: Report on Disability-Inclusive International Cooperation* (New York, NY: United Nations General Assembly, 2020) A/75/186.

26 World Health Organization, *Constitution of the World Health Organization* (Geneva: WHO, 2006), available online at https://apps.who.int/gb/bd/PDF/bd47/EN/constitution-en.pdf?ua=1 (accessed 16 November 2021).

belief, economic or social condition."[27] In a Fact Sheet jointly prepared by the WHO and the Office of the United Nations High Commissioner for Human Rights, this right to health is a complete and inclusive right, which includes within its scope, the rights to entitlement as well as availability, accessibility, acceptability and good quality of services, goods and facilities.[28]

Such is the importance of the right to health that it has been enumerated in numerous international conventions too. In the UN Universal Declaration of Human Rights 1948,[29] Article 25 states that "everyone has the right to a standard of living adequate for the health and well-being of himself and of his family, including foot, clothing, housing and medical care and necessary social services." The concept of the right to health is also further enumerated in Article 12 of International Covenant on Economic, Social and Cultural Rights 1966.[30] In Europe, under Title V, Article 35 of the EU Charter on Fundamental Rights,[31] health is presented in terms of healthcare: "Everyone has the right of access to preventive health care and the right to benefit from medical treatment under the conditions established by national laws and practices. A high level of human health protection shall be ensured in the definition and implementation of all Union policies and activities." It is safe to presume that the right of health is not disputed, and that this right must be accessible to every single human being in the world.

---

27 *Ibid.*

28 OHCHR and WHO, *supra* note 10.

29 *Universal Declaration of Human Rights* (New York, NY: United Nations, 1948), available online at http://www.un.org/en/universal-declaration-human-rights/ (accessed 1 August 2018).

30 OHCHR, *International Covenant on Economic, Social and Cultural Rights* (New York, NY: UN OHCHR, 16 December 1966), available online at https://www.ohchr.org/en/professionalinterest/pages/cescr.aspx (accessed 29 September 2021). Article 12 reads:

"The States Parties to the present Covenant recognize the right of everyone to the enjoyment of the highest attainable standard of physical and mental health. The steps to be taken by the States Parties to the present Covenant to achieve the full realization of this right shall include those necessary for:

The reduction of the stillbirth-rate and of infant mortality and for the healthy development of the child;

The improvement of all aspects of environmental and industrial hygiene;

The prevention, treatment and control of epidemic, endemic, occupational and other diseases;

The creation of conditions which would assure to all medical service and medical attention in the event of sickness."

31 *Charter of Fundamental Rights of the European Union 2000/C 364/01* (Brussels: Official Journal of the European Communities, 2000), available online at https://www.europarl.europa.eu/charter/pdf/text_en.pdf (accessed 21 November 2019).

In respect of persons with disabilities, CRPD also provides for a right to health. The relevant Article 25 provides for this, where "State Parties recognize that persons with disabilities have the right to the enjoyment of the highest attainable standard of health without discrimination on the basis of disability."[32] This has been reiterated by the UN Special Rapporteur in report number A/73/161 on the rights of persons with disabilities[33] where special attention was drawn to Article 25. In the report, the UN Special Rapporteur highlighted the keen knowledge of the history of persons with disabilities being treated as patients, and not active participants to their own health and well-being.[34] Central to the recommendations made in this report[35] is the acknowledgement of shared decision making and informed consent of persons with disabilities[36] (which is consistent with the arguments made in this

32 Article 25 of the CRPD reads:

"States Parties recognize that persons with disabilities have the right to the enjoyment of the highest attainable standard of health without discrimination on the basis of disability. States Parties shall take all appropriate measures to ensure access for persons with disabilities to health services that are gender-sensitive, including health-related rehabilitation. In particular, States Parties shall:

a) Provide persons with disabilities with the same range, quality and standard of free or affordable health care and programmes as provided to other persons, including in the area of sexual and reproductive health and population-based public health programmes;

b) Provide those health services needed by persons with disabilities specifically because of their disabilities, including early identification and intervention as appropriate, and services designed to minimize and prevent further disabilities, including among children and older persons;

c) Provide these health services as close as possible to people's own communities, including in rural areas;

d) Require health professionals to provide care of the same quality to persons with disabilities as to others, including on the basis of free and informed consent by, inter alia, raising awareness of the human rights, dignity, autonomy and needs of persons with disabilities through training and the promulgation of ethical standards for public and private health care;

e) Prohibit discrimination against persons with disabilities in the provision of health insurance, and life insurance where such insurance is permitted by national law, which shall be provided in a fair and reasonable manner;

f) Prevent discriminatory denial of health care or health services or food and fluids on the basis of disability."

33 C. Devandas-Aguilar, *Report of the Special Rapporteur on the Rights of Persons with Disabilites: Report on the Impact of Ableism in Medical and Scientific Practice* (New York, NY: United Nations General Assembly, 2019), A/HRC/43/31, available online at https://www.ohchr.org/EN/Issues/Disability/SRDisabilities/Pages/BioethicsDisabilities.aspx (accessed 17 October 2021).

34 *Ibid.*, p. 4.

35 *Ibid.*, pp. 20–22.

36 *Ibid.*, p. 6.

chapter). What has also been acknowledged in practice is the struggle faced by persons with disabilities: "poorer access to health care and poorer health outcomes than the general population owing to several structural factors, such as stigma and stereotypes, discriminatory legislation and policies, barriers to accessing primary and secondary care, limited availability of disability-specific services and programs, poverty and social exclusion."[37]

With particularized emphasis on emerging technologies in biomedicine, such as genome editing, this chapter identifies that Article 26 of the CRPD concerning the right to habilitation and rehabilitation, must work in complementarity with the right to health under Article 25. The complementarity nature of Article 25's right to health is also recognized in the UN Special Rapporteur's report.[38] Hence, this chapter reiterates that persons with ID need equitable access to genome technologies, so that they can fully realize their right to health (broadly), which is complemented by a right to habilitation (narrowly) under Article 26 of the CRPD.

2.3 *Epigenome Editing to Reverse Genetic Mutations: Examples of Treatment of Intellectual Disabilities*

This section now provides examples where genome editing has been used for the treatment of some IDs. In this regard, these examples represent possibilities for persons with ID to engage with technologies as part of their right to health (Article 25 CRPD) and right to habilitation (Article 26 CRPD). There are currently specific points of interest around the potential use of epigenome editing therapies for treating, or even reversing some genetic mutations that cause cognitive or ID. Some recent studies have shown that it is possible to use CRISPR-Cas9 for targeted in-vitro editing and can be very effective in mammalian and human tissue-derived disease models.[39]

For example, a modified CRISPR system may be used to reverse the genetic mutations that cause WAGR Syndrome. According to the National Human Genome Research Institute, WAGR Syndrome is a rare genetic condition "caused by a deletion of a group of genes located on chromosome number 11."[40] Children who are born with WAGR Syndrome suffer from eye problems and are at a higher risk of developing mental and intellectual retardation and

37 *Ibid.*, pp. 21–22.

38 *Ibid.*, p. 7.

39 M. Ilyas, A. Mir, S. Efthymiou and H. Holden, 'The Genetics of Intellectual Disability: Advancing Technology and Gene Editing', *F1000Research* 9 (2020) 22.

40 National Human Genome Research Institute, 'WAGR Syndrome', *Genome.gov* (2021), available online at https://www.genome.gov/Genetic-Disorders/WAGR-Syndrome (accessed 9 July 2021).

developing some types of cancer, including Wilms' Tumors.[41] However, there appears to be great promise in using a modified CRISPR genome editing system to treat this condition, conducted by researchers at the Johns Hopkins University School of Medicine.[42] This epigenome editing approach "reversed a brain abnormality that is common in individuals with WAGR Syndrome"[43] by changing the epigenome that regulates the gene without changing its genetic code. It appears that this approach was very successful in mice, and could be very useful for humans.

Another promising area of research utilizing CRISPR is in the treatment of Fragile-X Syndrome. Fragile-X Syndrome is another genetic condition where a single gene, the FMR1, shuts down and causes a range of ID and learning and behavioral challenges.[44] In 2018, researchers from the MIT's Whitehead Institute for Biomedical Research reported that CRISPR-Cas9 was used to "remove the molecular tags that keep the mutant gene shut off in Fragile-X neurons."[45] The results of the study[46] demonstrated that some of the neurons began to produce protein normally and continued to do so even when the cells were transferred into mice.[47] Whilst these studies were conducted in a petri dish, and not in live mice, the researchers had used CRISPR in such a way that reactivated the FMR1 gene without damaging the gene itself, nor make any changes to the coding sequence.[48] Another study published in Nature Biomedical Engineering[49] used an alternatively developed version of CRIPSR,

---

41 *Ibid.*

42 C.J. Peter, A. Saito, Y. Hasegawa, Y. Tanaka, M. Nagpal, G. Perez, E. Alway, S. Espeso-Gil, T. Fayyad, C. Ratner, A. Dincer, A. Gupta, L. Devi, J.G. Pappas, F.M. Lalonde, J.A. Butman, J.C. Han, S. Akbarian and A. Kamiya, 'In Vivo Epigenetic Editing of Sema6a Promoter Reverses Transcallosal Dysconnectivity Caused by C11orf46/Arl14ep Risk Gene', *Nature Communications* 10 (2019) 4112.

43 International WAGR Syndrome Association, *Epigenome Editing Could Lead to Treatment of Brain Abnormalities in WAGR Syndrome* (2014), available online at http://wagr.org/research-updates/epigenome-editing-could-lead-to-treatment-of-brain-abnormalities-in-wagr-syndrome (accessed 20 October 2021).

44 D. Whiting, 'Fragile X 101', *National Fragile X Foundation* (2021), available online at https://fragilex.org/understanding-fragile-x/fragile-x-101/ (accessed 20 October 2021).

45 K. Clapp, 'Can CRISPR Cure Fragile X Syndrome?', *Fragile X Research — FRAXA Research Foundation* (28 February 2018), available online at https://www.fraxa.org/can-crispr-cure-fragile-x-syndrome/ (accessed 7 October 2021).

46 X.S. Liu, H. Wu, M. Krzisch, X. Wu, J. Graef, J. Muffat, D. Hnisz, C.H. Li, B. Yuan, C. Xu, Y. Li, D. Vershkov, A. Cacace, R.A. Young and R. Jaenisch, 'Rescue of Fragile X Syndrome Neurons by DNA Methylation Editing of the FMR1 Gene', *Cell* 172 (2018) 979–992.

47 Clapp, *supra* note 45.

48 *Ibid.*

49 B. Lee, K. Lee, S. Panda, R. Gonzales-Rojas, A. Chong, V. Bugay, H.M. Park, R. Brenner, N. Murthy and H.Y. Lee, 'Nanoparticle Delivery of CRISPR into the Brain Rescues a Mouse

called CRISPR-Gold[50] to "effectively edit an autism-associated gene in a mouse model of Fragile-X."[51]

Whilst these are only a couple of examples where CRISPR has shown promise in the treatment of genetic ID, what this means for persons with ID is the likelihood that more types of hereditary genetic conditions that result in ID may be reversed, corrected, or treated in the future.

Bearing in mind that there are still other types of ID that are not yet adequately researched into, with levels of disabilities ranging from mild to severe to profound, these examples are only the tip of the iceberg in terms of genome editing therapies being developed to treat genetic ID. It may also be that ID and the research conducted thus far, are difficult to define, and to quantify in terms of severity, and how it may impact on a person's life.[52] For example, whilst WAGR Syndrome and Fragile-X Syndrome appear to be ID that could someday be treated, the same may not be true of more profound ID where a basic awareness of the self and surroundings are completely impaired, where round-the-clock care is necessitated, and where there is full dependence on others for daily care. In such instances, this impacts their ability to participate in democratic decision-making processes.

There may also be instances of ID, coupled with mental illness such as schizophrenia, which may be "maximally disabling."[53] The complexities that enter the picture, linking human rights, health, and biomedical laws, demonstrate to us that if there is an opportunity for technologies to be accessed as part of these persons' right to health, then we should enable access and enlarge the measures that can be taken to enjoy this right.

Model of Fragile X Syndrome from Exaggerated Repetitive Behaviours', *Nature Biomedical Engineering* 2 (2018) 497–507.

50 L. Duan, O. Kan, X. Xu, L. Xu, C. Wen, X. Zhou, Z. Qin, Z. Xu, W. Sun and Y. Liang, 'Nanoparticle Delivery of CRISPR/Cas9 for Genome Editing', *Frontiers in Genetics* 12 (2021) 673286.

51 I. Mumal, *CRISPR-Gold Edits Fragile X Gene in Mice to Ease Exaggerated Behaviors* (18 April 2019), available online at https://fragilexnewstoday.com/2019/04/18/crispr-gold-using-non-viral-carrier-edits-fragile-x-gene-in-mouse-model-to-ease-exaggerated-behaviors/ (accessed 6 October 2021).

52 *Intellectual Disability and Severity Codes*, available online at https://www.mentalhelp.net/intellectual-disabilities/and-severity-codes/ (accessed 14 November 2021).

53 P.K. Chaudhury, K. Deka and D. Chetia, 'Disability Associated with Mental Disorders', *Indian Journal of Psychiatry* 48 (2006) 95–101.

3 Legal Provisions in the CRPD and Other International Instruments: Adequacy and Efficiency in Light of Genome Editing Technologies for Persons with Intellectual Disabilities

In the Introduction of this chapter it was highlighted that the CRPD is the most comprehensive and updated international convention that addresses the rights of persons with disabilities.[54] It is acknowledged that the CRPD has advanced the rights of persons with disabilities in transformative ways, treating such persons as rights-holders in ways that superseded the previous medical model of disability. It is, indeed a convention that "highlights the need to remove all societal structures, barriers and practices that limit the full and equal enjoyment of the right to the highest attainable standard of health by all persons with disabilities."[55] Notwithstanding, there has also been equal amount of criticism directed towards the CRPD. The key of these criticisms center on the inadequacy of the CRPD in dealing with issues of mental health in persons with ID. For example, one study (amongst many others[56]) employing a systematic literature review finds that there is not enough research in mental health "reflecting the importance of the [CRPD]"[57] and that "empirical research on the aspects of CRPD are still scarce."[58] Another study highlights the reality that ill mental health factored amongst the highest in persons with ID compared with the rest of the population[59] and is attributable to reasons ranging from the biophysical to psychosocial.[60]

Another criticism levied against the CRPD raises questions about the manner in which the CRPD frames "practices of inclusion and accommodation at the individual, rather than the structural level"[61] and this invites the risk of

54 G. Szmukler, '"Capacity," "Best Interests," "Will and Preferences" and the UN Convention on the Rights of Persons with Disabilities', *World Psychiatry* 18 (2019) 34, pp. 34–41.

55 Devandas-Aguilar, *supra* note 23, p. 6.

56 J. Buckles, R. Luckasson and E. Keefe, 'A Systematic Review of the Prevalence of Psychiatric Disorders in Adults With Intellectual Disability, 2003–2010', *Journal of Mental Health Research in Intellectual Disabilities* 6 (2013) 181–207.

57 C. Steinert, T. Steinert, E. Flammer and S. Jaeger, 'Impact of the UN Convention on the Rights of Persons with Disabilities (UN-CRPD) on Mental Health Care Research — a Systematic Review', *BMC Psychiatry* 16 (2016) 166, p. 4.

58 *Ibid.*

59 E.L. Whittle, K.R. Fisher, S. Reppermund, R. Lenroot and J. Trollor, 'Barriers and Enablers to Accessing Mental Health Services for People With Intellectual Disability: A Scoping Review', *Journal of Mental Health Research in Intellectual Disabilities* 11 (2018) 69–102.

60 *Ibid.*, p. 69.

61 J. Grue, 'Inclusive Marginalisation? A Critical Analysis of the Concept of Disability, Its Framings and Their Implications in the United Nations Convention on the Rights of Persons with Disabilities', *Nordic Journal of Human Rights* 37 (2019) 3–17, p. 3.

"inclusive marginalization."[62] Hence, whilst the intention is noble, a lack of action to address the structural and systemic inequalities for persons with disabilities may be seen as an inadequacy gap to counter discrimination.

In the meantime, this chapter argues that where new and emerging technologies are concerned (that could be of benefit to persons with ID), the provisions in the CRPD currently do not account for this evolution of technologies, especially where genome editing technologies such as CRISPR is concerned. If this is the case, this chapter further argues that the lack of will or effort to address genome editing technologies for persons with disabilities *vis-à-vis* Article 26 CRPD, is akin to restricting their rights to full enjoyment of health under Article 25.

3.1 *Legal Provisions in the CRPD in the Context of Genome Editing Technologies*

As briefly mentioned in the preceding section, this chapter argues that the CRPD currently does not consider the impact of technologies such as genome editing technologies, and how this might be used or adapted to assist persons with disabilities. As far as existing literature[63] on genome editing and persons with disabilities is concerned,[64] much of the legal scholarship has been focused on human germline genome editing[65] and the manner in which this can affect persons with disabilities.[66] Indeed, much of the headlines of mainstream newspaper articles also weigh in on the impact of human germline genome editing.[67] A cursory search using the keywords 'human germline gene editing' and 'disability' will reveal the voluminous amount of scholarship on the subject matter; but there is much less when considering *somatic genome editing for persons with disabilities*, and that which is not determined from a pre-implantation embryonic level.

There are several areas in the CRPD where there are manifest shortcomings. First, the CRPD does not appear at all to envisage the impact of any new

62 *Ibid.*

63 F. Boardman, 'Human Genome Editing and the Identity Politics of Genetic Disability', *Journal of Community Genetics* 11 (2020) 125–127.

64 D.J.H. Mathews and R. Lovell-Badge, 'A Path Through The Thicket', *Nature* 527 (2015) 159–161.

65 D. Flaherty, 'Human Germline Modification Is Coming', *Columbia Science and Technology Law Review* 22 (2017), available online at https://journals.library.columbia.edu/index.php/stlr/blog/view/169 (accessed 25 May 2018).

66 Mathews and Lovell-Badge, *supra* note 64.

67 K. Hafner, 'Once Science Fiction, Gene Editing Is Now a Looming Reality', *The New York Times* (22 July 2020), available online at https://www.nytimes.com/2020/07/22/style/crispr-gene-editing-ethics.html (accessed 15 January 2022).

forms of biomedical interventions, emerging technologies, or genome therapies (including genome editing)[68] which may apply to persons with disabilities. Conti surmises that the absence of words such as 'eugenics', 'genetics' or 'bioethics' are telling of the fact that the CRPD has not considered how tools such as CRISPR-Cas9 may shift a balance of human rights considerations for persons with ID. Since the disability discourse is a continually evolving one, it is uncanny that the key legislation that seeks to protect persons with disabilities, does not also evolve contemporaneously.

Conti also highlights the disparity of Article 10 of the CRPD,[69] which provides for the "inherent right to life" and "to ensure its effective enjoyment by persons with disabilities on an equal basis with others." Whilst this is a crucial consistency in human rights instruments for the protection of lives, it presents an apparent incongruence with the genetic engineering therapies targeted at eradicating mutations that cause disabilities,[70] or with other diagnostic reproductive technologies such as PGD that involve selecting healthy embryos for implantation.

Finally, Article 26 of the CRPD (as highlighted in some of the preceding sections herein) does not appear to adequately address clear and proper measures of habilitation for persons with disabilities. Habilitation can be defined as a "process aimed at helping people gain certain new skills, abilities and knowledge"[71] whilst rehabilitation refers to "regaining skills, abilities or knowledge that may have been lost or compromised as a result of acquiring a disability, or due to a change in one's disability or circumstances."[72] Not only is there a lack of representation in the voices of persons with disabilities in science and technology[73] — there is also a lack of representation of the kind of measures of habilitation in which persons with disabilities may partake.

The CRPD attempts, as far as it is possible, to enunciate the removal of barriers that may prevent a person with ID to exercise their full human rights under the convention. In this instance, with the advancements that have been

68 Conti, *supra* note 12, p. 10.

69 *Ibid.*, p. 11.

70 *Ibid.*

71 J.E. Lord, K.N. Guernsey, J.M. Balfe, V.L. Karr and A.S. deFranco, *Human Rights. Yes!: Action and Advocacy on the Rights of Persons with Disabilities* (Minneapolis, MN: University of Minnesota Human Rights Resource Center, 2012) 106.

72 *Ibid.*

73 S. Burgstahler, 'Increasing the Representation of People with Disabilities in Science, Engineering, and Mathematics', *Disabilities, Opportunities, Internetworking, and Technology* (December 1994), available online at https://www.washington.edu/doit/increasing-representation-people-disabilities-science-engineering-and-mathematics (accessed 16 January 2022).

made in research, development and scientific and clinical experiments of CRISPR-Cas9, there should be more that is done to equip an individual with ID with specific tools, information, knowledge and resources[74] that would be needed to access genome editing technologies.

3.2 *Legal Provisions in Various International Instruments in the context of Genome Editing Technologies*

In the Introduction, this chapter mentions the WHO Committee's Recommendations. Prior to these Recommendations, there are over-arching international human rights law[75] that deal with the governance of genome editing technologies. These include the 1997 Convention for the Protection of Human Rights and Dignity of the Human Being with regard to the Application of Biology and Medicine: Convention on Human Rights and Biomedicine (the Oviedo Convention). Other soft law instruments include the UNESCO Universal Declaration on the Human Genome and Human Rights, and the UNESCO Universal Declaration on Bioethics and Human Rights.

The text in Article 13 of the Oviedo Convention[76] has always been the subject of enquiry as to whether human genome editing is prohibited. Additionally, Article 3 of the Oviedo Convention is also consistent with the premise upon which this chapter is based — that is, equitable access to health care for all persons.[77]

Genome editing is also addressed in the international soft law instruments, continuing the theme of a human rights paradigm. In the 1997 UNESCO Universal Declaration on the Human Genome and Human Rights, the emphasis is on "internationally agreed standards and good practices concerning genetic interventions, which were supported by a broad international consensus at the time of its adoption."[78] This Declaration, in Article 1 particularly, stipulates that:

74 Lord et al., *supra* note 71, p. 107.

75 R. Yotova, 'Regulating Genome Editing under International Human Rights Law', International and Comparative Law Quarterly 69 (2020) 653–684, p. 658.

76 Article 13 of the Oviedo Convention, titled "Article 13 — Interventions on the Human Genome" reads as follows: "An intervention seeking to modify the human genome may only be undertaken for preventive, diagnostic, or therapeutic purposes and only if its aim is not to introduce any modification in the genome of any descendants."

77 P.L. Lau, *Comparative Legal Frameworks for Pre-Implantation Embryonic Genetic Interventions* (Chem: Springer International, 2019), p. 193, available online at http://link.springer.com/10.1007/978-3-030-22308-3 (accessed 19 November 2019).

78 Yotova, *supra* note 75, p. 671.

> The human genome underlies the fundamental unity of all members of the human family, as well as the recognition of their inherent dignity and diversity. In a symbolic sense, it is the heritage of humanity.[79]

Article 10 of this Declaration continues by emphasizing that human rights, fundamental freedoms and liberties, and human dignity, must always prevail over any research or applications that pertain to the human genome. This illustrates the respect given to key values such as personal autonomy, integrity and informed choice, especially where biology, genetics and medicine are concerned.

Similarly, the 2005 UNESCO Universal Declaration on Bioethics and Human Rights, in Article 2, aims "to provide a universal framework of principles and procedures to guide States in the formulation of their legislation, policies or other instruments in the field of bioethics."[80] Of particular interest in Article 2 are sub-sections (d) and (f), explaining, respectively, the importance of freedom of scientific research (that must take into account human rights and fundamental freedoms and liberties), and equitable access to medical, scientific and technological developments.

Hence, as far as governance frameworks go, prior to the Recommendations, there has been some recognition and foresight of the trajectory that biomedical technologies, such as genome editing tools, may take. The reality, however, is of limited applicability, particularly where the technologies evolve rapidly, and the law tries to keep up with such change. However, it is now implicit upon us to adapt the international human rights framework in tandem with the new Committee Recommendations, including working to build "an inclusive global dialogue on frontier technologies."[81]

In addition, whilst these regulations are meant to be neutral in nature, it would now be appropriate as human rights legislation that they also take into consideration the rights of persons with disabilities, and their access to these technologies.

---

79 Universal Declaration on the Human Genome and Human Rights (New York, NY: UNESCO, 2017), available online at http://portal.unesco.org/en/ev.php-URL_ID=13177&URL_DO=DO_TOPIC&URL_SECTION=201.html (accessed 18 December 2017).

80 H. ten Have and M. Jean, *The UNESCO Universal Declaration on Bioethics and Human Rights: Background, Principles and Application* (New York, NY: UNESCO, 2009), available online at https://unesdoc.unesco.org/ark:/48223/pf0000146180 (accessed 17 February 2017.

81 World Health Organisation, *WHO Issues New Recommendations on Human Genome Editing for the Advancement of Public Health* (12 July 2021), available online at https://www.who.int/news/item/12-07-2021-who-issues-new-recommendations-on-human-genome-editing-for-the-advancement-of-public-health (accessed 13 October 2021).

3.3 *Suggested Habilitation Measures under Article 26 CRPD*

This chapter has consistently maintained that access to genome technologies for persons with ID would be compatible with an exercise of their right to health under Article 25 and 26 CRPD. Nevertheless, there is inadequate scholarship that has been devoted to what might be encompassed under the right of habilitation in Article 26. In most literature regarding the right to habilitation and rehabilitation,[82] these two concepts are almost always intertwined and considered as if they were one, but the reality cannot be further from the truth. The precarity of this intertwinement means that the right to habilitation is often overlooked in favor of the right to rehabilitation. Any efforts, steps or actions that can be taken on "adapting the social, legal, political and physical environments are often inadequate to create equal opportunities for each person with a disability."[83]

Now, repositioned within the concept of genome editing technologies, efforts must be made to ensure that an individual with ID, as an example, be granted equal access and information to the use of such technologies, which may entail additional support, specific training or information session, education and awareness, and on a technical basis, perhaps even skills development. If there is a manner in which genome editing technologies may be available to a person with ID, then such measure must be made available accordingly. Dependent on the level of disabilities that is being suffered by a particular individual, this also means that information about habilitation must be provided in an accessible format,[84] otherwise it would defeat the purposes of Article 26 entirely.

Broadly considered, Wolbring and Diep present some pertinent questions which may help to plan the specific measures necessary for habilitation under Article 26. For example:

> Who will provide for the societal environment that allows disabled people to take part which includes physical access, accessibility of the information material, and access to education that allows disabled people to identify problems? Will disabled people have the ability to provide and inform the network of groups involved in the governance of science, technology and innovation and who within the networks will decide who

82 OHCHR, 'Report on Habilitation and Rehabilitation of Persons with Disabilities under Article 26 of the CRPD, Including List of Submissions from States and Stakeholders', *United Nations Human Rights Office of the High Commissioner* (21 January 2019), available online at https://www.ohchr.org/EN/Issues/Disability/Pages/Article26.aspx (accessed 16 January 2022).

83 Lord et al., *supra* note 71, p. 107.

84 *Ibid.*, p. 110.

> that network includes? Will disabled people have the ability to access the information needed for them to know that they should get involved and to be able to evaluate the situation? Will disabled people have the ability to know early enough that they have to be informed so that they can influence the anticipatory governance discourse of topics such as gene editing before the trajectory is already set? Will disabled people have the ability to get involved; that is, will they not be hindered by the struggles of daily life.[85]

Additionally, from the perspective of persons with ID, there is even less scholarship or resources that inform how habilitation may take place. Given the fact that persons with ID are particularly vulnerable to human rights violations committed in the name of 'rehabilitation',[86] it becomes even more acute why a holistic and inclusive participatory, and emancipatory process is employed to enable them to achieve their personal goals.

It may be that genome editing technologies could be adapted in a similar way as assistive technologies, which helps with habilitation and rehabilitation. By adaptation, this means that firstly, concerted efforts should be made to provide awareness and education on the use of genome editing technologies for treating ID, and secondly, by applying the 'solution' of emancipatory, participatory and transformative research and innovation measures *with* (and not *for*) persons with ID. Whilst it is likely that addressing the reversal or eradication of ID may take place vis-à-vis pre-birth stages, and less likely to be prevalent in adults with ID, the benefits that may be afforded to them through technological adaptations of genome editing tools should further be studied and given equal weight as research and studies into other aspects of human genome editing. For this reason, this chapter wishes to draw attention to how we may now think about Article 26 in the context of genome editing technologies, and to find efficacy in this line of thinking. For example, inspiration can be drawn from similar examples for the treatment of other diseases in adults[87] that have also used genome editing technologies.[88] If similar adaptations can be made

85 G. Wolbring and L. Diep, 'The Discussions around Precision Genetic Engineering: Role of and Impact on Disabled People', *Laws* 5 (2016) 37, p. 9.

86 Lord et al., *supra* note 71, p. 112.

87 J. Kaiser, 'A Human Has Been Injected with Gene-Editing Tools to Cure His Disabling Disease. Here's What You Need to Know', *Science* (2017), doi: 10.1126/science.aar5098 (accessed 15 January 2022).

88 B. Walsh, 'Scientists Used CRISPR inside an Adult Patient's Body for the First Time', *Axios* (4 March 2020), available online at https://www.axios.com/crispr-gene-editing-patient-ac724626-05cf-4584-b802-62e0e83388aa.html (accessed 15 January 2022).

for persons with IDs, then this would be one of the first steps towards true disability-inclusion approaches.[89]

Additionally, assistive technologies (ATs)[90] could be technologies that are quite sophisticated, or even quite low-key, and their purpose would be to support persons with disabilities, such as supporting organization, memory, or other cognitive functions. For different types of disabilities, ATs can be adapted to be much more specialized, using computer software and other networking capabilities to support a user. In this way, ATs enables a person with ID to access technologies that can help them in their daily lives, thereby markedly improving how they are able to exercise their full rights to health.[91] The European Parliament recognizes the importance of these ATs.[92] Whilst genome editing tools may still be in a developmental stage *vis-à-vis* ATs, taking other steps, such as "targeting wide attitudinal and social change, encouraging co-creation of future ATs, and promoting the emergence of AT professionals"[93] are some ways that could be promoted.

4 Expanding the Social Model of Disability: Emancipatory, Participatory and Transformative Research and Innovation for Persons with Disabilities

4.1 *Removing Ableism and Emphasizing the Voices of Persons with Disabilities*

A big point of contention that is prevalent in disability discourse revolves around the 'ableism' arguments, and the equity of technologies viewed from the perspective of the abled and through the lens of disability as a problem that must be solved. This is a point that is emphasized in this chapter as an extension of the social model of disability. There is a wealth of scholarship that demonstrate disability — positive arguments, where persons with disabilities may not necessarily wish for their disabilities to be eradicated or "edited" because this creates the (wrongful) narrative that persons with disabilities are

89 Devandas-Aguilar, *supra* note 25.

90 P. Boucher, 'Assistive Technologies for People with Disabilities', *European Parliament* (January 2018), available online at https://www.europarl.europa.eu/RegData/etudes/IDAN/2018/603218/EPRS_IDA(2018)603218_EN.pdf (accessed 16 November 2021).

91 World Health Organization, *Assistive Technology* (18 May 2018), available online at https://www.who.int/news-room/fact-sheets/detail/assistive-technology (accessed 16 January 2022).

92 Boucher, *supra* note 90.

93 *Ibid.*

less than, trailing on the fringes of 'other'. Lennard J. Davis, one of the most important, leading disabilities studies scholar whose work focuses on the construction of disability[94] states: "… the 'problem' is not the person with disabilities; the problem is the way that normalcy is constructed to create the 'problem' of the disabled person."[95] What is needed is a change in how we interrogate our participation in the disability — ability system, and that as able-bodied persons, we will need to rethink how we might impose on persons with disabilities our own presumed values, practices, and experiences.

This is where honest and experiential stories like *Unspeakable Conversations*[96] becomes relevant. This essay by Harriet Johnson, in all its simplicity, presents conversations had between the author and Peter Singer, extrapolating on the value of the disabled body. Whilst the essay has not been intended to be a piece of critical academic work and critiques are likely to express some confusion about the writing, it nevertheless does shed light on the bodily experiences of persons with disabilities, and the fallacies of Singer's philosophical arguments about disability. Johnson states: "As a disability pariah, I must struggle for a place, for kinship, for community, for connection"[97] — further reinforcing Davis' arguments that assessments of normalcy continue to pervade and be accepted as justification to unconsciously 'other' a disabled body.

Is there, however, a difference between physical disabilities and ID viewed from the perspective of therapeutic genome editing? It appears that a majority of disability activism seems to be significantly more opposed to suggestions that physical disabilities such as deafness[98] and dwarfism[99] should be eradicated. In France, one of its most prolific cases, argued on the basis of a violation of human dignity, is the Conseil d'Etat's decision in *Commune de Morsang-sur-Orge v Societe Fun Production et M. Wackenheim*.[100] In this case,

94 L.J. Davis (ed.), *The Disability Studies Reader* (Abingdon: Routledge, 2017).

95 L.J. Davis, 'Introduction: Disability, Normality and Power' in: L.J. Davis (ed.), *The Disability Reader* (Abingdon: Routledge, 2017) p. 16.

96 H. McBryde Johnson, 'Unspeakable Conversations' *The New York Times* (16 February 2003), available online at https://www.nytimes.com/2003/02/16/magazine/unspeakable-conversations.html (accessed 17 October 2021).

97 *Ibid.*

98 O. Feeney and V. Rakić, 'Genome Editing and "Disenhancement": Considerations on Issues of Non-Identity and Genetic Pluralism', *Nature Humanities and Social Sciences Communications* 8 (2021) 116.

99 L. Marshall, *Why This Disability Activist Fears CRISPR* (11 May 2021), available online at https://st-0059284.stprod.webmd.com/children/story/centerpiece-crispr-sidebar (accessed 23 October 2021).

100 *Commune de Morsang-sur-Orge v Societe Fun Production et MWackenheim* [1995] Conseil d'Etat 136727, Cons Etat.

the court stipulated that the activity of dwarf-tossing outweighs freedom of livelihood and commerce, because the violation of their human dignity is much more acute.[101] This decision is consistent with the protection of human dignity as a fundamental principle[102] in France, and indeed, in many countries within the jurisdiction of the European Court of Human Rights. The protection of human dignity can also be found in Article 1 of the EU Charter of Fundamental Rights,[103] Article 2 of the Treaty of European Union[104] and the jurisprudence of the Court of Justice of the EU.[105] Conversely, this may be viewed by some disability activists that disabled bodies need special protection through the notions of human dignity.

The tensions between voices in the disability community and the scientific research genetics community have been palpable, and this may largely be due to the under-representation of the disability community in the future developments of genome editing.[106] Recent studies conducted[107] have also indicated that persons with genetic disabilities feel that "it would be a loss to society to have fewer people with their particular condition coming into the world"[108] and that a 90% majority of family members would not be comfortable with terminating pregnancies that reveal disabilities.[109]

Scholars have consistently highlighted the importance of considering the views and voices of the disability community.[110] Even with advancements in genomic technologies such as CRISPR-Cas9, the prioritization of persons with disabilities would remain focused on combatting discrimination and prejudice.[111] Felicity Boardman reminds that "the core ethical and social issues that genetic disability eradication and/or minimization present will invariably remain the same."[112]

101 Lau, *supra* note 77, p. 197.

102 C. McCrudden, 'Human Dignity and Judicial Interpretation of Human Rights', *European Journal of International Law* 19 (2008) 655–724.

103 'Charter of Fundamental Rights of the European Union 2000/C 364/01' (n 32).

104 'Treaty on European Union C326/15', *Official Journal of the European Union* (26 October 2012).

105 *C-34/10 — Oliver Brustle v Greenpeace eV* [2011] Court of Justice of the EU (Grand Chamber) ECLI:EU:C:2011:669.

106 Wolbring and Diep, *supra* note 85.

107 Boardman, *supra* note 63.

108 *Ibid.* 125.

109 *Ibid.* 126.

110 Mathews and Lovell-Badge, *supra* note 64.

111 T. Shakespeare, 'Gene Editing: Heed Disability Views', *Nature* 527 (2015) 446.

112 Boardman, *supra* note 63, p. 127.

4.2 *Enablement for the Enjoyment of a Right to Health* (*and a Right to Habilitation through Science*)

Instead of questioning if we should encourage the eradication of disabilities — what might be advantageous is to find an alternative way of guiding our understanding of ID, and calculating its relationship with inclusionary and solidifying access to the benefits of genome editing therapies. Framing the narrative for persons with ID, in terms of their access to a right to health, and conversely, the right to habilitation *vis-à-vis* scientific and biomedical developments, is a strong measure that considers the UN Special Rapporteur's report on how disability — inclusion[113] needs to be on the forefront for the immediate futures.

One way in which we can do so is the following: to suffuse the contemporary evolution of disabilities with much more emancipatory, participatory and transformative disabilities studies research.

Returning to the notion that we should not be framing disability as a problem with bodies and therefore needing to associate these bodies with harmful and unsolicited medical treatment or interventions based on a paternalistic model[114] — it should be noted that disability has been recognized as an evolving concept, which may continue to include future types of disabilities, under the CRPD.[115] Because of this evolution — then it also logically follows that a framework for protecting persons with disabilities must also evolve. This involves viewing persons with disabilities as actors and active contributors in disability discourse — as opposed to victims, or the subject matter of regulation. According to Nicola Martin:

> An understanding of the social construction of disability is required in order to engage with the process of eradicating barriers and to pave the way for inclusive practice to minimize disadvantage. Inclusive practice needs to be embedded in institutions' routine practices rather than as compensatory or additional. Inclusive practice starts with the creation of awareness and a non-intimidating environment.[116]

113 Devandas-Aguilar, *supra* note 25.

114 Devandas-Aguilar, *supra* note 33.

115 Conti, *supra* note 12.

116 N. Martin, 'Brief Reflections on Disability Theory, Language, Identity, Equality and Inclusion', *Equity, Diversity and Inclusion* (13 May 2011), available online at https://blogs.lse.ac.uk/equityDiversityInclusion/2011/05/brief-reflections-on-disability-theory-language-identity-equality-and-inclusion/ (accessed 24 October 2021).

Further, contemporary disabilities studies research is much more emancipatory, participatory and transformative than they used to be — acknowledging that power is a fundamental aspect of all research relationships[117] and conversely, research must also "empower the subjects of social inquiry."[118] It is also useful to further navigate these waters through empathy for understanding persons with disabilities — where scholars study the conception of empathy in the design of technologies, and call for "reimagining empathy as guided by the lived experiences of people with disabilities who are traditionally positioned as those to be empathized."[119] To orient empathy with disability activism, the authors proposed the following commitments: first, partnership in the design encounter;[120] secondly, a process of ongoing attunement;[121] thirdly, recognizing and working with asymmetry.[122]

Enabling the enjoyment of the right to health is also something that can be exemplified through biology, science, and medicine. In the context of this chapter looking at how science can be democratized, and therefore, be accessed more easily, is one of the ways in which we may couple the reimagination of ID. From the perspective of the consumption market, when products of science are placed in a sphere enabling access by 'consumers', some scholars have pointed out that public participation in science and technology has democratizing effects. Where non-experts are involved and are allowed to provide input into processes such as "agenda setting, decision-making, policy forming, and knowledge production processes regarding science,"[123] this has the effect of changing narratives and creating more inclusion — depending on the categories of the kind of participation. Additionally, it makes sense for

---

117 V. Jupp (ed.), *The Sage Dictionary of Social Research Methods* (Thousand Oaks, CA: SAGE, 2006), p. 88.

118 *Ibid.*

119 C.L. Bennett and D.K. Rosner, 'The Promise of Empathy: Design, Disability, and Knowing the "Other"', *Proceedings of the 2019 CHI Conference on Human Factors in Computing Systems* (ACM 2019), available online at https://dl.acm.org/doi/10.1145/3290605.3300528 (accessed 24 October 2021).

120 *Ibid.*, p. 9.

121 *Ibid.*, p. 10.

122 *Ibid.*

123 N. Invernizzi, 'Public Participation and Democratization: Effects on the Production and Consumption of Science and Technology', *Tapuya: Latin American Science, Technology and Society* 3 (2020) 227–253.

persons with ID to be part of the conversation that democratizes science, so that they may move towards improvement of public health.[124]

Particularly in the context of persons with disabilities and the democratization of science more broadly, Ruha Benjamin states the following:

> To fully "interrogate equity," we must foster deliberation that moves beyond questions of access to treatment, however important, and think very seriously about the design of research — who does it and with what guiding questions and assumptions— because how research is framed is never neutral, universal, or inevitable. Gene editing techniques are seeded with values and interests — economic as well as social — and without careful examination, they will easily reproduce existing hierarchies, including assumptions about which lives are worth which lives are worth living and which are worth "editing" out of existence.[125]

Ruha Benjamin further reminds us that an expansive approach to genetic technologies includes disabled people "at the table and not just on the table of the life sciences."[126] If we are to truly partake in the democratization of science, and allow the benefits of health technologies for all, then we must exert the creative will to address these social complexities and be open to regeneration of new ideas of body politics.[127]

5 Conclusion

The promise and potential of genome editing tools and technologies must continue to be refined to contemplate the voices, needs and concerns of persons with ID. A paradigm shift in disability studies discourse must be adequately facilitated in the light of changing definitions of disabilities, and compliance with international law instruments. Whilst existing genome editing tools may

124 F. Kurtulmuş, 'The Democratization of Science', in: D. Ludwig, I. Koskinen, Z. Mncube, L. Poliseli and L. Reyes-Galindo, *Global Epistemologies and Philosophies of Science*, 1st edn. (Abingdon: Routledge, 2021), Chapter 12, available online at https://www.taylorfrancis.com/books/9781003027140/chapters/10.4324/9781003027140-16 (accessed 16 November 2021).

125 R. Benjamin, 'Interrogating Equity: A Disability Justice Approach to Genetic Engineering', *Issues in Science and Technology* 32 (2021) 51–54, p. 52.

126 *Ibid.*, p. 54.

127 *Ibid.*

not yet be fully ready to treat a wide range of IDs — this does not mean that this sectional group of society should be excluded from basic habilitation measures that can be useful for future deployment. Research and innovations in genome editing should continue to be creative and inclusive, recognizing that persons with ID are no less important. Recognizing the diversity and vulnerabilities of our human population means that we must also be in a position to activate actions and measures that center upon the enablement of technological adaptations in genome editing to remove discrimination, inequalities, segregation and seclusion of persons with disabilities.

Regulating Heritable Human Genome Editing: Drawing the Line between Legitimate and Controversial Use

Noemi Conditi | ORCID: 0000-0002-2209-7777
Department of Legal Studies, University of Bologna,
Via Zamboni 33, 40126 Bologna, Italy
noemi.conditi3@unibo.it

Abstract

In general, to modify the human germline is prohibited. However, regulating the use of HHGE might be a more efficient method than the actual ban. Indeed, when genome editing is safe for introduction in clinical practices, it is frequently proposed that the prohibition is lifted solely for therapeutic purposes, i.e., to eliminate serious genetic diseases. Definitions of the concepts of *health* and *disease* are controversial and may only be reached by adopting a value-laden approach, which may rise concerns about legal certainty and have possible discriminatory effects. Nor the threshold of the *seriousness of the disease* might be used to solve these issues. A different model might then be adopted for the assessment of the permissibility of HHGE, i.e., the PGD model. However, such model should not be implemented as the only criterion, but should rather be a "minimum threshold": HHGE should be allowed whenever used to correct a genetic defect for which PGD is possible.

Keywords

germline editing – therapy – enhancement – serious genetic disease

1 Introduction

The history of human development is characterised by man's desire to improve and somehow gain control over their human biological destiny.[1] The field of human genome editing is no exception in this respect. Indeed, since the discovery of DNA, the scientific community has been focusing on trying to achieve the capacity to make targeted changes to the human genome, particularly in order to cure genetic diseases. The development of systems like ZFNS, TALENS and especially CRISPR-Cas9 family of genome-editing tools, often referred to as "the Breakthrough to Genome Editing,"[2] has brought us closer to this aim by making it possible to perform genome modifications in a precise, efficient, and cost-effective way.[3] These are exceptional tools for achieving great therapeutic purposes, but at the same time they raise issues related to the social consequences and the ethical permissibility of their use.

This is particularly the case for heritable human genome editing (HHGE), i.e., when changes are made to germline cells, and thus to the genetic material of eggs, sperm or any germ cells, including the cells of early embryos.[4] The genetically modified embryo is then transferred to a uterus in order to initiate a pregnancy and give birth to a child with a modified genome. Unlike modifications made to somatic cells, which are all other cells in the human body, alterations of the germline cells are then inherited by the descendants of the modified person,[5] a peculiarity that raises fervent hope for future therapeutic treatments, but also great societal, ethical and legal concerns.[6]

Indeed, in general terms, HHGE may be used to alter the human genome at least for the following aims: (1) the prevention or treatment of genetic

1 B. Fantini, 'Il fantasma dell'eugenetica', in S. Rodotà (ed.) *Questioni di bioetica* (Bari: Laterza, 1993).

2 M. Mcnutt, 'Breakthrough to Gernome Editing', *Science* 350 (6267) (2015) 1445, doi: 10.1126/science.aae0479.

3 A. Boggio, 'Introduction', in A. Boggio, C. Romano and J. Almqvist (eds.), *Human Germline Genome Modification and the Right to Science: A Comparative Study of National Laws and Policies* (Cambridge: Cambridge University Press, 2020), pp. 1–21, doi: 10.1017/9781108759083.002.

4 National Academy of Sciences, *Heritable Human Genome Editing* (Washington, DC: The National Academies Press, 2020), https://doi.org/10.17226/25665.

5 Boggio, *supra* note 3.

6 For an extensive analysis of the ethical and legal concerns related to the use of HHGE for enhancement see, among others, National Academies of Sciences, Engineering, and Medicine, *Human Genome Editing: Science, Ethics, and Governance* (Washington, DC: The National Academies Press, 2017), doi: 10.17226/24623; Nuffield Council on Bioethics, Genome Editing and Human Reproduction: social and ethical issues (London: Nuffield Council on Bioethics, 2018); C Gyngell, T. Douglas and J. Savulescu, 'The ethics of germline gene editing', *Journal of Applied Philosophy*, 32 (4) (2017) 498–513, doi: 10.1111/japp.12249.

disorders (therapeutic purpose), and (2) the optimisation of certain traits or abilities, and more broadly the attempt to modify desired traits in offspring that are not directly related to a disease (enhancement).[7] However, the dividing line between these different purposes is far from being clear. Even though it is unrealistic to think that we will ever be able to alter complex human traits such as strength or intelligence, mainly because of their multifactorial and extremely complex nature,[8] interventions in the human genome such as increasing athletic performance by altering the erythropoietin receptor gene or ensuring disease resistance may not always be considered medically necessary. Consequently, modifications of this kind might still qualify as enhancement and thus raise enormous concerns related to, among the others, the protection of the human genome, possible violations of the right to self-determination of the future person, and of human dignity.[9]

For these reasons, and because of the unsolved societal, ethical, legal, and technical issues,[10] the HHGE is sometimes referred to as "a red line that should never be crossed."[11] Currently, this restrictive approach is reflected in the European and International legal instruments applicable to HHGE, as well as that of the vast majority of the countries, that mainly prohibit the use of HHGE for reproductive purposes.[12] However, in recent years international scholars' and institutions' opinion on the matter started to increasingly ask for the establishment of a responsible and prudent pathway to an effective regulation on the matter. Indeed, nowadays the main question appears to be less *whether* HHGE should be pursued and more *how and under which circumstances*.[13] In

7 For a more in-depth analysis, see German Ethics Council, *Intervening in the Human Germline. Opinion — Executive Summary & Recommendations* (Berlin: German Ethics Council, 2019) and European Group on Ethics in Science and New Technologies, *Opinion on Ethics of Genome Editing — Opinion n. 34* (Brussels: European Group on Ethics in Science and New Technologies, 2021).

8 German Ethics Council, *supra* note 7.

9 Nuffield Council on Bioethics, *supra* note 6.

10 Nuffield Council on Bioethics, *supra* note 6.

11 R. Andorno and E.A. Yamin, 'The Right to Design Babies? Human Rights and Bioethics', *OpenGlobalRights* (2019), available online at https://www.openglobalrights.org/the-right-to-design-babies-human-rights-and-bioethics/. In this regard, see also in particular Parliamentary Assembly of the Council of Europe, 'The Use of New Genetic Technologies in Human Beings', Recommendation 2115 (2017) where it is stated: "3. Deliberate germ-line editing in human beings would cross a line viewed as ethically inviolable."

12 For an extensive analysis of the national regulations on HHGE see F. Baylis, M. Darnovsky, K. Hasson and T.M. Krahn, 'Human Germline and Heritable Genome Editing: The Global Policy Landscape', *The CRISPR Journal* 3(5) (2020) 365–377, doi: 10.1089/crispr.2020.0082.

13 J.B. Hurlbut, 'Human Genome Editing: Ask Whether, Not How', *Nature* 565 (135) (2019) 135, doi: https://doi.org/10.1038/d41586-018-07881-1; D. Dickenson and M. Darnovsky,

this regard, it is frequently suggested to use the *therapeutic purpose* as a threshold for the permissibility of HHGE and as one of the guidance principles for a regulatory pathway on the matter, especially in its meanings of "correction of *serious* (*monogenic*) *diseases*" or "restoration of *health*." However, there is no consensus on the definition of these terms.

Therefore, after an overview of the current legal framework applicable to HHGE and a brief analysis of the shift in public perspective over a call for a responsible pathway in Section 2, in Section 3 I argue that the distinction between "therapy" and "enhancement" is still somehow valuable in itself for the purpose of assessing the permissibility of HHGE and that at least two opposite approaches may be adopted to define the concepts of *disease* and *health* on which that distinction relies: naturalism (value-free) and normativism (value-laden). While the first approach might be preferrable, value-free definitions of these concepts appear difficult to be reached. Therefore, only a value-laden approach seems feasible, which however raises concerns in terms of legal certainty and possible discriminations. Neither it appears feasible to adopt a value-free definition of the threshold of the *seriousness* of the disease, with the aim of reducing the discretion on decisions about the permissibility of HHGE.

Then, in Section 4 I analyse an alternative method to discern between permissible and unlawful use of HHGE: the so called preimplantation genetic diagnosis (PGD) model, i.e., to adopt the same thresholds used to assess whether PGD might be undergone in a given case.[14] PGD is a procedure used to examine cells from oocytes or in vitro fertilized embryos to detect genetic alteration responsible for possible genetic diseases and thus enable prospective parents to choose to implant only "healthy" embryos.[15] I argue that because of the differences between PGD and HHGE it may be problematic to adopt exclusively the PGD model to assess the permissibility of HHGE. On the contrary, such model might be used as a complementary one, meaning that HHGE might be

'Did a Permissive Scientific Culture Encourage the "CRISPR Babies" Experiment?', *Nature Biotechnology* 37 (2019) 355–357, doi: 10.1038/s41587-019-0077-3; E.Y. Adashi and I.G. Cohen, 'Heritable Genome Editing: Is a Moratorium Needed?', *Journal of the American Medical Association* 322 (2) (2019) 104–105, doi: 10.1001/jama.2019.8977. Admittedly, Stock and Campbell were already asking the same question back in 2000; G. Stock and J. Campbell, *Engineering the Human Germline: An Exploration of the Science and Ethics of Altering the Genes We Pass to Our Children* (Oxford: Oxford University Press, 2000), p. 6.

14 R. Isasi, E. Kleiderman and B.M. Knoppers, 'Editing policy to fit the genome', *Science* 351 (6271) (2016) 337–339, doi: 10.1126/science.aad6778.

15 L. Lu, 'Recent advances in preimplantation genetic diagnosis and screening', *Journal of Assisted Reproduction and Genetics* 33 (2016) 1129–1134, doi: 10.1007/s10815-016-0750-0.

allowed at least for preventing the occurrence of any of the genetic diseases for which PGD is already permissible.

As an introductory and general remark, the whole analysis starts from the assumption that at some point in the future the use of HHGE for reproductive purposes will be found safe and effective enough for standard clinical application.[16] However, like any other medical intervention, HHGE for reproductive purposes will always entail an unavoidable degree of risk and possible side effects. Therefore, as a general criterion, HHGE may be said to be safe and effective when the benefit/risk ratio of their use is deemed appropriate under scientific terms for clinical application.

2 The Framework Applicable to HHGE

2.1 *Legal Instruments Applicable to HHGE*

At the International level, the Universal Declaration on Human Genome and Human Rights forms "the basis of 'soft law' in the area of human genome governance,"[17] with the aim of preserving the human genome from improper manipulations.[18] Illustrative of this goal is Article 1, which qualifies the human genome as "the heritage of humanity" in a symbolic sense. Even though the Declaration recognises the importance of research on the human genome and the resulting applications, in the Preamble it is emphasized that "such research should fully respect human dignity, freedom and human rights." Therefore, Article 11 prohibits the performance of practices which are contrary to human dignity, among which Article 24 includes germ-line interventions.[19] However, these instruments made no reference to the purpose of HHGE as a criterion for assessing its permissibility.

At the regional level, already in 1997 the so called Oviedo Convention, the first multilateral treaty and regional binding legal instrument in the field of biomedical law,[20] established in Article 13 what is considered to be a ban on

16 E. Kleiderman, V. Ravitsky and B.M. Knoppers, 'The "serious" factor in germline modification', *Journal of Medical Ethics* 45 (2019) 508–513.

17 C Kuppuswamy, *The International Legal Governance of the Human Genome* (Abingdon: Routledge, 2009).

18 R. Andorno, *Principles of International Biolaw: Seeking Common Ground at the Intersection of Bioethics and Human Rights* (Brussels: Bruylant, 2013).

19 This position was then reaffirmed in 2003 by the Report of the IBC on pre-implantation genetic diagnosis and germ-line intervention.

20 J. Almqvist, 'The Regulation of Human Germline Genome Modification in Europe', in A. Boggio, C. Romano and J. Almqvist (eds.), *Human Germline Genome Modification and the Right to Science: A Comparative Study of National Laws and Policies* (Cambridge:

HHGE for reproductive purposes, with no distinction between therapeutic aims and enhancement, and at the same time it recognises the legitimacy of therapeutic somatic interventions.[21] Reasons for such approach may be found in the Oviedo Convention's Explanatory report, where it is stated that HHGE "may endanger the individual and the species itself" and that "the ultimate fear is of intentional modification of the human genome so as to produce individuals or entire groups endowed with particular characteristics and required qualities."[22]

Moreover, a more permissible approach is adopted in some European soft law instruments. Indeed, Recommendation 934 on genetic engineering explicitly states that the right to inherit a genetic pattern not artificially modified[23] "must not impede development of the therapeutic applications of genetic engineering (gene therapy), which holds great promise for the treatment and eradication of certain diseases which are genetically transmitted,"[24] thus suggesting that in principle therapeutic applications of HHGE do not violate such right. In this regard, this Recommendation further asks for "the boundaries of legitimate therapeutic application of genetic engineering techniques [to] be clearly drawn" and calls for regulations on the protection of "individuals against non-therapeutic applications of these techniques."[25] Along the same line, in 2017 Recommendation 2115 recognises that HHGE raises "complex ethical and human rights questions, including — but not limited to — unintended harm which may result from the techniques used, access and consent to such techniques, and their potential abuse for enhancement or eugenic purposes."[26]

Cambridge University Press, 2020), pp. 155–216, doi: 10.1017/9781108759083.007. However, it is worth noticing that the Convention is binding exclusively upon the States that fully ratify it. Nowadays, the Convention has been ratified by 29 countries and signed, but not yet fully ratified, by a further 7.

21 Article 13: "An intervention seeking to modify the human genome may only be undertaken for preventive, diagnostic or therapeutic purposes and only if its aim is not to introduce any modification in the genome of any descendants." On the interpretation of this Article as a categorical ban on HHGE see Oviedo Convention, Explanatory Report (no. 20), para. 90. On a more in-depth analysis of Article 13 and different interpretations of its meaning, see Almqvist, *supra* note 20.

22 Explanatory Report to the Convention on Human Rights and Biomedicine, *European Treaty Series, no. 164*, sub 89.

23 Parliamentary Assembly of the Council of Europe, 'Recommendation on Genetic Engineering', Recommendation 934 (1982), sub 4a.

24 *Ibid.*, sub 4.

25 *Ibid.*, sub 4e and 4f.

26 Parliamentary Assembly of the Council of Europe, *supra* note 11.

At the national level, the legal approaches adopted by different legislators vary greatly. By way of example, and by no means attempting to be exhaustive,[27] some Member States prohibit the use of HHGE for whatever purpose, such as Germany,[28] while others permit their use exclusively when the aim is therapeutic. For instance, Italy prohibits the selection of embryos for eugenic purposes, by selecting, manipulating, or using other artificial technical measures, whose aim is to modify the genetic heritage of the embryo or predetermine its genetic characteristics.[29] By way of exception, however, interventions for therapeutic or diagnostic purposes are allowed, when used to safeguard the health and development of the embryo itself, and if there are no alternatives available.[30] Furthermore, some legislations impose a general ban on HHGE while at the same time allowing to conduct research in that regard if the aim is therapeutic. Indeed, the French Civil Code establishes both a prohibition to intervene in the genetic characteristics of a person so as to also modify its descendants, and an exception in this regard for research when aimed at the prevention, diagnosis, or treatment of diseases.[31] An analogous categorical ban is in force in Greece.[32]

2.2 *Scholars' and Institutions' Approach to HHGE — The Call for an Effective Regulation*

In the first major round in the debate surrounding HHGE, when these technologies still had a high rate of side effects and inaccuracies,[33] international scholars, institutions and legal experts were almost unanimously in favour of an international ban for both research and clinical use, without making any

27 For a more comprehensive analysis of the different national regulations on HHGE, A. Boggio, C. Romano and J. Almqvist (eds.), *Human Germline Genome Modification and the Right to Science: A Comparative Study of National Laws and Policies* (Cambridge: Cambridge University Press, 2020); and Baylis et al., *supra* note 12.

28 ESchG para. 5(1) and (2).

29 Law 40/2004 Article 14.

30 Law 40/2004 Article 13 para. 3 lett. b.

31 Code Civile Article 16–4.

32 Act 3148/2005 Article 34.

33 X. Kang, W. He, Y. Huang, Q. Yu, Y. Chen, X. Gao, X. Sun and Y. Fan, 'Introducing precise genetic modifications into human 3PN embryos by CRISPR/Cas-mediated genome editing.' *Journal of Assisted Reproduction and Genetics* 33 (5) (2016) 581–588, doi: 10.1007/s10815-016-0710-8; P. Liang, Y. Xu, X. Zhang, C. Ding, R. Huang, Z. Zhang, J. Lv, X. Xie, Y. Chen, Y. Li, Y. Sun, Y. Bai, S. Zhou, W. Ma, C. Zhou and J. Huang, 'CRISPR/Cas9-mediated gene editing in human tripronuclear zygotes.' *Protein & Cell* 6 (5) (2015) 363–372, doi: 10.1007/s13238-015-0153-5.

distinction between therapeutic purpose and enhancement.[34] While recognizing the tremendous potential of these techniques,[35] the fear that HHGE could violate fundamental human rights and challenge existing values prevailed over the possible (therapeutic) benefits,[36] and the adoption of a restrictive approach on the matter was perceived as the best suitable solution to protect the different rights and interests at stake.

However, this restrictive approach came soon under pressure. Indeed, first in 2016 UK licensed a research project on HHGE,[37] and then in 2015 and 2019 both UK[38] and Greece[39] granted permissions to clinically use mitochondrial replacement technique (MRT), a technique which results in modifications of the germline that can be inherited.[40] MRT is an *in vitro* fertilization technique used to replace a woman's pathogenic mitochondrial DNA (mtDNA) with the one of an healthy donor, thus preventing the transmission of serious mitochondrial DNA-based diseases.[41] These scientific developments were

34 By way of example, S. Chan, P.J. Donovan, T. Douglas, C. Gyngell, J. Harris, R. Lovell-Badge, D.J.H. Mathews, A. Regenberg and On Behalf of the Hinxton Group, 'Genome Editing Technologies and Human Germline Genetic Modification: The Hinxton Group Consensus Statement', *The American Journal of Bioethics* 15(12) (2015) 42–47, doi: 10.1080/15265161.2015.1103814; D. Baltimore, P. Berg, M. Botchan, D. Carroll, R.A. Charo, G. Church, G.Q. Daley, J.A. Doudna, M. Fenner, H.T. Greely, M. Jinek, G.S. Martin, E.Penhoet, J. Puck, S.H. Sternberg, J.S. Weissman and K.R. Yamamoto, 'Biotechnology. A prudent path forward for genomic engineering and germline gene modification', *Science* 348 (6230) (2015) 36–38, doi: 10.1126/science.aab1028; Lanphier, F. Urnov, S. Ehlen Haecker, M. Werner and J. Smolenski, 'Don't edit the human germ line', *Nature* 519 (2015) 410–411, doi: 10.1038/519410a; Berlin-Brandenburg Academy of Sciences and Humanities (BBAW), *Human Genome Surgery — Towards a Responsible Evaluation of a New Technology* (Berlin: BBAW, 2015); Leopoldina, Acatech and Union, *The opportunities and limits of genome editing* (Halle/Saale: Leopoldina, 2015).

35 Chan et al., *supra* note 34.

36 *Ibid.*

37 E. Callaway, 'UK scientists gain licence to edit genes in human embryos', *Nature* 530 (2016) 18, doi: 10.1038/nature.2016.19270.

38 'Human Germline Genome Editing', *UK Parliament Post* 611 (January 2020).

39 H. Devlin, 'Baby with DNA from three people born in Greece', *The Guardian* (2019).

40 *Supra* note 4.

41 Extensively on this topic, Committee on the Ethical and Social Policy Considerations of Novel Techniques for Prevention of Maternal Transmission of Mitochondrial DNA Diseases, *Mitochondrial Replacement Techniques: Ethical, Social, and Policy Considerations* (Washington, DC: National Academies Press, 2016), doi: 10.17226/21871; H. Sharma, D. Singh, A. Mahant, S.K. Sohal, A.K. Kesavan and Samiksha, 'Development of mitochondrial replacement therapy. A review', *Heliyon* 6 (9) (2020) e046043, doi: 10.1016/j.heliyon.2020.e04643; National Academy of Sciences, *supra* note 4.

perceived as first cracks in the existing legal framework in the field.[42] Moreover, in November 2018 the controversial experiment of the Chinese researched He Jiankui led for the first time to the birth of twin girls whose genomes had been edited at the embryonic stage with the aim to confer them resistance to HIV infection.[43]

Eventually, through time scholars started to question the prohibitive approach on HHGE thus far adopted,[44] and to call for the establishment of a responsible and prudent pathway to an effective regulation on the matter, labelled as "more realistic and effective than a prohibitive model."[45] Illustrative examples of this change in trend are the 2017 Report issued by the National Academy of Sciences and the final statement of the Second International Summit held in Hong Kong, where Dr. He presented his experiment. On the one hand, the former, often referred to as "the game changer,"[46] enshrines a fundamental permission on HHGE guided by formal and material criteria, as long as the risks associated with its use could be addressed more reliably.[47] On the other hand, in its final statement, the organizing committee reaffirmed that "the scientific understanding and technical requirements for clinical practice remain too uncertain and the risks too great to permit clinical trials of

42 B.C. van Beers, 'Rewriting the human genome, rewriting human rights law? Human rights, human dignity, and human germline modification in the CRISPR era', *Journal of Law and the Biosciences* 7 (1) (2020) lsaa006, doi: 10.1093/jlb/lsaa006.

43 J. He, *About Lulu and Nana: Twin girls born healthy after gene surgery as single-cell embryos* (2018), available online at https://www.youtube.com/watch?v=thovnOmFltc&t=18s (accessed 28 December 2020).

44 E.S. Lander, 'Brand new genome', *The New England Journal of Medicine* 373 (1) (2015) 5–8, doi: 10.1056/NEJMp1506446.

45 R. Alta Charo, 'Rogues and regulation of germline editing', *The New England Journal of Medicine* 380 (2019) 976–980, doi: 10.1056/NEJMms1817528. Along the same line of reasoning, P. Sykora and A. Caplan, 'The Council of Europe should not reaffirm the ban on germline genome editing in human', *EMBO Reports* 18 (2017) 1871–1872, doi: 10.15252/embr.201745246; G. De Wert, B. Heindryckx, G. Pennings, A. Clarke, U. Eichenlaub-Ritter, C.G. van El, F. Forzano, M. Goddijn, H.C. Howard, D. Radojkovic, E. Rial-Sebbag, W. Dondorp, B.C. Tarlatzis and M.C. Cornel, 'Responsible innovation in human germline gene editing: background document to the recommendations of ESHG and ESHRE', *European Journal of Human Genetics* 26 (2018) 450–470; Nuffield Council on Bioethics, *supra* note 6.

46 P. Dabrock, 'Who? What? How? Why? If You Don't Ask, You'll Never Know … On Criticism of the New Uproar about Germline Editing — Discourse Analytical and Socioethical Metaperspectives', in: M. Braun, H. Schickl, P. Dabrock (eds.), *Between Moral Hazard and Legal Uncertainty — Ethical, Legal and Societal Challenges of Human Genome Editing* (Wiesbaden: Springer Nature, 2018), pp. 163–186.

47 National Academies of Sciences, Engineering, and Medicine, *supra* note 6.

germline editing at this time."[48] However, at the same time, it was stated that scientific progresses in the field suggested that "it is time to define a rigorous, responsible translational pathway," because "germline genome editing could become acceptable in the future" if the risks associated with these techniques are addressed and certain criteria are met, which include the existence of "a compelling medical need."[49]

Even though there are international scholars and institutions still in favour of a general ban on HHGE, whatever the purpose,[50] the request for an effective regulation on the matter may be said to have started to emerge.

3 The Therapeutic Purpose Threshold

Traditionally, the debate on the ethical and legal legitimacy of HHGE pivoted around the distinction between its use for therapeutic purposes and that for enhancement.[51] However, in recent years, this approach has been challenged, especially by those who believe that such distinction should be abandoned altogether[52] or replaced by the principle of the *best interest of the (future) child*.[53]

I believe that the therapy/enhancement distinction is still a relevant one in the debate on the permissibility of HHGE.[54] Indeed, as demonstrated in

48 National Academies of Sciences, Engineering, and Medicine, '*Second International Summit on Human Genome Editing: Continuing the Global Discussion: Proceedings of a Workshop — in Brief*' (Washington, DC: The National Academies Press, 2019), doi: 10.17226/25343.

49 *Ibid.*

50 Berlin-Brandenburg Academy of Sciences and Humanities (BBAW), *Fourth Gene Technology Report — Review of a High-Tech Sector* (Berlin: BBAW, 2019); E. Lander, F. Baylis, F. Zhang, E. Charpentier, P. Berg, C. Bourgain, B. Friedrich, J.K. Joung, J. Li, D. Liu, L. Naldini, J.-B. Nie, R. Qiu, B. Schoene-Seifert, F. Shao, S. Terry, W. Wei and E.-L. Winnacker, 'Adopt a moratorium on heritable genome editing' *Nature* 567 (2019) 165–168, doi: 10.1038/d41586-019-00726-5.

51 Among many others, E. Juengst, 'Can enhancement be distinguished from prevention in genetic medicine?' *Journal of Medicine and Philosophy* 22 (1997) 125–142, doi: 10.1093/jmp/22.2.125; W. Anderson, 'Human gene therapy: scientific and ethical considerations', *Journal of Medicine and Philosophy*, 10 (1985) doi: 10.1093/jmp/10.3.275.

52 A.M. Gouw, 'Challenging the Therapy/Enhancement Distinction in CRISPR Gene Editing', in: *The Palgrave Handbook of Philosophy and Public Policy* (Basinstoke: Palgrave, 2018), pp. 493–508, doi.org/10.1007/978-3-319-93907-0_38; B. Cwik, 'Moving Beyond "Therapy" and "Enhancement" in the Ethics of Gene Editing', *Cambridge Quarterly of Healthcare Ethics* 28 (4) (2019) 695–707, doi: 10.1017/S0963180119000641.

53 Nuffield Council on Bioethics, *supra* note 6.

54 Of a different opinion, see, among others, Cwik, *supra* note 52; R. Bjerregaard Mikkelsen, H. Reventlow S Frederiksen, M. Gjerris, B. Holst, P. Hyttel, Y. Luo, K. Freude and P. Sandøe, 'Genetic Protection Modifications: Moving Beyond the Binary Distinction Between

Section 2, scholars and international institutions calling for a regulation on HHGE frequently refer to the *therapeutic purpose* as the theoretical threshold for assessing the permissibility of HHGE and one of the guidance principles for a regulatory pathway on the matter.[55] Such purpose is then often translated into the prevention or cure of *serious genetic diseases*. For instance, the 2017 report of the National Academy of Sciences expressly suggested in Recommendation 5.1 to include "the prevention of serious diseases" among the criteria to guide the permissibility of HHGE, and the National Academy of Sciences in 2020 proposed that at least at the beginning "1) the use of HHGE [should be] limited to serious monogenic diseases," defined as one that causes severe morbidity or premature death.[56] The distinction between therapy and enhancement is also mentioned as a relevant one in those previous or recent opinions calling for a moratorium on HHGE.[57] Furthermore, such dichotomy is also embedded in regulations and public opinions on biomedical technologies which raise concerns similar to those related to HHGE (e.g., PGD, as explained further in Section 4). Finally, consensus among scholars is almost unanimous in recognising that if HHGE technologies are to be allowed in the future, it will be for therapeutic purposes, and specifically for the "*treatment of serious genetic disease*," at least at first.[58]

Therapy and Enhancement for Human Genome Editing', *CRISPR Journal* 2 (6) (2019) 362–369, doi: 10.1089/crispr.2019.0024.

55 Along the same line, but in general for biomedical interventions, A. Giubilini, 'Normality, Therapy, and Enhancement: What Should Bioconservatives Say about the Medicalization of Love?', *Cambridge Quarterly of Healthcare Ethics* 24(3) (2015) 347–354. doi: 10.1017/S0963180114000656. However, it is worth mentioning that the Nuffield Council of Bioethics rejected the therapy/enhancement distinction and stated that the guiding principle in deciding on the permissibility of HHGE should be the best interest of the (future) child. It goes without saying that this line of reasoning led the Council to declare that at least in principle HHGE may also be used for enhancement. See Nuffield Council on Bioethics, *supra* note 6.

56 National Academy of Sciences *supra* note 4. The purpose of the Report was to determine criteria for developing sufficient safety and efficacy of genome editing methodology for responsible clinical use, and not to establish whether HHGE techniques should in principle be permitted.

57 BBAW, Leopoldina, Acatech and Union *supra* note 34. For some scholars, we have a moral obligation to use HGGE for disease prevention. On this further topic, Gyngell et al, *supra* note 6.

58 T. Ishii, 'Germ Line Genome Editing in Clinics: The Approaches, Objectives and Global Society', *Briefings in Functional Genomics* 16 (2017) 46–56; C. Long, J.R. McAnally, J.M. Shelton, A.A. Mireault, R. Bassel-Duby and E.N. Olson, 'Prevention of Muscular Dystrophy in Mice by CRISPR/Cas9-Mediated Editing of Germline DNA', *Science* 345 (2014) 1184–1188; National Academies of Sciences, Engineering, and Medicine, *supra* note 6, p. 159.

For all these reasons and letting aside further considerations on the theoretical suitability of the distinction between *therapy* and *enhancement* for the purposes of identifying permissible uses of HHGE, I believe that it is worth trying to define the concept of *therapy*, and those strictly related of *disease* and *health*.

3.1 *The Definitions of Therapy, Health, and Disease*

Definitions of "enhancement" may be sorted into 4 broad categories: (a) enhancement defined as the use of a technique originally developed for therapeutic purposes, but that goes beyond it ("beyond therapy views"); (b) quantitative approach, when the technique is used to increase or add certain capabilities; (c) qualitative approach, i.e., making human traits somehow better; and (d) enhancement defined as an "umbrella term" for a number of particular potential changes.[59] Indeed, enhancement has been defined as "interventions different from treating human disease,"[60] "interventions that extend targeted traits or capabilities beyond the normal range,"[61] or "intervention with the primary aim of overcoming those biological limitations that afflict the average person,"[62] and as an intervention used for gaining an "increase of overall well-being rather than an augmentation of single capacities or functions."[63] Finally, Parens defines enhancement as "interventions that improve bodily condition or function beyond what is needed to restore or sustain health,"[64] thus focusing on both the technique itself and the aim of its use.[65]

Similarly, even though definitions of "therapy" vary greatly, they somehow always pivot around the definition of the related concepts of "disease," "normality/normal functioning" and "health."[66] Indeed, examples of such definitions are the following: "the use of medicine to restore the normal functions

59 R. Chadwick, 'Therapy, Enhancement and Improvement', in: B. Gordijn, R. Chadwick (eds.) *Medical Enhancement and Posthumanity* (Berlin: Springer, 2009), pp. 25–37.

60 *Ibid.*

61 Bjerregaard Mikkelsen et al., *supra* note 54.

62 D. Greenbaum and L.Y. Cabrera (eds.), *ELSI in Human Enhancement: What Distinguishes it from Therapy?* (Lausanne: Frontiers Media, 2020), p. 1, doi: 10.3389/978-2-88966-221-0.

63 J. Savulescu, 'Justice, fairness, and enhancement', *Annals of the New York Academy of Sciences* 1093 (2006) 321–338, doi: 10.1196/annals.1382.021; B.D. Earp, A. Sandberg, G. Kahane and J. Savulescu, 'When is diminishment a form of enhancement? Rethinking the enhancement debate in biomedical ethics', *Frontiers in Systems Neuroscience* 8 (12) (2014) 1–8, doi: https://doi.org/10.3389/fnsys.2014.00012.

64 National Academies of Sciences, Engineering, and Medicine, *supra* note 6, p. 159.

65 *Ibid.*

66 Giubilini, *supra* note 55.

of our organism"[67] or, specifically for genetic therapy, "manipulation of the genome to treat individuals or their progeny with known diseases, disabilities or impairments to restore them to a normal state of health."[68]

Consequently, to properly assess the contours of therapy, it appears that those of "health" and "disease" shall be defined.

3.1.1 Normativist and Naturalist Approach to the Definitions of Health and Disease

In general terms, three approaches might be adopted when it comes to defining what health and disease mean.[69] At the two ends of the spectrum, (1) the "naturalist" approach aims at identifying a purely descriptive and value-free definition of health and disease, based exclusively on scientific theories, while (2) the "normativist" approach starts from the assumption that health and disease are concepts inherently value-laden.[70] Somehow in between, (3) the hybrid approach tries to reach definitions of these concepts that contain both normativist and naturalist elements.[71]

Indeed, on the one hand, normativists believe that health and disease are concepts inherently value-laden, because based on the notion of adaptation and environment, and thus an attempt to objectively define them will be vain.[72] Indeed, for them the "disease" concept is based on social, moral, and cultural norms,[73] and thus absence of diseases is the condition of whoever falls within the boundaries set by such norms.[74] By way of example, Downie states that health always requires reference to a certain concept of good life,[75] and as for Nordenfelt, "health" is "the ability, given standard circumstances, to reach

67 *Ibid.*

68 Gouw, *supra* note 52.

69 M. Ereshefsky, 'Defining "Health" and "Disease"', *Studies in History and Philosophy of Science Part C: Studies in History and Philosophy of Biological and Biomedical Sciences* 40 (3) (2009) 221–227, doi: 10.1016/j.shpsc.2009.06.005.

70 R.P. Hamilton, 'The concept of health: beyond normativism and naturalism', *Journal of Evaluation in Clinical Practice* 16 (2) (2010) 323–329, doi: 10.1111/j.1365-2753.2010.01393.x.

71 *Ibid.*

72 J. Kovács, 'The concept of health and disease', *Medical Health Care Philosophy* 1 (1998) 31–39, doi: 10.1023/A:1009981721055.

73 D.B. Resnik, 'The moral significance of the therapy-enhancement distinction in human genetics', *Cambridge Quarterly of Health Ethics* 9 (3) (2000) 365–377, doi: 10.1017/s0963180100903086.

74 *Ibid.*

75 K.M. Boyd, 'Disease, illness, sickness, health, healing, and wholeness: exploring some elusive concepts', *Medical Humanities* 26 (1) (2000) 9–17, doi: 10.1136/mh.26.1.9.

all his or her vital goals,"[76] with "vital goals" being defined as "the set of goals which are necessary and jointly sufficient for a person's minimal happiness."[77] Along a similar line, the World Health Organisation defines "health" as "a state of complete physical, mental and social wellbeing and not merely the absence of disease or infirmity."

On the other hand, 'naturalist' approaches aim at defining concepts in a purely descriptive manner, thus trying to avoid any kind of evaluative judgements.[78] The most prominent influential version of a naturalistic conception of health is Boorse's biostatistical theory of health (BST),[79] with which he aims at defining "health" and "disease" as value-free concepts with an empirical, factual basis in human biology.[80] In doing so, he rests on an account of normal physiology, which he considers the basic medical science.

BST defines "disease" as the departure from "species-typical normal functioning," i.e., the statistically typical contribution of some parts or processes in individuals of a given reference class to survival and reproduction.[81] Therefore, the definition of "normality" depends on the statistical distribution of a given characteristics in human beings. Boorse presents his BST according to the following definition schema:[82]

---

76 L. Nordenfelt, 'The Concepts of Health and Illness Revisited', *Medicine, Healthcare and Philosophy* 10 (2007) 5–10.

77 L. Nordenfelt, *On the Nature of Health. An Action Theoretic Approach* (Dordrecht: Kluwer Academic Publishing, 1995). Various critiques were made through time by scholars. Indeed, it has been pointed out that a broad definition of this kind '*leaves most of us unhealthy most of the time*', as pointed out by R. Smith, 'The end of disease and the beginning of health', *The BMJ Opinion* (8 July 2008), available online at https://blogs.bmj.com/bmj/2008/07/08/richard-smith-the-end-of-disease-and-the-beginning-of-health/.

78 R. Powell and E. Scarffe, 'Rethinking "Disease": a fresh diagnosis and a new philosophical treatment', *Journal of Medical Ethics* 45 (2019) 579–588.

79 J.D. Guerrero, 'On a naturalist theory of health: a critique', *Studies in History and Philosophy of Science Part C41* (3) (2010) 272–278, doi: 10.1016/j.shpsc.2009.12.008; T. Schramme, 'What a Naturalist Theory of Illness Should Be', in: E. Giroux (ed.), *Naturalism in the Philosophy of Health* (Berlin: Springer, 2016), pp. 63–77, doi: 10.1007/978-3-319-29091-1; Powell and Scarffe, *supra* note 78.

80 R.M. Sade, 'A Theory of Health and Disease: The Objectivist-Subjectivist Dichotomy', *The Journal of Medicine and Philosophy* 20 (1995) 513–525.

81 Powell and Scarffe, *supra* note 78. Indeed, they firmly state that the only biological mechanisms relevant to properly defined health and disease are those that contribute to individual survival and reproduction. Such assumption, far from being normative or value-laden, derives from the evidence that '*human physiologists have as yet found no functions clearly serving species survival rather than individual survival and reproduction*'. C. Boorse, 'A rebuttal on health', in: J.M. Humber and R.F. Almeder (eds.), *What is disease?* (Totowa, NJ: Humana Press, 1997), pp. 3–134. Of a different opinion, Ereshefsky, *supra* note 69.

82 Boorse, *supra* note 81.

(a) The reference class is a natural class of organisms of uniform functional design, specifically, an age group of a sex of a species.
(b) A normal function of a part or process within members of the reference class is a statistically typical contribution by it to their individual survival and reproduction.
(c) A disease is a type of internal state which is either an impairment of normal functional ability, i.e., a reduction of one or more functional abilities below typical efficiency, or a limitation on functional ability caused by environmental agents.
(d) Health is the absence of disease.

Therefore, in simplified terms, an individual is

- diseased when one of the relevant functions is performed below the statistical norm of the same species reference class on species-typical occasions;[83]
- healthy in the absence of diseases as above defined and thus if "all the functions that contribute to the species member's survival and reproduction today are capable of performing in a way that is species-typical (i.e., the statistical norm of the relevant functions of the same species, sex and age at time t) on species typical occasions."[84]

Consequently, "therapeutic" is any intervention whose aim is to restore an individual's function capability to the species-typical normal range, defined in statistical, naturalistic,[85] and objective terms.[86]

Therefore, it seems that in his BST Boorse resorts to physiology and statistics (and statistical normalcy) to avoid value-laden judgements on the concept of "health" and "disease."

However, through time, this approach has been the target of many criticisms.

First of all, it has been asserted that, because of the reliance of Boorse's BST on statistical normalcy, changes in the status of an individual as healthy or diseased depend not only on physiological changes in the individuals themselves, i.e., on the fact that now a relevant function fails to perform in a way that is species-typical differently from before, but also on mere "Cambridge changes."[87] Changes of this kind occur in the absence of "real" *physiological* changes in the individual, but whenever there is a *statistical* change in the

83 Guerrero, *supra* note 79.

84 *Ibid.*

85 M. Lemoine and É. Giroux, 'Is Boorse's Biostatistical Theory of Health Naturalistic?', in: E. Giroux (ed.), *Naturalism in the Philosophy of Health* (Berlin: Springer, 2016), pp. 19–38.

86 For a more in-depth analysis of this theory, see *supra* notes 72, 73, and 80.

87 Guerrero, *supra* note 79.

norm of a relevant function for a reference class.[88] This tendency to be prone to Cambridge changes undermines the objectivity of Boorse's approach.

Secondly, scholars highlighted the difficulties in defining which human traits shall be deemed to be "normal." Indeed, human traits and their development are the result of interactions between genotypes and various complex non-genetic environmental factors.[89] Even though we can identify different statistical patterns of traits development, we cannot objectively define which of these is normal for a given species.[90] Therefore, it has been argued that Boorse's theory rests on some idealized standard which has been developed recurring to moral values and against which dysfunctions are measured. Indeed, also the choice of the appropriate degree of departure from normal functionality (if ever defined) may, in fact, be normatively determined.[91] For this reason too, Boorse's naturalistic approach has been criticized as being in fact value-laden and thus failing to achieve a properly objective notion of disease.[92]

Finally, with the intention of building a middle ground approach for defining "disease," which includes both bio-functional and value elements of the disease concept, Wakefield proposed the category of "harmful dysfunction." In this proposal, harmfulness shall be interpreted according to social values, while the existence of disfunctions shall be evaluated in biological terms as the failure to perform one's evolutionary function.[93]

3.2 *On the Definitory Approach to be Adopted for Assessing the Permissibility of* HHGE

When it comes to define *health* and *disease* for the purpose of assessing the lawfulness of HHGE, naturalism seems to be the preferable option, at least theoretically. Indeed, "there seems good reason, (…) to seek an objective framework, so that judgments of health and disease are removed from the subjective domain where contentious disputes leading to personal or social abuses are more likely."[94] However, as extensively discussed above, only value-laden approaches for defining concepts such as therapy, health, and disease appears

88 *Ibid.*
89 R. Amundson, 'Against normal function', *Studies in History and Philosophy of Science Part C* 31 (2000) 33–53.
90 Kovács, *supra* note 72.
91 Powell, *supra* note 78.
92 *Ibid.*
93 Powell and Scarffe, *supra* note 78; J.C. Wakefield, 'Disorder as harmful dysfunction: a conceptual critique of DSM-III-R's definition of mental disorder', *Psychology Reviews* 99 (1992) 232–247.
94 Sade, *supra* note 80.

to be possible. Indeed, any attempt to reach naturalistic definitions of such concepts seems to fail its original purpose of being entirely value-free.

Therefore, a normative approach seems to be the only feasible option, which however might be problematic for at least two different reasons.

First of all, as we have seen normativism prioritizes an approach which takes into account also the person's perception of his/her health condition. However, in the context of HHGE "disease" and "health" are concepts referred to a future person, and therefore it is impossible to include such parameter in the decision of whether to permit specific interventions. Thus, such evaluation would be performed by third parties on behalf of the person to be born. It would then become possible for prospective parents to choose to alter some traits for no scientific medical reason, if driven by the belief that this genetic modification would enable their child to live an appropriate life. Decisions of this kind may be in contrast with the right to an open future of the future person,[95] and his/her human dignity.[96]

Moreover, in the context of HHGE normativism might lead to discriminatory decisions by public authorities and be considered as a step towards state-driven eugenics. Indeed, "if definitions of health and disease are based on judgments of what is desirable and undesirable, on approval or disapproval, without reference to objective standards, there is considerable potential for mistreatment of individuals or groups."[97] The lack of clear, predetermined criteria based on empirical evidence might lead to a discretionary sorting between desirable and undesirable traits by public authorities, as well as arbitrary decision on the social, moral, and cultural norms to be taken as parameters to evaluate whether to correct a specific genetic alteration might be said to prevent the occurrence of a disease, thus being therapeutic.

However, it might be said that the impact of the issues arising from the adoption of a value-laden definition of health and disease might be mitigated by the introduction of the threshold of the *seriousness of the disease* when assessing the legitimacy of HHGE interventions. By doing so, HHGE would be lawfully used to correct not any genetic alteration responsible for the outbreak of a disease (value-laden defined), but only those that would cause a *serious disease*. However, even though the seriousness of the disease is often cited by scholars or institutions in international documents or statements as a threshold for assessing the permissibility of HHGE, and sometimes included in regulations

95 J. Feinberg, 'The child's right to an open future', in: J. Feinberg (ed.), *Freedom and Fulfilment* (Princeton, NJ: Princeton University Press, 1992), pp. 221n235.

96 Resnik, *supra* note 73.

97 Sade, *supra* note 80.

on other IVF technologies, I will now argue that it could not serve the goal of limiting the discretion embedded in a value-laden definition of the concepts of health and disease.

3.3 *The Threshold of the Seriousness of the Disease*

The *seriousness of the disease* is a cornerstone notion in many public policies.[98] As outlined above, it has been used on different occasions also in the debate on the permissibility of HHGE in the NASEM[99] Report and by the German Ethics Councils,[100] to cite a few, and it is often referred to as a criterion to sort between legitimate and unlawful uses of many biomedical interventions, in the sense that permissible uses of a given technology are only those aiming at treating (genetic) diseases that meet a certain level of seriousness. Indeed, as a matter of example, this "serious factor" is embedded in regulations on PGD and therapeutic abortion, biomedical interventions which raise moral and legal concerns like those surrounding HHGE.

The reason for its introduction may be linked to the need of somehow protecting the *in-vitro* embryos. Indeed, in this regard, while not answering the question of whether an embryo may be qualified as "person" for the meaning of Article 2 of the ECHR,[101] the European Court of Human Rights stated in the case *Vo.* v. *France* that embryos "are beginning to receive some protection in the light of scientific progress and the potential consequences of research into genetic engineering, medically assisted procreation or embryo experimentation."[102] Being worth of protection, some regulations allow the use of certain IVF techniques that directly affect the embryo only in relation to diseases that meet a certain level of seriousness.

However, I believe that the "serious factor" should not be used in the context of HHGE as a mean for limiting the level of discretion included in a value-laden definition of health and disease, because of two reasons: (1) a value-free and empirical definition of this concept cannot be reached, and (2) the creation of a list of diseases that meet such threshold may in itself lead to further discrimination and stigmatization.

98 D.C. Wertz and B.M. Knoppers, 'Serious genetic disorders: can or should they be defined?' *American Journal of Medical Genetics* 108(1) (2002) 29–35, doi: 10.1002/ajmg.10212.

99 National Academies of Sciences, Engineering, and Medicine, *supra* note 6.

100 German Ethics Council, *supra* note 7.

101 ECtHR 8 July 2004, no. 53924/00 (Vo v. France), para. 85.

102 *Ibid.*, para. 82.

Indeed, on the one hand regulations and public opinions never attempt to properly define what *seriousness* means.[103] It has been thus suggested that lawmakers might have referred to a hypothetical "common public understanding of what constitutes a serious disorder," which has been proved to be absent.[104] Scholars on the matter are almost unanimous in asserting that a value-free or empirical definition of *seriousness* is impossible to be reached. Indeed, the threshold of *seriousness of the disease* is often criticised for being an ontologically vague, subjective, and arbitrary concept,[105] because of the lack of consensus on its core elements, the heterogenous perception of diseases,[106] and its reliance on socio-economic factors.[107] Moreover, from a critical disability rights perspective, Asch, Parens, and Saxton claimed that such concept is socially construed and reflects existing biases and misconceptions in society.[108]

On the other hand, a list of diseases that meet the threshold of the *seriousness of the disease* may be drawn up to avoid the need to provide for an abstract definition of the concept, as for example suggested by Recommendation 934 of the Council of Europe.[109] A similar approach has been adopted in the UK, where the HFE Authority is responsible for drawing up and updating a list of serious genetic diseases for which undergoing PGD is considered lawful.[110]

103 However, see Isasi, Kleiderman, and Knoppers, *supra* note 14, where it is stated that "The U.S. Food and Drug Administration defines 'serious' as 'a disease or condition associated with morbidity that has substantial impact on day-to-day-functioning. Short-lived and self-limiting morbidity will usually not be sufficient, but the morbidity need not be irreversible, provided it is persistent or recurrent. Whether a disease or condition is serious is a matter of clinical judgement, based on its impact on such factors as survival, day-to-day functioning, or the likelihood that the disease, if left untreated, will progress from a less severe condition to a more serious one.'"

104 Wertz and Knoppers, *supra* note 98.

105 Isasi, Kleiderman, and Knoppers, *supra* note 14.

106 *Ibid*, and F.K. Boardman and C.C. Clark, 'What is a "serious" genetic condition? The perceptions of people living with genetic conditions', *European Journal of Human Genetics* (2021) 160–169, doi: 10.1038/s41431-021-00962-2.

107 Wertz and Knoppers, *supra* note 98.

108 M. Saxton, 'Disability rights and selective abortion', in: L.J. Davis (ed.), *The Disability Studies Reader* (Hove: Psychology Press, 2006), pp. 105–116; E. Parens and A. Asch, 'The Disability Rights Critique of Prenatal Genetic Testing Reflections and Recommendations', *The Hastings Center Report* 29 (5) (1999) S21–S22, doi: 10.2307/3527746.

109 Parliamentary Assembly of the Council of Europe, *supra* note 23.

110 V. English and P. Braude, 'Regulation of PGD in the UK and Worldwide', in: T. El-Toukhy and P. Braude (eds.), *Preimplantation Genetic Diagnosis in Clinical Practice* (Berlin: Springer, 2014); E. Jackson, 'Statutory Regulation of PGD in the UK: unintended consequences and future challenges', in: S.A.M. McLean and S. Elliston (eds.), *Regulating Pre-implantation Genetic Diagnosis — A Comparative and Theoretical Analysis* (Abingdon: Routledge, 2013), pp. 71–88.

The decision on the granting of the licenses to conduct PGD were originally taken on a case-by-case basis, while nowadays this assessment is being conducted on a condition-by-condition basis: Once a condition has been included in the list of those for the detection of which PGD may be performed, subsequent requests for undergoing PGD for the same disease may rely on this first assessment.[111]

However, in general, Member States that allow PGD usually refuse to draw up a list of this kind because of the fear of possible stigmatization and discrimination.[112] Letting aside questions on the criteria to be defined to assess whether a specific disease qualifies as "serious," the very idea of creating a list of diseases that meet the "serious" threshold is problematic.[113] Indeed, the disability community raised concerns on the possible discriminatory effects that a list of this kind may generate.[114] As Parens and Asch stated "it increases the likelihood that an explicitly devaluing message will be sent about people whose conditions are listed as 'serious enough to avoid'."[115]

4 Alternative Methods to Assess the Permissibility of HHGE — The PGD Model

As extensively discussed above, adopting a value-laden definition of the concepts of *therapy*, *health*, and *disease* may raise issues mainly related to (1) the lack of legal certainty on the criteria used to assess the permissibility of HHGE, (2) possible arbitrary decisions and discriminatory effects. Moreover, these issues cannot be mitigated or solved through the use of the "serious factor."

The aim of this Section is thus to evaluate a different method for assessing when HHGE might be permissible, namely, to adopt the same legal boundaries and thresholds delineated by the regulation on PGD (the so-called "PGD model").[116]

111 *Ibid.*

112 W. Manon, *Le diagnostic Préimplantatoire et le diagnostic prénatal en Belgique et en France: droit comparé et confrontation aux droits fondamentaux* (Louvain: Université Catholique de Louvain, 2019).

113 In this regard, the International Bioethics Committee asserted that professional organisations of genetics and reproductive technologies, as well as advisory groups on bioethics, opposed to the idea of establishing a list of diseases considered serious enough to justify the use of PGD. See, Comité international de bioéthique, *Rapport du CIB sur la mise à jour de sa réflexion sur le génome humain et les droits de l'homme* (Paris: CIB, 2015).

114 J.R. Botkin, 'Fetal Privacy and Confidentiality', *Hastings Centre Report* 25 (5) (1995) 32–39.

115 Parens, *supra* note 108.

116 Kleiderman, *supra* note 14.

Regulations on PGD among national legislations vary greatly, and even among EU Member States.[117] However, in those countries where it is a lawful procedure, its use is mainly restricted to the detection (and thus avoidance) of *serious genetic diseases*.[118] By way of example, in France an authorization to undergo PGD may be granted only if the couple has a high probability of giving birth to a child affected by a particularly serious genetic disease recognized as incurable at the moment of the diagnosis.[119] Moreover, in Germany PGD is allowed only in case of high risk of a serious hereditary genetic disease.[120]

Therefore, applying the PGD model would mean to decide whether to allow HHGE by using exactly and only the same line of reasoning adopted to determine whether a certain genetic condition is serious enough to permit the screening, and subsequent discard, of an *in-vitro* embryo. No other elements would be considered in the evaluation. However, this approach might be subject to the following criticisms.

Firstly, PGD is an invasive procedure for the embryo tested, and it is undergone with the only purpose of operating a negative selection, namely to discard those embryos that are affected by the unwanted genetic alteration.[121] On the contrary, the purpose of HHGE "is clearly therapeutic,"[122] in the sense that it may be used to prevent the birth of a child with a genetic disease of which he/she was a carrier. While it is true that both PGD and HHGE permit to avoid the birth of an unhealthy person, only HHGE may be used to allow the birth of a healthy child.[123] Consequently, on the one hand it seems reasonable to restrict the permissible use of PGD to the avoidance of only *serious genetic diseases*. In this way, the range of possible defects that permits the use PGD are limited to those cases where the seriousness of the condition justifies the decision not to implant an (unhealthy) embryo with the aim of safeguarding

117 Isasi, Kleiderman, and Knoppers, *supra* note 14.

118 *Ibid.*

119 Article L2131–4 Code de la Santé Publique.

120 Section 3a (2) Embryonenschutzgesetz.

121 R. Ranisch, 'Germline genome editing versus preimplantation genetic diagnosis: Is there a case in favour of germline interventions?', *Bioethics* 34 (1) (2020) 60–69, doi: 10.1111/bioe.12635.

122 *Ibid.* Holding the opposite view, T. Rulli, 'Reproductive CRISPR does not cure disease', *Bioethics* 33 (2019) 1072–1082, doi: 10.1111/bioe.12663.

123 This assumption is based on the *subjective* evaluation of the effects of PGD and HHGE. Indeed, it is true that also PGD may be used to select healthy embryos to be implanted in a woman, and thus that also such technology may serve the *objective* purpose of giving birth to a healthy individual. However, the born child (A) is different from the embryo (B) discarded after the diagnosis. On the other hand, HHGE intervenes on the embryo (A) and by correcting its genetic defect enables its birth as a healthy child (A).

parental rights and interests. Among the latter, it is worth mentioning the right to conceive a child unaffected by a specific genetic disease, which is worth of protection under Article 8 of the ECHR, even though not directly enshrined in the Convention.[124] On the other, the same cannot be said for HHGE, which may be used to promote the life and health of a future person by allowing her birth.

Therefore, considering that "the value of HHGE comes mainly from its ability to go much further than what PGD is and will be able to accomplish," "limiting its applicability to serious diseases is depriving the technique of its raison d'être."[125]

However, I believe that a possible solution might be to adopt the PGD model not as the only method to assess the permissibility of HHGE, but as a complementary one. Indeed, I propose to use the PGD model as a "minimum threshold," namely, to allow HHGE at least whenever used to correct a genetic defect for which PGD is possible.

This approach derives from the idea that, as explained above, unlike PGD HHGE may be used to correct a genetic defect responsible for a specific genetic disease and thus to enable the birth of a healthy child who otherwise would never have come into existence. Indeed, if PGD detects a genetic defect, the "unhealthy" embryos are usually discarded and not chosen for implantation. In this regard, some national regulations even explicitly prohibit to choose to implant "unhealthy" embryos over healthy ones if the latter are available after an IVF cycle.[126] Even if it is true that this is not the case for every regulatory framework on PGD, and thus that some countries may permit to implant an "unhealthy" embryo, it seems unreasonable to establish that for certain genetic diseases PGD and the subsequent decision not to implant affected embryos are permissible, while eliminating such genetic defect and consequently implant the modified embryo afterwards are not.[127]

Indeed, it seems reasonable to allow HHGE whenever used for correcting genetic diseases for which it is permissible to undergo PGD and discard the "unhealthy" embryos in case of positive result. In these eventualities, HHGE would not only be a form of prevention of diseases and promotion of health of the person-to-be, but also a mean to the end of giving birth to a healthy child.

---

124 *Costa and Pavan* v. *Italy*, No. 54270/10, 28 August 2012.

125 I. De Miguel Beriain, 'Is the "serious" factor in germline modification really relevant? A response to Kleiderman, Ravitsky and Knoppers', *Journal of Medical Ethics* 46 (2019) 151–152, doi: 10.1136/medethics-2019-105744.

126 HFE Act Section 13 (9).

127 It is worth reminding that the precondition enshrined in the analysis as a whole is the technique being safe and effective enough for being introduced into clinical practice.

5 Conclusion

In this chapter I have advocated that the distinction between therapeutic purpose and enhancement is still worth studying for the purposes of assessing permissible uses of HHGE. However, there is still no agreement on the definition of such concepts.

In particular, the notion of *therapy* rests on two further concepts, those of *health* and *disease*, which shall firstly be defined to determine the contours of the notion of *therapeutic purpose*. Two main approaches might be identified to this end, the value-free/naturalistic and the value-laden ones. While in theory the first is preferrable for the purpose of identifying permissible uses of HHGE, value-free approaches fail in principle to completely avoid the use of value-laden concepts. However, adopting a "normativist" approach may raise concerns related to the lack of legal certainty on the elements to be considered when conducting such assessment and may possibly result in arbitrary decisions with discriminatory effects. Neither the adoption of the threshold of the *seriousness of the disease* may serve the goal of reducing such discretion and eliminating the problems raised by a value-laden approach, given the impossibility to define such concept in value-free terms and the fact that drawing up a list of possible diseases for which HHGE is in principle admissible may contribute to further stigmatization and increase in itself possible discriminatory effects.

Indeed, a different method might be proposed, that of the so called PGD model, i.e., to apply the regulation on PGD to assess the permissibility also of HHGE. However, existing differences between the two techniques may jeopardize this approach, if the PGD model is used as the only criterion for assessing the permissibility of HHGE. Indeed, only HHGE may be used to allow the birth of a healthy child, while PGD may exclusively serve the goal of avoiding the birth of a (possibly) unhealthy one. However, finally, I suggest that this model should not be abandoned altogether. In fact, if the technique is found safe and effective for clinical application, HHGE should be permitted *at least* for correcting those genetic diseases for which PGD is legitimate, thus implementing the PGD model as a minimum threshold for HHGE.

The European Court of Human Rights and the Emergence of Human Germline Genome Editing – 'The Right to Life' and 'the Right to (Artificial) Procreation'

Merel M. Spaander | ORCID: 0000-0002-7137-5462
Department of Law, University of Amsterdam, Nieuwe Achtergracht 166, 1018 WV Amsterdam, The Netherlands
m.m.spaander@uva.nl

Abstract

The field of human germline genome editing (HGGE) offers a promising reproductive potential to prevent inheritance of genetic diseases, yet also opens the door to undesirable eugenics. This stirred the debate about the acceptability of HGGE in light of human rights, particularly human dignity. The European Convention of Human Rights (ECHR) and the European Court of Human Rights (ECtHR) use human dignity as a guiding principle. Therefore, this chapter examined the clinical implementation of HGGE in light of relevant case-law regarding Article 2 and Article 8 ECHR. The analysis illustrates that the ECtHR broadens the scope of artificial reproductive rights under Article 8, however, Contracting States of the Council of Europe can limit these rights and the accessibility to reproductive techniques, such as HGGE. The ECtHR remains elusive about the legal status of unborn life, but protection under Article 2 with the introduction of HGGE should not be ruled out.

Keywords

germline genome editing – human rights – right to life – right to respect for private and family life

1 Introduction

The term 'genome editing' refers to a group of techniques that has the ability to modify the DNA.[1] Human germline genome editing (HGGE) involves modifying the human germline cells, or reproductive cells,[2] and has the potential to prevent inheritance of a genetic disease of which prospective parents are (both) carrier. The field of HGGE has rapidly evolved since the introduction of the CRISPR-Cas9 technique, which is considered easier and more efficient than existing techniques.[3] Once considered safe and effective, clinical implementation of HGGE has the promising potential to fulfil the wish of prospective parents to bring a healthy child in the world that would otherwise be born with a genetic disease. On the contrary, it opens the door to undesirable possibilities of 'human enhancement' and 'selection of persons' as well. This has stirred the debate about the acceptability of HGGE in light of human rights protection in Europe.

The main legal argument of opponents of clinical implementation of HGGE is its incompatibility with (respect to) human dignity.[4] This was first mentioned by the Parliamentary Assembly of the Council of Europe (CoE) that speaks of "the right to inherit a genetic pattern which has not been artificially changed."[5] From this perspective — that the human genome should be protected — interventions on the genome that enact modifications that are passed on to descendants are not acceptable. On the other hand, once considered safe and effective, the question is raised whether it is justifiable to potentially breach the procreative rights of parents by withholding them from the possibility to bring a healthy child into the world. This is often associated with the concept of human dignity as autonomy: the individual as independent, being capable of self-determination, free to make his/her own decisions and consciously

1 M.L. Maeder and C.A. Gersbach, 'Genome-editing technologies for gene and cell therapy', *Molecular Therapy* 24 (2016) 430–446.

2 Germline cells or reproductive cells consist of stem cells, gametes, egg and sperm cells and embryos.

3 M. Jinek, K. Chylinski, I. Fonfara, M. Hauer, J.A. Doudna and E. Charpentier, 'A programmable dual-RNA — guided DNA endonuclease in adaptive bacterial immunity' *Science* (2012) 816–821.

4 J. Harris, 'Germline Modification and the Burden of Human Existence', *Cambridge Quarterly of Healthcare Ethics* 25 (2016) 6–18; J. Halpern, S.E. O'Hara, K.W. Doxzen, L.B. Witkowsky and A.L. Owen, 'Societal and Ethical Impacts of Germline Genome Editing: How Can We Secure Human Rights?', *CRISPR Journal* 2 (2019) 293–298; S. Segers and H. Mertes, 'Does Human Genome Editing Reinforce or Violate Human Dignity?', *Bioethics* 34 (2020) 33–40.

5 Council of Europe, Parliamentary Assembly, *Recommendation 934* (1982) para. 4.

determine his/her own life.[6] Consequently, at the moment, the human rights debate does not provide a clear direction as to the acceptability of HHGE for reproductive purposes.

Although HGGE is still facing preclinical challenges, it is realistic that further development of HGGE will eventually lead to safe and effective reproductive use. Therefore, consistent legal frameworks should be established within Europe in order to adequately regulate the clinical implementation in accordance with human rights. Within Europe, human rights are mainly protected by the European Convention of Human Rights (ECHR). Although the ECHR does not explicitly safeguard human dignity, case-law of the European Court of Human Rights (ECtHR) indicates the use of human dignity as a guiding principle.[7] In the past decades, the ECtHR has played an important role in bridging the gap between medical-scientific developments within the field of assisted procreation and unresolved legal questions that are raised under Article 2 ('right to life') and most often, Article 8 ('right to respect for private and family life') of the ECHR. It is expected that the clinical potential of HGGE will raise important questions under these articles as well.[8] Consequently, the ECtHR will likely become a central player in the legal debate surrounding acceptability of HHGE-techniques for prospective parents. It is therefore important to examine existing case-law on both Article 2 and Article 8 in relation to (artificial) procreative rights and examine how the position of the ECtHR may be of relevance in light of regulating clinical implementation of HGGE.

This article aims to analyse the ECtHR's case-law in order to provide guidance for developing a clear human rights-based legal framework for HHGE in Europe. In order to achieve this objective, the second paragraph will discuss relevant background information regarding HGGE. Subsequently, Section 3 lays down the principle of *human dignity* in relation to the ECHR and its importance in the legal and ethical discussions surrounding HHGE. The fourth and the fifth paragraph will focus on Article 2 and Article 8 of the ECHR and relevant caselaw that has been examined by the ECtHR in the field of assisted

6 R. Bronsword and D. Beyleveld, *Human dignity in bioethics and biolaw* (Oxford: Oxford University Press, 2001).

7 Up to October 2016, the ECtHR has referred to 'human dignity' in 876 cases. A. Buyse, *The role of human dignity in ECHR case-law* (21 October 2016), available online at https://www.echrblog.com/2016/10/the-role-of-human-dignity-in-echr-case.html (accessed 16 January 2022); ECtHR 4 October 2016, 2653/13 (*Yaroslav Belousov v. Russia*) para. 92.

8 Council of Europe/European Court of Human Rights, Research report: bioethics and the case-law of the Court (20 October 2016), available online at https://www.coe.int/t/dg3/healthbioethic/texts_and_documents/Bioethics_and_caselaw_Court_EN.pdf (accessed 16 January 2022).

procreation. Section 6 will analyse the decisions of the ECtHR in light of clinical implementation of HGGE. Lastly, the conclusion will summarize the findings within the relevant caselaw of the ECtHR in relation to HGGE.

2 Background

An important distinction within the field of genome editing, the ability to *treat* or *prevent* genetic disorders. For treatment purposes, genome editing is performed on somatic cells (or other cells) in order to alleviate or treat the symptoms of a disease that existing patients are suffering from. On the contrary, germline therapy, or HGGE, involves modifying the germline cells, which are stem cells, gametes, egg and sperm cells and embryos. The difference is that with HGGE, the applied changes will be passed on to future generations. Thus, in a hypothetical situation, HGGE would be applied to an *in vitro* human embryo to cleave the DNA that is responsible for a genetic disease. The edited embryo would be implanted in the woman's womb and develops into a human being. Once the baby is born, it will not have inherited the genetic disease, nor will it be able pass on the disease to its (prospective) offspring. Somatic genome editing only modifies the somatic cells, which does not have consequences in case of reproduction, and is considered less controversial.[9] This chapter focuses on the ethical controversy around HGGE, which does have reproductive consequences for further generations as well.

2.1 *HGGE for Research Purposes*

The use of HGGE for research purposes is non-reproductive, but rather focuses on the development and improvement of gene-editing technology (basic research), or addressing and solving issues that may arise with clinical implementation of HGGE for reproductive purposes (preclinical research). Basic research enables scientists to gain better understanding of the early

9 K. Saha, E.J. Sontheimer, P.J. Brooks, M.R. Dwinell, C.A. Gersbach, D.R. Liu, S.A. Murray, S.Q. Tsai, R.C. Wilson, D.G. Anderson, A. Asokan, J.F. Banfield, K.S. Bankiewicz, G. Bao, J.W.M. Bulte, N. Bursac, J.M. Campbell, D.F. Carlson, E.L. Chaikof, Z.-Y. Chen, R.H. Cheng, K.J. Clark, D.T. Curiel, J.E. Dahlman, B.E. Deverman, M.E. Dickinson, J.A. Doudna, S.C. Ekker, M.E. Emborg, G. Feng, B.S. Freedman, D.M. Gamm, G. Gao, I.C. Ghiran, P.M. Glazer, S. Gong, J.D. Heaney, J.D. Hennebold, J.T. Hinson, A. Khvorova, S. Kiani, W.R. Lagor, K.S. Lam, K.W. Leong, J.E. Levine, J.A. Lewis, C.M. Lutz, D.H. Ly, S. Maragh, P.B. McCray Jr, T.C. McDevitt, O. Mirochnitchenko, R. Morizane, N. Murthy, R.S. Prather, J.A. Ronald, S. Roy, S. Roy, V. Sabbisetti, W.M. Saltzman, P.J. Santangelo, D.J. Segal, M. Shimoyama, M.C. Skala, A.F. Tarantal, J.C. Tilton, G.A. Truskey, M. Vandsburger, J.K. Watts, K.D. Wells, S.A. Wolfe, Q. Xu, W. Xue, G. Yi, J. Zhou and The SCGE Consortium, 'The NIH Somatic Cell Genome Editing program', *Nature* 592 (2021) 195–204.

developmental stages of the human embryo, for example, to improve infertility treatment.[10] The general aim of preclinical research is to responsibly introduce new assisted reproduction techniques in the clinic.[11] Specifically with regard to HGGE, it aims to clarify the editing efficiency and the safety of clinical implementation. The first preclinical studies showed that that HGGE is not yet deemed safe nor (always) efficient.[12] Mosaicism, on-target and off-target mutations are important challenges. Although strategies have been developed to detect and reduce both mosaicism and off-target effects, and more advanced techniques have reached technical improvements and higher levels of efficiency, it is not guaranteed that all the effects are eliminated.[13] Due to serious health risks for the embryo and the human being it will develop into, it is essential to conduct preclinical research on HGGE before introduction to the fertility industry.

---

10 R.A. Lea and K.K. Niakan, 'Human germline genome editing', *Nature Cell Biology* 21 (2019) 1479–1489.

11 A. van Steirteghem, 'What next for assisted reproductive technology? A plea for an evidence-based approach' *Human Reproduction* 23 (2008) 2615–2616; J. Harper, M.C. Magli, K. Lundin, C.L.R. Barratt and D. Brison, 'When and how should new technology be introduced into the IVF laboratory?', *Human Reproduction* 27 (2012) 303–313; D.R. Brison, S.A. Roberts and S.J. Kimber, 'How should we assess the safety of IVF technologies?', *Reproduction Biomed Online* 27 (2013) 710–721; V. Provoost, K. Tilleman, A. D'Angelo, P. De Sutter, G. de Wert, W. Nelen, G. Pennings, F. Shenfield and W. Dondorp, 'Beyond the dichotomy: a tool for distinguishing between experimental, innovative and established treatment', *Human Reproduction* 29 (2014) 413–417.

12 X. Kang, W. He, Y. Huang, Q. Yu, Y. Chen, X. Gao, X. Sun and Y. Fan, 'Introducing precise genetic modifications into human 3PN embryos by CRISPR/Cas-mediated genome editing', *Journal of Assisted Reproduction and Genetics* 33(5) (2016) 581–588; H. Ma, N. Marti-Gutierrez, S.-W. Park, J. Wu, Y. Lee, K. Suzuki, A. Koski, D. Ji, T. Hayama, R. Ahmed, H. Darby, C. Van Dyken, Y. Li, E. Kang, A.-R. Park, D. Kim, S.-T. Kim, J. Gong, Y. Gu, X. Xu, D. Battaglia, S.A. Krieg, D.M. Lee, D.H. Wu, D.P. Wolf, S.B. Heitner, J.C. Izpisua Belmonte, P. Amato, J.-S. Kim, S. Kaul and S. Mitalipov, 'Correction of a pathogenic gene mutation in human embryos', *Nature* 548 (7668) (2017) 413–419. P. Liang, Y. Xu, X. Zhang, C. Ding, R. Huang, Z. Zhang, J. Lv, X. Xie, Y. Chen, Y. Li, Y. Sun, Y. Bai, S. Zhou, W. Ma, C. Zhou and J. Huang, 'CRISPR/Cas9-mediated gene editing in human triponuclear zygotes', *Protein & Cell* 6 (2015) 363–372.

13 T. Koo, J. Lee and J. Kim, 'Measuring and reducing off-target activities of programmable nucleases including CRISPR-Cas9', *Molecules and Cells* 38 (6) (2015) 475–481; S.Q. Tsai and J.K. Joung, 'Defining and improving the genome-wide specificities of CRISPR — Cas9 nucleases', *Nature Reviews Genetics* 17 (5) (2016) 300–312; H. Ledford, 'CRISPR gene editing in human embryos wreaks chromosomal mayhem, *Nature* 583 (2020) 17–18; G. Alanis-Lobato, J. Zohren, A. McCarthy, N.M.E. Fogarty, N. Kubikova, E. Hardman, M. Greco, D. Wells, J.M.A. Turner and K.K. Niakan, 'Frequent loss-of-heterozygosity in CRISPR-Cas9-edited early human embryos', *Proceedings of the National Academy of Sciences of the United States of America* 118 (22) (2020) e2004832117.

2.2 *HGGE for Reproductive Purposes*

Prospective parents that are carrier of a disease with a high genetic risk for their offspring have various reproductive options to eliminate or reduce the risk of passing on their genetic disease: the couple could opt for adoption, use a gamete donor, or undergo prenatal or preimplantation genetic diagnosis (PGD). Once HGGE is effective and safe, its addition to this range of options has important (medical) advantages. HGGE is a preventive intervention that could correct or erase disease-causing mutations around the stage of fertilization, thereby eliminating the risk of passing the genetic disease to offspring and further descendants.[14] This will have profound effects on the well-being of the future child, given that it is born without the disease it would otherwise have inherited, as well as on parents that are satisfied in their desire for a healthy child that is genetically related to both of them. Currently, due to the safety and efficiency challenges as described in Section 2.1., clinical use of HGGE for reproductive purposes has been prohibited or restricted in most European countries.[15]

2.3 *HGGE for Human Enhancement Purposes*

Although the concept of 'human enhancement' is hard to define, it often refers to alternating the genome to enhance *normal* human traits, such as muscularity or intelligence.[16] Associated terms such as 'designer babies', 'trait selection' and 'eugenics',[17] are the foundation of existing legal bans on HGGE in various legal frameworks.[18] Albeit this concern is not completely unjustified, it is extremely difficult to modify the genome in such an advanced manner. Genetics are complex — as is inheritability — which is often overlooked when it comes to the practical implementation of HGGE.[19] Biological conditions

14 M. Viotti, A.R. Victor, D.K. Griffin, J.S. Groob, A.J. Brake, C.G. Zouves and F.L Barnes, 'Estimating demand for germline genome editing: an in vitro fertilization clinic perspective', *The CRISPR Journal* 2 (2019) 304–315.

15 F. Baylis, M. Darnovsky, K. Hasson and T.M. Krahn, 'Human germline and heritable genome editing: the global policy landscape', *The CRISPR Journal* 3(5) (2020) 365–377.

16 N. Bostrom and J. Savulescu, *Human enhancement ethics: The state of the debate* (Oxford: Oxford University Press, 2009).

17 S.M. Suter, 'A Brave New World of Designer Babies', *Berkeley Techology Law Journal* 22 (2007) 897–915.

18 Explanatory report to the Convention on Human Rights and Biomedicine, *European Treaty Series, nr. 164*; International Bioethics Committee, *Report of the International Bioethics Committee (IBC) on Updating Its Reflection on the Human Genome and Human Rights* (New York, NY: International Bioethics Committee, 2015).

19 A.C.W. Janssens, 'Designing babies through gene editing: science or science fiction?', *Genetics and Medicine* 18 (2016) 1186–1187.

limit the possibilities of 'human enhancement', yet attempts to make simpler modifications to less complex traits should not be ruled out.

3 Human Dignity as a Guiding Principle in European Human Rights

After the second World War, the concept of human dignity begun to play an important role in different fields, including philosophy, politics and law.[20] In law, human dignity is often assumed to be the foundation of human rights.[21] It has been attributed a central role in various international legal human rights frameworks. UNESCO's Universal Declaration of Human Rights states in its first article that "all human beings are born free and equal in dignity and rights."[22] Other legal instruments, such as the EU Charter of Fundamental Rights (EU Charter) and the International Covenant on Economic, Social and Cultural Rights (ICESCR) associate human dignity with similar notions of inviolability, alienability, equality and freedom. A coherent and single conceptualization of human dignity remains elusive — legal doctrine and practice continue to apply various variants of definitions. These definitions roughly amount to two main understandings about human dignity: either that human dignity is about respect for individual human being that is capable of making his/her own autonomous decisions ('empowerment'), or that human dignity is based on respect for and protection of the human being, and is a safeguard against inhuman or degrading treatment and practices ('constraint').[23] Albeit these approaches appear to be contradicting, one understanding does not necessarily exclude the other.[24]

In bioethics, there is a strong tendency to link human dignity to the human genome. The Universal Declaration on the Human Genome and Human Rights (1997) notably refers to this association in its first heading 'Human Dignity and the Human Genome'. Article 1 specifically indicates the human genome as "underlying the fundamental unity of all members of the human family, as well as the recognition of their inherent dignity and diversity. In a symbolic

20 C. McCrudden, 'Human Dignity and Judicial Interpretation of Human Rights', *European Journal of International Law* 664 (19) (2008) 655–724.

21 Preamble of the EU Charter: "the Union is founded on the indivisible, universal values of human dignity, freedom, equality and solidarity."

22 UN General Assembly, 'Universal Declaration of Human Rights', 10 December 1948, 217 A (I).

23 Bronsword and Beyleveld, *supra* note 6.

24 R. Andorno, 'Human dignity and human rights as a common ground for a global bioethics', *Journal of Medicine and Philosophy* 34 (2009) 223–240, p. 232.

sense, it is the heritage of humanity."[25] This has led to different views on the acceptability of technologies that aim to modify the genome. In light of human dignity, the question raises whether we should either refrain from altering the human genome ('constraint') or respect an individual's autonomous decision to do or do not so ('empowerment')? Current human rights frameworks regarding bioethics tend to pursue the 'constraint' dimension of human dignity by restricting the alteration of the human genome, particularly because of concerns related to dehumanisation and objectification. For instance, the Oviedo Convention posits that preventive, diagnostic or therapeutic interventions of the genome are allowed under the condition that "its aim is not to introduce any modification in the genome of any descendants."[26] The rationale behind this in light of human dignity is explained by "the ultimate fear of intentional modification of the human genome so as to produce individuals or entire groups endowed with particular characteristics and required qualities," which seems to refer to 'human enhancement.'[27] Similar concerns about 'long term effects of HGGE' and 'selection of persons' have been expressed in the Universal Declaration of the Human Genome and Human Rights and the EU Charter as an explanation to restrict interventions on the human genome.[28]

In the ECHR, the concept of human dignity is remarkably absent. Nevertheless, the caselaw of the ECtHR often refers to human dignity as a guiding principle — more specifically has it stated that "the very essence of the Convention is respect for human dignity and freedom."[29] Furthermore, Article 3 of the ECHR is most often applied in reference to human dignity — as it prohibits inhuman or degrading treatment that may offend human dignity.[30] Yet, other articles are associated to human dignity as well. Particularly regarding bioethical

25 Article 1 UNESCO 'Universal Declaration on the Human Genome and Human Rights' (11 November 1997), available online at https://en.unesco.org/themes/ethics-science-and-technology/human-genome-and-human-rights (accessed 11 January 2022).

26 Article 13 Convention for the Protection of Human Rights and Dignity of the Human Being with regard to the Application of Biology and Medicine (Oviedo Convention), 4 April 1997, *ETS no. 164*.

27 Explanatory report to the Convention on Human Rights and Biomedicine, *ETS no. 164*, para. 89.

28 Article 25 in conjunction with International Bioethics Committee, 'Report of the International Bioethics Committee (IBC) on Updating Its Reflection on the Human Genome and Human Rights' 2 October 2015, para. 107; Article 3 (2) of the EU Charter: "[…] prohibition of eugenic practices, in particular those aiming at the selection of persons."

29 ECtHR 11 July 2002, 28957/95 (*Christine Goodwin v. United Kingdom*) para. 90 in conjunction with ECtHR 29 April 2002, 2346/02 (*Pretty v. United Kingdom*).

30 Article 3 ECHR: "No one shall be subjected to torture or to inhuman or degrading treatment or punishment."

developments and assisted procreation, the ECtHR often refers to Article 2 and Article 8 in its caselaw.[31] Human dignity is expressed in Article 2 — right to life — as protection of (unborn) human life against dehumanisation and objectification ('constraint'), whereas under Article 8 — right to private and family life — it is referred to as the right self-determination or personal autonomy regarding the body and person ('empowerment').[32] In the context of the expanding assisted procreation possibilities, various cases have been examined by the ECtHR about reproductive rights under Article 8 and the legal status of an embryo under Article 2. These decisions — that are guided by the concept of human dignity — potentially provide legal guidance on how Contracting States of the Council of Europe (thereafter: Contracting States) should shape their legislation in response to the clinical implementation of HGGE.

4 Article 8 ECHR: 'The Right to Respect for Private and Family Life'

This paragraph will further elaborate on Article 8 in the context of assisted procreation. As HGGE can be used for reproductive purposes, it is important to establish whether reproductive rights fall within the scope of Article 8 — and if so — whether and when it is possible to limit these rights under circumstances. Section 4.1 describes the normative framework of Article 8. Next, Section 4.2 discusses the relevant caselaw in the context of assisted procreation within this normative framework.

4.1 *Normative Framework of Article 8 ECHR*

"1. Everyone has the right to respect for his private and family life, his home and his correspondence"

The objective of Article 8 of the ECHR is protection against interferences by national authority with private and family life, home and correspondence. The scope of this article is not limited to the four interests as described in the article — as mentioned — the right to self-determination and personal autonomy are also considered to be protected by Article 8.[33] Although Article 8 holds a negative obligation for a public authority to abstain from intervening with

31 ECtHR 10 April 2007, 6339/05 (*Evans v. United Kingdom*); ECtHR 4 December 2007, 44362/04 (*Dickson* v. *United Kingdom*); ECtHR 3 November 2011, 57813/00 (*S.H. and others* v. *Austria*); ECtHR 28 August 2012, 54270/10 (*Costa & Pavan* v. *Italy*).

32 For instance, regarding sexual orientation, end of life choices and assisted procreation.

33 ECtHR 11 July 2002, 28957/95 (*Christine Goodwin v. the United Kingdom*).

private and family life, home and correspondence,[34] the second paragraph of this article describes an exception.

"2. *There shall be no interference by a public authority with the exercise of this right except such as is in accordance with the law and is necessary in a democratic society* [...]"[35]

According to this exception, infringement of Article 8 is allowed with legitimate consideration of the competing interests of the individual and society, under the conditions that this is (a) in accordance with the law and (b) necessary in a democratic society. The first condition requires that the national legislation is clear, foreseeable and adequately accessible, and pursues one or more of the legitimate aims listed therein.[36] With regard to the second condition, the interference must correspond to a pressing social need and must remain proportionate to the legitimate aim pursued. In case of sensitive moral and ethical issues on which there is no consensus within Contracting States, a wide *margin of appreciation* is afforded. Within this *margin of appreciation*, Contracting States are allowed discretion to interpret the ECHR in light of their national interests regarding the subject.

4.2 *The Right to (Medically Assisted) Procreation*

Although it has been established by the ECtHR that the right to self-determination and personal autonomy fall within the scope of Article 8, this does not explicitly indicate that this is also the case for reproductive rights. This leads to the following question:

4.2.1 Is There a Right to (Medically Assisted) Procreation under Article 8?

In 2007, the ECtHR specifically examines reproductive rights in relation to Article 8 in the case of *Evans v. United Kingdom*.[37] Mrs. Evans wished to use the embryos that had been created with her eggs and the sperm of her ex-partner before she had her ovaries removed. After their break-up, the ex-partner withdrawals his consent to use the sperm. Mrs. Evans complains that this is in violation with her rights as protected by Article 8, as this prevents her from ever having genetically related offspring. The ECtHR recognizes that the decision

34 ECtHR 22 February 2018, 588/13 (*Libert v. France*), paras 40–42.

35 [...] in the interests of national security, public safety or the economic wellbeing of the country, for the prevention of disorder or crime, for the protection of health or morals, or for the protection of the rights and freedoms of others.

36 ECtHR 25 March 1983, 5947/72; 6205/73; 7052/75; 7061/75; 7107/75; 7113/75; 7136/75 (*Silver and others v. the United Kingdom*), para. 87.

37 ECtHR 10 April 2007, 6339/05 (*Evans v. United Kingdom*).

to have and to not have a child in the genetic sense falls within the scope of the right to respect for private life as protected by Article 8.[38] This was reaffirmed in the case of *Dickson v. United Kingdom*, which involved a prisoner and his wife who were refused access to artificial insemination facilities by the U.K. Secretary of State. The prisoner was still serving his prison sentence, which withheld them from inducing a natural pregnancy. Given the age of his wife, the chance at conception would be considerably low by the time the prisoner would be released. The couple complained that this refusal breached their rights under Article 8. The ECtHR decided that this concerned the right to respect for family and private life under Article 8, which includes the right to respect for the applicants' decision to become a parents in the genetic sense.[39] Given the fact that the case concerned artificial insemination, the access to assisted procreation techniques seems to fall within the scope of Article 8 as well. This approach was confirmed in the case of *S.H. and others v. Austria*, which concerned two infertile couples wished to use ova donation and sperm donation for medically assisted procreation (ivf). The Austrian law prohibits the use of (donated) sperm for ivf and includes a general ban for ova donation. The couples argued a violation of their rights under Article 8. The ECtHR considers that the choice to use medically assisted procreation is an expression of private and family life. Therefore, the right of a couple to make use of medically assisted procreation is protected under Article 8.[40]

The case of *Costa & Pavan v. Italy* specifically concerns the use of medically assisted procreation to become parents of a child unaffected by a genetic disease. Costa and Pavan are both healthy carriers of cystic fibrosis and resort to use assisted reproduction technology (ivf) and preimplantation genetic diagnosis (PGD) with the purpose to select an embryo that does not carry the disease.[41] However, the Italian law forbids the use of PGD and allows ivf treatment exclusively for specific reasons.[42] The Italian regulation does not consider the risk of transferring a genetic disease as one of these reasons. The law does provide the opportunity to terminate the pregnancy on medical grounds, such as a genetic disease.[43] This leaves Costa and Pavan with only one option: inducing natural pregnancy with the possibility for abortion on medical grounds in case the prenatal tests confirm that the child is affected by cystic fibrosis. They complained that this violated their rights under Article 8. The

38 *Ibid.*, para. 60.

39 ECtHR 4 December 2007, 44362/04 (*Dickson* v. *United Kingdom*) para. 62.

40 ECtHR 3 November 2011, 57813/00 (*S.H. and others* v. *Austria*) para. 82.

41 ECtHR 28 August 2012, 54270/10 (*Costa & Pavan* v. *Italy*).

42 Article 4(1) and 5 Law 40/2004 on medically assisted reproduction.

43 Article 6 para. 1 letter b Law 194/1978 on social protection of motherhood and abortion.

ECtHR finds the desire to use medically assisted procreation as to conceive a child that is unaffected by a genetic disease of which the (prospective) parents are healthy carriers, to be protected under Article 8.

However, what if the *initial* decision to become parents in the genetic sense changes due to certain circumstances, and so does the wish to use assisted reproduction techniques in order accomplish this? In the case if *Parrillo v. Italy*, Ms. Parrillo wished to donate the embryos that were initially intended for an ivf treatment, to scientific research. Given that her partner had passed away, Ms. Parrillo no longer had the intention to start a family. The ECtHR finds the choice to donate embryos to scientific research an aspect of the personal life, related to the right to self-determination. From a standpoint of the right to respect for private life, the case of Ms. Parrillo was applicable under Article 8.[44]

These cases indicate that the ECtHR considers (medically assisted) procreation to be protected under Article 8. In fact, the scope appears to broaden in accordance with the advancing scientific developments within the field of assisted procreation. This increasing focus on personal autonomy with regard to assisted procreation accentuates the 'empowering' dimension of human dignity.[45] Even more so, because it appears to expand outside the field of assisted procreation into a broader field of embryo donation (*Parrillo v. Italy*). However, the right to (assisted) procreation is not an absolute right. In these cases, the ECtHR refers to the moral and ethical sensitivity of the subject of assisted procreation and the little consensus between the Contracting States. It has assigned a wide *margin of appreciation* to the Contracting States to shape their reproductive laws and intervene with the right to medically assisted procreation if they consider this necessary.[46] In order to decide whether a Contacting State has not exceeded this wide *margin of appreciation*, the ECtHR balances the interests at stake.

4.2.2 A Positive Obligation or an Interference: 'In Accordance with the Law' and 'Necessary in a Democratic Society'?

In the case of *Evans v. United Kingdom*, the ECtHR examines the conflicting interests of Ms. Evans, who wishes to become a parent in the genetic sense, and her ex-partner, who does not want to become a parent in the genetic sense.[47]

44 ECtHR 27 August 2015, 46470/11 (*Parrillo* v. *Italy*), para. 156.

45 Case of Evans v. U.K., *supra* note 37. In the case of *Evans v. the United Kingdom*, the ECtHR literally refers to 'personal autonomy' under Article 8.

46 Case of S.H. and others v. Austria, *supra* note 40 para. 83; Case of Costa & Pavan v. Italy, *supra* note 41, paras 77–79.

47 These are two conflicting individual rights, rather than conflicting private and public rights.

First, UK's Human Fertilisation and Embryology of 1990 (HFEA) is based on the principles of respect for human dignity and free will: the wishes of the donor are prioritized. The required consent of the donor before usage holds no exceptions, in order to ensure that donated gametes are not used without continuing consent, as well as to promote legal certainty. The ECtHR finds these general interests pursued by the law legitimate as well as consistent with Article 8.[48] With regard to the conflicting interests, the ECtHR decided that the interests of Ms. Evans did not outweigh the interests of her ex-partner. Otherwise stated, the competing interests were fairly balanced and did not violate the rights of Ms. Evans under Article 8 of the ECHR.

The relevance of balancing competing private and public interests became clear in the case of *Dickson v. United Kingdom*. The policy of the Secretary of State stated that requests for artificial insemination by prisoners are only granted in exceptional circumstances, yet, according to the ECtHR, the threshold for 'exceptionality' was set so high that it excluded actual balancing of competing interests and a proportionality test of the restriction.[49] Given the importance of this assessment for the prisoner and his wife — artificial insemination was the only realistic hope on conceiving a child — the ECtHR finds that the national authority has exceeded the afforded *margin of appreciation*, and therefore violated Article 8 of the ECHR.

In the case of *S.H. and others v. Austria*, the ECtHR examines whether the bans on ova donation for assisted reproduction and sperm donation for the purpose of ivf were sufficiently justified to restrict the applicants' procreative rights under Article 8.[50] The Austrian legislation approaches the advances in medically assisted procreation with particular care, given the complexity of split motherhood and the risks for other undesired objectives such as 'selection' of children and exploitation of women in case of ova donation.[51] As to the specific prohibition to donate sperm for *in vitro* fertilisation, but not for *in vivo* fertilisation, it was stated that *in vivo* fertilisation had been clinically implemented for a while and gained societal acceptance over time — it would be hard to monitor a prohibition. To the question whether the latter argument by itself outweighs the procreative interests of the individual, the ECtHR answered that this argument is part of balancing interests in seeking to reconcile social realities with the general legislative framework that has

48 Case of Evans v. U.K., *supra* note 37, para. 89.

49 Case of Dickson v. U.K., *supra* note 39, para. 82.

50 There is a clear legal basis and the legitimate aim of the protection of health or morals and the protection of rights and freedom of others is pursued — hence that this was not in dispute.

51 Case of S.H. and others v. Austria, *supra* note 40, para. 101.

been adopted by the Austrian authorities. The ECtHR understands the careful and cautious approach, yet it criticizes the Austrian authority for not taking sufficient steps to monitor the dynamic developments in science and society regarding gamete donation. Nevertheless, despite the prohibitions, the ECtHR notes that assisted procreation is not completely excluded, given that homologous methods are allowed, as is seeking the desired treatment abroad.[52] Both the ban on ova donation for assisted reproduction as well as the ban on sperm donation for the purpose of ivf are considered compatible with Article 8.

In the case of *Costa & Pavan v. Italy*, the important question is not whether the Italian law is compatible with Article 8 of the ECHR — the prohibition itself is not incompatible with Article 8 — but concerns the proportionality of the prohibition on PGD in conjunction with other reproductive laws. The ECtHR observes a clear inconsistency in Law 40/2004, as PGD in case of a genetic disease (cystic fibrosis) is prohibited, but termination of the pregnancy on medical grounds (cystic fibrosis) is allowed. The ECtHR recognizes the negative impact on the health of the individual who only has a choice to conceive an affected child and terminate the pregnancy after the prenatal tests. This restriction on the individuals' procreative rights as protected under Article 8 is considered disproportionate — and therefore a violation of Article 8 of the ECHR.[53]

4.3 *Concluding Remarks*

As mentioned, the scope of artificial reproductive rights is expanded with the medical-scientific possibilities. Yet the decisions of the ECtHR in the aforementioned cases imply these rights are not absolute. Given the wide *margin of appreciation*, interference by Contracting States is allowed under the conditions of a *coherence* within the reproductive laws (*Costa & Pavan v. Italy*), proportionality as well as legitimate consideration of the interests at stake (*Dickson v. United Kingdom*) and review of the highly dynamic science and society regarding assisted procreation (*S.H. and others v. Austria*). Although the increasing focus on the 'empowering' dimension of human dignity is notable in these decisions of the ECtHR, the *margin of appreciation* allows the Contracting States to decide to what extent their reproductive laws either respect the individual's autonomous decisions or limit reproductive rights in order to prevent that artificial reproduction becomes commodification or objectification of human life. On the other hand, the case of *Costa & Pavan v. Italy* illustrates that the ECtHR does no longer limit herself to the judgement whether the national legislation on assisted procreation itself is in accordance

52 *Ibid.*, para. 114.

53 Case of Costa & Pavan v. Italy, *supra* note 41, para. 70.

with Article 8, but rather examines the concrete content of the Italian legislation regarding its proportionality and coherence in the context of other reproductive laws. Further cases should confirm whether this indicates a shift from a reluctant approach of the ECtHR to more strict scrutiny of the *margin of appreciation* that is afforded to Contracting States regarding bioethical matters that fall within the scope of Article 8.

5 Article 2 ECHR: 'The Right to Life'

The following paragraph focusses on Article 2 of the ECHR, which aims to protect the right to life. The expanding possibilities to artificially procreate raises questions about the protectability of unborn life, or embryo — even more so in case of HGGE given that this introduces modifications to the unborn human being and its possible descendants. Section 5.1 describes the normative framework of Article 2. Subsequently, Section 5.2 explains this framework from the perspective of relevant caselaw of the ECtHR about the protectability of the human embryo.

5.1 *Normative Framework of Article 2 ECHR*

"1. Everyone's right to life shall be protected by law [...]*"*

The right to life is considered as one of the most basic fundamental human rights. Derogation of this right under Article 15 of the ECHR is inadmissible. The only exceptions are described in the second paragraph of Article 2, which requires an absolute necessity (a) in defence of any person from unlawful violence, (b) in order to effect a lawful arrest or to prevent the escape of a person lawfully detained or (c) in action lawfully taken for the purpose of quelling a riot or insurrection. The Article positively obligates the Contracting States to refrain from intentional deprivation of the lives of those who fall within its jurisdiction, as well as to take legal measures to protect those lives.[54] From caselaw of the ECtHR, in can be inferred that the scope of this obligation is rather broadly applied, such as in environmental context,[55] in the context of accidents[56] and in the context of both beginning and end of life.[57]

---

54 R.C.A. White and C. Ovey, *The European Convention of Human Rights* (Oxford: Oxford University Press, 2014), p. 145.

55 ECtHR 30 November 2004, 48939/99 (*Öneryıldız v. Turkey*).

56 ECtHR 15 December 2009, 4314/02 (*Kalender v. Turkey*); ECtHR 3 December 2009, 60255/00 (*Pereira Henriques v. Luxembourg*).

57 ECtHR 29 April 2002 (*Pretty v. the United Kingdom*), ECtHR 5 June 2015, 46043/14 (*Lambert and others v. France*); ECtHR 8 July 2004, 53924/00 (*Vo v. France*).

5.1.1 The Legal Status of a Human Embryo

Article 2 does not provide a definition of 'everyone' whose life is protected under the ECHR, neither does it specify when 'life' begins. Thus, it should first be established what is considered the beginning of 'life' to determine the protectability of a human embryo under Article 2. There are various moral and legal views on when and to what extent legal protection should be granted to the human embryo. Some consider the embryo a human being and argue that it should enjoy complete protection from the point of fertilization. Others state that this protectability is dependent on the developmental stage of the embryo, or that the embryo is not considered a human being at all and should not be afforded any legal protection.[58] As for the ECtHR, it has examined various cases that concerned the protectability of unborn human life under Article 2, particularly in connection with abortion.[59] In these cases, the ECtHR consistently addresses the European divergence regarding the definition of the 'beginning of life', yet it refrains from clarifying whether the embryo enjoys protection under Article 2. Instead, it decides that the definition of the 'beginning of life' as well and the extent to which it is legally protected fall within the *margin of appreciation* enjoyed by the Contracting States. Moreover, it observes that most reproductive laws of the Contracting States[60] do not regard the unborn child as a 'person' directly protected under Article 2 and that even if the existence of a certain 'right to life' of the unborn child would be assumed, that this right is implicitly limited by the mother's rights and interests.[61] However, this does not necessarily rule out the possibility that there are circumstances in which the ECtHR considers unborn life to fall within the scope of protection under Article 2 which will imply a positive obligation on national authorities to take preventive measures to protect this life.[62]

A remarkable case in relation to the right to life of unborn human life — that did not concern abortion — is the case of *Vo v. France*.[63] Mrs. Vo intended to carry her pregnancy to term, but when the foetus was 20 to 21 weeks old,

58 Steering Committee on Bioethics (CDBI), 'The protection of the human embryo in vitro', Strasbourg, 19 June 2003; Human Embryo Research Panel of the National Institutes of Health, 'Report of the Human Embryo Research Panel (Vol. 1)', 27 September 1994, p. 39.

59 ECtHR 13 May 1980, 8416/79 (*X v. the United Kingdom*), ECtHR 19 May 1992, 17004/90 (*H. v. Norway*); ECtHR 8 July 2004, 53924/00 (*Vo v. France*); ECtHR 16 December 2010, 25579/05 (*A, B and C v. Ireland*); ECtHR 20 March 2007, 5410/03 (*Tysiac v. Poland*).

60 For instance, Belgium, Denmark, Finland, France, Greece, Ireland, Italy, Luxembourg, Netherlands, Portugal and Sweden.

61 ECtHR 13 May 1980, 8416/79 (*X v. the United Kingdom*), para. 19; ECtHR 19 May 1992, 17004/90 (*H. v. Norway*) para. 168; ECtHR 5 September 2002, 50490/99 (*Boso v. Italy*).

62 ECtHR 5 September 2002, 50490/99 (*Boso v. Italy*).

63 ECtHR 8 July 2004, 53924/00 (*Vo v. France*).

her pregnancy was involuntarily terminated due to medical negligence by the attending doctor. Mrs. Vo stated that this should be considered as unintentional homicide of her child, however, the unborn child (foetus) is not regarded as a 'person' under the French Criminal Code. Subsequently, Mrs. Vo appeals to the ECtHR with her complaint — raising the question whether harming the unborn child should be considered a criminal offence in light of Article 2.[64] Due to the lack of consensus on the nature and status of the embryo, the ECtHR decides that it is "neither desirable, nor even possible" to specify whether the unborn child should be considered a person as protected under Article 2.[65] The ECtHR did state that embryos are beginning to receive some protection in light of the scientific progress in the field of genetic engineering, medically assisted procreation and embryo experimentation.[66] However, this may only indicate that the human embryo is regarded as belonging to the human race and requires protection in light of human dignity, but not necessarily under Article 2 as a 'person'. As for the question whether harming the unborn child should be considered a criminal offence in light of Article 2, the ECtHR concludes that Mrs. Vo did not seize the alternative legal opportunity to bring an action for damages against authority on account of the doctor's alleged negligence. Had she done so, this would have enabled her to prove the medical negligence and obtain full redress for the damage.[67] The ECtHR sees no necessity in instituting criminal proceedings. Although the case is applicable under Article 2, the complaint of violation is dismissed.

Interestingly, in the case of *Evans v. United Kingdom*, which involved *in vitro* embryos generated for an ivf treatment rather than a foetus of 20 to 21 weeks, the ECtHR comes to a more straightforward conclusion. In reference to the British legislation, which reads that "an embryo does not have independent rights or interests and cannot claim — or have claimed on its behalf — a right to life under Article 2," the ECtHR concludes that the embryo did not fall within the scope of protection under Article 2.[68] This rather extreme position has later been described as the *Evans* anti-life principle in the case of *Parrillo v. Italy*.[69] Given the fact that the *Evans* case concerned *in vitro* embryos, it has been questioned whether the ECtHR considers the embryo *in vitro* to be different from an *in vivo* embryo (foetus) with regard to legal status.

64 *Ibid.*, para. 81.
65 *Ibid.*, para. 85.
66 *Ibid.*, para. 84.
67 *Ibid.*, para. 91.
68 Case of Evans v. U.K., *supra* note 37, para. 54.
69 Case of Parillo v. Italy, *supra* note 44, para. 31.

5.2 *Concluding Remarks*

As to the legal status of the embryo, the ECtHR attempts to refrain from taking a position on questions regarding Article 2. Instead, it leaves the decision on the 'beginning of life' and the scope of protection under Article 2 to the Contracting States. Nevertheless, it is not ruled out that there are certain well-defined circumstances in which the embryo will be granted protection under Article 2. In light of advancing medical-scientific developments, the ECtHR has observed that embryos are beginning to receive more protection under in light of human dignity. In fact, research that has been commissioned by the Nuffield Bioethics Committee has found that under international law, recent decisions indicate a trend of acknowledging that while embryos and foetuses are not generally recognised as holders of human rights, they are becoming increasingly recognised as having human dignity.[70] This increasing recognition indicates the relevance of human dignity as a 'constraint', as it aims to protect the human embryo against medical-scientific developments that have the potential to objectify or commodify the embryo.

6 Articles 2 and 8 ECHR in Light of the Emergence of HGGE

Needless to say there have been no decisions of the ECtHR regarding HGGE, given that it has not been clinically implemented yet. Nevertheless, when further development results in safe and effective reproductive use of HGGE, this requires a consistent legal framework in consideration of human rights — in particular human dignity. The case-law on both Article 2 and Article 8 may provide relevant guidance to shape national legal frameworks regarding HGGE. This paragraph discusses how both articles and related caselaw could be interpreted in light of HGGE. Section 6.1 focuses on the question whether there would be a right to medically assisted procreation with use of HGGE, whereas Section 6.2 examines the right to life of a gene-edited embryo and the potential positive obligation to protect the life of the human being it develops into.

6.1 *The Right to Medically Assisted Procreation with Use of HGGE*

Albeit the scope of artificial reproductive rights appears to expand with the possibilities for assisted reproduction, this does not necessarily imply that HGGE will fall within the scope of Article 8 as well. Moreover, it should be

70 R. Yotova, *The regulation of genome editing and human reproduction under international law, EU law and comparative law* (Nuffield: Nuffield Council of Bioethics, 2017).

taken into account that the rights under Article 8 are not absolute. Within their *margin of appreciation*, the Contracting States can decide to intervene with the right to respect private and family life if this is considered necessary in a democratic society. The first question that should be answered:

6.1.1 Is There a Right to Medically Assisted Procreation with Use of HGGE?

Given the cases that have been discussed under the fourth paragraph that were applicable under Article 8, the applicability of a case that concerns the access to HGGE under this Article would be based on the following:

Does the Case Involve a Choice or Decision to Become Parents in the Genetic Sense by Means of an Assisted Procreation Technique?[71]

The ECtHR has specifically examined various assisted reproduction techniques and decided that IVF, artificial insemination, ova donation, sperm donation and PGD are applicable under Article 8. In these decisions, the ECtHR emphasizes that the decision to become parents in the genetic sense and the choice to use one of these techniques, are expressions of the right to respect for family and private life. Thus, for the use of HGGE to be applicable under Article 8, it is important that it concerns a decision of (prospective) parents to become parents in the genetic sense and the wish to use HGGE to accomplish this.

However, as the case of *Parrillo v. Italy* has illustrated, if an *initial* decision to become parents in the genetic sense by using assisted reproduction, changes to a wish to donate the generated embryos to research, this would be applicable under Article 8 as an aspect of the right to respect for private life as well. This indirectly enables the opportunity that the wish to donate embryos to (preclinical) research on HGGE also falls within the scope of Article 8. Although the case of *Parrillo v. Italy* concerned the donation of embryos to research on pluripotent stem cells, the reasoning that this scientific development opens new possibilities for research and therapeutic applications to treat diseases that are incurable or difficult to cure, is applicable to research on HGGE as well.[72] After all, as has been set out in the first paragraph, HGGE opens new possibilities for research as well as for clinical application to treat genetic diseases.

---

71 Cases of Evans v. U.K., Dickson v. U.K., S.H. and others v. Austria, *supra* notes 37, 39, 40.

72 Case of Parillo v. Italy, *supra* note 44, para. 90.

Does the Case Involve the Desire to Use Medically Assisted Procreation as to Conceive a Child that is Unaffected by a Genetic Disease of Which the (Prospective) Parents Are Carriers?[73]

In the case of *Costa & Pavan v. Italy* the ECtHR has recognized the right of parents to procreate a child who is not affected by the disease of which they are carriers. This indicates that if HGGE would be used for reproductive purposes with the objective to procreate an unaffected child, this would fall under the scope of Article 8. The purpose would be to modify the genome of the *in vitro* embryo in order to eliminate the risk that the child is born with a genetic disease of which the (prospective) parents are carriers. This objective is similar to PGD — which selects rather than modifies — and HGGE can be considered as effective, if not more effective. After all, PGD cannot be used in all cases of (prospective) parents who are carriers of a genetic disease and wish to conceive healthy offspring. For instance, when both parents suffer from the same or two different genetic diseases it is simply not possible to select an embryo that has a high chance of developing into a healthy child. On the other hand, HGGE does not only impact the embryo that is edited and the person that results from it, but also his or her descendants, and so forth. Albeit this is an important difference, given the caselaw currently available, the use of reproductive HGGE would still meet the condition that there should be a desire to use medically assisted procreation as to conceive a child that is unaffected by a genetic disease of which the (prospective) parents are carriers. On the contrary, the use of HGGE for reproductive purposes with the objective of human enhancement would not be protected by Article 8 based on the case of *Costa & Pavan v. Italy*. Ultimately, this does not concern a genetic disease nor parents that desire to conceive a child that is unaffected by this disease.

Thus, based on existing caselaw of the ECtHR, both the use of HGGE for reproductive purposes as well as research purposes could fall within the scope of Article 8, either under 'private and family life' or solely under 'private life'. This indicates that there would be a right to medically assisted procreation by using HGGE under Article 8. However, the wide *margin of appreciation* with regard to sensitive moral and ethical issues on which there is no European consensus allows the Contracting States to intervene in the right to respect for private and family life, under the conditions that this is in accordance with the law and necessary in a democratic society.

---

73 Case of Costa & Pavan v. Italy, *supra* note 41.

6.1.2 A Positive Obligation or an Interference: 'In Accordance with the Law' and 'Necessary in a Democratic Society'?

The European landscape is (already) highly divergent with regard to HGGE, ranging from prohibitive or restrictive to intermediate to permissive.[74] Contracting States that have signed and ratified the Oviedo Convention are bound to implement Article 13, which explicitly prohibits the use of HGGE for reproductive purposes. As mentioned, this approach is based on the 'constraint' dimension of human dignity: "the ultimate fear of intentional modification of the human genome so as to produce individuals or entire groups endowed with particular characteristics and required qualities."[75] Given the explicit reference to HGGE, it would not be disputed whether this measure is provided for by law and can be regarded as pursuing the legitimate aims of protecting morals and the rights and freedoms of others.

However, 'in accordance with the law' under Article 8 may not always be undisputed. For instance, the Contracting States that are also EU Member States are directly bound to the Clinical Trials Regulation and the EU Charter. Article 90 of the Clinical Trials Regulation on research with medicinal products prohibits gene therapy clinical trials that lead to alternations in the participant's germline genetic identity.[76] Similarly, the second paragraph of Article 3 of the EU Charter speaks about respecting "the prohibition of eugenic practices, in particular those aiming at the selection of persons." In order for a measure to be considered in accordance with the law, it should be clear, foreseeable and adequately accessible.[77] Yet, these provisions raise questions: when exactly is the germline genetic identity modified?[78] What exactly is meant by 'eugenic practices' and 'selection of persons'? Does that specifically refer to HGGE?[79] If a Contracting State would implement reproductive laws that prohibit HGGE for reproductive purposes, it is important to take into account these requirements.

---

74 Prohibitive or restrictive (Germany) to intermediate (Italy and Austria) to permissive (Belgium, Sweden and United Kingdom).

75 Explanatory report to the Convention on Human Rights and Biomedicine, *supra* note 27.

76 Article 9 Regulation (EU) 536/2014 of the European Parliament and of the Council of 16 April 2014 on clinical trials on medicinal products for human use, and repealing Directive 2001/20/EC. *Official Journal of the European Union*, 27 May 2014.

77 Case of Silver and others v. U.K., *supra* note 36, para. 87.

78 COGEM and the Dutch Health Council, '*Editing Human DNA: Moral and social implications of germline genetic modification*' (Bilthoven: COGEM, 2017) pp. 37–38; B.C. van Beers, 'Rewriting the human genome, rewriting human rights law? Human rights, human dignity, and human germline modification in the CRISPR era', *Journal of Law and Biosciences* 7(1) (2020) lsaa006.

79 *Ibid.*

The next question would be whether a prohibition is necessary in a democratic society. In the case of *S.H. and others v. Austria*, the reasoning of the public authority to prohibit ovum donation for ivf was based on the inherent risk that medically assisted procreation techniques carried the risk of being employed for other purposes than therapeutic, such as 'selection' of children.[80] The ECtHR acknowledges that shaping legislation regarding rapidly evolving artificial procreation techniques is a complex process, as these techniques might have consequences that become apparent after a longer period. For this reason, the ECtHR finds it understandable that the Contracting States are cautious regarding the field of artificial procreation.[81] This indicates that the ECtHR does not exclude that the risk that HGGE may be used for eugenic practices, such as 'human enhancement', is considered a valid argument on the necessity to restrict the right to artificially procreate using HGGE. After all, similar concerns about long term effects have been expressed.[82] However, as emphasized in the case of *Costa and Pavan v. Italy*, the Contracting States should clarify how these restrictions avert the risk of eugenic selection and affecting the dignity and freedom of conscience of the medical professions.[83] Whether the prohibition is proportionate, depends on other reproductive laws of the Contracting States. In the case of *Costa & Pavan v. Italy*, the ECtHR considers the fact that the use of PGD in case of a genetic disease was prohibited, but the termination of pregnancy on similar medical grounds was an option, a disproportionate restriction on the individuals procreative rights under Article 8. It is not unthinkable that a similar scenario with the use of HGGE will transpire. In order to prevent this, it is important to shape coherent national reproductive laws and keep the dynamic developments in science and law under review.

It becomes clear that the ECtHR increasingly acknowledges personal autonomy and self-determination with regard to assisted procreation, yet the current legal frameworks with regard to HGGE tend to be prohibitive or restrictive. This illustrates tension between the 'empowering' dimension of human dignity with regard to reproductive rights and the 'constraint' dimension in light of the fear for eugenic practices and long term effects of HGGE.

80 Case of S.H. and others v. Austria, *supra* note 40, para. 101.

81 *Ibid.*, para. 103.

82 International Bioethics Committee, *supra* note 28, para. 107.

83 Case of Costa & Pavan v. Italy, *supra* note 41, para. 63.

6.2 *The Right to Life of a Gene-Edited Embryo*

The ECtHR tends to steer clear of the questions whether unborn life should be protected under Article 2. Yet, the determination of the legal status of an embryo and its protectability may become more important with the introduction of HGGE, given that this introduces modifications to the embryo that affect not only the unborn child, but future generations as well. Moreover, in light of the tendency in bioethics to link human dignity to the human genome, the 'constraint' dimension of human dignity that is based on respecting and safeguarding the human being against dehumanisation and objectification becomes more relevant with the clinical implementation of HGGE.

6.2.1 The Legal Status of the Gene-Edited Embryo

In the case of *Vo v. France*, the ECtHR has observed the changing perspective with regard to the protectability of the human embryo. With the advancing medical-scientific developments, embryos and foetuses are being increasingly acknowledged as having human dignity. As has been described in the third paragraph, the concept of human dignity can be interpreted both 'empowering' as well as 'constraining'. With regard to HGGE, current legal frameworks are prohibitive or restrictive, which is in line with the latter dimension of human dignity. It should be noted that these laws are founded by the concerns about HGGE (enhancement purposes), rather than by the medical advantages for the prospective human being in case of safe and effective application (reproductive purposes). Furthermore, the acknowledgement that an embryo should be protected in light of human dignity, does not necessarily afford it protection under Article 2 as well. This will still be dependent on the definition of the 'beginning of life' that is decided by the Contracting State within its *margin of appreciation*.

Although it is not ruled out that the ECtHR will consider the introduction of HGGE as a 'certain circumstance in which the unborn life does fall within the scope of protection under Article 2', the existing caselaw provides no concrete guidance on the conditions for such a circumstance, nor on the context in which such a circumstance might occur. In the case of *Costa & Pavan v. Italy*, it appears that the ECtHR indirectly considers the *in vivo* embryo as 'other' — or bearer of legal status — when it refers to the Italian law that limits accessibility to PGD as pursuing the legitimate aims of protecting morals and the rights and freedoms of 'others'.[84] However, it also stresses that the concept of 'child' cannot be put in the same category as that of 'embryo'.[85] This position regard-

84 *Ibid.*, para. 59.
85 *Ibid.*, para. 62.

ing the legal status of an *in vivo* embryo appears conflicting and, additionally, leaves the question whether the ECtHR distinguishes between *in vivo* and *in vitro* embryos, unanswered.

In light of association between the human genome and human dignity, the 'constraint' dimension of human dignity aims to respect and protect the human being against dehumanization and objectification. Hypothetically, if human enhancement were to be categorized as dehumanizing and objectifying, it could be argued that the unborn life should be protected under Article 2 in this 'certain circumstance' — the use of HGGE for enhancement purposes — on this basis of human dignity.

6.2.2 The Positive Obligation of Article 2 in Light of HGGE

Thus, if the clinical implementation of HGGE is categorized as a 'certain circumstance' in which unborn life is protected by Article 2, this would positively obligate a Contracting State to (i) protect the right to life by law and (ii) refrain from intentional deprivation of life.[86] The first obligates the Contracting States to take appropriate measures in order to protect the lives of those within its jurisdiction, which raises the question whether — in light of the right to life of the unborn child — a Contracting State should or should not refrain from providing the legal opportunity to apply HGGE in order to prevent an inheritable disease. On the one hand, there are potential risks to health and life that result from HGGE. On the other hand, health problems in the form of the genetic disease will manifest nonetheless. Is the Contracting State obligated to take preventive measures for health risks to the prospective child's life as a result of HGGE or will it fail to aspire its obligations by deprivation of access to a treatment that would save or substantially improve life?

Importantly, the ECtHR considers the obligation to take preventive measures under Article 2 as an obligation of means, not of result. If the appropriate measures have been taken by a Contracting State in response to a 'risk of life', and the risk materialises either way, this does not necessarily imply a violation of the right to life under Article 2. The circumstances will be assessed in light of what was known to the authorities at the relevant time.[87] For instance, in the case of *L.C.B. v. United Kingdom*, a patient suffering from leukaemia claims that she became sick because her father had been exposed to nuclear radiation

86 Council of Europe/European Court of Human Rights, *Guide on Article 2 — right to life* (31 December 2021), available online at https://www.echr.coe.int/documents/guide_art_2_eng.pdf (accessed 20 January 2022).

87 ECtHR 15 June 2021, 62903/15 (*Kurt v. Austria*) para. 160; ECtHR 28 October 1998, 23452/94 (*Osman v. the United Kingdom*) para. 116.

before she was born. She complains to the ECtHR that her right to life has been violated because the authorities did not warn her parents about the health risks for their prospective children. The ECtHR found no link between the information available to the authorities at the relevant time concerning the likelihood of the patient's father having been exposed to dangerous levels of radiation and of this having created a risk to the health of the applicant. Therefore, there was no reason to assume that the authorities could, or should have taken measures. The ECtHR decided that Article 2 was not violated.[88] If a similar approach is adopted for complaints under Article 2 regarding the potential risks for life and health for a gene-edited embryo, it is important to consider what information was known to the Contracting State. Indeed, if it can be established that the authorities knew or ought to have known of the existence of certain risks of life of HGGE that should have triggered their obligation to take measures, a complaint under Article 2 would be legitimate. Nevertheless, as shown in the case of *L.C.B. v. the United Kingdom*, successful liability of the Contracting State requires causality between the application of HGGE and the materialised health risk, which will be difficult to establish, given that it is not possible to verify that the risk would not have materialised if the genome had not been modified.

With regard to deprivation of a treatment that would be life-saving, the ECtHR has emphasized in various cases that an issue under Article 2 may arise when an authority denies health care, thereby putting the life of an individual at risk.[89] Whether HGGE is considered 'life-saving' and therefore puts the life of the unborn child at risk in case of deprivation depends on various aspects. First, the life of the prospective child is not necessarily at risk without the treatment — this depends on the genetic disease — although the quality of life may be substantially lower. Second, if the treatment would be considered as life-saving, the ECtHR has formulated cumulative conditions for a 'denial of access to life-saving treatment' under Article 2.[90] The first condition focusses on mere error or medical negligence of the medical health-care providers in the awareness that the person's life is at risk if the treatment is not given. This is not directly applicable for HGGE application. Lastly, the access to HGGE is closely related to reproductive rights under Article 8 and the ability of Contracting States to restrict the accessibility to assisted procreation techniques. Thus,

88 ECtHR 9 June 1998, 23413/94 (*L.C.B. v. the United Kingdom*).

89 ECtHR 4 May 2000, 45305/99 (*Powell v. the United Kingdom*); ECtHR 10 May 2001, 25781/94 (*Cyprus v. Turkey*); ECtHR 13 November 2012, 47039/11 and 358/12 (*Hristozov and others v. Bulgaria*).

90 ECtHR 19 December 2017, 56080/13 (*Lopes de Sousa Fernandes v. Portugal*).

whether a Contracting State fails to aspire its obligations by deprivation of access to HGGE is difficult to establish based on existing case-law.

In short, whether a gene-edited embryo should be provided protection under Article 2 is difficult to deduct from existing caselaw, particularly because the ECtHR explicitly refrains from specifying 'the beginning of life' and the protectability of unborn life under Article 2. The ECtHR did not rule out 'certain circumstances' under which unborn life could be afforded legal protection, yet future caselaw should specify these circumstances. If, with the implementation of HGGE, the unborn life is afforded protection under Article 2, this will give rise to positive obligations for the Contracting States. How these positive obligations should be interpreted in light of the potential risk to health and life due to application or denial of HGGE, depends on various aspects, including the circumstances at the relevant time and the definition of 'risk of life'.

7 Conclusion

Due to the promising reproductive opportunities, the clinical implementation of HGGE is highly anticipated by both science and society. However, it is important to shape a coherent legal framework, based on human rights, particularly human dignity. Although human dignity remains an elusive concept, it runs like a thread through the ECHR and existing case-law of the ECtHR that addresses the advancing medical-scientific advances within assisted procreation. This chapter has provided insights on how the existing case-law on Article 2 and Article 8 could provide guidance in regulating the clinical implementation of HGGE. The analysis indicates that the ECtHR consistently broadens the scope of artificial reproductive rights that fall under Article 8, yet it leaves room for the Contracting States to limit these rights and therefore the accessibility to artificial reproduction techniques such as HGGE. The ECtHR tends to steer clear of the question whether unborn life falls under Article 2, but it has not ruled out 'certain circumstances' in which unborn life will be granted protection. Moreover, if unborn life would fall within the scope of Article 2 with the clinical implementation of HGGE, it remains debatable how Contracting States should interpret their positive obligations under Article 2. There is no clear answer to the question how the clinical implementation of HGGE should be interpreted in light of the ECHR and its existing case-law on Article 2 and Article 8. If anything, it shows that the process to develop regulation is a complex interaction between various human rights aspects that need to be balanced.

The Object-Based and Process-Based Regulation of Genome Editing

Michal Koščík | ORCID: 0000-0002-9243-6391
Department of Public Health, Faculty of Medicine, Masaryk University, Kamenice 753/5, 625 00 Brno, Czech Republic
Institute of Law and Technology, Faculty of Law, Masaryk University, Veveří 158/70, 611 80 Brno, Czech Republic
Corresponding author, e-mail: michalkoscik@gmail.com

Eliška Vladíková | ORCID: 0000-0003-3953-3122
Department of Public Health, Faculty of Medicine, Masaryk University, Kamenice 753/5, 625 00 Brno, Czech Republic
eliska.vladikova@med.muni.cz

Abstract

The chapter explores whether the broader regulatory framework applicable to the member states of the EU contains suitable tools to react to the rapid advances in science, especially as to the question of germline editing technologies. From the perspective of EU member states, the regulatory framework is fragmented between norms of international law, secondary EU law and national legislation. The rules and their interpretation are strongly influenced by the concept of precaution, which reflects the concern that there is not enough knowledge to assess the impact of genome editing technology on individuals, society and future populations. However, the argument of precaution loses its strength with every new scientific discovery. The expanding knowledge in the field creates the need to replace regulation, which is based on the lack of knowledge (such as precautionary moratoriums) by the regulation that is based on the actual knowledge. The chapter reaches a conclusion that the EU framework for advanced treatments and medicinal products is in a state where it can, in principle, address the questions associated with the safety and efficacy of germline editing technologies. The EU framework is, however, not suitable to assess the moral and societal impacts of new technology, which should be left for member states.

 | DOI:10.1163/9789004526136_009

Keywords

genome editing – germline genome editing – EU law

1 Introduction

The debate on the regulation of gene editing is driven by three central concerns. The first concern is the concern for societal order. It is driven by fear that the technology might be abused for non-healthcare purposes and thus undermine the fundamental moral values of society and change the society irreversibly. The most notable demonstration of this concern is the fear of overuse in editing the human genome for nonmedical reasons, for example designing children (known as "designer babies") and the resulting social conflicts.[1] On a more general level, this concern is reflected in the complex debate on determining the line between the treatment of disease and enhancement of a human.[2] The second concern is the fear that the technology is not safe enough. Concerns are raised about technology's technical limitations, such as possibilities of unexpected mutations after gene editing,[3] apprehension whether modified organisms will be affected indefinitely, and whether the edited genes will be transferred to future generations, potentially affecting them in unexpected ways.[4] The gene-editing technology also raises concerns that it could be weaponised,[5] even if this concern is mostly discussed in the context of genetic engineering of biological pathogens or species.[6]

1 S. Shen, T.J. Loh, H. Shen, X. Zheng and H. Shen, 'CRISPR as a strong gene editing tool', *BMB Reports* 50 (1) (2017) 20–24, doi:10.5483/bmbrep.2017.50.1.128.

2 K. Doxzen and J. Halpern. 'Focusing on Human Rights: a framework for CRISPR germline genome editing ethics and regulation', *Perspectives in Biology and Medicine* 63 (1) (2020) 44–53, doi: 10.1353/pbm.2020.0003.

3 K. Schaefer, W.H. Wu, D.F. Colgan, S.H. Tsang, A.G. Bassuk and V.B. Mahajan, 'Unexpected mutations after CRISPR–Cas9 editing in vivo'. *Nature Methods* 14 (2017) 547–548, https://doi.org/10.1038/nmeth.4293.

4 C. Brokowski and M. Adli, 'CRISPR Ethics: Moral Considerations for Applications of a Powerful Tool', *Journal of Molecular Biology* 431 (2019) 88–101. doi: https://doi.org/10.1016/j.jmb.2018.05.044.

5 C.M. Fraser, M.R. Dando, 'Genomics and future biological weapons: the need for preventive action by the biomedical community', *Nature Genetics* 29 (3) (2001) 253–256, doi:10.1038/ng763.

6 K. Gronlund, 'Genome editing and the future of biowarfare: A conversation with Dr. Piers Millett', *Future of Life Institute* (12 December 2018), available online at https://futureoflife.org/2018/10/12/genome-editing-and-the-future-of-biowarfare-a-conversation-with-dr-piers-millett/.

The focus of this chapter is the regulatory framework for using gene-editing technology in healthcare. From the perspective of EU member states, the debate on how the clinical application of gene editing should be regulated is shaped by the three above mentioned concerns and framed by the complex framework of international treaties, EU legislation, national rules, and rules of soft law, most of which were not drafted with the gene-editing technology in mind. The discussion on the appropriate regulatory model for genome editing has two dimensions. The first dimension is whether the technology should be regulated by the tools of international, EU or national law. The second dimension is whether the regulation should focus on the *object*, such as the device or product or on the *process*, such as the course of treatment and the conduct of the healthcare provider.

The advantage of the *object-based* approach is the concentration of expertise. The products are assessed by experts who have better knowledge than the workers who use them. The disadvantage of this approach is that it does not focus on how the healthcare workers or laypersons actually use the regulated products. To ensure safety and tackle the ethical concerns of gene therapies, the "object-based" regulation needs to be complemented by "process-based regulation" that focuses on the conduct of healthcare providers. Whereas the "object-based" regulation is focused on alleviating doubts on the safety of a technology ("how the technology should look like"), the "process-based" regulation is focused on the protection of societal values from negative impacts of a newly developed technology ("how the technology should be used").

The precautionary principle could be applied as a strategy to deal with the concern of unforeseen consequences for both societal orders, public safety or individual safety. According to this principle, if there is a potential for harm from the activity and if there is uncertainty about the magnitude of impacts or causality, then anticipatory action should be taken to avoid harm.[7] The precautionary principle is a variation of the ethical non-maleficence principle.[8] In practice, however, this can lead to a consequence called an 'uncertainty paradox', which is a situation where there is a discrepancy between a promise of scientific knowledge and the lack thereof in a specific case.[9] This prin-

7 C. Raffensperger and J. Tickner (eds.), 'Introduction: to foresee and forestall', in: *Protecting Public Health and the Environment: Implementing the Precautionary Principle* (Washington, DC: Island Press, 1999), pp. 1–11.

8 T. Peters, 'CRISPR, the Precautionary principle, and bioethics', *Theology and Science* 13(3) (2015) 267–270, doi: 10.1080/14746700.2015.1056583.

9 Ch. Tannert, H.D. Elvers and B. Jandrig, 'The ethics of uncertainty: In the light of possible dangers, research becomes a moral duty', *EMBO Reports* 8(10) (2007) 892–896, doi: https://doi.org/10.1038/sj.embor.7401072.

ciple is applied mainly in environmental law, where it is even considered fundamental,[10] but it can also be used in the application of new technology or product.

The chapter seeks to assess whether the international, supranational and national rules relevant for the EU area are prepared for the rapid advancement of technology in the field of genome editing, especially as to the question of germline editing technologies. The chapter also discusses which regulatory levels are suitable for object-based regulation and which are more suitable towards regulating the processes of gene therapy.

2 Rapid Development Induced by CRISPR

The discovery of methods for programming CRISPR to edit genomic DNA was made in 2012[11,12] and started a new era in biology and in related fields. The intensive research eventually leads to practical applications. Genome editing technologies have already taken over the field of plant breeding.[13] The deployment of genome editing in the production of eggs, poultry and livestock is foreseen in the near future.[14] At the time of writing, the US Patent Collection database contains 6745 CRISPR related patents[15] and European Patent Register contains 777 patents or applications that contain CRISPR as keyword.[16] The Core collection of the Web of Science[17] contains 30523 documents mentioning CRISPR between years 2012–2021.

10 J. Cameron and J. Abouchar, 'The precautionary principle: a fundamental principle of law and policy for the protection of the global environment', *Boston College International and Comparative Law Review* 14 (1) (1991) 1–27.

11 M. Jinek, K. Chylinski, I. Fonfara, M. Hauer, J.A. Doudna and E. Charpentier, 'A programmable dual-RNA–guided DNA endonuclease in adaptive bacterial immunity', *Science* 337 (6096) (2012) 816–821, doi: 10.1126/science.1225829.

12 J.A. Doudna and E. Charpentier, 'The new frontier of genome engineering with CRISPR-Cas9', *Science* 346 (6213) (2014), doi: 10.1126/science.1258096.

13 J. Metje-Sprink, J. Menz, D. Modrzejewski and T. Sprink, 'DNA-Free Genome Editing: Past, Present and Future', *Frontiers in Plant Science* 9 (2019), doi: 10.3389/FPLS.2018.01957.

14 C.N. Khwatenge and S.N. Nahashon, 'Recent Advances in the Application of CRISPR/Cas9 Gene Editing System in Poultry Species', *Frontiers in Genetics* 12 (2021) 627714, doi: 10.3389/FGENE.2021.627714.

15 Search performed by United States patent and trademark office full-text and image database on 21 January 2022 at https://patft.uspto.gov/.

16 Search of European patent register smart search on 21st of January 2022 https://register.epo.org/.

17 Search of https://mjl.clarivate.com/.

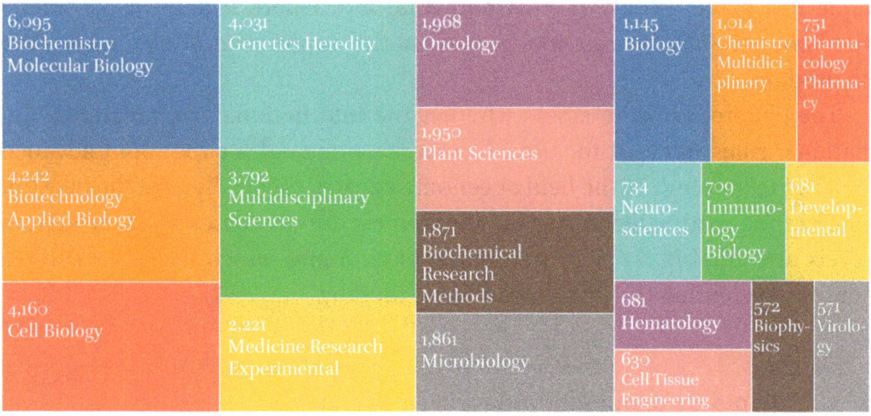

FIGURE 1 Tree bar chart generated from Web of Science

Arguably, CRISPR has started a new era in the field of healthcare. Figure 1 shows the proportion of peer-reviewed articles indexed in the Web of Science database that contained CRISPR as a keyword between 2012 and 2020 categorised into respective research fields.

The tree bar chart demonstrates that the research activity in cell biology and biochemistry has spilled over towards research in clinical medicine. The first discoveries associated with CRISPR brought hopes to treat both communicable as well as non-communicable diseases, which gave impulse to frenetic research activity searching for potential clinical applications. Less than three years after its discovery, the CRISPR methods were used to successfully modify human embryos.[18] In the immediate reaction to this experiment, the research community generally accepted that mankind needed a moratorium on clinical applications of CRISPR until "*the ethical and safety concerns of human-embryo editing are worked out.*"[19] The international summit was held in 2015 with a concluding statement: "*It would be irresponsible to proceed with any clinical use of germline editing unless and until (i) the relevant safety and efficacy issues have been resolved, based on appropriate understanding and balancing of risks, potential benefits, and alternatives, and (ii) there is broad societal consensus about the*

18 P. Liang, Y. Xu, X. Zhang, C. Ding, R. Huang, Z. Zhang, J. Lv, X. Xie, Y. Chen, Y. Li, Y. Sun, Y. Bai, S. Zhou, W. Ma, C. Zhou and J. Huang, 'CRISPR/Cas9-Mediated Gene Editing in Human Tripronuclear Zygotes' *Protein & Cell* 6 (2015) 363372. DOI: 10.1007/S13238-015-0153-5.

19 D. Cyranoski, 'Reardon Embryo editing sparks epic debate', *Nature* 520 (7549) (2015) 593–594, doi: 10.1038/520593A.

appropriateness of the proposed application."[20] At the time of the conference, these criteria had not been met for any proposed clinical use.

Three years later, in 2018, the first genetically engineered babies were born, which was met with "*universal condemnation by scientists and international organizations*."[21] Fast forward further three years to 2021, and we are witnessing an abundance of CRISPR related research that is aimed for clinical application. According to a summary article published by innovative genomics institute in 2020, there were ongoing successful clinical trials for using genome editing technologies for treating cancer, eye diseases, chronic infections and rare 'protein-folding' disease.[22] The first use of CRISPR technology injected into the blood of a patient was reported in June 2021.[23] Private and public institutions dedicate significant amounts of resources to clinical applications of genome editing, and regulators all over the world are currently allowing clinical trials involving gene editing to happen.[24] It can be observed that the moratorium on any clinical applications of genome editing technologies is coming to its *de facto* end if it ever factually existed. The genie of genome editing therapies is out of the bottle. The calls for a global moratorium on heritable genome editing from the science community are still vocal and prevalent.[25] However, the conclusions of the Second International Summit on Human Genome Editing acknowledge the transition towards regulated heritable human genome

20 S. Olson, National Academies of Sciences, Engineering, and Medicine. 'International summit on human gene editing: A global discussion', *International Summit on Human Gene Editing: A Global Discussion* (2016).

21 R. Yotova, 'Regulating Genome Editing Under International Human Rights Law', *International & Comparative Law Quarterly* 69 (3) (2020) 653–684, doi: 10.1017/S0020589320000184.

22 'CRISPR Clinical Trials: A 2021 Update, *Innovative Genomics Institute*' (*IGI*) (n.d.), available online at https://innovativegenomics.org/news/crispr-clinical-trials-2021/ (accessed 14 October 2021).

23 'CRISPR injected into the blood treats a genetic disease for first time', *Science AAAS* (n.d.), available online at https://www.science.org/content/article/crispr-injected-blood-treats-genetic-disease-first-time (accessed 14 October 2021).

24 Current trials are underway in areas: blood disorders, cancers, eye disease, chronic infections, and protein-folding disorders. Source: https://crisprmedicinenews.com/clinical-trials/.

25 See: E.S. Lander, F. Baylis, F. Zhang, E. Charpentier, P. Berg, C. Bourgain, B. Friedrich, J.K. Joung, J. Li, D. Liu, L. Naldini, J.-B. Nie, R. Qiu, B. Schoene-Seifert, F. Shao, S. Terry, W. Wei and E.-L. Winnacker, 'Adopt a moratorium on heritable genome editing', *Nature* 567 (2019) 165–168.

editing[26] and formulate eleven recommendations for countries that intend to permit its clinical use.[27]

3 The Reactive Approach to Genome Editing in the EU

Due to the rapid progress in science, the EU and its member states are now in a position where they need to react to the actual development in genome editing rather than anticipating it and using regulation as an incentive to reach policy objectives. The question of whether there should be a moratorium on at least some of the clinical applications of gene editing technologies has not been resolved in a systematic way across the EU. Currently, each member state can make its own decision whether to put in place the moratorium or specific regulation on clinical applications of somatic or germline genome editing. The compatibility of "object-based" and "process-based" regulations is an issue. The rules on market access of medicinal products and medical devices are centralised or harmonised,[28] but the rules on the actual provision of healthcare remain in the competence of the member states.[29] Part of "process-based" regulation often has the form of non-binding guidelines issued by professional organisations.

The international human rights treaties play an important role in Europe. Yotova observes that international law already plays a role in regulating genome editing through more general treaties and soft law instruments[30] and identifies main limits of international law's regulation, which can be summarised as (1) use of genome editing for medical purposes only; (2) respect for the dignity and human rights; (3) management of risks and their proportionality to

26 National Academies of Sciences, Engineering, and Medicine, *Second International Summit on Human Genome Editing: Continuing the Global Discussion: Proceedings of a Workshop — in Brief* (2019).

27 National Academies of Sciences, Engineering, and Medicine, *Report recommendations: Heritable Human Genome Editing* (2020).

28 Most notably within the framework of Regulation (EU) 2017/745 on medical devices OJ L 117 5 May 2017, p. 1 and Regulation (EU) 2017/746 on in vitro diagnostic medical devices OJ L 117 5 May 2017, p. 176, Regulation (EC) No 1394/2007 on advanced therapy medicinal products OJ L 324, 10 December 2007, pp. 121–137, Regulation (EU) No 536/2014 on clinical trials on medicinal products for human use OJ L 158, 27 May 2014, pp. 1–76 OJ L 117 of 5 May 2017.

29 In accordance with the Article 168 on the Treaty on the Functioning of the European Union the health policy and the organisation and delivery of health services and medical care, the management of health services and medical care and the allocation of the resources remains within the competence of Member states.

30 Yotova, *supra* note 21, p. 658.

benefits; (4) patient autonomy; and (5) rights of future generations,[31] with a lack of international consensus concerning the particularities of genome editing. Whilst current international law sets out common minimum standards, the decisive part of the process-based regulation currently lies at the national level.

Seventeen EU countries are bound by the Article 13 of the Oviedo Convention,[32] which prohibits interventions that aim to introduce any modification in the genome of any descendants. Other member states where the intensity of biomedical research is high (such as Germany, Italy, Netherlands, Belgium and Sweden) did not ratify this convention.[33] This does not necessarily mean, that the countries which did not ratify Oviedo Convention have a liberal stance towards human germline editing.

A specific form of germline editing moratorium is contained in Article 90 of the Clinical trials regulation,[34] which says "*no gene therapy clinical trials may be carried out which result in modifications to the subject's germ line genetic identity*." This provision does not offer a complex solution because it regulates only clinical trials and does not cover the registration of medicinal product or the actual application of medicinal product in case its clinical trials proceeded outside the EU. The Clinical trials regulation also contains very little reasoning of why this provision is included, as it only refers to the similar provision in the revoked Clinical trials directive.[35]

European Union and the Member states are yet to create a workable legislative framework that will balance the safety and ethical concerns with the benefits of the new technology with a wide scope of practical application. In its "horizon scan report," the EMEA called for stakeholder dialogue to address the new challenges of new technologies upfront.[36]

---

31 *Ibid.*

32 Convention for the protection of Human Rights and Dignity of the Human Being with regard to the Application of Biology and Medicine: Convention on Human Rights and Biomedicine Oviedo, 1997, ETS 164.

33 The largest European states (including states outside EU) that did not ratify the Oviedo convention are the Russian Federation, Germany, United Kingdom, Italy, Ukraine, Poland, The Netherlands, Belgium and Sweden.

34 Regulation (EU) No 536/2014 on clinical trials on medicinal products for human use OJ L 158, 27 May 2014, pp. 1–76.

35 Directive 2001/20/EC on the approximation of the laws, regulations and administrative provisions of the Member States relating to the implementation of good clinical practice in the conduct of clinical trials on medicinal products for human use OJ L 121, 1 May 2001, p. 34.

36 European Medicines Agency, *Genome Editing EU-IN Horizon Scanning Report* (2021), available online at https://www.ema.europa.eu/en/documents/report/genome-editing-eu-horizon-scanning-report_en.pdf.

4 The Transition from Moratoriums Based on Precaution

The concept of the legal moratorium on the new technology based on precaution is not alien to EU law. The EU rules on genetically modified organisms,[37] genetically modified food and genetically modified feeds[38] are put in place with the objective to protect human health, animal health and the environment in accordance with the precautionary principle. The precautionary principle is explicitly mentioned in the first paragraph of the Cartagena Protocol on Biosafety to the Convention on Biological Diversity to which the EU is a member.[39] The precautionary principle is explicitly mentioned in the first recital of the Directive 2001/18/EC on the deliberate release into the environment of genetically modified organisms as well as in the recital no. 22 of the Regulation (EC) No 1946/2003 on transboundary movements of genetically modified organisms. The GMO framework is also applicable to modern biotechnological methods, including CRISPR.[40] It is important to stress that the GMO legislative framework does not apply to humans.[41]

When it comes to the regulation of human genome editing, the application of the precautionary principle is more nuanced. The strictness of the regulation depends on the criterion, whether the induced genetic changes are heritable or non-heritable. There is a distinction between somatic gene editing, which targets only some of the cells of a patient and is believed not to affect

37 Directive 2001/18/EC of the European Parliament and of the Council of 12 March 2001 on the deliberate release into the environment of genetically modified organisms and repealing Council Directive 90/220/EEC OJ L 106, 17 April 2001, pp. 1–39; Directive 2009/41/EC of the European Parliament and of the Council of 6 May 2009 on the contained use of genetically modified micro-organisms OJ L 125, 21 May 2009, pp. 75–97; Regulation (EC) No 1946/2003 of the European Parliament and of the Council of 15 July 2003 on transboundary movements of genetically modified organisms OJ L 287, 5 November 2003, pp. 1–10.

38 Regulation (EC) No 1829/2003 on genetically modified food and feed OJ L 268, 18 October 2003, p. 1.; Regulation (EC) No 1830/2003 concerning the traceability and labelling of genetically modified organisms and the traceability of food and feed products produced from genetically modified organisms OJ L 268, 18 October 2003, p. 24.

39 EU became a member in 2003. See https://bch.cbd.int/protocol/parties/.

40 See Judgment in Case C-528/16 Confédération paysanne and Others v Premier ministre and Ministre de l'Agriculture, de l'Agroalimentaire et de la Forêt.

41 See CJEU Article 2(2) of Directive 2001/18/EC, on the deliberate release into the environment of genetically modified organisms which defines genetically modified organism (GMO) as 'an organism, *with the exception of human beings*, in which the genetic material has been altered in a way that does not occur naturally by mating and/or natural recombination.'

future generations and germline editing, which *affects all cells in an organism, including eggs and sperm, and so is passed on to future generations.*[42]

A significant degree of precaution is required for both kinds of genome editing. Whereas somatic editing brings risks of adverse events to a single patient, germline editing brings risks also to the future population. As a result, somatic gene editing for medical purposes is in general accepted, albeit strongly regulated, whereas germline editing is in general prohibited as a measure of precaution by EU law[43] as well as laws of individual member states, especially the states that transposed the Article 13[44] of the Oviedo Convention[45] into their national legislation.

The precautionary approach that puts emphasis on the general prohibition of a certain technology loses its validity over time as science advances. The underlying argument for the precautionary approach is based on the *lack of knowledge*[46] about the implications of new technology. Therefore, it loses strength with every new piece of information brought by science. We argue that any potential general prohibition based on a precautionary approach must be perceived as a temporary moratorium, where the rules based on *lack of knowledge* on the implications of new technology are inevitably going to be replaced by the rules based on the knowledge of beneficial and harmful implications of the technology.

The advance of science, however, does not weaken only the regulation underlined by a precautionary approach. We agree with the argument raised by Schleidigen et al.[47] that the parties to the European Convention of Human Rights are under the obligation to revisit their rules in accordance with the development of science. Even if a moratorium on any technology is based

---

42 M.T. Bergman, *Perspectives on gene editing* (9 January 2019), available online at https://news.harvard.edu/gazette/story/2019/01/perspectives-on-gene-editing/ (accessed 22 October 2021).

43 The clinical trials in germ line gene therapy are allowed to be carried out under the provisions of Article 90 of the regulation no. 536/2004 on medicinal products.

44 Oviedo Convention, *supra* note 32, Article 13: "An intervention seeking to modify the human genome may only be undertaken for preventive, diagnostic or therapeutic purposes and only if its aim is not to introduce any modification in the genome of any descendants."

45 Biomedicine Convention, *supra* note 32.

46 See, for example, Articles 10.6 and 11.8 of the Cartagena Protocol on Biosafety which mention "lack of scientific certainty due to insufficient relevant scientific information and knowledge" on potential adverse effects.

47 S. Schleidgen, H.G. Dederer, S. Sgodda, S. Cravcisin, L. Lüneburg, T. Cantz and T. Heinemann, 'Human germline editing in the era of CRISPR-Cas: Risk and uncertainty, inter-generational responsibility, therapeutic legitimacy', *BMC Medical Ethics* 21 (1) (2020) 87, doi: 10.1186/S12910-020-00487-1/METRICS.

on moral and ethical values, these values will have to be balanced by a right of individuals to enjoy the benefits of scientific progress and its applications granted by Article 15(1)(b) of the International Covenant on Economic, Social and Cultural Rights.

Any argument for a precautionary moratorium of any form of genome editing within the EU also loses validity in time when considering the global perspective. If a state enforces a moratorium on the development of new technology, knowledge and discoveries will arise in different parts of the world. There are already 11 countries in the world that explicitly permit germline editing for other purposes than reproduction.[48] These include research-intensive countries like China, the UK and the USA[49] It can be argued that countries that stick to the precautionary moratorium relinquish the opportunity to have a say on research priorities and policy in the field of genome editing. In the end, the countries that preserve the moratorium may end up having too little expertise to formulate their own rules and will most likely copy the regulatory mechanisms of the countries that made further progress in adopting new technology once the technology becomes too advanced to be ignored.

5 Object-Based Regulation as the First Step out of the Moratorium

The regulatory approach of the EU is predominantly object-based and focuses on the efficiency and safety of medicinal products and medical devices. The first possible step out of the precautionary moratorium is the regulation of market access for individual products, where it is up to the manufacturer to put forward scientific evidence on the safety of the new product. This approach respects the principle of precaution because no product is considered safe to use unless proven otherwise. A good example of this approach is a clinical trial of a medicinal product. The precaution, which is based on a lack of knowledge on the effects of a given product, is eased when the manufacturer brings convincing information on the risks and benefits of a new product or its new application.[50] The manufacturer's reward for creating new knowledge is the right to access the market with the newly developed product.

---

48 See: F. Baylis, M. Darnovsky, K. Hasson and T.M. Krahn, 'Human Germline and Heritable Genome Editing: The Global Policy Landscape', *The CRISPR Journal* 3 (5) (2020) 365–377, doi: 10.1089/crispr.2020.0082.

49 The list of 11 countries according to Baylis et al. (*supra* note 48) includes: Burundi, China, Congo, India, Iran, Ireland, Japan, Norway, Thailand, United Kingdom, United States.

50 Under EU law, a good example of this may be the provisions of Article 8 of the Directive 2001/83/EC on the Community code relating to medicinal products for human use OJ L 311 28 November 2001, p. 67.

The approach based on the market authorisation of individual products, such as medicinal products or medical devices, emphasises the safety of the consumer or patient. The objective is not to introduce products with zero risks to patients or end users because this is, in most cases, impossible. The approach is based on risk management[51] where the benefits and risks of each product introduced to a market must be known and transparently documented so that only products where there is scientific evidence that benefits outweigh the risks are made available for use. The most common tool for object-based regulation is standardisation. The standards are documented agreements containing technical specifications or other precise criteria to be used consistently to ensure that products are fit for their purpose.[52]

The EU utilizes this approach for marketing authorisation of new medicines, medical devices and diagnostic methods to incentivise investments in research and development. Furthermore, this approach can be paired with other legal tools which follow further societal, political, or environmental objectives. The most notable of these tools are research policy, research subsidies, rules for state aid in research,[53] clinical trials regulation, IP rights, design standards and performative rules for manufacturers of medical devices. Policymakers can use this toolbox to channel the flow of innovation in the direction needed by society. The approach of incentivising innovation towards societal objectives is in general preferable to the precautionary moratorium.

5.1 *Clinical Trials and Medicinal Products Policy*

The EU legislation on clinical trials distinguishes between somatic and germline gene editing. The clinical trials directive from the year 2001[54] anticipated the need for clinical trials involving medicinal products for gene therapy, somatic cell therapy, xenogenic cell therapy and the development of medicinal products containing genetically modified organisms. However, the directive explicitly excluded the option of trials that may result in modifications to

51 See, for example, World Health Organization, *Medical device regulations: global overview and guiding principles* (Geneva: World Health Organization, 2003).

52 *Ibid.*

53 European Commission, Joint Research Centre, H. Kebapci, B. Wendland and S. Kaymaktchiyski, 'State aid rules in research, development & innovation: addressing knowledge and awareness gaps among research and knowledge dissemination organisations: decision tree', *Publications Office* (2020), available online at https://data.europa.eu/doi/10.2760/675525.

54 Clinical Trials Directive, *supra* note 35, Article 9(6).

the subject's germ line genetic identity. The current Clinical trials Regulation[55], which replaces the Clinical trials Directive in 2022, preserves this policy.[56] The prohibition of clinical trials which result in modifications to the subject's germ line genetic identity is contained in Article 90 of the Clinical trials Regulation.

The legislative framework of secondary law that impacts somatic gene therapies contains the Regulation on advanced therapy medicinal products[57] and the Directive on the Community code relating to medicinal products for human use.[58] This is further developed by overarching and specific guidelines published by the European Medicines Agency[59] that cover practical aspects of safety, efficiency, quality and pharmacovigilance. The complexity of the framework and systematic expert work of the European Medicines Agency demonstrates that EU institutions are capable of developing rules that manage the safety, efficacy and risks of advanced medicinal products.

5.2 *Design Standards and Performative Rules in* MDR

The products that are delivered into the body of patients to change their genes would, in most cases, fall outside the scope of Medical Device Regulation, as they would most likely fall under the definition of advanced therapy medicinal products. However, this may happen in connection with the parallel use of a medical device. For example, intravitreal injection of medicinal product can be combined with special optronic goggles to enhance effects.[60]

---

55 Regulation (EU) No 536/2014 of the European Parliament and of the Council of 16 April 2014 on clinical trials on medicinal products for human use, and repealing Directive 2001/20/EC.

56 Recital no. 75 of the Clinical trials regulation states "Directive 2001/20/EC provides that no gene therapy trials may be carried out which result in modifications to the subject's germ line genetic identity. It is appropriate to maintain that provision," without any further elaboration.

57 Regulation No 1394/2007 of the European Parliament and of the Council of 13 November 2007 on advanced therapy medicinal products and amending Directive 2001/83/EC and Regulation (EC) No 726/2004, OJ L 324, 10 December 2007.

58 Directive 2001/83/EC of the European Parliament and of the Council of 6 November 2001 on the Community code relating to medicinal products for human use OJ L 311, 28 November 2001.

59 Such as the "Guideline on the quality, non-clinical and clinical aspects of gene therapy medicinal products (EMA/CAT/80183/2014)" or "Guideline on safety and efficacy follow-up and risk management of Advanced Therapy Medicinal Products (EMEA/149995/2008)."

60 See Gene therapy with new medical device', EuroTimes (n.d.), available online at https://www.escrs.org/eurotimes/gene-therapy-with-new-medical-device (accessed 13 November 2022).

Medical Device Regulation[61] is an example of regulation where the policymaker anticipates that the new products will be developed in accordance with predefined standards[62] and specifications.[63] Another useful tool used by Medical Device Regulation is the application of so-called performative rules, where the manufacturer is not bound by a certain predefined standard but is asked to achieve a generally defined objective. A good example is an obligation to have measures in place to provide sufficient financial coverage in respect of their potential liability.[64]

5.3 *Patent Rules and Morality Exception Article 53 of the European Patent Convention*

Another form of object-based regulation are intellectual property rights. Intellectual property policy can incentivise or de-incentivise investment into the research and development of new technologies. The EU law is framed by the European patent convention,[65] which has broader geographical coverage. Article 53 of the European patent convention denies patent rights to inventions that would be contrary to '*ordre public*' or morality. Guidelines for Examination in the European Patent Office explain that the purpose of this provision is "*to deny protection to inventions likely to induce riot or public disorder, or to lead to criminal or other generally offensive behaviour.*"[66] This provision is based on moral concerns only. The precaution and individual safety are not mentioned in Article 53 or in guidelines.[67] The secondary EU legislation provides a further specification of what is considered to be contrary to ordre public or morality in the Directive on the legal protection of biotechnological inventions.[68] Article 6

61 Regulation (EU) 2017/745 of the European Parliament and of the Council of 5 April 2017 on medical devices, amending Directive 2001/83/EC, Regulation (EC) No 178/2002 and Regulation (EC) No 1223/2009 and repealing Council Directives 90/385/EEC and 93/42/EEC OJ L 117, 5 May 2017, pp. 1–175.

62 See *Ibid.*, Article 8.

63 See *Ibid.*, Article 9.

64 See *Ibid.*, Article 10(6).

65 Convention on the Grant of European Patents (European Patent Convention) of 5 October 1973 as revised by the Act revising Article 63 EPC of 17 December 1991 and the Act revising the EPC of 29 November 2000.

66 See Part G, Chapter II, 4.1 of the Guidelines for Examination in the European Patent Office, 16 December 2021, OJ EPO 2022 A10.

67 *Ibid.*

68 Directive 98/44/EC of the European Parliament and of the Council of 6 July 1998 on the legal protection of biotechnological inventions OJ L 213, 30 July 1998, pp. 13–21.

of the Directive explicitly includes *processes for modifying the germ line genetic identity of human beings*.[69]

The concept where the patent offices serve as guardians of public order and morality is broadly criticised. The research of Plomer showed that the panels of the European patent office are, in practice, not well equipped to tackle questions of dignity and morality[70] and that they have questionable legitimacy as opposed to governments and courts.[71] Sherkow goes even further with criticism of limitations of "ordre public" when he claims that the removal of "ordre public" exception will be more appropriate since the patent holder could step in and prevent unethical use or exploitation of a biotechnological patent by private action.[72] Keeping certain technology out of patent protection frees the inventor from accountability for the actual use and abuse of the invention. Feeney at all observed the current trend of *ethical licensing*, where the patent holder controls the ethical use of potentially exploitable technology and reached a conclusion that this tool is a commendable albeit insufficient solution to a problem, which can be solved only by international legislation.[73] On the other hand, Pila argues against the approach where the responsibility for ethical use is given to the hands of patent owners.[74] Instead, she calls for a more elaborate form of risk assessments aimed at "*recognising and confronting the uncertain consequences of new technologies and their implications for society*."[75]

Even if the abovementioned authors propose different solutions, they all agree that the current regulation of patent exceptions based on morality is problematic. All authors propose the shift of focus from assessing whether a

69 The list is non exhaustive and contains processes for cloning human beings; processes for modifying the germ line genetic identity of human beings; uses of human embryos for industrial or commercial purposes; processes for modifying the genetic identity of animals which are likely to cause them suffering without any substantial medical benefit to man or animal, and also animals resulting from such processes.

70 A. Plomer, 'Human Dignity and Patents', *SSRN Electronic Journal* (2013) doi: 10.2139/SSRN.2360999.

71 *Ibid.*

72 J.S. Sherkow, E.Y. Adashi and I.G. Cohen 'Governing Human Germline Editing Through Patent Law', *Journal of the American Medical Association* 326 (12) (2021) 1149–1150. DOI: 10.1001/JAMA.2021.13824.

73 O. Feeney, J. Cockbain and S. Sterckx, 'Ethics, Patents and Genome Editing: A Critical Assessment of Three Options of Technology Governance', *Frontiers in Political Science* (2021) 731505, doi: 10.3389/FPOS.2021.731505.

74 J. Pila, 'Adapting the ordre public and morality exclusion of European patent law to accommodate emerging technologies', *Nature Biotechnology* 38 (2020) 555–557, doi: https://doi.org/10.1038/s41587-020-0504-5.

75 *Ibid.*

certain technology is moral or immoral per se towards the consideration of how such technology will be actually used in society.

6 Process-Based Regulation

The regulation of genome editing technologies needs to go beyond answering the question of whether the individual product or procedure is reasonably safe to use or whether a certain object or technology is per se moral or immoral. The regulation needs to keep perspective on the whole process of treatment, not only on the object that is used to treat a patient. Every application of genome-editing technology needs to be embedded into the broader regulatory framework, which protects various societal values, such as human dignity, equity, the welfare of an individual, patients' autonomy or public health. These values are, in general, shared across all member states, declared in Charter of Fundamental Rights of the European Union and reinforced by commitments to international treaties.[76] However, the examples of euthanasia, abortions and in-vitro fertilisation of single parents demonstrate that shared values do not lead to unanimous answers to questions whether a specific treatment is morally acceptable and legal. De Ruijter observes that "*the EU is de facto balancing fundamental rights and values relating to health, implicitly taking on obligations for safeguarding fundamental rights in the field of health and affecting individuals' rights sometimes without an explicit legal competence to do so*,"[77] but also observes that the decision at what level these values and rights should be protected is ultimately political.[78] As a consequence, it remains the competence of the member states to determine which forms of treatment are considered acceptable and ultimately legal. It is still up to the Member states to determine under what circumstances will the actual healthcare be provided, how the rights of a patient will be protected and how the oversight over individual healthcare providers will be exercised. The regulation on national level may take form of binding legislation as well as the form of soft law in the form of clinical guidelines and good practices.

76 For broader analysis how societal values and health values interact with international treaties and the of Charter of Fundamental Rights of the European Union we refer to A. De Ruijter, EU Health Law & Policy: The Expansion of EU Power in Public Health and Health Care (Oxford: Oxford University Press, 2019), especially pp. 37–38.

77 *Ibid.*, p. 15.

78 *Ibid.*, p. 225.

7 Discussion

As we mentioned above, the debate on the regulation of gene editing is driven by three concerns, which are fears for public safety, individual (patient) safety and moral values. These concerns can be addressed on the international level, EU level and national level. The current regulatory framework that affects EU member states is based on the state of professional knowledge (or better said, lack of it) from the late 20th and early 21st century. While the basic principles[79] and mechanics[80] of the regulatory framework are sound, the rapid advancements of technology brought by the use of CRISPR pose a challenge. We argue that adaptations of the regulatory framework are needed.

The existing instruments of international law remain relevant for addressing certain concerns in the field of public safety[81] and moral values, especially in the area of so-called first-generation human rights.[82] Considering the global perspective, where individual states took very different approaches in regulation of gene-editing technology, it seems that the only globally shared position is the prohibition of germline genome editing for the purposes of mere reproduction where no treatment is involved.[83] There is little hope for a global international treaty that would address other issues, such as germline genome editing for treatment purposes, standards for somatic treatments or ethical guidance and transparency of research.

The member states of EU share basic values codified in CFREU, but the political decision must be made on which levels should be these values protected when it comes to practical questions connected with patient safety and morality. We suggest that the division line between the competence of the EU and member states should be based on object-based versus process-based regulations. The EU should focus on object-based regulation, and process-based regulation should be left in the competence of member states. The division of competencies on core issues on gene editing can be summarized in Table 1.

---

79 Such as respect to human life, dignity, access to healthcare and social security.

80 Such as mechanisms to ensure safety and efficiency of medicinal products.

81 For the analysis on the applicability of the Convention on the Prohibition of the Development, Production and Stockpiling of Bacteriological (Biological) and Toxin Weapons and on their Destruction see M.E. Kosal, 'Emerging life sciences and possible threats to international security', *Orbis* 64 (4) (2020) 599–614.

82 See Yotova, *supra* note 21, p. 658.

83 Baylis et al., *supra* note 48.

TABLE 1 The division of competencies on core issues on gene editing

	International law	Secondary EU law	National law
Object-based regulation (how the technology should be designed and manufactured)	IP rights	Safety and efficacy of medicinal products and devices Standardisation of products and market authorisation Qualification of medical professionals IP rights	IP rights
Process-based regulation (how the technology should be used)	Use of genome editing for medical purposes only Prohibition of eugenics Prohibition of weaponisation Respect for the dignity of a patient Definition of human dignity and fundamental rights		Standard of care Ethical acceptability of individual therapies Ethical acceptability of research Access to treatment and reimbursement Patient's rights before, during and after care Liability for malpractice Professional ethics

We analysed two cases where secondary EU law attempts to assess technologies on other criteria than their technical function and efficiency. The first case is the moratorium on clinical trials that involve germline editing,[84] and the second case is the *ordre public* exception on the patentability of processes for modifying the germ line genetic identity of human beings.[85] The former provision creates a moratorium based on precaution. The latter penalises certain technologies on the basis of a moral principle. We demonstrated that both provisions are problematic. The rationale of these provisions is based on the

84 Article 9(6) of the Clinical Trials Directive and Article 90 of the Clinical Trials Regulation.

85 Article 6 of the directive on legal protection of biotechnological inventions.

presumption that there is a lack of knowledge on the potential safety or moral consequences of the technology. Paradoxically, they work against creating better knowledge by putting a moratorium on research activities and disincentivising investments into the development of technology, but they are not suitable to prevent the development of germline editing treatments outside of EU borders and their subsequent deployment in Europe.

We suggest, that in the case of genome editing, the secondary EU law should not address the questions of morality and ethics, as these questions can be adequately addressed by the international fundamental rights treaties and national law. The EU law should focus on the scientifically backed efficiency and safety of new technology and developing standards that will shape the future technology. The policy that removes obstacles in research and incentivises new knowledge progress does not lead to the regulatory race to the bottom. Moral and ethical reservations against certain applications of genome editing technologies are certainly legitimate, and as our research showed, some of them are shared globally. More profound knowledge will, however, lead to better arguments for ethical constraints and better regulation based on societal values. It can be also assumed, that better understanding of the technology will lead to its greater social acceptance, as it was in similar cases, like dispensing Human Growth Hormone (HGH) to the children, that used to be controversial from a moral and ethical points of view,[86] but is currently considered as common treatment.

8 Conclusions

Somatic genome editing is widely accepted as a legitimate treatment across the EU states, whereas germline editing is prohibited mainly on the grounds of precaution and morality. The legal basis of the moratorium on germline genome editing differs among the individual member states, depending on the ratification status of the Oviedo Convention. As the countries outside the EU are becoming more open to human germline editing (albeit not for reproduction purposes), it is important to discuss whether the EU and its member states should adapt their current policy.

The increasing amount of knowledge on genome editing, including human germline editing, erodes regulation based on the precautionary principle and

86 J. Lantos, M. Siegler and L. Cuttler, 'Ethical Issues in Growth Hormone Therapy', *Journal of the American Medical Association* 261 (7) (1989) 1020–1024. doi:10.1001/jama.1989.03420070070033.

can even change the moral perspective on specific therapies. The current regulatory framework, which is based on the lack of knowledge on future implications of the technology, needs to be replaced by the regulation based on knowledge and risk-based approach. The regulatory framework on the EU level should acknowledge the possibility of using germline editing technology in treatment in case it is proven safe and efficient. This will create further incentives to research activity and create knowledge, which can be used as a basis for political decisions on the moral acceptability of individual treatments.

We, therefore, suggest that the member states of EU should pool their resources to expertly assess the efficiency and safety of germline editing procedures similarly as they do with medicinal products, medical devices and innovative therapies and focus on the products (objects) that are used for the treatment. On the other hand, the member states should keep the competence to decide on the acceptability of individual treatments (processes) within their borders and on conditions under which these treatments will be provided.

PART 2

Bringing Genome Editing to the Market and Making It Available to Patients

A Room with a View (and with a Gene Therapy Drug): Gene Therapy Medicinal Products and Genetic Tourism in Europe

Vera Lúcia Raposo | ORCID: 0000-0001-7895-2181
Nova School of Law
Campus de Campolide 18, 1099-032 Lisboa Portugal
vera.lucia.raposo@novalaw.unl.pt

Abstract

In contrast to the extreme caution that has been imposed on genetic medical procedures, in European law genetic drugs, or medications, have found a legal loophole that allows flexible (perhaps too flexible) access to these drugs. In Europe, Gene Therapy Medicinal Products are a form of Advanced Therapy Medicinal Products and as such submitted to the marketing authorization procedure. However, there are legal mechanisms in place — such as compassionate use, named patient use, and hospital exception — that allow for their provision to patients without proper approval. This is not, de per se, problematic; the problem arises, though, because such mechanisms are neither properly regulated nor monitored, and their application differs substantially according to the jurisdiction. This disparity and lack of control have given rise to situations of genetic tourism, where patients in desperate need travel to so-called genetic paradises, looking for a miraculous, and extremely expensive cure. The outcome is sometimes tragic, endangering patients' safety and undermining confidence in genetic products.

Keywords

gene therapy medicinal products – advanced therapy medicinal products – compassionate use – named patient use – hospital use – genetic tourism

1 Introduction

European countries have traditionally had a very cautionary approach towards gene editing when it operates as a medical procedure,[1] not only because it is an innovative therapy,[2] but also, *et pour cause*, there are many unknowns in these therapies.[3] There is some acceptance of genetic interventions if they meet two criteria: i) that they are somatic (i.e., they do not affect any offspring) and ii) that they are therapeutic (even though the exact contour of the concept 'therapeutic' is unclear).[4] Such genetic procedures are allowed by Article 13 of the Oviedo Convention[5] and therefore by several European national laws.[6] Still, several restrictions are in place and medical procedures involving gene editing somatic therapies are highly regulated.[7]

However, gene therapy can also operate through medication rather than a medical procedure, and when that is the case the legal regime becomes much looser due to various loopholes on European pharma regulations. This chapter will address how the loopholes in pharma laws are allowing unproven genetic therapies to reach the market, exploiting the fragilities of vulnerable patients. Moreover, this scenario is harmful to the steady development of

1 European Group on Ethics in Science and New Technologies, *Ethics of Genome Editing* (Luxembourg: Publications Office of the European Union, 2021).

2 A. Loche, W. Mossmann, L. Van der Veken and G. Yang, 2020, 'COVID-19 and cell and gene therapy: How to keep innovation on track', *McKinsey and Company* (2020), available online at https://www.mckinsey.com/industries/life-sciences/our-insights/covid-19-and-cell-and-gene-therapy-how-to-keep-innovation-on-track, p. 2 (accessed 15 December 2021).

3 Reporting some of the uncertainties involved in gene therapies, S. Tunis, E. Hanna, P.J. Neumann, M. Toumi, O. Dabbous, M. Drummond, F.-U. Fricke, S.D. Sullivan, D.C. Malone, U. Persson and J.D. Chambers, 'Variation in Market Access Decisions for Cell and Gene Therapies Across the United States, Canada, and Europe', *Health Policy* 125 (12) (2021) 1550–1556, https://doi.org/10.1016/j.healthpol.2021.10.003.

4 This is a question discussed in V.L. Raposo, 'Gene Editing, the Mystic Threat to Human Dignity', *Journal of Bioethical Inquiry* 16 (2) (2019) 249–257, doi: 10.1007/s11673-019-09906-4; V.L. Raposo, 'When Parents Look for A "Better" Child (Reproductive Choices and Genetic Planning)', *BioLaw Journal/Rivista de Biodiritto* 15 (2021) 407–427, http://dx.doi.org/10.15168/2284-4503-796.

5 The Convention for the Protection of Human Rights and Dignity of the Human Being with regard to the Application of Biology and Medicine. Cf., V.L. Raposo, 'The Convention of Human Rights and Biomedicine Revisited: Critical Assessment', *International Journal of Human Rights* 20 (8) (2016) 1277–1294, doi: 10.1080/13642987.2016.1207628.

6 E.g., in Portugal, Article 8 of Law No. 12/2005, from 26 January; in Spain, Article 158 of the Criminal Code, together with Article 74 of Law No. 14/2007 from 3 July. In some other jurisdictions, it is not expressly allowed but also not expressly banned.

7 For an overview of EU laws in this regard, see http://www.genetherapynet.com/europe.html.

genetic technologies, jeopardizes funding and social credibility of legitimate gene editing drugs.[8]

2 The Qualification of Gene Therapies as Drugs

2.1 *ATMPs and Pharma Laws*

Usually, we tend to think about gene therapies as medical procedures. However, they are increasingly being provided as drugs. In Europe, Gene Therapy Medicinal Products (GTMPs)[9] are a form of Advance Therapy Medicinal Products (ATMPs).[10]

Commonly available drugs are able to treat the symptoms of genetic diseases, but they cannot cure them, whereas GTMPs can, by modifying and repairing the disease-causing gene. GTMPs involve the insertion of genetic material (DNA or RNA) into the target cell, using a carrier (the 'vector', usually modified versions of natural viruses), either in vivo or in vitro.[11]

As with any other drug, GTMPs are regulated by Directive 2001/83/EC, relating to medicinal products for human use,[12] and Regulation (EC) 1394/2007,[13] which introduced the ATMPs in the referred Directive. According to Part IV

8 J. Poulos, 'The Limited Application of Stem Cells in Medicine: A Review', *Stem Cell Research & Therapy* 9 (2018) 1, doi: 10.1186/s13287-017-0735-7.

9 It should be noted that these drugs are exclusively aimed at somatic (not germinal) gene therapy (not enhancement).

10 This chapter will only deal with GTPM's. However, many of the considerations presented apply to ATMPs in general, as GTPM's do not have relevant specificities regarding the issues here discussed. Likewise, several bibliographic references quoted in the chapter analyse other types of ATMPs (mostly stem cell products), but their consideration can easily be transposed to the GTPM discussion.

11 More details in A. Sinclair, S. Islam and S. Jones, 'Gene Therapy: An Overview of Approved and Pipeline Technologies'. in *CADTH Issues in Emerging Health Technologies* (Ottawa, ON: Canadian Agency for Drugs and Technologies in Health, 2016), at p. 171; K. Bulaklak and C.A. Gersbach, 'The Once and Future Gene Therapy', *Nature Communications* 11 (2020) 5820, doi: 10.1038/s41467-020-19505-2; X. Pan, H. Veroniaina, N. Su, K. Sha, F. jiang, Z. Wu and X. Qi, 'Applications and Developments of Gene Therapy Drug Delivery Systems for Genetic diseases', *Asian Journal of Pharmaceutical Sciences* 16 (2021) 687–703, doi: 10.1016/j.ajps.2021.05.003.

12 Directive 2001/83/EC of the European Parliament and of the Council of 6 November 2001 on the Community code relating to medicinal products for human use, OJ L 311, 28 November 2001, pp. 67–128, which rules ATMPs (hereafter, 'the Directive').

13 Regulation (EC) 1394/2007 of the European Parliament and of the Council of 13 November 2007 on advanced therapy medicinal products and amending Directive 2001/83/EC and Regulation (EC) No 726/2004 (hereafter, the 'ATMP Regulation').

of Annex I[14] of Directive 2001/83, GTMPs are 'a biological medicinal product which has the following characteristics: (a) it contains an active substance which contains or consists of a recombinant nucleic acid used in or administered to human beings with a view to regulating, repairing, replacing, adding or deleting a genetic sequence; (b) its therapeutic, prophylactic or diagnostic effect relates directly to the recombinant nucleic acid sequence it contains, or to the product of genetic expression of this sequence.[15] Gene therapy medicinal products shall not include vaccines against infectious diseases'.

2.2 *The Approval of GTMPs*

GTMPs (as all remaining ATMPs) follow the general drug approval procedure.[16] As with any drug, they are subject to the process of drug approval set forth in the 2001 Directive, which involves an assessment of the quality, safety, and efficacy of the product. If the assessment is positive a marketing authorisation (MA) is granted, and the drug can finally reach the market.[17]

A specificity feature of ATMPs is mandatory submission to the centralised approval procedure, i.e., it is up to the European Medicines Agency (EMA) to grant the respective MA and not to national drug authorities. Only some drugs are eligible for centralised approval:[18] these are the ones that are particularly risky and/or particularly innovative. ATMPs meet both requirements.

Centralised approval assures uniform assessment, to guarantee that all GTMPs provided in Europe follow the same standards of safety and efficacy. However, this apparent uniformity of criteria has a relevant loophole that

14 Commission Directive 2009/120/EC of 14 September 2009 amending Directive 2001/83/EC of the European Parliament and of the Council on the Community code relating to medicinal products for human use as regards advanced therapy medicinal products.

15 Note that the requisites are cumulative.

16 The first GTMP approved in Europe was Glybera, in 2012, a 'drug' aimed at treating adult patients with a condition known as familial lipoprotein lipase deficiency (S. Ylä-Herttuala, 'Endgame: Glybera Finally Recommended for Approval as the First Gene Therapy Drug in the European Union', *Molecular Therapy: The Journal of the American Society of Gene Therapy* 20 (10) (2012) 1831–1832, doi: 10.1038/mt.2012.194).

17 On the drug approval process in Europe see M.I. Manley and M. Vickers, *Navigating European Pharmaceutical Law* (Oxford: Oxford University Press, 2015).

18 This category included human medicines containing a new active substance to treat particular diseases; medicines derived from biotechnology processes, such as genetic engineering; advanced-therapy medicines, such as gene-therapy, somatic cell-therapy or tissue-engineered medicines; orphan medicines (medicines for rare diseases); veterinary medicines for use as growth or yield enhancer (European Medicines Agency, *Authorisation of Medicines* (10 February 2020), available online at https://www.ema.europa.eu/en/about-us/what-we-do/authorisation-medicines#scope-of-the-centralised-procedure-section (accessed 4 November 2021)).

allows patients to receive GTMPs even before the granting of the MA: the so-called early access pathways.[19] Even though a MA is required for the GTMP (or any other drug) to enter the market, there are legal mechanisms in place aimed at allowing patients in need to have earlier access to these medicines, under the discretion of national authorities, without an MA and consequently without the technical assessment of the drug authority in charge.

2.3 *Non-Approved GTMPs*

Early access to drugs — that is, before the MA is granted, while the drug is still under development — is not unusual in European Union (EU) law.[20] The 2001 Directive allows for that possibility in Article 5 (see also Article 83 of the ATMP Regulation), under the name of 'compassionate use',[21] based on humanitarian considerations. Similar to this one is the 'named-patient use', but while the former procedure is initiated by pharmaceutical companies for a group of patients in a selected clinic or hospital, the latter originates from a request presented by a physician on behalf of specific or 'named' patient directly to the manufacturer. In the case of ATMPs, there is an additional mechanism to allow early access to these drugs, which is the so-termed hospital exception. It refers to 'medicinal products which are prepared on a non-routine basis according to specific quality standards, and used within the same Member State in a hospital under the exclusive professional responsibility of a medical practitioner, to comply with an individual medical prescription for a custom-made product for an individual patient' (Article 3(7) of Directive 2001/83; Article 28 of Regulation (EC) 1394/2007).[22]

In all these cases — compassionate use, named patient use and the hospital exception — the procedure is such that national authorities are allowed

19 'Early access' pathways or schemes are common designation for these procedures that allow patients to have access to medicines before they obtain the respective MA. Cf. M. Mills, O. Efthymiadou, V. Tzouma, F. Grimaccia and P. Kavanos, 'PHP15 — Early Access to Medicines Pathways — Results of a Global Survey', *Value in Health* 20 (9) (2017) A654, doi: 10.1016/j.jval.2017.08.1548.

20 An overview in D.G.M. Coppens, J. Hoekman, M.L. De Bruin, I.C.M. Slaper-Cortenbach, H.G.M. Leufkens, P. Meij and H. Gardarsdottir, 'Advanced Therapy Medicinal Product Manufacturing Under the Hospital Exemption and Other Exemption Pathways in Seven European Union Countries', *Cytotherapy* 22 (2020) 592–600, doi: 10.1016/j.jcyt.2020.04.092, at 593.

21 Cf. J. Borysowski, H.-J. Ehni and A. Górski, 'Ethics Review in Compassionate Use', *BMC Medicine* 15 (2017) 136, doi: 10.1186/s12916-017-0910-9.

22 K. Yano and M. Yamato, 'Compassionate Use and Hospital Exemption for Regenerative Medicine: Something Wrong to Apply the Program for Patients in a Real World', *Regenerative Therapy* 8 (2018) 63–64, https://doi.org/10.1016/j.reth.2018.03.002.

some discretion in their decisions[23] and so the problem arises here: these mechanisms are applied quite differently among the Member States, providing European patients GTMPs with (very) different degrees of safety and reliability.[24] The hospital exception reveals an additional problem in this regard, caused by the fact that it targets medicines prepared for individual patients, or at least for a restricted circle of patients in a given hospital, under the exclusive professional responsibility of a medical practitioner (magistral formulas) and so the treatment is usually a custom-made product, prepared on a non-routine basis and adhering to specific quality standards.[25] The diverse 'composition' of every single product adds another layer of complexity, as they are so complex that even slight differences in their composition and/or structure can condition the respective safety profile of each one.[26] Another factor hampering the control over these genetic products is the fact that some of the concepts that materialise in the hospital exception — 'non-routine basis', 'industrial manner' and 'custom made' — have still to reach an agreed uniform definition among the Member States.[27] Let's take the example of 'non-routine basis'.[28] The

---

23 T. Ivaskiene, M. Mauricas and J. Ivaska, 'Hospital Exemption for Advanced Therapy Medicinal Products: Issue in Application in the European Union Member States', *Current Stem Cell Research & Therapy* 12 (1) (2017) 45–51, doi: 10.2174/1574888X11666160714114854, at pp. 46–49; J. Mansnérus, 'Encountering Challenges with the EU Regulation on Advance Therapy Medical Products', *European Journal of Health Law* 22 (5) (2015) 426–461, doi: 10.1163/15718093-12341369, at 442–444.

24 An analysis of how France and the United Kingdom interpret the requisites set up by the Regulation is provided in A. Dupraz Poiseau, and N. Thomas, 'The EU hospital Exemption Scheme for Advanced Therapies: A Valuable Tool to Support Innovation or a Regulatory Path Leading to a Fragmented Market? Examples of National Implementation in France and UK', *Cytotherapy* 16 (4) (2014) S52, doi: 10.1016/j.jcyt.2014.01.189.

25 C. MacGregor, A. Petersen and M. Munsie, 'Regulation of Unproven Stem Cell Therapies — Medicinal Product or Medical Procedure?', *EuroStemCell* (30 August 2015), available online at https://www.eurostemcell.org/regulation-unproven-stem-cell-therapies-medicinal-product-or-medical-procedure (accessed 5 December 2021).

26 D. Horgan, A. Metspalu, M.C. Ouillade, D. Athanasiou, J. Pasi, O. Adjali, P. Harrison, C. Hermans, G. Codacci-Pisanelli, J. Koeva, T. Szucs, V. Cursaru, I. Belina, C. Bernini, S. Zhuang, S. McMahon, D. Toncheva and T. Thum, 'Propelling Healthcare with Advanced Therapy Medicinal Products: A Policy Discussion', *Biomed Hub* 5 (3) (2020) 130–152, doi: 10.1159/000511678, at p. 140.

27 C. Eder and C. Wild, 'Technology Forecast: Advanced Therapies in Late Clinical Research, EMA Approval or Clinical Application Via Hospital Exemption', *Journal of Market Access & Health Policy* 7 (1) (2019), doi: 10.1080/20016689.2019.1600939.

28 A. Hills, J. Awigena-Cook, K. Genenz, M. Ostertag, S. Butler, A.-V. Eggimann and A. Hubert, 'An Assessment of the Hospital Exemption Landscape Across European Member States: Regulatory Frameworks, Use and Impact', *Cytotherapy* 22 (12) (2020) 772–779, doi: https://doi.org/10.1016/j.jcyt.2020.08.011, at p. 773.

British Medicines and Healthcare Products Regulatory Agency, for instance, issued a guidance note on the concept of 'non-routine basis', which recognises the difficulty in committing to a specific number of uses and states as an alternative that 'the scale and frequency of HE ['hospital exception'] ATMP production will be considered'. In Germany, following the guidance of the Paul Ehrlich Institute, the concept 'non-routine basis' is commonly understood as referring to drugs 'manufactured and used on such a small scale that it cannot be expected that sufficient clinical experience will be gained to enable the medicinal product to be fully evaluated'.[29] Most jurisdictions, however, shine no light on this issue. In essence, how many patients can be treated with the drug without it being considered a 'routine basis' is not defined.[30] Similar doubts involve the remaining concepts used to describe the hospital exception.

The flexibility that early access pathways provide for the rigid mechanism of MA approval is much appreciated. However, the extreme novelty and complexity of GTPM's cannot be underestimated. These features would require strict control on the way gene therapy drugs are provided to patients in the whole of European territory. This is not, however, what happens. Under the pretence of expediting medical care, GTMPs provided under early access pathways largely escape the required checks and controls.

3 The Risks of Unproven and Unregulated GTMPs

Medical procedures involving gene therapies are still a 'work in progress'. What we already know is that many potential hazards may take place: tumour formation, tissue rejection, autoimmunity, permanent disability and even death.[31]

29 Paul Ehrlich Institute, German Medicinal Products Act (Arzneimittelgesetz AMG) (2019), available online at at http://www.gesetze-im-internet.de/englisch_amg/englisch_amg.html#p0060 (accessed 23 November 2021).

30 Medicines and Healthcare Products Regulatory Agency, *Guidance on "Non Routine"* (2021), available online at https://assets.publishing.service.gov.uk/government/uploads/system/uploads/attachment_data/file/397739/Non-routine_guidance_on_ATMPs.pdf (accessed 2 November 2021).

31 M. Carvalho, B. Sepodes, and A.P. Martins, 'Regulatory and Scientific Advancements in Gene Therapy: State-of-the-Art of Clinical Applications and of the Supporting European Regulatory Framework', *Frontiers in Medicine* 4 (2017) 182, doi: 10.3389/fmed.2017.00182; G. Műzes and F. Sipos, 'Issues and Opportunities of Stem Cell Therapy in Autoimmune Diseases', *World Journal of Stem Cells* 11 (4) (2019) 212–221, doi: 10.4252/wjsc.v11.i4.212; Z. Wang, X. Liu, F. Cao, J.A. Bellanti, J. Zhou and S.G. Zheng, 'Prospects of the Use of Cell Therapy to Induce Immune Tolerance', *Frontiers in Immunology* 11 (2020) 792, doi: 10.3389/fimmu.2020.00792.

When such therapies are used before being properly approved and certified, the risks dramatically increase.[32]

All around the world we can find alarming incidents related to the provision of unproven GTMPs without proper monitoring, based on a market logic and not on a healthcare logic. Europe is no exception.

An infamous episode in Europe involved the Stamina Foundation, a charitable entity based in Italy, which was providing allogenic intravenous injections — classified as an ATMP — to patients with different medical conditions, under the payment of 'generous' amounts.[33] The norms on compassionate use were invoked as a basis for the use of these drugs, but an inspection by the Italian drug authorities found out that the requirements had not been met, mostly because the ATMP lacked sufficient clinical evidence (the existing evidence was merely testimony from 'treated' patients). Surprisingly, and despite these findings, the Stamina Foundation managed to get a judicial ruling allowing its activity, later confirmed by a governmental decree.[34] However, later on, several individuals with connections to the Stamina Foundation ended up facing court proceedings and some of them were even arrested.[35]

Another example of what happens when ATMPs are not properly monitored refers to X-Cell, for long the largest stem cell clinical network in Europe, based in Germany. It built a name for itself by providing unproven transplantations of autologous bone marrow stem cells for neurological disorders, injecting them into the brain, spinal cord or other body parts of patients. The price of those treatments was around 26 000 euros. From the beginning, the practice of these clinics generated suspicions, but not even the entry into force of

32 P. Bianco, 'Don't Market Stem-Cell Products Ahead of Proof', *Nature* 499 (7458) (2013) 255, doi: 10.1038/499255a; P. Foong, 'Regulating Unproven Stem Cell Interventions: How Effective Are the ISSCR Guidelines?', *Biotechnology Law Report* 39 (3) (2020) 196–203; L. Richardson, 'Harms Linked to Unapproved Stem Cell Interventions Highlight Need for Greater FDA Enforcement', *PEW* (1 June 2021), available online at https://www.pewtrusts.org/en/research-and-analysis/issue-briefs/2021/06/harms-linked-to-unapproved-stem-cell-interventions-highlight-need-for-greater-fda-enforcement (accessed 12 December 2021).

33 Cf. Emmanuelle Rial-Sebbag, and Alessandro Blasimme, 'The European Court of Human Rights' ruling on unproven stem cell therapies: a missed opportunity?' *Stem Cells and Development* 23(1) (2014) 39–43, doi: 10.1089/scd.2014.0361, at 16–17.

34 C. Hornby, 'Scientists Criticize Italy for Allowing Unproven Stem Cell Therapy', *Reuters* (29 March 2013), available online at https://www.reuters.com/article/us-italy-stemcell-idUSBRE92R0UD20130328 (accessed 23 October 2021); P.J. Zettler, 'Compassionate Use of Experimental Therapies: Who Should Decide?', *EMBO Mol Med* 7(10) (2015) 1248–1450, doi: 10.15252/emmm.201505262.

35 A. Abbott, 'Disgraced Stem-Cell Entrepreneur Under Fresh Investigation', *Nature* 539 (2016) 340, doi: 10.1038/539340a.

the ATMP Regulation (in 2009 in Germany) managed to shut them down, as the Regulation came with an 18-month transition period. After that period the clinics failed to ask for a license to operate and they were finally shut down, but they moved to Lebanon, where they continue with their doubtful 'therapeutic' procedures. Its medical practice was mired in scandal: severe internal bleeding in the head of a 10-year-old boy following cell injections into the brain; and the death of an 18-month-old infant after receiving a stem cell treatment with brain injections.[36] Money was a central element in the clinics' daily practice and they were managed more as a tourist destination than a medical one (e.g., X-Cell representatives were waiting for patients at train stations or airports to drive them to their hotel).

These two cases specifically relate to stem cell drugs, but the legal framework that facilitated its occurrence is the same one that rules gene therapy drugs, and thus it is fair to assume that it can lead to the same results. Up until now, specialised literature has not revealed high profile cases with genetic unauthorised drugs.

4 Are Pharmaceutical Norms Promoting Unsafe Genetic Tourism?

All the three early access pathways — compassionate use, named patient use and the hospital exception — fall under the competence of national authorities, which decide their requirements without the desired consistency.[37] Manipulated by less scrupulous providers of genetic 'treatments', the norms

36 A. Abbott, 'Notorious Stem Cell Therapy Centre Closes in Germany', *Blogs Nature* (9 May 2011), available online at http://blogs.nature.com/news/2011/05/notorious_stem_cell_therapy_ce_1.html (accessed 12 December 2021); C. MacGregor, A. Petersen and M. Munsie, 'Stem Cell Tourism: Selling Hope Through Unproven Stem Cell Treatments — Lessons from the X-Cell Center Controversy', *EuroStemCell* (30 April 2015), available online at https://www.eurostemcell.org/stem-cell-tourism-selling-hope-through-unproven-stem-cell-treatments-lessons-x-cell-center (accessed 3 January 2022); J. Yee, 'Europe's Biggest Stem Cell Clinic Shut Down After Baby's Death' *Bioedge* (14 May 2011), available online at https://bioedge.org/uncategorized/europes-biggest-stem-cell-clinic-shut-down-after-babys-death/ (accessed 4 December 2021).

37 An additional problem linked to the abuse of these special procedures is that they (especially the hospital exception) are being used to circumvent the drug approval procedure, discouraging investment in fully approved ATMPs. More details in Alliance for Regenerative Medicine, *Recommendations for the use of Hospital Exemption* (10 October 2020), available online at http://alliancerm.org/wp-content/uploads/2020/10/ARM-position-on-HE-final-Oct-2020.pdf (accessed 30 November 2021).

on early access pathways gave rise to genetic paradises, where control is loose and profits flow.

One would think that unapproved ATMPs were only possible in jurisdictions with little regulation in this area, but actually there are reports of clinics offering unapproved ATMPs in apparently highly regulated pharmaceutical jurisdictions, such as the ones we have in Europe.[38] Several reasons justify this regulatory loophole. Some national drug authorities — AIFA (Italy), AEMPS (Spain), ANSM (France) and IGJ (the Netherlands) — merely require ATMPs manufactured under a hospital exception to comply with the EU regulations for ATMPs. This may seem enough, but as those norms are based on a risk-based approach, they leave a wide margin of discretion for national authorities to assess what is being provided to patients and it remains unclear how demanding (or how flexible) the procedure is.[39] Moreover, in some jurisdictions — France, Germany, Italy, Poland, The Netherlands — regulatory authorities do not explicitly require ATMPs provided within the hospital exception to have been previously clinically tested.[40]

Disparities in the way ATMPs (including GTMPs) are provided have fostered a kind of 'genetic tourism' (a specific form of medical tourism)[41] in Europe, whereby desperate patients look for the more 'genetically-loose' jurisdictions, i.e., the ones in which access to ATMPs is simpler, cheaper and more loosely controlled. This phenomenon was identified long ago. Back in 2010, the Committee for Advanced Therapies expressed its concerns 'about a phenomenon known as stem-cell tourism[42] in which severely ill patients travel to clinics around the world where unauthorised stem-cell-based treatments are offered in the absence of rigorous scientific and ethical requirements. Some clinics offer these unauthorised therapies to desperate patients with incurable diseases at a high cost without ethics approval from independent bodies and potentially without documentation of adequate quality standards necessary for the protection of patients' safety'.[43]

38 Z. Master, K.R.W. Matthews and M. Abou-el-Enein, 'Unproven Stem Cell Interventions: A Global Public Health Problem Requiring Global Deliberation', *Stem Cell Reports* 16 (6) (2021) 1435–1445, doi: 10.1016/j.stemcr.2021.05.004.

39 Hills et al., *supra* note 28, at 773–774.

40 *Ibid.*, at 775.

41 B. Gharaibeh, J. Anderson and B.M. Deasy, 'Combating the Threat of Stem Cell Tourism through Patient Education and Government Regulation', *Innovation and Entrepreneurship in Health* 3 (2016) 15–24, doi: 10.2147/IEH.S56239, at pp. 15–16.

42 The concerns about 'stem cell tourism' also apply top genetic tourism.

43 Committee for Advanced Therapies and CAT Scientific Secretariat, 'Use of Unregulated Stem-Cell Based Medicinal Products', *The Lancet* 376 (9740) (2010) 514, doi: 10.1016/S0140-6736(10)61249-4.

Patients in need, and frequently losing hope, are willing to leave their homes and travel to such dubious 'genetic resorts', many unaware of the lack of clinical data supporting their genetic adventure. They engage in procedures at best ineffective and possibly even unsafe.[44] Due to the lack of transparency — we do not have accurate data on how many ATMPs are being provided to patients nor about their safety and effectiveness[45] — only more serious outcomes become public, but it is fair to assume that several minor incidents might take place with these non-approved drugs.

5 Should We Abolish Unproven GTMPs?

GTMPs offer promising possibilities in terms of personalised medicine[46] and, overall, hope for many patients afflicted by serious diseases — either caused by one single gene or by multiple genes — for which there are no other therapeutic alternatives available.[47]

Even unproven ATMPs might bring benefits to patients and in some cases they are the only option. However, because of the long wait for the MA they might arrive too late on the market. All drugs (each and every one) require lengthy approval procedures; when genes are involved the assessment becomes even more complex.[48] Due to the particularities of GTMPs, the procedure for drug authorization cannot be as standardized as with other drugs. To circumvent some of the obstacles posed by these GRMP's (and ATMPs in general), EMA drafted a risk-based approach, 'based on the identification of various risks associated with the clinical use of an ATMP and risk factors inherent to the

44 S. Jawad, A. Al-Yassin, D. Herridge, W.K.L. Lai, N. Rozario and J. Hendy, 'Safeguarding Patients Against Stem Cell Tourism', *British Journal of General Practice* 62 (598) (2012) 269–270, doi: 10.3399/bjgp12X641591, at p. 269.

45 Cf. Al Alliance for Regenerative Medicine, *supra* note 37 (the Alliance urges doctors involved in these practices to collect more data to increase transparency).

46 Horgan et al., *supra* note 26.

47 Carvalho et al., *supra* note 31, at p. 182; A. Elsanhoury, R. Sanzenbacher, P. Reinke and M. Abou-El-Enein, 'Accelerating Patients' Access to Advanced Therapies in the EU', *Molecular Therapy: Methods & Clinical Development* 7 (2017) 15–19, doi: 10.1016/j.omtm.2017.08.005, at 15.

48 Coppens et al., *supra* note 21; A. Loche, N. Paolucci, N. Peters and L. Van der Veken, 'A Call to Action: Opportunities and Challenges for CGTs in Europe', *McKinsey and Company* (2021), available online at https://www.mckinsey.com/industries/life-sciences/our-insights/a-call-to-action-opportunities-and-challenges-for-cgts-in-europe (accessed 4 December 2021); S. Ylä-Herttuala, 'The Need for Increased Clarity and Transparency in the Regulatory Pathway for Gene medicines in the European Union', *Molecular Therapy* 20 (3) (2012) 471–472, doi: 10.1038/mt.2012.1.

ATMP with respect to quality, safety and efficacy'.[49] this strategy profiles each risk that is inherent to the product (not the general risk of a product),[50] and thus is quite complex and time-consuming. These barriers end up restricting access until drug authorities are satisfied with the scientific evidence, even in cases where sound data on these products' safety and efficiency are already available. For these reasons, an absolute ban on unproven GTMPs — that is, gene therapy drugs provided under early access pathways — would prevent patients in need from having easier and faster access to gene editing therapies that might save their lives.

6 Some Suggestions for the Future

There are several scenarios in which patients receive unproven gene editing therapies in a legitimate way. This usually happens in the framework of standardised, clinically sanctioned and legally based clinical trials. It might also happen within early access pathways. However, the very rules of those legal mechanisms give rise to practices in a grey area,[51] that might take advantage of the lack of control, raising a clear public health problem.[52]

This outcome is a complete subversion of the original intents of early access pathways. They were not created to break the strict rules on drug approval, but to confer some flexibility on their (most criticised) rigidity.[53] However, they should only operate regarding gene therapy drugs that, though still under development, have already proven to be reasonably safe to be used by humans. Otherwise, it is pure human experimentation and, more than that, economic exploitation of people in very fragile situations.

---

49 European Medicines Agency, *Guideline on the Risk-Based Approach According to Annex I, Part IV of Directive 2001/83/EC Applied to Advanced Therapy Medicinal Products [EMA/CAT/CPWP/686637/2011]* (2013), available online at http://www.ema.europa.eu/docs/en_GB/document_library/Scientific_guideline/2013/03/WC500139748.pdf (accessed 12 December 2021), at p. 3.

50 *Ibid.*, at p. 4.

51 Claiming for more regulation, P. Bianco, '"Commercial Stem Cells" Damage Medicine: Medicine is Aware', *Recenti Progressi in Medicina* 106 (11) (2015) 538–539, doi: 10.1701/2074.22484.

52 Master et al., *supra* note 38.

53 European Federation of Pharmaceutical Industries and Associations, *The Root Cause of Unavailability and Delay to Innovative Medicines: Reducing the Time Before Patients Have Access to Innovative Medicines* (2020), available online at https://www.efpia.eu/media/554527/root-causes-unvailability-delay-cra-final-300620.pdf (accessed 11 December 2021).

The problem is not so much the fact that these therapies are unproven, but the fact they are unregulated.[54] When regulated, even therapies without the entire set of clinical evidence can be beneficial. The original aim guiding the implementation of early access pathways was, in my perspective, to allow access to unproven therapies, but in a regulated manner. However, the regulation part of the equation was lost along the way. National states, which run these mechanisms of early access, failed to establish clear practices and adequate control in this regard.

The provision of GTMPs within early access pathways should not be banned due to the benefits referred to in the previous sections. However, I do advocate two types of measures to circumvent potential health hazards: i) transparency and specific information duties; ii) proper monitoring by the different entities in charge.[55]

6.1 *Trustworthy Information*

6.1.1 A Duty to Provide Transparent Information

In the medical field in general there can be no misinformation, no false expectations, no deception. Right now, many cases of early access pathways involving GTMPs are pure quackery and non-enlightened patients are an easy target. Therefore, patients should be provided with trustworthy information about what they can expect from non-approved GTPM's.[56]

Studies show that patients who have received clear explanations and who have informed participation in medical decision making are less willing to accept risky treatments.[57] However, often patients do not realise that drugs provided under these early access pathways are still experimental procedures, as they have not been fully tested and assessed by the competent drug

54 The distinction between the two in L. Riva, L. Campanozzi, M. Vitali, G. Ricci and V. Tambone, 'Unproven Stem Cell Therapies: Is It my Right to Try?', *Annali Istituto Super Sanita* 55 (2) (2019) 179–185, doi: 10.4415/ANN_19_02_10, at 181.

55 Other measures that have been suggested to circumvent medical tourism (and that can also be applicable to genetic tourism) is patent law to restrict the use of technology. See J.S. Sherkow, E.Y. Adashi, and I.G. Cohen, 'Governing Human Germline Editing Through Patent Law', *Journal of the American Medical Association* 326 (12) (2021) 1149–1150, doi: 10.1001/jama.2021.13824.

56 A. Zarzeczny, H. Atkins, J. Illes, J. Kimmelman, Z. Master, J.M. Robillard, J. Snyder, L. Turner 7, P.J. Zettler, and T. Caulfield, 'Stem Cell Market and Policy Options: A Call for Clarity', *Journal of Law and the Biosciences* 5 (3) (2018) 743–758, doi: 10.1093/jlb/lsy025, at pp. 753–756.

57 L. Fraenkel and E. Peters, 'Patient Responsibility for Medical Decision Making and Risky Treatment Options', *Arthritis and Rheumatism* 61 (12) (2009) 1674–1676, doi: 10.1002/art.24947.

authorities. Moreover, patients are not able to fully understand the risks and benefits of such therapies,[58] and thus they create great expectations that in the end are frustrated, sometimes causing severe damage.[59]

Information in this regard has two dimensions: (a) the real benefits of gene editing treatments,[60] which at this moment are not totally clear, and the potential hazards involved, so that patients do not overestimate the outcomes; (b) the particular risks they incur when taking non-authorised drugs, for which there are not enough data available, any or not enough clinical evidence and no final assessment from a drug authority.

6.1.2 Should Informed Patients Still Be Protected from Their Own Decision?

A basic premise of modern health law is patients' self-determination regarding the treatments they want (or do not want) to receive. Therefore, informed patients should be allowed to use unproven medical treatments if that is their desire.

However, many have spoken out against the right of terminally ill patients to use risky treatments, such as non-approved drugs, even when there are no other therapeutic alternatives.[61] It has been stated that because patients who resort to these therapies are usually extremely vulnerable[62] — they have reached the end of the line — they should not be allowed to make such choices.[63]

Likewise, some court decisions have upheld this understanding. In Hristozov and others v. Bulgaria,[64] and in Durisotto v. Italy[65] (related to the Stamina

---

58 Therefore, patient education is a must. Cf. Z. Master and D.B. Resnik, 'Stem-Cell Tourism and Scientific Responsibility', EMBO *Reports* 12 (10) (201) 992–995.

59 Poulos, *supra* note 8.

60 Gharaibeh et al., *supra* note 41, at pp. 17–18.

61 See the considerations of Rial-Sebbag and Blasimme (*supra* note 33, at p. 41): 'The fact that a patient has exhausted all other therapeutic options is not enough to overlook those considerations'.

62 'Exposing the weakest people to unknown risks is ethically unacceptable', P. Bianco, R. Barker, O. Brüstle, E. Cattaneo, H. Clevers, G.Q. Daley, M. De Luca, L. Goldstein, O. Lindvall, C. Mummery, P.G. Robey, C. Sattler de Sousa e Brito and A. Smith, 'Regulation of Stem Cell Therapies Under Attack in Europe: For Whom The Bell Tolls', *EMBO Journal* 32 (11) (2013) 1489–1495, doi: 10.1038/emboj.2013.114, at 1491.

63 'There should not be a "right to try" something that is unsafe but rather approved treatments and in line with good clinical practic' (Riva et al., *supra* note 54, at p. 179). It is not clear from the paper if the authors would be willing to accept the so called 'right to try' if these therapies present more safety tests or if patients were more enlightened.

64 *Hristozov and others v. Bulgaria*, 2013, nos. 47039/11 and 358/12.

65 *Durisotto vs Italy*, Application no. 62804/13, European Court of Human Rights (HUDOC), 2014. A comment to this case in Rial-Sebbag and Blasimme, *supra* note 33.

Foundation) the ECHR gave precedence to the patient's protection (including from their own 'reckless' decisions) rather than personal self-determination. In Durisotto, the ECHR was asked to ascertain whether a governmental decree could establish the conditions under which the compassionate use of ATMPs could be provided to new patients (that is, patients not previously included in the treatment). The case was presented as a violation of the ECHR's norms — Article 2 (right to life), Articles 8 (right to respect for private life) and 14 (prohibition of discrimination) — to sustain the person's right to freely decide what experimental treatments to receive (more specifically, the right of the father to decide about the experimental treatments to be provided to the daughter, of whom he was the legal guardian). The Court, however, dismissed the claimants' arguments. As regards the right to private life, the Court stated that 'the interference with the right of the applicant's daughter to respect for her private life may therefore be considered necessary in a democratic society' (para. 41) and that the judicial decision preventing access to the Stamina treatment 'pursued the legitimate aim of protecting health and was proportionate to it (...) the scientific value of the method in question has not been established at the present time' (para. 48).

If this premise were true, informed consent would have to be abolished for a myriad of medical acts performed on severely ill patients. I believe that the particular vulnerability of these patients justifies further protection than in normal situations, but the law cannot be paternalistic. Additional protection from reckless decisions cannot lead to a ban on their free choice, even when it comes to risky treatments.[66]

6.2 *Greater Control by Authorities in Charge*

The different authorities in charge — drug authorities, health regulatory agencies and medical associations — should exercise greater control over the provision of GTPM's under early access pathways. This cannot be under the pure responsibility of the medical practitioner, nor be purely dependent on national governments decisions. There are recommendations from the EMA

66 In the US the so called 'right to try' — that is, the patient's right to use drugs under development — was claimed for a long time and it was finally passed in law in 2018. Cf. R. Agarwal and L.B. Saltz, 'Understanding the Right to Try Act', *Clinical Cancer Research* 26 (2) (2020) 340–343, doi: 10.1158/1078-0432.CCR-19-2015.

More radically, Flanigan (J. Flanigan, 'Three Arguments Against Prescription Requirements', *Journal of Medical Ethics* 38 (2012) 579–586) argued in favour of a right to self-medicate oneself based on personal autonomy. In this paper I speak in favour of personal autonomy, but not to the extent that the patient should be allowed to medicate himself/ herself.

on compassionate use (including the type of patients who can benefit from it), but when it comes to the other mechanisms the EMA's intervention is almost nil. It is crucial to set up guidelines/recommendations, or, eventually, binding documents, which, therefore, would hold those in non-compliance responsible. Such scientific guidelines should establish minimum thresholds of demonstrable safety for GTMPs to be provided to patients, which, in turn, require a certain amount of clinical evidence to base such threshold. Right now, there are no minimum requirements regarding the safety and efficacy of GTMPs under early pathways procedures, so, in theory, even gene editing products without any clinical evidence can be provided.

In addition to monitoring the gene editing product itself, the physicians who prescribe it should also be under stricter control by the authorities in charge of regulating the medical profession. These authorities should quickly identify and stop medical practitioners carrying out deceitful practices involving GTMPs.[67] A strict ban on misleading adverting should also be in place.

Up until now, disciplinary medical boards have acted reactively to sanction doctors, but failed to act proactively to monitor such practices, perhaps due to the lack of resources, namely, of staff with expert knowledge in the particular domain of gene editing products.[68]

Control and sanctioning by medical professionals has the advantage of allowing a technical assessment of each case by experts in the field, instead of leaving matters to a court of law. The appearance of expert witnesses might not be enough to assist judges — laymen in the matter — in such complex and technical (in scientific terms) issues, for which specific expertise is required.[69] There is, however, a downside: professional regulation tends to vary a lot across jurisdictions, so we might end up with the very same problem raised by early access pathways, that is, disparity in assessment, giving rise to very different practices.

7 Concluding Notes

The use of unproven GTMPs under a fragmentary legal framework is leading to genetic paradises and 'genetic no man's land', which threaten patient

---

67 A. Zarzeczny, T. Caulfield, U. Ogbogu, P. Bell, V.A. Crooks, K. Kamenova, Z. Master, C. Rachul, J. Snyder, M. Toews and S. Zoeller, 'Professional Regulation: A Potentially Valuable Tool in Responding to "Stem Cell Tourism"', *Stem Cell Reports* 3 (2014) 379–384, http://dx.doi.org/10.1016/j.stemcr.2014.06.016, at pp. 381–382.

68 *Ibid.*, at pp. 381–382.

69 *Ibid.*, at p. 381.

safety and discredit genetic therapies by spreading a general mistrust about them. The lack of clear regulation and proper monitoring of these early access mechanisms leaves desperate patients unprotected from unscrupulous health care providers.

To avoid this outcome the simplest solution would be to abolish any provision of GTMPs that are not duly approved and only allow GTMPs with their respective MA. However, by doing so we would be depriving patients in extreme need of what could be their last chance of survival. Not all non-authorised GTPM's are dangerous. The key is not to simply to abolish early access pathways, but to impose more reliable information requirements and more checks and controls.

What Would It Take to Enable Germline Editing in Europe for Medical Purposes?

Santa Slokenberga | ORCID: 0000-0002-5621-8485
Department of Law, Faculty of Law, Uppsala University, Box 256, 751 05 Uppsala, Sweden
santa.slokenberga@jur.uu.se

Abstract

Commonly, the regulation on germline editing in Europe is described through the two prohibitions: the prohibition set out in Article 13 of the Convention for the protection of Human Rights and Dignity of the Human Being with regard to the Application of Biology and Medicine: Convention on Human Rights and Biomedicine and the prohibition that is set out in the EU Clinical Trials Regulation. These prohibitions reflect the European regional position regarding the ethical and legal questions raised by the technology, and an unwillingness to enable such interventions in Europe. Simultaneously, these prohibitions have been shaped prior to the recent breakthroughs in the field, such as the discovery of the CRISPR-Cas technology, which has initiated a new era in the field. This contribution examines what it would take to enable human germline gene editing in Europe for medical purposes. It scrutinises in detail the content and context of the existing bans, as well as mechanisms to lift them. It argues that the bans that are prescribed by each of the European regional legal orders are embedded in strong structures, composed of values and principles. For the human germline gene editing to be enabled in Europe for health-related purposes, the approach to these values and principles needs to change. Only then can the machinery to lift the bans lead to a change.

Keywords

Biomedicine Convention Article 13 – Clinical Trials Regulation Article 90 – gene therapy – germline gene editing

1 Introduction

Commonly, the regulation on germline editing in Europe is described through the two prohibitions: one set out in Article 13 of the Convention for the protection of Human Rights and Dignity of the Human Being with regard to the Application of Biology and Medicine: Convention on Human Rights and Biomedicine (Biomedicine Convention)[1] and the other set out in the EU clinical trials framework, Clinical Trials Directive and Clinical Trials Regulation repealing the directive.[2] These bans date back to 1997 for the Council of Europe and, at least in so far as the EU clinical trials framework is concerned, to 2001; moreover, they shape the national legal requirements and medical practice in European national legal orders.[3]

The recent scientific advances[4] as well as their extraordinary practical applications, resulting in the birth of the first children whose genomes have been edited despite a *consensus*[5] in the field, have led to a renewed discussion and positions on the moral acceptability of human germline editing and future directions of the field. While there is a general reservation towards premature use of technology on humans, there is also an interest in exploring and eventually harvesting the potential benefits that germline editing could offer. In the health context, it has the potential to correct disease-causing mutations early in the development of a human being when the mutation is present in one

1 Convention for the Protection of Human Rights and Dignity of the Human Being with regard to the Application of Biology and Medicine: Convention on Human Rights and Biomedicine, ETS 164.

2 Directive 2001/20/EC of the European Parliament and of the Council of 4 April 2001 on the approximation of the laws, regulations and administrative provisions of the Member States relating to the implementation of good clinical practice in the conduct of clinical trials on medicinal products for human use OJ L 121, 1 May 2001, pp. 34–44, Article 9(6). Regulation (EU) No 536/2014 of the European Parliament and of the Council of 16 April 2014 on clinical trials on medicinal products for human use, and repealing Directive 2001/20/EC Text with EEA relevance OJ L 158, 27 May 2014, pp. 1–76, Article 90.

3 In the EU, a reserved attitude towards interventions in human germline can be observed even earlier, for example, in 1998, in the Biotechnology Directive, Directive 98/44/EC of the European Parliament and of the Council of 6 July 1998 on the legal protection of biotechnological inventions OJ L 213, 30 July 1998, p. 13–21, Article 6(2)(b).

4 Particular milestones are the work of Liang et al., published in 2015, which uses CrisprCas on non-viable human embryos to investigate the efficacy and specificity of the method, initiated an international debate on the permissibility of such research as well as future clinical. P. Liang, Y. Xu, X. Zhang, C. Ding, R. Huang, Z. Zhang, J. Lv, X. Xie, Y. Chen, Y. Li, Y. Sun 1, Y. Bai, S. Zhou, W. Ma, C. Zhou and J. Huang, 'CRISPR/Cas9-Mediated Gene Editing in Human Tripronuclear Zygotes', *Protein & Cell* 6 (2015) 363–372.

5 F. Baylis, 'Human Germline Genome Editing and Broad Societal Consensus', *Nature Human Behaviour* 1 (2017) 0103.

of few embryonic cells. Moreover, it promises to not only prevent passage of genetic disease to a child but also to break the genetic inheritance chain and prevent it from passing on to future generations.[6]

As with any issue in biology and medicine, arguments for and against the eventual use of human germline gene editing in humans are put forward. In support of germline interventions, such arguments as that society should not be deprived of the possibility of benefitting from scientific advances in the field are invoked.[7] Often, this argument is also accompanied by a proposed constrained application of the technology, e.g. for the cases where pre-implantation genetic diagnostics is not an adequate alternative,[8] or enable the use (at least) as far as pre-implantation genetic diagnosis is permitted.[9] Arguments such as the safety of the intervention and risks associated with,[10] for example, off-target edits and scientific uncertainties are invoked against the use of germline gene editing.[11] Other arguments are that alternative interventions for most of the cases are available and hence, there is a limited necessity for the interventions,[12] and that the intervention creates concerns of eugenics, and is problematic from a moral standpoint.[13]

6 D.P. Wolf, P.A. Mitalipov and S.M. Mitalipov, 'Principles of and Strategies for Germline Gene Therapy', *Nature Medicine* 25 (2019) 890–897.

7 See, for example, H.I. Miller, 'Germline Gene Therapy: We're Ready', *Science* 348 (6241) (2015) 1325.

8 See, for example, G.Q. Daley, R. Lovell-Badge and J. Steffann, 'After the Storm — A Responsible Path for Genome Editing', *The New England Journal of Medicine* 380 (2019) 897–899. D. Cyranoski, 'The CRISPR-Baby Scandal: What's next for Human Gene-Editing', *Nature* 566 (2019) 440–442.

9 See A.L.V. Hammerstein, M. Eggel and N. Biller-Andorno, 'Is Selecting Better than Modifying? An Investigation of Arguments against Germline Gene Editing as Compared to Preimplantation Genetic Diagnosis', *BMC Medical Ethics* 20 (2019) 83.

10 C. Brokowski, 'Do CRISPR Germline Ethics Statements Cut It?', *The CRISPR Journal* 1 (2018) 115–125.

11 Hammerstein et al., *supra* note 9. Insight into uncertainties also here, National Academies of Sciences, Engineering, and Medicine, *Statement by the Organizing Committee of the Second International Summit on Human Genome Editing | National Academies* (28 November 2018), available online at https://www.nationalacademies.org/news/2018/11/statement-by-the-organizing-committee-of-the-second-international-summit-on-human-genome-editing (accessed 8 February 2022).

12 G. De Wert, B. Heindryckx, G. Pennings, A. Clarke, U. Eichenlaub-Ritter, C.G. van El, F. Forzano, M. Goddijn, H.C. Howard, D. Radojkovic, E. Rial-Sebbag, W. Dondorp, B.C. Tarlatzis and M.C. Cornel, 'Responsible Innovation in Human Germline Gene Editing: Background Document to the Recommendations of ESHG and ESHRE', *European Journal of Human Genetics* 26 (2018) 450–470.

13 On analysis of how eugenics relates to germline gene editing, see N. Agar, 'Why We Should Defend Gene Editing as Eugenics', *Cambridge Quarterly of Healthcare Ethics* 28 (2019) 9–19.

Different stakeholders, including law and policymakers, have also taken a stand on the issue. For example, in 2015, the National Academies of Sciences, Engineering, Medicine issued a statement emphasising that it would be irresponsible to proceed with any clinical use of germline editing until the intervention can be deemed sufficiently safe and is acceptable.[14] Three years later, in 2018, they emphasised that the time was not ripe for clinical trials in the field,[15] but the recent progress requires defining a rigorous, responsible translational pathway towards such trials.[16] In 2015, the UNESCO International Bioethics Committee issued the Report on Updating Its Reflections on the Human Genome and Human Rights and called for 'a moratorium on genome engineering of the human germline, at least as long as the safety and efficacy of the procedures are not adequately proven as treatment'.[17] In 2017, the Council of Europe Parliamentary Assembly urged the signatories of the Biomedicine Convention to proceed with a ratification or 'as a minimum, to put in place a national ban on establishing a pregnancy with germ-line cells or human embryos having undergone intentional genome editing'.[18] In 2021, the Council of Europe affirmed that a revision is not currently on the Council of Europe's agenda.[19] In comparison, in 2018, Nuffield Council on Bioethics report Genome

14 National Academies of Sciences, Engineering, and Medicine, *On Human Gene Editing — International Summit Statement | National Academies* (3 December 2015), available online at https://www.nationalacademies.org/news/2015/12/on-human-gene-editing-international-summit-statement (accessed 8 February 2022).

15 'Statement by the Organizing Committee of the Second International Summit on Human Genome Editing | National Academies' *supra* note 11.

16 *Ibid.*

17 International Bioethics Committee, *Report of the IBC on updating its reflection on the Human Genome and Human Rights* (2015), p. 3.

18 Recommendation 2115 (2017) The use of new genetic technologies in human beings. Parliamentary Assembly Origin — Assembly debate on 12 October 2017 (35th Sitting) Text adopted by the Assembly on 12 October 2017 (35th Sitting), available online at https://assembly.coe.int/nw/xml/XRef/Xref-XML2HTML-en.asp?fileid=24228&lang=en, 5.1.

19 The Committee on Bioethics of the Council of Europe, *Genome Editing Technologies: Some Clarifications but No Revision of the Oviedo Convention* (7 June 2021), available online at https://www.coe.int/en/web/human-rights-rule-of-law/newsroom/-/asset_publisher/UORLPrekXNpu/content/genome-editing-technologies-some-clarifications-but-no-revision-of-the-oviedo-convention (accessed 8 February 2022). Later in 2022, a clarification was adopted. Steering Committee for Human Rights in the fields of Biomedicine and Health (CDBIO), Intervention on the human genome, Re-examination process of Article 13 of the Oviedo Convention, Conclusions and Clarifications https://rm.coe.int/cdbio-2022-7-final-clarifications-er-art-13-e-2777-5174-4006-1/1680a87953 (accessed 13 November 2022).

Editing and Human Reproduction: Social and Ethical Issues concluded that the intervention should be permitted under some restrictive circumstances.[20]

In the existing scholarly debates and policy documents, fundamental biomedical law principles and human rights, such as human dignity, right to health, and right to benefit from the scientific advances, are tweaked in both directions. Ultimately, once science has progressed and such central intervention-related practical issues like the safety of the intervention are no longer a concern, for example, due to off-target effects[21] and the interventions have established positive risk-benefit ratio, it could be argued to be a policy choice. At the core lies considerable, and potentially irresolvable moral questions — regarding enabling clinical trials and thereafter providing access to human germline genetic interventions and subordinated to that regarding the scope of that access as part of healthcare services.[22]

This contribution acknowledges the significant controversies regarding permissibility of human germline gene editing, and it sets aside the difficult question of whether and under what circumstances human germline gene editing should be permitted. It assumes that eventually the question of *removing* the hurdles for clinical trials and ultimately *enabling* the medical application of the technology could be put on the agenda of the two European legal orders more fiercely. It, thus, examines what it would take to enable human germline gene editing in Europe for medical purposes. To address this question, this

---

20 Nuffield Council on Bioethics in 2018 concludes that germline gene editing could be ethically acceptable if "reproductive cells that have been subject to heritable genome editing interventions are (should only be) only used for purposes that are consistent with the welfare of the future person" and if "the use of heritable genome editing interventions is (should be) consistent with social justice and solidarity so that it should not be expected to increase disadvantage, discrimination, or division in society" Bioethics, N. Co., *Genome Editing and Human Reproduction: social and ethical issues* (London: Nuffield Council on Bioethics, 2018).

21 See the ongoing discussions regarding off-target effects, M.V. Zuccaro, J. Xu, C. Mitchell, D. Marin, R. Zimmerman, B. Rana, E. Weinstein, R.T. King, K.L. Palmerola, M.E. Smith, S.H. Tsang, R. Goland, M. Jasin, R. Lobo, N. Treff and D. Egli, 'Allele-Specific Chromosome Removal after Cas9 Cleavage in Human Embryos', *Cell* 183 (2020) 1650–1664. These off-target effects could be passed on to the next generations, see I. Höijer, A. Emmanouilidou, R. Östlund, R. van Schendel, S. Bozorgpana, M. Tijsterman, L. Feuk, U. Gyllensten, M. den Hoed and A. Ameur, 'CRISPR-Cas9 Induces Large Structural Variants at on-Target and off-Target Sites in Vivo That Segregate across Generations', *Nature Communications* 13 (2022) 627.

22 For example, the right to benefit from scientific advances as protected under Article 15(1)(b) can be subject to limitations under Article 4 of the Covenant, such as through protecting from participation in scientific research that is deemed unethical, *see* UN General Assembly, International Covenant on Economic, Social and Cultural Rights, 16 December 1966, *United Nations, Treaty Series* vol. 993, p. 3.

chapter examines the existing prohibitions in detail to ascertain what specific interventions in the human genome are prohibited through the two bans. It scrutinises the context in which these bans operate as well as mechanisms to lift them within each of the European legal orders. This chapter shows the limited reach of these bans; furthermore, it argues that the bans which are prescribed by each of the European regional legal orders are embedded in strong structures composed of values and principles. For the human germline gene editing to be enabled in Europe for health-related purposes, the approach to these values and principles needs to change. Only then can the machinery to lift the bans lead to a change.

2 On the Two Bans in European Regional Legal Fora

The Biomedicine Convention is a universal human rights instrument in the area of biology and medicine. It provides a common framework for the protection of human dignity and human rights to its contracting parties. While its effects could stretch beyond the borders of the Council of Europe, to this day, there is no country outside the Council of Europe that would have acceded to the convention.[23] It has 29 ratifications[24] and thus unites only slightly more than half of the members of the Council of Europe. However, the limited number of ratifications does not do justice to the impact of the principles set out in the convention across the Council of Europe. The powerful adjudication under the ECHR established by the ECtHR, and the structured approach crafted by the Council of Europe, whereby sectorial treaties and soft-law tools are anchored in the rights protected by the ECHR, render the ECtHR an indirect enforcer of the convention.[25] Although the ECtHR has not had a chance to consider on Article 13 of the Biomedicine Convention yet, given the important human rights questions that interventions in human genome pose, it cannot be precluded that a question will eventually land before the court.

23 See Article 34 of the Biomedicine Convention and Council of Europe, *Chart of Signatures and Ratifications of Treaty 164*, status as of 8 February 2022, available online at https://www.coe.int/en/web/conventions/full-list?module=signatures-by-treaty&treatynum=164 (accessed 8 February 2022).

24 *Ibid.* Seven countries have signed the convention and have not proceeded with the ratification.

25 See F. Seatzu and S. Fanni, 'The Experience of the European Court of Human Rights with the European Convention on Human Rights and Biomedicine', *Utrecht Journal of International and European Law* 31 (2015) 5–16.

The EU does not possess any general powers regarding health care. However, health matters trigger diverse competences of the EU.[26] Through the principle of conferral, the Member States have entrusted the EU to legislate for setting high standards of quality and safety for medicinal products.[27] As stipulated in declaration 32 attached to the Lisbon treaty, the EU shall be acting on quality and safety matters where national standards affecting the internal market would otherwise prevent a high level of human health protection being achieved. However, this provision is not in itself sufficient for enacting comprehensive legislation on clinical trials and regulation of the market-related aspects for medicinal products generally or advanced therapy medicinal products specifically. Central to the regulation of the medicinal products are rules on internal market, and consequently, the legal basis set out in Article 114 TFEU. These are also the two legal bases on which the Clinical Trials Regulation rests,[28] and which are examined in greater detail in the subsequent sections.

Generally, gene therapy falls within the scope of the EU Regulation on Advanced Therapy Medicinal Products.[29] However, the rules pertaining to clinical trials are set out in the Clinical Trials Regulation. The regulation applies to all clinical trials in the EU, whereby an integral part of a clinical trial is presence of a medicinal product for investigation in a clinical study.[30] This suggests that the EU Clinical Trials Regulation applies only to such gene editing that satisfies the definition of a medicinal product. What is a medicinal product and thus is captured under this ban is examined in the next section. Here, it suffices to note that other interventions that do not fall within the scope of Clinical Trials Regulation can be regulated differently, for example, under the general product safety requirements.[31]

For the national legal orders, the Biomedicine Convention as well as the EU law place different obligations. The Biomedicine Convention is an

26 For an insight into the EU competences, *see* K.P. Purnhagen, A. De Ruijter, M.L. Flear, T.K. Hervey and A. Herwig, 'More Competences than You Knew? The Web of Health Competence for European Union Action in Response to the COVID-19 Outbreak', *European Journal of Risk Regulation* 11 (2020) 297–306.

27 Article 168(4)(c) Consolidated version of the Treaty on the Functioning of the European Union OJ C 326, 26.10.2012, pp. 47–390.

28 Clinical Trials Regulation *supra* note 2.

29 Regulation (EC) No 1394/2007 of the European Parliament and of the Council of 13 November 2007 on advanced therapy medicinal products and amending Directive 2001/83/EC and Regulation (EC) No 726/2004 (Text with EEA relevance) OJ L 324, 10 December 2007, pp. 121–137.

30 Clinical Trials Regulation, *supra* note 2, Article 1 and Article 2(2).

31 See Directive 2001/95/EC of the European Parliament and of the Council of 3 December 2001 on general product safety (Text with EEA relevance), OJ L 11, 15 January 2002, pp. 4–17.

international treaty, and its effectiveness at the national level rests on the effectiveness of measures taken by the national legal orders in order to give them effect. Although Article 13 of the Biomedicine Convention is a non-derogable prohibition,[32] and the signatories are required to provide appropriate sanctions for infringements,[33] its effect can be compromised by the countries failing to take measures to give full effect to the provisions. Generally, from the international law perspective, a distinction can be drawn between monism and dualism traditions.[34] The monist school regards international and national law in a system of unity, whereas the dualist school sees them as a separate system. Additional challenges relating to implementation could emerge in the dualist traditions and limited direct impacts that the convention could create. However, as a matter of international law, disregarding whether a state follows a monist or dualist tradition, it shall ensure that it lives up to its international commitments, and violations of the ban prescribed in Article 13 do not take place.

The EU law obligations are subsumed under the principle of primacy of EU law.[35] As the Clinical Trials Regulation takes a form of a regulation — a directly applicable legal instrument — and Article 90 is capable of meeting the requirements of direct effect as the norm is sufficiently clear, precise and does not require further implementation measures,[36] there is nothing from hindering its application in regard to each clinical trial. Hence, its effects can reach down to, for example, each sponsor responsible for a clinical trial. However, unlike, for example, in the area of data protection, the Clinical Trials Regulation does not prescribe uniform sanctions for violations. It merely requires the Member States to adopt 'effective, proportionate and dissuasive' penalties for the infringements of the regulation,[37] leaving it up to each Member State to define the content of these penalties.

3 What Is Prohibited and Why?

3.1 *Article 13 of the Biomedicine Convention*

Article 13 of the Biomedicine Convention reads as follows:

---

32 Biomedicine Convention, *supra* note 1, Article 26.

33 *Ibid.*, Article 15.

34 J.G. Starke, 'Monism and Dualism in the Theory of International Law', *British Year Book of International Law* 17 (1936) 66–81.

35 Case 6/64, *Flaminio Costa v E.N.E.L*, ECLI:EU:C:1964:66.

36 See Case 26/62, *Van Gend en Loos v Administratie der Belastingen*, ECLI:EU:C:1963:1.

37 Clinical Trials Regulation, *supra* note 2, Article 94(1).

> An intervention seeking to modify the human genome may only be undertaken for preventive, diagnostic or therapeutic purposes and only if its aim is not to introduce any modification in the genome of any descendants.

This provision only allows for 'modifications' of the human genome for 'preventive, diagnostic or therapeutic purposes', except for when such modifications seek to introduce any changes to the genome of any descendants. It is neutral to the genome editing technique that is involved in introducing the modification; instead, it focuses on the prohibited behaviour and its intention. The provision is intended to enable only somatic, health-related genome editing. However, it tolerates that somatic, health-related genome editing could have implications for germ cells, and it could result in heritable changes.[38] It does not put any hinders to the basic research in the field using surplus embryos.[39] However, in line with Article 18 of the convention, embryos for research purposes shall not be created. The ban that is set forth in Article 13 becomes applicable if the potential of life is attempted to be realised, for example, through using gametes that have been subject to editing interventions in *in vitro* fertilisation or through insemination of a fertilised edited egg in a woman's body.

At the time this provision was adopted, it was the first of its kind. Work on this provision within the Council of Europe took place from November 1992 to June 1996, and the preparatory works provide an insight into central considerations that lie behind the wording of the provision. They include reluctance to assume risks that human beings could differ from one generation to the next,[40] interest to enable diagnostic and therapeutic somatic interventions and acceptance of eventual risks in that regard to the germline,[41] acknowledgements of the limitations relating to science underlying interventions in the human genome at the time of drafting the convention, as well as some

38 Explanatory Report to the Convention for the protection of Human Rights and Dignity of the Human Being with regard to the Application of Biology and Medicine: Convention on Human Rights and Biomedicine, para. 91.

39 See Steering Committee on Bioethics (CDBI) Convention on the Protection of Human Rights and Dignity of the Human Being with Regard to the Application of Biology and Medicine: Convention on Human Rights and Biomedicine (Ets No. 164), Preparatory Work on the Convention, CDBI/INF (2000) 1, pp. 63–68.
See also I. de Miguel Beriain, E. Armaza and A. Duardo Sánchez, 'Human Germline Editing Is Not Prohibited by the Oviedo Convention: An Argument', *Medical Law International* 19 (2–3) (2019) 226–232.

40 Preparatory Work on the Convention, *supra* note 38, ORED 9-12/11/92, p. 63.

41 See *ibid.*, pp. 63–68.

openness to the revisions of the wording of the provision.[42] While the interest in the openness to the revisions is traceable in the preparatory works at the early stages of the development of the convention, the preparatory works following November 1995 are silent on this issue.[43] *Expressis verbis* rejection of the idea that the provision could be revised is not documented. It might well be that some parallels can be drawn regarding the discussions on the state of scientific knowledge and state of art and the needs to revise the provision in that light, which had taken place at the earlier stages of the development of the provision, versus the principle-based discussions regarding the permissibility of interventions in the human genome.[44] One could also speculate that the revision consideration has some parallels with the development of Article 32 of the convention that focuses on the amendments to the convention, but the preparatory works are silent on that.[45] More conclusive answers from the preparatory works regarding the intentions are difficult to draw.

Explanatory Report to the Biomedicine Convention, on the other hand, emphasises only the fear of misuse that could endanger not only individuals but also the human species. As the ultimate fear in that regard, it points out the fear 'to produce individuals or entire groups endowed with particular characteristics and required qualities'.[46] It addresses safety of the interventions to the extent that they are allowed under Article 13, and in so far as they are part of scientific research, wherein they should be conducted accordingly. It could be argued that the Explanatory Report to the Biomedicine Convention addresses the central concern motivating the prohibition set out in Article 13. Since that is a matter of principal concern, the question of safety then was no longer relevant.

3.2 *Article 90 of the Clinical Trials Regulation*

Article 90 of the Clinical Trial Regulation states:

> No gene therapy clinical trials may be carried out which result in modifications to the subject's germ line genetic identity.

42 See *ibid.*, in particular CORED 14-16/12/92, pp. 63–64, CDBI 27/06-1/07/94, pp. 65–66, and CDBI 20-22/1195, p. 66.

43 See Preparatory Work on the Convention, *supra* note 39, pp. 63–68. See also preparatory works regarding Article 32, pp. 124–125.

44 See nature of discussions and the transition to the agreement on the substance of the issues, *ibid.*, CDBI 26/02-1/03/96, p. 67.

45 *Ibid.*, pp. 124–125.

46 Explanatory Report to the Biomedicine Convention *supra* note 38, para. 89.

This provision contains a prohibition that has existed in the EU law for a considerable time.

In its predecessor, Article 9(6) of the Clinical Trials Directive, it was included in the second reading, following the recommendation of the Committee on the Environment, Public Health and Consumer Policy on the Council, giving a common position for the directive.[47] Justification of the inclusion was motivated with at that time the existing EU policy in the field. More specifically, it was argued that '[t]he prohibition of germ line gene therapy is in line with stated EU policy'.[48] No further information is provided regarding the policy that the committee refers to. It was then adopted in the 2nd reading.[49] In 2012, the European Commission launched a proposal for the Clinical Trials Regulation, and this proposal did not contain any consideration regarding the germ line. However, already in the first reading, this was rectified, and the ban set out in the Clinical Trials Directive found also its place in the proposed regulation, with a motivation that '[t]he regulation may not fall behind the existing directive. Therefore, we should adopt the formulation of the present directive'.[50] The available preparatory works are silent on whether this was a mere administrative slip, or the European Commission had a particular intention of not including the ban in its proposal. The context of EU law in the field, however, speaks of the former.[51]

One of the central features of the EU legal framework in the field is that it applies to medicinal products. This is a general rule, taming the EU competences and the application of the Clinical Trials Regulation, as well as the

47 European Parliament Recommendation for Second Reading Final A5-0349/2000, 22 November 2000.

48 *Ibid.*, amendment 19, p. 17.

49 See European Parliament legislative resolution on the Council common position for adopting a European Parliament and Council directive on the approximation of the laws, regulations and administrative provisions of the Member States relating to the implementation of good clinical practice in the conduct of clinical trials on medicinal products for human use (8878/1/2000—C5-0424/2000—1997/0197(COD)), Amendment 42.

50 On the proposal for a regulation of the European Parliament and of the Council on clinical trials on medicinal products for human use, and repealing Directive 2001/20/EC (COM(2012)0369—C7-0194/2012—2012/0192(COD)), Amendment 257.

51 Such a ban is also set out in other EU legal acts, for example, on EU funding for scientific research, *see* Regulation (EU) 2021/695 of the European Parliament and of the Council of 28 April 2021 establishing Horizon Europe — the Framework Programme for Research and Innovation, laying down its rules for participation and dissemination, and repealing Regulations (EU) No 1290/2013 and (EU) No 1291/2013 (text with EEA relevance) PE/12/2021/INITOJ L 170, 12.5.2021, pp. 1–68, Article 18(1)(b). Another example is Directive 98/44/EC of the European Parliament and of the Council of 6 July 1998 on the legal protection of biotechnological inventions OJ L 213, 30.7.1998, pp. 13–21, Article 6(2)(b).

Regulation on Advanced Therapy Medicinal Products.[52] Consequently, it is also a limitation on the application of Article 90 of the Clinical Trials Regulation and the interventions that can be subjected to the ban on heritable genetic changes set therein.

The Clinical Trials Regulation applies to all clinical trials conducted within the EU.[53] From Article 2(2) of the Clinical Trials Regulation derives that in order for a clinical trial to be subject to the regulation, it shall involve assessment of a medicinal product or a 'therapeutic strategy' that falls outside the normal clinical practice in a Member State, or 'diagnostic or monitoring procedures' falling outside the normal clinical practice, whereby the 'therapeutic strategy' as well as 'diagnostic or monitoring procedures' relate to a medicinal product. The regulation does not define what a medicinal product is, but it indicates that the definition of a 'medicinal product' that is set out in Directive 2001/83/EC applies.[54] There, in Article 1(2), a medicinal product is defined as

> Any substance or combination of substances presented for treating or preventing disease in human beings.
>
> Any substance or combination of substances which may be administered to human beings with a view to making a medical diagnosis or to restoring, correcting or modifying physiological functions in human beings is likewise considered a medicinal product.

If a product falls within any of the two definitions (i.e. can be regarded as a medicinal product by presentation or by function), the product shall be regarded as a medicinal product.[55] However, the assessment of whether a particular substance shall be classified as a medicinal product is not straightforward. As explained by the Court of Justice of the European Union (CJEU), this assessment lies with the national authorities, acting under the supervision of the courts, to 'decide on a case-by-case basis, taking account of all the characteristics of the product, in particular its composition, its pharmacological, immunological or metabolic properties, to the extent to which they can be established in the present state of scientific knowledge, the manner in which it is used, the extent of its distribution, its familiarity to consumers and the risks which its use may entail'.[56] In regard to the advanced therapy medicinal

52 See recitals 2 and 3 in Advanced Therapy Medicinal Products Regulation, *supra* note 29.

53 Clinical Trials Regulation, *supra* note 2, Article 1.

54 *Ibid.*, Article 2(1). *See* C-27/08, *BIOS Naturprodukte GmbH v Saarland*, ECLI:EU:C:2009:278, paras 17–22.

55 See, for example, Joined Cases C-358/13 and C-181/14, *Markus D. and G.*, ECLI:EU:C:2014:2060, paras 26–28.

56 *Ibid.*, para. 42.

products, such as particular interventions in the human genome, however, this assessment lies with the European Medicines Agency.[57]

The assessment of a substance's classification as a medicinal product by presentation is rather straightforward — if a substance is presented as being intended for treating or preventing a disease in human beings, it shall be regarded as a medicinal product. However, the assessment of a substance being classified as a medicinal product by function is less straightforward. It requires a more sophisticated judgment, examining the central elements enlisted in the definition. More specifically, while restoration and correction are rather straightforward in the health context, questions emerge in regard to the meaning of the word modify, and consequently, what types of modifications are captured under the Clinical Trials Regulation.

The CJEU has explained that, in everyday language, the word modify appears neutral in terms of its effects, whether they are harmful or beneficial.[58] However, in the context of the EU objectives and competencies, and in particular, in the area of public health, as well as with due regard to the legal framework, in which this term is located, and associated terms in the definition imply the beneficial nature of the modification.[59] In a similar way, restoration and correction of functions are intended to capture the beneficial effects. In *Upjohn*, early on, the CJEU indicated that this wording covers 'all substances capable of having an effect on the actual functioning of the body'.[60] Thus, products, which alter physiological functions in the absence of disease, such as contraceptive substances, also fall within the scope of that definition.[61] More recently, in the joined cases *Markus D. and G.*, the CJEU clarified that this wording reflects the legislature's intention to capture substances producing 'beneficial effects ... on the functioning of the human organism and, as a consequence — be it immediately or over a period of time — on human health, even in the absence of disease'.[62] Thus, the wording modify 'must be

57 See the role of Committee for Advanced Therapies under Regulation (EC) No 1394/2007 of the European Parliament and of the Council of 13 November 2007 on advanced therapy medicinal products and amending Directive 2001/83/EC and Regulation (EC) No 726/2004 (Text with EEA relevance) OJ L 324, 10.12.2007, pp. 121–137.

58 Joined Cases C-358/13 and C-181/14, *Markus D. and G.*, *supra* note 55, para. 31.

59 *Ibid.*, paras 30–37.

60 C-112/89, *Upjohn Company and Upjohn NV v Farzoo Inc. and J. Kortmann*, ECLI:EU:C:1991:147, para 21.

61 *Ibid.*, para 19. Though, obviously, this is an outlier in the medicinal products regime, similarly as abortifacients. Joined Cases C-358/13 and C-181/14, *Markus D. and G.*, *supra* note 55, paras 40–41.

62 Joined Cases C-358/13 and C-181/14, *Markus D. and G.*, *supra* note 55, para 36.

interpreted as not covering substances whose effects merely modify physiological functions and which are not such as to entail immediate or long-term beneficial effects for human health'.[63] Thus, for example, interventions in the human genome that do not produce this effect fall outside the scope of the application of the respective ban.

4 Lifting the Ban Set Out in Article 13 of the Biomedicine Convention

4.1 *On the Procedure of Lifting the Ban*

Biomedicine Convention is an international treaty, concluded under the auspices of the Council of Europe. A treaty may be amended by agreement between the parties.[64] Vienna Convention on the Law of the Treaties of 1969,[65] a treaty governing treaties, allows that treaty amendment rules are set forth in a respective treaty. Article 32 of the Biomedicine Convention sets forth a 4-stage mechanism to make it happen.

To begin with, there are only three actors that are entitled to submit a proposal for a treaty amendment. It can be done by any party of the convention, the Steering Committee for Human Rights in the fields of Biomedicine and Health (CDBIO),[66] or the Committee of Ministers.[67] Thereafter, the text needs to be examined by the CDBIO. If the CDBIO is the one submitting, this step can be viewed as futile on the condition that two-thirds majority of the votes are present for the submission of the proposal. The CDBIO is composed of experts of the highest rank on matters pertaining to the areas of the Biomedicine Convention, and in that committee, each Council of Europe member state may be represented and have one vote.[68] If the proposal is approved by a two-thirds majority of the votes cast, it proceeds to the next step, the Committee of

63 *Ibid.*, para. 38.

64 Vienna Convention on the Law of Treaties (United Nations (UN)) 1155 UNTS 331 VCLT, Vienna Convention 1969, Article 39.

65 *Ibid.*

66 Council of Europe, *The Committee on Bioethics (DH-BIO) Becomes the Steering Committee for Human Rights in the Fields of Biomedicine and Health (CDBIO)* (13 December 2021), available online at https://www.coe.int/en/web/bioethics/news/-/asset_publisher/EV740sp47zWZ/content/the-committee-on-bioethics-dh-bio-becomes-the-steering-committee-for-human-rights-in-the-fields-of-biomedicine-and-health-cdbio- (accessed 8 February 2022).

67 Biomedicine Convention, *supra* note 1, Article 32(5).

68 *Ibid.*, Article 32(2).

Ministers, for approval.[69] The Committee of Ministers is the organ that acts on behalf of the Council of Europe, and it consists of Ministers for Foreign Affairs of the Council of Europe member states.[70] Each member of the Council of Europe is entitled to one representative on the Committee of Ministers, and each representative shall be entitled to one vote.[71] It is required that the decision is made by a two-thirds majority of the representatives casting a vote and a majority of the representatives entitled to sit on the Committee of Ministers.[72]

As evident from the above, there must be a considerable interest in furthering the changes, and this interest needs to stem from different directions and reach a considerable threshold. To begin with, there needs to be an interest among one of the key actors to proceed with amendments. Thereafter, there needs to be a majority of the Member States of the Council of Europe experts working at the CDBIO in favour of the amendment. Thirdly, it needs to pass the threshold assigned to the ministers of foreign affairs of the Council of Europe states, representing the political view at the national level. Only thereafter can it proceed to the ratification stage, and the lifting of the ban can get the full effect.

4.2 *On the Context of Lifting the Ban*

The ban on human germline editing rests on a number of pillars of the Biomedicine Convention. Among its cornerstones is 'need to respect the human being both as an individual and as a member of the human species' and wish to tackle the fact that 'the misuse of biology and medicine may lead to acts endangering human dignity'.[73] Substantively, the convention seeks to protect the dignity and identity of all human beings with regard to the application of biology and medicine.[74] Moreover, '[t]he interests and welfare of the human being shall prevail over the sole interest of society or science'.[75] Any intervention shall be 'carried out in accordance with relevant professional obligations and standards'.[76]

The context in which Article 13 is placed indicates that germline interventions can be argued to be disrespectful to an individual, be incompatible with dignity, and endanger the humanity. In that regard, it is not in the interests and

69 Biomedicine Convention, *supra* note 1, Article 32(6). The participation in the CDBIO is open also to parties to the convention that are not Members of the Council of Europe.
70 Statute of the Council of Europe, European Treaty Series No. 1, Article 14.
71 *Ibid.*, Article 14.
72 *Ibid.*, Article 20.
73 Biomedicine Convention, *supra* note 1, preamble.
74 *Ibid.*, Article 1.
75 *Ibid.*, Article 2.
76 *Ibid.*, Article 4.

welfare of the individual that such interventions, as part of research or care, take place.

The view behind these strong values and fundamental principles of the European bio law is somewhat complex. One of the significant critiques that the Biomedicine Convention has received is the fact that it places human dignity at its core, and dignity is informing different solutions presented in the convention. However, at the same time, nowhere in the convention is this notion defined.[77] It is true that the concept of human dignity is notoriously difficult to define.[78] However, failure to elaborate, at least in a functional way regarding values it accounts for, opens up room for questions and uncertainties regarding exactly what facets of human dignity that the ban set out in Article 13 upholds.

Regarding the respect of an individual as one of the central pillars of the Biomedicine Convention, at least two facets emerge. First, that of the gamete donor and prospective parent. Second, that of the prospective child. As the norms of the convention apply to everyone, the protection of a prospective child is not precluded.[79] However, then, freedom from a particular genetic condition is ranked lower as a possibility to be born with a particular genetic condition.[80] This line of reasoning could easily be rejected through systemic interpretation of the convention in regard to genetic conditions to which other biology and medicine applications are permissible under the convention.[81] What remains then is that this respect anchors in the control over gametes and embryos, as well as an embodiment of collective values — such as avoidance of eugenics — in the notion of "respect" and allowing that to trump any interest in making individually beneficial decisions, which could be at the detriment of society, on whatever scale.

Additionally, the Biomedicine Convention is not only an instrument to safeguard individual rights in the application of biology and medicine. It is also an instrument that seeks to safeguard humanity, at least, within the European regional fora. In this light, heritable interventions in the human genome, as banned by Article 13, are regarded as a risk to humanity, even if the application is health-related and thus entails positive individual health effects on the

77 V.L. Raposo, 'The Convention of Human Rights and Biomedicine Revisited: Critical Assessment', *The International Journal of Human Rights* 20 (8) (2016) 1277–1294, p. 1283.

78 For insights *see* C. McCrudden, 'Human Dignity and Judicial Interpretation of Human Rights', *European Journal of International Law* 19 (4) (2008) 655–724.

79 See Biomedicine Convention, *supra* note 1, Article 1; and Explanatory Report to the Biomedicine Convention, *supra* note 37, paras 16–19.

80 It should be noted that this question is fundamentally different from abortion debates.

81 See permissibility of predictive genetic tests under the convention. Biomedicine Convention, *supra* note 1, Article 12.

prospective child. If, however, the endangerment relates to, for example, concerns over eugenics, they are qualitatively different from restrictive applications of technology in isolated cases. This begs the difficult question added here as a side note, on the chosen means to tackle the challenges, and in particular, whether carefully regulated applications of the technology could lead to the materialisation of these fears.

Additionally, the convention sets forth a number of principles and rights relevant for scientific research and medical care. It is not sufficient that health-related gene editing interventions could be anchored into the above-mentioned pillars, they also need to comply with other norms. One such is the requirement for the health research and care to be in line with professional standards.[82] Thus, anchoring the health-related interventions in the fundamental pillars of the convention will not, in itself, be enough for enabling the interventions in research or care. Also, key actors, researchers and medical doctors need to be of the view that the intervention is compatible with the professional standards. Ultimately, it needs to be compatible with the research participant's and the patient's perspective under the clauses of informed consent or assent, so that the interventions can be applied in scientific research or care. While these largely relate to the application of techniques, once the ban is lifted, a lack of acceptance of the intervention, among the researchers, medical doctors and patients, risks depriving the lifting of the ban from its purpose.

5 Lifting the Ban Set Out in Article 90 of the Clinical Trials Regulation

5.1 *On the Procedure of Lifting the Ban*

Deregulation of a field is not regulated in the EU law in any particular way. Even though this phenomenon is rather unique, as it essentially requires the EU to take a step back from the depth of the integration, it has previously happened. An example of this is the area of genetically modified organisms.[83] Generally, there could be different reasons for deregulation of a field. One such reason is that the EU integration measure has not yielded the intended results. Another such reason is an arguable oversight of the legislature in failing to accommodate

---

82 Biomedicine Convention, *supra* note 1, Article 4.

83 See Directive (EU) 2015/412 of the European Parliament and of the Council of 11 March 2015 amending Directive 2001/18/EC as regards the possibility for the Member States to restrict or prohibit the cultivation of genetically modified organisms (GMOs) in their territory Text with EEA relevance, OJ L 68, 13.3.2015, p. 1–8 , recital 6.

in the secondary law the freedom that the Treaty on the Functioning of the European Union (TFEU) allows for the Member States. Another could be changes in reasons that underpin the ban. Even though the reasons behind lifting a ban could affect modalities within the procedure,[84] both of the basis of the Clinical Trial Regulations require a measure within the ordinary legislative procedure.

Within the ordinary legislative procedure, the European Commission has the task to submit a proposal to the European Parliament and the Council.[85] Additionally, in regard to the measures under Article 168(4)(c) TFEU, a consultation with the Economic and Social Committee and the Committee of the Region shall take place.[86] The European Commission, as a watchdog of the treaties and as the actor of furthering EU interests, shall put forward a proposal when it believes that it is in the interest of the EU that a ban on clinical trials involving germline gene editing be lifted.[87]

Following the proposal of the European Commission, the European Parliament — the representatives of the EU citizens — begins by adopting its position and communicating it to the Council — representatives of the EU Member States.[88] The Council can then either approve the Parliament's position motivating its reasons,[89] or adopt its own position.[90] In both instances, the Commission shall be informed. The adoption of its own position leads to the second reading and further dialogue between the two actors. That process can take up to three readings and involves a Conciliation Committee as a platform to work out the disagreements between the two parts.[91]

The European Parliament is composed of representatives of the EU's citizens, and it has the mandate to act in their interests.[92] The Council, however, has been assigned the task of carrying out policymaking and coordinating functions as laid down in the Treaties. It consists of a representative of each Member State at the ministerial level, who may commit the government of the Member State in question and cast its vote.[93] So, there should also be a

84 C-482/17 *Czech Republic v Parliament and Council*, ECLI:EU:C:2019:1035, para. 42.

85 Consolidated version of the Treaty on the Functioning of the European Union OJ C 326, 26.10.2012, pp. 47–390. Article 294(2) TFEU.

86 *Ibid.*, Article 168(4)(c).

87 Consolidated version of the Treaty on European Union OJ C 326, 26.10.2012, pp. 13–390, Article 17.

88 TFEU, *supra* note 85, Article 294(3).

89 *Ibid.*, Article 294(4) and (6).

90 *Ibid.*, Article 294(5)–(6).

91 *Ibid.*, Article 294(10)–(12).

92 TEU, *supra* note 87, Article 14.

93 *Ibid.*, Article 15.

prevailing opinion that lifting the ban set out in the Clinical Trials Regulation is the way to go. There must be a considerable interest in furthering the changes, and this interest needs to stem from different directions and reach a considerable threshold. Firstly, there needs to be an interest from the EU for this to happen. Secondly, there must be a support of the "people's representatives," and also the EU's policy agreement steered by the representatives of the Member States sitting in the Council.

5.2 *On the Context of Lifting the Ban*

Article 114 TFEU enables the EU to legislate in order to remove actual potential hinders to the internal market,[94] and in the context of germline editing, particularly, free movement of goods and services is of interest. Any measure that is prepared by the European Commission under this provision is required to have as a base a high level of protection in the fields of health, safety, environmental protection and consumer protection.[95] This needs to be done, considering particularly any new development, which is to be based on scientific facts.[96]

According to the established jurisprudence of the CJEU, legislation through Article 114 TFEU has some particularities that need to be accounted for. Since *Tobacco Advertising 1* case, it is well-established that the provision cannot be used to harmonise non-market objectives, if a market objective is lacking.[97] However, it is equally well established that if the divergences in the market exist (actual or potential), i.e. if the market precondition to engage Article 114 TFEU is met, the legislature can also make choices under Article 114(3) TFEU, including if those choices are decisive.[98] Once the field has changed, the EU legislature is not prevented from amending the existing legislation, to account for those changes.[99]

94 C-482/17 *Czech Republic v Parliament and Council supra* note 83 para 35. On the insufficiency of mere disparities between the national laws, *see* para 58 (and cited case law therein) in C-547/14 *Philip Morris Brands SARL and Others v Secretary of State for Health*, ECLI:EU:C:2016:325.

95 TFEU, *supra* note 85, Article 114(3).

96 *Ibid.*, Article 114(3).

97 C-376/98 *Federal Republic of Germany v European Parliament and Council of the European* Union, ECLI:EU:C:2000:544.

98 C-482/17 *Czech Republic v Parliament and Council, supra* note 83, para. 36.

99 *Ibid.*, paras 38–39. See also C-491/01 *The Queen v Secretary of State for Health, ex parte British American Tobacco (Investments) Ltd and Imperial Tobacco Ltd.*, ECLI:EU:C:2002:741 paras 77 and 78, as well as C-58/08 *The Queen, on the application of Vodafone Ltd and Others v Secretary of State for Business, Enterprise and Regulatory Reform (Vodafone and Others)*, ECLI:EU:C:2010:321, para. 34. *See* also C-477/14 *Pillbox 38 (UK) Limited, trading*

The consideration of lifting the existing ban on human germline gene editing in the EU, thus, requires at least two acknowledgements. First, tolerance of the possibilities that could be opened up through the divergences. This stems from two considerations. The already noted inherent nature of Article 114(1) TFEU that allows legislation in that regard. Interlinked to that, the possibilities of the Member States to invoke, for example, health or morality-related considerations for the purposes of putting obstacles to the free movement nationally.[100] Secondly, acceptance of the measure under Article 114(3) TFEU, and in particular that the lifting of the ban is considered compatible with the requirement for a high level of health and safety protection. While it is well-established that the EU legislature enjoys discretion under this provision,[101] it is difficult to see that a measure that is contrary to this standard would be tolerable under the legislature's discretion. In so far as health would be concerned, such a measure would be incompatible with the high level of health within the EU under Article 168(1) TFEU[102] as well as health as protected under Article 35 of the CFREU,[103] and general principles of EU law.[104]

Article 168(4)(c) enables measures for setting high standards of quality and safety for medicinal products. A possibility to legislate under this provision is a public health asset of the Lisbon Treaty and could be said to reflect the until-Lisbon established praxis to address public health concerns through an internal market regulation. At its very basic level, it required that the germline editing not pose risks to safety. In healthcare, it is not a question of an absolute safety, but a question of positive risk-benefit ratio that needs to be demonstrated.

Any EU law measure shall comply with the fundamental principles of EU law and the rights and principles set out in the CFREU. For example, the CFREU does not mention human germline gene editing, however, prohibits

---

as Totally Wicked v Secretary of State for Health, ECLI:EU:C:2016:324, para. 116, where the CJEU notes that the EU could be required to act in the changing circumstances.

100 See in that regard, e.g., TFEU *supra* note 84 Article 36, morality concerns, e.g., C-36/02 *Omega Spielhallen- und Automatenaufstellungs-GmbH v Oberbürgermeisterin der Bundesstadt Bonn*, ECLI:EU:C:2004:614. *See* also TFEU, *supra* note 84, Article 114(4).

101 See B. de Witte, 'Non-Market Values in Internal Market Legislation', in: N.N. Shuibhne (ed.), *Regulating the Internal Market* (Cheltenham: Edward Elgar, 2006), pp. 61–86.

102 For an explicit link between Article 114(3) TFEU and Article 168(1) TFEU see para. 61 in C-547/14 *Philip Morris Brands SARL and Others v Secretary of State for Health, supra* note 88.

103 See Charter of Fundamental Rights of the European Union OJ C 326, 26 October 2012, pp. 391–407, Article 51(1).

104 C-547/14 *Philip Morris Brands SARL and Others v Secretary of State for Health, supra* note 96, para. 62.

'eugenic practices, in particular those aiming at the selection of persons'.[105] Moreover, Article 1 of the CFREU safeguards human dignity. Hence, similar to the Biomedicine Convention, both of these values would need to be interpreted in a way to be compatible with germline gene editing for health-related purposes. Unlike Article 13 in the Biomedicine Convention, the prohibition of eugenic practices is set out much more broadly and vaguely in the context of germline gene editing. Hence, one could argue that the EU legislature is in a somewhat better position to push for changes than the Council of Europe is.

6 One at a Time or Both at the Same Time?

Both of the European regional legal orders set considerable restrictions for human germline gene editing to enter into the domain of clinical research and, subsequently, care. At the same time, neither the ban set out in Article 13 of the Biomedicine Convention, nor Article 90 of the Clinical Trials Regulation is set in stone. There are rather straightforward procedures within each of the legal orders that allow for the two bans to be lifted. The procedural requirements in both of the European regional legal orders require considerable agreement between different representatives of the states, representing different groups. There is room for tensions at the national level and between indifferent actors in the same country, and between states, and between states and institution representatives. Additionally, as the analysis in this chapter shows, the bans are located in a rather complex legal environment, and there are considerable thresholds that need to be met in order for the bans to be lifted.

Under the Biomedicine Convention, the ban *inter alia* seeks to uphold interest in safeguarding humanity. Hence, it is required that the understanding of risks associated with how heritable genome editing challenges that are reassessed, and a diametrically opposite conclusion of that which is valid today, is reached. Such an approach will inevitably open up discussions regarding the point of adopting the bans in the first place, and justification of the early critique of the bans. There is, however, a contra-argument to it, namely, the increased knowledge about the intervention, and consequently also control over it as well as minimisation of the negative effects it could create for the society.

The EU legal order, at least *expressis verbis*, does not prescribe such strong values that lie at the core of the prohibition. What has been traceable is that the prohibition reflects EU policy in the field. This, however, does not lead to a conclusion that the procedure for lifting the ban is much more straightforward.

105 CFREU, *supra* note 103, Article 3(2)(b).

To begin with, the intervention needs to be regarded as safe. Additionally, the Member States enjoy certain room for managing issues that can be anchored in the morality arguments, and the EU can be expected to tolerate that, provided, however, that the national legislation is overall coherent regarding the moral values it seeks to uphold.[106] Moreover, a ban aiming at safeguarding the germline is also set out in other EU legal acts, such as the mentioned Biotech Directive and the Research Regulation.[107] It could be argued that a more comprehensive action, rather than merely de-regulation of the field of clinical trials, will be necessary, and the restrictions set out in those laws will also need to be reconsidered.

The two bans, which are in effect in both of the European regional legal orders, are not mutually related. Therefore, one could question whether it suffices that one ban is lifted, whereas the other remains in effect. There is no requirement that lifting of the bans shall occur simultaneously. It is, however, neither practical nor sustainable from the state external accountability point of view and the doctrine of legal pluralism. It also cannot be argued to be possible if an account of the strong but not expressly regulated ties between the two legal orders is given.

The Council of Europe and the EU share the same set of 27 Member States. Not all Member States of the EU are parties to the Biomedicine Convention, but a significant portion of them are parties. A choice not to coordinate the actions and lift the two bans simultaneously risks resulting in a situation where a state has conflicting legal obligations. Some conflicts can be easier to resolve, but some are not as easy. For example, if the Biomedicine Convention lowers the standard and the EU retains it, then the EU Member States have a chance to envisage a higher level of protection under the Biomedicine Convention. However, if the EU lowers the standard, a question emerges as to whether it would then allow Member States to retain higher standards to remain in line with the Biomedicine Convention obligations. On the one hand, as has been already noted, it is a question of moral values where the EU has been generous in leaving leeway to the Member States. On the other hand, it needs to be acknowledged that it will end up being a market question, which is the EU's interest. Considering the free movement possibilities even under differing national laws, there could be limited room for national unilateral exemptions. This could suggest that the question of human germline gene editing for healthcare purposes is of a European concern. Hence, urgent, fruitful, multilevel policy discussions are needed on top of the dialogue with stakeholders and society.

---

106 See in that regard C-165/08 *Commission of the European Communities v Republic of Poland* ECLI:EU:C:2009:473.

107 See *supra*, note 51.

Genetics and Justice, Non-Ideal Theory and the Role of Patents: The Case of CRISPR-Cas9

Oliver Feeney | ORCID: 0000-0003-3585-448X
Research Unit 'Ethics of Genome Editing', Institute of Ethics and History of Medicine, University of Tübingen, Gartenstraße 47, 72074 Tübingen, Germany
oliver.feeney@uni-tuebingen.de

Abstract

There are ongoing concerns of social justice regarding inequalities in the distribution of access to potential genome editing technologies. Working within non-ideal theory, Colin Farrelly advances a justification for the use of patents to speed up the arrival of safe and effective interventions for all, including the socially disadvantaged. This chapter argues that such success is less assured when one considers the actual functioning of patents and the practical implications of the patent system in the context of biotechnological innovations. I suggest that non-ideal theoretical approaches risk reverting back to a form of ideal theory if they simply refer to such real-world constraints — e.g. patents — but do not critically assess and fully examine how such constraints manifest themselves in practice. I highlight some considerations that would be important in order to develop and foster a more robust non-ideal approach to justice in biotechnological developments.

Keywords

non-ideal theory – patents – genome-editing – distributive justice

1 Introduction

In the context of biotechnological developments, there are ongoing concerns of social justice regarding inequalities in the distribution of access to potential

DOI:10.1163/9789004526136_012

genome editing technologies.[1] Nevertheless, requiring an ideally just egalitarian distribution of costly technologies may be an unrealistic ideal and the alternative of forbidding access to those able to meet the costs, when others cannot, is a very morally problematic substitute.[2] The problem of ideal theory in political philosophy is that the goal of a just society is too far removed from the real-world. Non-ideal theory, on the other hand, takes seriously fact-sensitive considerations such as feasibility constraints — including the high costs of biotechnology and the (generally perceived) need for incentivising innovation and investment — and seeks to develop a more realistic social justice response that accepts and works within those constraints.

Working within this non-ideal theoretical framework, Colin Farrelly[3] advances a *broadly* egalitarian, or rather more specifically *prioritarian*, argument. The egalitarian-prioritarian distinction is well-known in political philosophy and studies of meaning of egalitarianism.[4] According to the Parfit, an 'egalitarian' (*strictly speaking*) is someone who thinks it is bad in itself, if some are *relatively* worse or better than others, regardless of their absolute levels of welfare or access to valuable resources.[5] Crucially, it is open to the levelling down objection which holds that strict egalitarians must believe that everybody being equally worse off, say due to a natural disaster, is in one way a good thing since it would remove the inequality.[6] One might assume that egalitarians generally desire equality because they care about the well-being of the worst off in society. Equality, and the egalitarianism that advocates it, seems good only insofar as it benefits the people who are absolutely worst off. This is akin to John Rawls argument for the Difference Principle in his renowned theory of justice, where one should seek equality *unless* an unequal distribution can be structured to the benefit of the worst off.[7]

1 O. Feeney, J. Cockbain, M. Morrison, L. Diependaele, K. Van Assche and S. Sterckx, 'Patenting Foundational Technologies: Lessons from CRISPR and Other Core Biotechnologies', *The American Journal of Bioethics* 18 (12) (2018) 36–48, DOI:10.1080/15265161.2018.1531160.

2 M.J. Mehlman. 'Genetic Enhancement: Plan Now to Act Later', *Kennedy Institute of Ethics Journal* 15 (1) (2005) 77–82.

3 C. Farrelly, *Biologically Modified Justice*. (Oxford: Blackwell, 2016).

4 D. Parfit, 'Equality or Priority?' the *Lindsay Lecture, University of Kansas, 21 Nov. 1991* (Lawrence, KS: University of Kansas, Department of Philosophy, 1995), in: J. Harris (ed.), *Bioethics* (Oxford: Oxford University Press, 2001), p. 364.

5 The form of egalitarianism advocated here is the telic egalitarianism developed by L. Temkin, *Inequality* (Oxford: Oxford University Press, 1993). Essentially, telic egalitarianism holds that "equality is valuable in itself, even if there is no one for whom it is good."

6 D. Parfit, 'Equality and priority', *Ratio*, 10 (3) (1997) 202–221, pp. 210–211.

7 J. Rawls, *A Theory of Justice*, revised edition (Oxford: Oxford University Press, 1999); J. Rawls. *Justice as Fairness: A Restatement* (Cambridge, MA: Harvard University Press, 2001). It should

Those egalitarians who view equality as merely instrumental to this end may be more accurately called prioritarians: those who think that those who are worse off than others should have increasing priority for their situation to be addressed and improved in absolute, not relative, terms. As Farrelly notes, "what underlies a concern for equality is a concern for the least advantaged [therefore] we should not object to inequalities that benefit the least advantaged."[8] Moreover, Farrelly advocates a form of pluralist prioritarianism which means (at least in this context) it recognises that there are multiple forms of disadvantage (and multiple forms of responses) and that there are other values — such as freedom — that are to be balanced with the prioritarian distributive argument itself. In short, pluralist prioritarians are not focused always on genomics nor only on optimal distributive issues all of the time.

In Rawlsian language, pluralist prioritarians (as Farrelly uses the term) endorse a 'lax genetic difference principle' where inequalities in the distribution of genes/genetic inequalities (we can read 'genetic interventions and related genetic research') important to the natural primary goods (e.g. health) are to be arranged so that they are to the greatest reasonable benefit of people who are genetically worst off. As Farrelly has more recently rephrased the lax genetic difference principle as the lax biological difference principle,[9] I will refer to both below as the lax genetic/biological difference principle — lax GDP/BDP.

It is important to note that *qua 'lax'*, unlike Rawls' Difference Principle, it does not maximin (*only* maximise the minimum, very worst-off position, not matter the cost to the other positions) and it takes seriously the trade-offs that need to be made with various empirical realities as well as other values. In keeping with this approach, Farrelly's *non-ideal* prioritarian moral justification for the use of patents is to speed up the arrival of safe and effective interventions for all, including the socially disadvantaged in need of, or standing to benefit from, access to such technologies. While some socially advantaged groups may have better access than less advantaged groups, due to the artificially higher costs of a patented technology, the less advantaged would not

be noted that Rawls' overall theory is far more complex, nuanced and is not reducible to this 'prioritarian' position.

8 C. Farrelly, 'Genes and equality', *Journal of Medical Ethics* 30 (2004) 587–592, p. 592. It can be argued that there is a different interpretation to the equality-priority distinction. See O. Feeney 'Egalitarianism and the Parfitian Equality-Priority Framework' [Spanish title: El igualitarismo según Derek Parfit: Una discusión], *Aesthetika: International Journal of Interdisciplinary Research on Subjectivity, Politics and Art* 13 (2) (2017) 65–75, available online at http://www.aesthethika.org/IMG/pdf/65-75_feeney_el_igualitarismo_a_la_luz.pdf.

9 Farrelly, *supra* note 3.

have legitimate complaint if this was the only feasible way to secure access for them too, albeit at a later point.

Whatever the merits of Farrelly's non-ideal approach if it were to succeed, I argue that such success is less assured when one considers the actual functioning of patents and the practical implications of the patent system in the context of biotechnological innovations. I suggest that any such non-ideal theoretical approaches risk reverting back to a form of ideal theory if they simply *refer* to (or gesture toward) such real-world constraints — in this case, the role of patents — but do not critically assess and fully examine how such constraints manifest themselves in practice. Reflecting on the (in)famous CRISPR-Cas9 patent dispute, I highlight some considerations that would be important in order to develop and foster a more robust non-ideal approach to social or distributive justice in biotechnological developments.

2 Social Justice Issues with Patenting CRISPR

Compared to previous techniques of genetic interventions, contemporary genome editing methods (such as CRISPR-Cas9, or Cas13 or Cas14, or other CRISPR-associated enzymes, such as base editors) has been steadily moving the possibilities of making effective and realistic genetic changes to emerging realities. To illustrate the revolutionary advances in technical capacities, it is worth highlighting that 22 years passed between the commencement of the Human Genome Project and Charpentier and Doudna's seminal 2012 paper highlighting CRISPR, and its possibilities.[10] From here, it was merely 6 years before the first confirmed cases of humans were born with their heritable genetic constitution genome-edited using CRISPR-Cas9. He Jiankui's germline reproductive genome-editing of twin girls consisted of inserting a variant of the CCR5 gene to attempt to confer immunity to HIV.

However, this case has been significant, not because of the technical possibilities it apparently illustrated, but due to the ethical and legal guidelines ignored in the process. Focussing not only on this case, but globally, it is clear that the international regulatory system when it comes to genome-editing, and CRISPR in particular, is insufficient and, worse, hardly present in any credible sense. While governments, international bodies and other relevant stakeholders, try to ensure that the legislative, regulatory and effective ethical, legal and

10 M. Jinek, K. Chylinski, I. Fonfara, M. Hauer, J.A. Doudna and E. Charpentier, 'A programmable dual-RNA-guided DNA endonuclease in adaptive bacterial immunity', *Science* 337 (6096) (2012) 816–821, doi:10.1126/science.1225829.

societal frameworks catch up to the technical possibilities, the concern is that the eventual outcome will be either an ineffective mix of partial regulation or an equally ineffective overreaction in terms of widespread prohibition and blunt overregulation.[11]

There are a number of potential issues over the powers of ownership (and thus the right of exclusion) over a fundamental, or 'foundational', technology, such as the genome-editing process exemplified by CRISPR (and related methods).[12] It is *both* potentially powerful in its individual application and potentially has an expansive range of such applications. In terms of human health, it can be applied directly to the development and research of human therapeutics. It can contribute to the development of new drugs (pharmacology) and new forms of immunotherapy.[13] It can be potentially applied to removing the genetic components to *some* disabling conditions.[14] More widely, it can improve the quality and quality of food needed for human health.[15] This has added importance given the forthcoming changes to the climate that seem all but unavoidable. The technology can be used to interfere in the wider ecology and can remove threats to human, via gene drives (malaria),[16] or, on the 'flip-side' it can potentially reduce other forms of interference in the wider ecology by genetically editing crop lines to be resistant to the diseases and reducing the need for harmful pesticides and herbicides.[17] More speculatively, it may even have some impact on extra-planetary exploration and colonization (e.g. Mars) as new forms of plants or humans will be needed to withstand the changes in gravity and other factors not encountered on Earth.[18]

11 A. Nordberg, T. Minssen, O. Feeney, I. de Miguel Beriain, L. Galvani and K. Wartiovaara, 'Regulating germline editing in assisted reproductive technology: An EU cross-disciplinary perspective', *Bioethics* 34 (1) (2020) 16–32, https://doi.org/10.1111/bioe.12705.

12 Feeney et al., *supra* note 1.

13 X. Ou, Q. Ma, W. Yin, X. Ma and Z. He, 'CRISPR/Cas9 Gene-Editing in Cancer Immunotherapy: Promoting the Present Revolution in Cancer Therapy and Exploring More', *Frontiers in Cell Development Biology* 9 (2021) 674467, doi: 10.3389/fcell.2021.674467.

14 I. de Miguel Beriain, 'Gene editing and disabled people: a response to Felicity Boardman', *J Community Genetics* 11 (2020) 241–243, https://doi.org/10.1007/s12687-020-00460-w.

15 N.G. Karavolias, W. Horner, M.N. Abugu and S.N. Evanega, 'Application of Gene Editing for Climate Change in Agriculture', *Frontiers in Sustainable Food Systems* 5 (2021) 685801, doi: 10.3389/fsufs.2021.685801.

16 K.M. Esvelt, 'Rules for sculpting ecosystems: Gene drives and responsive science', in: I. Braverman (ed.), *Gene editing, law, and the environment* (New York, NY: Routledge, 2018), pp. 21–37.

17 K. Yin and J.-L. Qiu. 'Genome editing for plant disease resistance: applications and perspectives'. *Philosophical Transactions of the Royal Society B* 374 (2019) 20180322, http://dx.doi.org/10.1098/rstb.2018.0322.

18 For instance (in terms of potential human genome editing), see: K. Szocik, M. Shelhamer, M. Braddock, F.A. Cucinotta, C. Impey, P. Worden, T. Peters, M.M. Ćirković, K.C. Smith,

Within the current context of the chapter such possibilities also have to be supplemented with other less technologically based (or idealistically based) possibilities that are likely to arise. Political, ethical and social justice issues will accompany and play an additional effect on the far-reaching decisions over the nature, type, extent and timescale of the aforementioned applications. The context of the chapter is focused on the role of patents and, more generally, the effect of such technologies being 'privately' owned and controlled by purely non-idealistically minded, altruistic individuals or institutions over a significant period of time. Affecting the above technical possibilities, a range of political, ethical and social justice issues can arise.[19] For one thing, the patenting itself would likely raise costs, especially given the litigation that has been involved and the sums already invested.[20] This would likely lead on to less affordable treatments for the end-user or patent (or medication user) — especially the relatively socially disadvantaged — for instance, entailing an exacerbation of their ill-health or prolonging their disability. As well as the intrinsic badness of ill-health and suffering, as health is fundamental to equality of opportunities,[21] this may have consequences in the competition for jobs and positions of advantage in society, and as a consequence, further solidifying the initial social disadvantage.[22]

Another related scenario might arise where a relatively small group of key players have the control — due to patents — to effectively set the agenda of subsequent research, be it by their approaches to exclusive licences, decisions over potential recipients of licences and the permitted purposes of licences or, as above, to do with the level of cost involved and the decisions researchers might have to therefore make regarding research priorities.[23] The possible resulting narrowing or delays to research and applications could have

K. Tachibana, M.J. Reiss, Z. Norman, A.M. Gouw and G. Munévar, 'Future space missions and human enhancement: Medical and ethical challenges', *Futures* 133 (2021) 102819, https://doi.org/10.1016/j.futures.2021.102819.

19 Feeney et al., *supra* note 1.

20 H. Ledford, 'Major CRISPR patent decision won't end tangled dispute', Nature 603 (2022) 373–374.

21 N. Daniels. *Just Health: Meeting Health Needs Fairly.* (New York: Cambridge University Press, 2008).

22 Feeney et al., *supra* note 1. There is a voluminous literature on this issue, hugely influenced by a now canonical text: A. Buchanan, D.W. Brock, N. Daniels and D. Wikler, *From Chance to Choice: Genetics and Justice* (Cambridge: Cambridge University Press; 2000).

23 O. Feeney, J. Cockbain and S. Sterckx, 'Ethics, Patents and Genome Editing: A Critical Assessment of Three Options of Technology Governance', *Frontiers in Political Science* 3 (2021) 731505. doi: 10.3389/fpos.2021.731505; S. Hilgartner, 'Foundational technologies and accountability', *The American Journal of Bioethics* 18/12 (2018) 63–65; Feeney et al., *supra* note 1.

consequences for the availability of treatments leading to unnecessary exacerbation of ill-health, with similar consequences. Given the level of investment and hype already involved, this may adversely affect efforts for adequate democratic oversight, or certainly increase tensions between such oversight and commercial goals.[24]

Issues of huge societal and commercial expectation of a given technology may also have wider, less explicit, effects such as a reduction of focus and funding for non-CRISPR alternatives. On a global level, especially in terms of medicine or agricultural food seeds, such issues of costs and control may not only affect groups of individuals, but entire countries in a similar imbalanced way (with historical precedent), contributing to a continuation of dependant development. Regardless of the rhetoric used by the various players, the prospects of royalty stacking and evergreening practices would remain likely within a context involving huge investments and profit. Such practices will have knock-on effects to both uncertainty for other companies to work out when it would be possible to work on certain areas (e.g. using apparently expired patents but finding that they are effectively extended) or further consequences for availability and cost of treatments.

A key problem is that the assorted problems outlined above are not just unconnected possibilities, but that a key part of the potential issue is directly related to the fact that they are related to each other, with one factor causing or exacerbating others and a narrowing of pathways and control leading back to the original, small group of key entities with control. The interconnections are not incidental but tied to the fact that the technology is a foundational one — the basis for an ever-widening range of technical possibilities (such as the potential benefits noted above) but with an ever-widening scope of control and associated problems just mentioned.[25]

How likely some problems, and therefore their subsequent resulting problems, will arise will be affected by the licencing decisions of the patent holders. For instance, the licencing approach of Broad/Editas consists of a mix of non-exclusive licences in research and tools while pursuing an Inclusive Innovation Model with regard to exclusive licences in human therapeutics.[26] Broad's CRISPR-Cas9 licences are also devised to prevent their use in tobacco crops, gene drives, and human germline modification. This 'ethical licencing' is where

24 Feeney et al., *supra* note 23; Feeney et al., *supra* note 1.

25 Feeney et al., *supra* note 1.

26 Broad Institute, *Information about licensing CRISPR genome editing systems*, available online at https://www.broadinstitute.org/partnerships/office-strategic-alliances-and-partnering/information-about-licensing-crispr-genome-edi (accessed 30 March 2022).

institutions, researchers and companies have used their patent control over CRISPR (and related) techniques (especially in the case of fundamental patents), to create a form of private governance over some uses of genome-editing through ethical constraints built into their licensing agreements.[27] Unlike the partial, ineffective patchwork of uncoordinated and outdated regulatory and legislative systems across different jurisdictions at the international level, the patenting system has global and legally enforceable scope (through the 1994 WTO TRIPS Agreement).

While ethical licencing may be a welcome initiative (at least on the face of it), there are significant, and possibly insurmountable, challenges to relying on it as an alternative form of regulation, in place of the more traditional political-legal systems of regulation. Firstly, there is the issue of wider coordination difficulties and likely disagreements between different private actors (in different jurisdictions). There are issues over how long such ethical stances last — particularly over time in a private arena where profitability, for instance, is an alternative and competing value. Without meaning to insinuate ulterior motives underpinning current examples of ethical licencing, there is also the problematic issue of self-regulation by the patent holders over their own research and commercial activities. The actual practice, which may change over time one way or the other and would be the result of the decisions by a few powerful groups, in addition to other powerful entities/commercial companies, would seem insufficient from a social justice perspective not to require some additional controls over this patent-permitted system.[28]

3 Forming a Realistic Non-Ideal Response

Given the range of potential benefits and social justice issues that may be involved, the current, and the most likely future trajectories of genome editing techniques and the patent-based regulatory system surrounding them, will raise questions of to what degree they are, or can be, justifiable with regard to social justice concerns. As argued elsewhere, the moral justification of patents — and the supporting ethical arguments — are problematic.[29] The search for a moral justification of patents in the field of biotechnology is not

27 C. Guerrini, M.A. Curnutte, J.S. Sherkow and C.T. Scott, 'The rise of the ethical license', *Nature Biotechnology* 35 (2017) 22–24.

28 Feeney et al., *supra* note 23; Feeney et al., *supra* note 1.

29 S. Sterckx, 'The Moral Justifiability of Patents', *Ethical Perspectives* 13 (2) (2006) 249–265; Feeney et al., *supra* note 1.

only to assess existing practices to see if they are justifiable or not; it is, importantly, to offer guidance as to the measures that would have to be taken if such justification was to be forthcoming.

Whatever moral justification that would be advanced would have to be reasonably realistic in terms of its requirements and the guidance to achieve this. If such moral guidance is too far in the realm of ideal theory (or, to be more pointed, if it is too idealised) and if the moral demands ask too much of people in the 'real world' (and not just people, but research institutions, companies, etc) — it would risk, as Mason notes, turning into wishful thinking:[30] injustice would effectively become misfortune; social justice recommendations into empty slogans. If, as John Dunn argues, the purpose of political theory is to diagnose practical predicaments while also identifying the best ways to confront them, this cannot be from an idealized perspective but rather political theorists must take as fundamental the more restraining perspective of where we currently are.[31]

In recent years, the approach known as non-ideal theory has been growing in relevance in the context of normative approaches to addressing environmental and migration issues. In the context of emerging, and increasingly significant in predicted societal impact, developments in biotechnology and genetics, Colin Farrelly has been the leading non-ideal normative theorist and who has advanced a particular response that is defined by seeking to encourage the further development of biotechnology in a manner that addresses the social justice challenges insofar that is realistically achievable in the broader contemporary context.[32] In short, what would seem needed would be a social justice approach that would offer a morally justifiable form of patent or patent system/practice that is reasonably achievable, with realistic guidance, from the current 'real-world' context.

Farrelly takes the following non-ideal assumptions to form parameters to the biotechnological context and related social justice responses:[33] whatever

30 A. Mason, 'Just Constraints', *British Journal of Political Science* 34 (2004) 251–268, p. 253.

31 J. Dunn, *Interpreting Political Responsibility* (Cambridge: Cambridge University Press, 1990), p. 193.

32 Farrelly, *supra* note 3; C. Farrelly, 'Genetic Justice Must Track Genetic Complexity', *Cambridge Quarterly of Healthcare Ethics* 17 (2008) 45–53; C. Farrelly, 'Gene Patents and Justice', *The Journal of Value Inquiry* 41 (2007) 147–163; C. Farrelly, 'Justice in Ideal Theory: A Refutation', *Political Studies* 55 (4) (2007) 844–864; C. Farrelly, 'The Genetic Difference Principle', *The American Journal of Bioethics* 4 (2) (2004) W21–W28; Farrelly, *supra* note 8.

33 Farrelly, *supra* note 3, pp. 199–200. Farrelly uses the phrase 'gene patents' which would be dated and oddly narrow if referring to patents on gene sequences. A more appropriate interpretation of Farrelly's gene patents — which would still be true to the spirit of the argument — would be patents on genetic processes, methods, products, interventions, tools, research and so on.

the benefits that new genetic technologies could hold for people, including the socially disadvantaged, in terms of health, avoidance of disability and related improved life chances, such benefits are:

(a) not certain given (i) the multiplicity of non-genetic factors affecting well-being, even if the appropriate genetic treatments (or associated 'tools' and research) were developed and (ii) it is not certain which genetic developments will arise (whether appropriate treatments will actually be pursued, or achieved, or, if both, to what level of efficiency, etc).

(b) likely to be costly (at minimum, relatively costlier on balance than the other costs of social justice-related commitments that the public budget could be directed toward) and would require a huge investment, thereby requiring private investment to be buttressed, by

(c) pursuing an overall flexible regulatory framework that would be defined by being a form of pluralist prioritarianism (lax genetic/biological difference principle — lax GDP/BDP)[34] which would hold a 'conditional' moral presumption in favour of patents that satisfy a stringent utility requirement.

Farrelly explains this *conditional moral presumption in favour of patents that satisfy a stringent utility requirement*, as entailing a twofold condition. Firstly, any specific application for patents should satisfy the legal criteria for patentable material (e.g. novelty, usefulness, non-obviousness[35]) and, secondly, there is only a presumption in favour of 'gene patents' *if and when* permitting the private appropriation is actually efficient in speeding up the 'arrival of safe and effective genetic interventions'.[36] For instance, if after due consideration, given patents contributed to an anticommons situation, the relevant legislators should intervene to eliminate such inefficiencies[37]

While Farrelly only refers to the anticommons argument in general, such inefficiencies can also be seen to include the phenomena of royalty stacking, evergreening and so on. While 'costs' (for instance, the final costs to the

34 As noted above in the Introduction.

35 Or, according to EPC and TRIPS terminology, novelty, inventive step and industrial application (Article 27 TRIPS Agreement; Article 52 (1) EPC).

36 Farrelly, *supra* note 3, pp. 199–200.

37 Farrelly, *supra* note 3, p. 200, further specifies the 'stringent utility requirement of gene patents' by referring to the US PTO 1999 guidelines that "investors must state definite, specific and plausible uses for the sequences of DNA they plan to patent." As noted in note 32 above, it would seem necessary, but justifiable, to refine the notion of 'gene patents' that Farrelly is using and to view such sentences in terms of the broader point that they make. To contribute to the speeding up of biological developments, Farrelly also notes the role of legislative activism (he seems to approve of the Bayh-Dole Act in this regard, with some fine tuning), governments role in 'marching in' rights to get certain technologies developed and commercialised.

end-user) is largely used here, this is shorthand for the collection of problems that may arise, as noted in the previous section: for instance, it would not only be concerned with raising monetary costs, thereby restricting access and the consequences for health and life itself. Such costs also include wider knock-on effects from inequalities of health access, to inequality of health and inequalities of opportunities that would follow in the person's life.

In this respect, it would also risk a permanent magnification of an economic inequality that causes perpetuation of (relatively) lower living conditions more widely, not just within society, but between global societies. This risks a further exacerbation of the dependant development, or underdevelopment, of developing countries with regard to developed nations likely to encompass the main CRISPR (or related) innovations. These costs also include a version of the opportunity costs as used in economics where the agenda is set by the main players, with less profitable research reduced in focus (regardless of its true impact) as well as possible reduction in novel research directions by a fear that such patents will become more strictly enforced and thereby begin to adversely scientific research.

Overall, Farrelly seeks to justify patents but with a reasonable limitation that should be imposed if required by the lax GDP/BDP. We can situate this within the following classification of social justice approaches:

(a) The moral justification and guidance is so weak that it justifies things as they are.
(b) The moral justification and guidance is too strong that it falls back into ideal theory
(c) The moral justification and guidance would need to offer a morally justifiable form of patent or patent system/practice that is reasonably achievable, with realistic guidance, from the current 'real-world' context.

4 Defining a Reasonable Limitation?

To illustrate what would seem an appropriate test case for Farrelly's approach, it might be instructive to look to a recent empirical study into the justification for the current high prices of new cancer drugs in the US context[38] which might also give some indications for the broader context of the (potential)

38 V. Prasad and S. Mailankody, 'Research and Development Spending to Bring a Single Cancer Drug to Market and Revenues after Approval', *Journal of the American Medical Association Internal Medicine* 177(2017) 1569–1577, doi: 10.1001/jamainternmed.2017.3601.

treatments under consideration in this chapter.[39] In their widely publicised analysis of 10 pharmaceutical firms, the Tufts Centre for the Study of Drug Development stated that it cost approximately 2.7 billion USD to bring a single cancer drug to the US market. This is compared to the 'Public Citizen' analysis which gives the lower figure of 320 million USD (2017: E2).[40] The difference is notable while the resulting end costs are growing, where each drug is regularly priced between 100 000 and 200 000 USD.[41]

Prasad and Mailankody noted that "one persistent argument in justification of high drug prices is the sizable outlay made by biopharmaceutical firms to develop new drugs."[42] The author's method, seeking to find a more accurate estimation of development costs, including cost of failure, permitted the examination of a single drug (in most cases, an orphan drug) that was FDA approved in the case of each company and found that the median cost per drug was 648 million USD with the mean cost as 719.8 million USD.[43] Of the ten cases Prasad and Mailankody examined, nine had higher revenues compared to research and development costs and this amounted to an overall conclusion of total spending on development to be 9 billion USD with the total revenue to date as 67 billion USD.[44] The authors anticipated the upward trend in revenue would continue for some years as all 10 drugs were currently protected by patents or another form of market exclusivity.[45]

To what degree the overall costs are protected by patents (it could be assumed that they play a significant role), the above may highlight what would be a reasonable level of patent protection — it would be enough to cover the likely development costs outlined above and this figure would need to be identified as best as possible. In any case, the difference between this approximate figure and the final cost seems too dramatic to be permitted by Farrelly's approach. Even in the case of commercial entities, a Farrelly-endorsed patent system would likely permit some amount that would still take into account some level of commercial profit that is more than the likely development costs

39 At least relevant for the significant US market for CRISPR. The authors also note how they had a small sample and how the focus on cancer could not be extrapolated to treatments for every disease due to disease-related differences in drug development difficulties, as between cancer and Alzheimer's Disease (Prasad and Mailankody, *supra* note 37, pp. 1573–1574).

40 Different methodologies were used.

41 Prasad and Mailankody, *supra* note 38, p. 1570.

42 *Ibid.*

43 Prasad and Mailankody, *supra* note 38, pp. 1570–1571.

44 Prasad and Mailankody, *supra* note 38, pp. 1572.

45 Prasad and Mailankody, *supra* note 38, p. 1573, also noted how significant returns were possible despite incredibly small market shares.

but far lower than the aforementioned actual costs to the end-users, such as patients, hospitals and insurance companies. Turning to the CRISPR situation, a Farrelly-endorsed patent system would seem to require a much lower figure (or much less patent protection) given the relative inexpensiveness of the development and application of the CRISPR technology.

Returning to the apparent commitments (however they will eventually transpire) of Broad and Editas above, the more they pursue the non-exclusivity in research, tools and reagents sales, the more justifiable they would seem to be. In terms of human therapeutics, the argument for exclusive rights seems to use a similar justification as Farrelly uses and could be similarly held to account in the non-ideal approach. Insofar as the inclusive innovation model was the goal, it would also seem justifiable in this regard. While the rhetoric is to be seen translating into reality, there seems a prima facie case where a non-ideal approach, such as Farrelly's, could be a form of useful lens to assess adherence to non-ideal justice and to offer guidance as to better approximate it.

Within the non-ideal approach, the secondary step is to offer guidance as to how to get to a situation that is desired or argued to be a 'just' situation. If the approach is too weak — and it was satisfied with the prospect of some benefits at some stage from the existing patenting system — then it simply leaves things as they are (a). If it — as it appears to — require significant reductions in costs to patients, including the extent of protection[46] offered under the current patent system, then it risks being too ideal (b). How do we get to, and how do we even identify, the conditions for (c)?[47] To this end, perhaps we can also incorporate a version of a Senian insight with the modest approach to incremental improvements in achieving social justice — of two realistic (or actual) scenarios, the one that is more just should be pursued (not the most ideal).[48] The level of difference between income generated from the patents and the actual development costs is the degree that the level of patent protection could be challenged in terms of Farrelly's approach.

Notwithstanding the ambiguous assessments of how limited the resulting spread and uses of the technologies actually was due to patent protections, it could be predicted that the spread would be wider, quicker and with less costs to the final-users if there was less patent protection. While it would still need

46 Where 'extent of protection' could be interpreted as reduction of years of patent control, reducing patent scope, replacing patents with alternative incentives, complement patents with alternative incentives, or a mix of the aforementioned.

47 The moral justification and guidance would need to offer a morally justifiable form of patent or patent system/practice that is reasonably achievable, with realistic guidance, from the current 'real-world' context.

48 A. Sen, *The Idea of Justice* (Cambridge, MA: Harvard University Press, 2009).

to be seen how this level would be calculated, and how realistic it would be to get there, we could still perhaps see one realistic step. Recalling the rhetoric of Broad and Editas, perhaps this is an achievable, minimal, marker to pursue in terms of a non-ideal social justice approach.

5 The Slippery Slope of Norms

There is another (more problematic) non-ideal interpretation that could be taken out of Farrelly's approach to patents that would not just be guided by seeking to minimise the difference between the final costs and related issues and the approximate/actual costs of development (of contemporary and emerging genome editing techniques). Given the overarching market economy, and the possible increasing likelihood that such a non-ideal proposal would be arising in an era and in a wider context already marked much more by commercial activities and norms, including in the academic setting,[49] a more 'realistic' non-ideal approach might have to take account not just of the actual R&D costs involved, but also, as I propose:

> (d) The moral justification and guidance would need to offer a morally justifiable form of patent or patent system/practice that is reasonably achievable, with realistic guidance, from the current 'real-world' context and given the likelihood that the best placed entities who have the power to pursue such development are those whose profit motivations 'as they are' must be taken into account or even as parameters (and the starting point with which one must give realistic guidance from).

This would seem to reduce the scope of the possibilities of much progress from non-ideal theory, or an approach such as Farrelly's, perhaps with some minimal exceptions. If this (Farrelly, or similar non-ideal approaches) is the most promising normative theoretical position to take to the social justice issues of new biotechnological developments of immense societal impact as may be the case with CRISPR (and related techniques), it may be a pessimistic point to reach. This would be further pessimistic if we were to view the possibility that norms and motivations are constantly changing and may be fostered in one way or the other by policy decisions. In Richard Titmuss' examination of the motivations behind blood donations, it was observed that the decision to use explicit incentives to encourage blood donation had the perverse effect of

49 Guerrini et al., *supra* note 27.

reducing the pre-existing altruistic motivations to do so.[50] Perhaps the trajectory and policy decisions in the case of academic patents could be seen in a similar light.

In an ideal collaborative world, patents would not be necessary. However, the world isn't ideal and some technologies are so expensive to develop that business won't invest unless some IPR protection is granted. The Cohen-Boyer patents and the licensing programme pursued by Stanford University, has been hailed as one of the most successful university technology transfer cases.[51] A key reason behind Stanford's decision to patent and license the powerful, and commercially viable, new technology was, as Cook-Deegan and Heaney[52] note, to act as a spur for innovation and a source of university income. Stanford's then Vice President for public affairs, Robert Rosenzweig, highlighted the difficulties of private university funding that would likely persist for the future and which would encourage the pursuit of the significant income from exploiting technological developments such as rDNA.[53] If one was to start with the *ideal* of Robert Merton's view of science as a collaborative enterprise, one might wish to minimise the need for the patent system in the first place[54] and any move away from this ideal would create ethical and social (and likely social justice) problems. One might question whether this view can ever fully be the case, or if, within the broader contemporary world, it is appropriate or relevant.

Nevertheless, it would be incorrect to suggest that the Cohen-Boyer patents and the licensing programme Stanford pursued necessarily had problematic negative implications for the ideal of science collaboration and the role of academic institutions in this regard (in effect, replacing an academic model of scientific collaboration with a more profit driven private commercial model). Robert Rosenzweig's positive view of encouraging the pursuit of income from new technological innovations developed within his institution had the

50 R. Titmuss, *The Gift Relationship: From Human Blood to Social Policy* (New York, NY: Pantheon Books, 1971).

51 M.P. Feldman, A. Colaianni and C. Liu. 'Lessons from the Commercialization of the Cohen-Boyer patents: The Stanford University Licensing Program', in: A. Krattiger, R.T. Mahoney, L. Nelsen, J.A. Thomson, A.B. Bennett, K. Satyanarayana, G.D. Graff, C. Fernandez and S.P. Kowalski (eds.) *Intellectual Property Management in Health and Agricultural Innovation: A Handbook of Best Practices* (Oxford: MIHR and Davis, CA: PIPRA, 2007), Chapter 17.22.

52 R. Cook-Deegan and C. Heaney, 'Patents in Genomics and Human Genetics', *Annual Review of Genomics and Human Genetics* 11 (2010) 383–425.

53 *Ibid.*

54 R.K. Merton. 'The Normative Structure of Science', in his The Sociology of Science: Theoretical and Empirical Investigations. (Chicago, IL: University of Chicago Press, 1942).

important qualifier that the pursuit would be "from activity that is legal, ethical, *and not destructive of the values of the institution.*"[55]

While Stanford University designed licences to include incentives for private investment to bring products to market and to generate revenue for the university, it did so with a public service mission in mind. Feldman et al.[56] note four goals guiding the Cohen-Boyer licence strategy: to be consistent with the university's goals of public service; to provide appropriate incentives for such technology to be commercialized for public benefit in an adequate and timely manner; to minimize the potential for biohazards; and to provide income for educational and research purposes. In short, profit was *not* Stanford's primary motive, as exemplified by their decision not to try to extend their patent coverage and not to require non-profit research institutions to take licences to pursue research using rDNA.[57]

It thus seems that Stanford behaved as one would perhaps expect where profit was not the driving factor (as opposed to collaboration) in, at least, a further four important respects: by consulting widely to build a consensus from a wide range of what one might call 'would be' competitors; by rejecting the arguments for exclusive licences from commercial respondents; by seeking transparency as opposed to the secrecy normally encountered in the patent process; and by refraining from behaving opportunistically. The resulting licence policy seems to have been partly constituted with a goal of building of long-term relationships with the licensees, while keeping licence fees to relatively modest levels.[58] Overall, one could argue that, in light of the need for investment for the development and expansion of such technologies as rDNA, and the resulting need for patent protection, while not 'ideal', Stanford's licensing policy may have reasonably balanced the problems of lack of access (to some extent, for some time, and for those unable to pay the licensing fees), on the one hand, with the encouraged spread of a valuable technology and the resulting medical and other benefits, on the other hand.

However, according to Cook-Deegan and Heaney,[59] an important aspect of the Cohen-Boyer patents was that it signalled an important shift in norms in the wider biotechnical context. Other researchers at the time were pursuing research and developing methods that could have been patented but which were not (such as the work of Gilbert and Sanger on DNA sequencing methods

55 Cook-Deegan and Heaney, *supra* note 52, emphasis added.

56 Feldman et al., *supra* note 51, p. 1798.

57 Feldman et al., *supra* note 51.

58 Feldman et al., *supra* note 51, p. 1799.

59 Cook-Deegan and Heaney, *supra* note 52.

and Bolivar and Rodriguez's work on the Pbr322 plasmid). There was an academic reluctance, also expressed by Cohen, to patent scientific techniques as it would run counter to the prevailing norms where pure university science (quest for truth) and commercial industry (quest for profit) should not mix.[60]

To whatever degree that the shift in norms would have an impact on future decisions regarding patents, and consequently whatever impact such patents had on access to the relevant biotechnological developments, would need to be considered. While the Bayh-Dole Act (1980)[61] — which allowed US universities to pursue ownership of inventions developed using US federal funds — came into effect after the Cohen-Boyer patents, Cook-Deegan and Heaney noted that it was less a "cause of a revolution [in the world of patents and universities] and more a codification of emerging practices"[62] such as in the Stanford case.[63]

Perhaps the Stanford decision was an example of an emerging practice that also contributed to this rise. While the 'shift' risks being overblown, Lee notes that through "a long (and still ongoing) process of norm contestation, academic culture has become much more receptive to exclusive rights and the commercial exploitation of scientific knowledge."[64] With regard to the emergence of the centrality of patents — whether exemplified by Cohen-Boyer, or codified by Bayh-Dole — the important question is to what degree does this move a significant group of actors (e.g. academics, scientists and inventors) into a more commercial setting (with its own norms and priorities) or into a setting with commercial-like use of patents/licencing/enforcement and to what degree does this increase issues of social justice in so doing.

Again, it should be noted that this is not to state that the commercial setting is to be equated with a setting of social injustice, nor to say that commercial actors are not concerned about issues of social justice as well as wider ethical issues. For instance, as long as international regulation efforts in the

---

60 Feldman et al., *supra* note 50.

61 Policymakers "began to question the linear theory of technological advance that largely segregated upstream academic research from downstream commercialization. A consensus emerged that knowledge flow between academic science and industry is bidirectional and that innovation was best served by collaborative relationships spanning the "triple helix" of government, academia, and industry. As a result, federal science policy began to focus more on downstream research, technology transfer, and commercialization." See P. Lee, 'Patents and the University', *Duke Law Journal* 63 (1) (2013) 1–87, p. 30 — thinking which Lee saw as culminating in the Bayh-Dole Act (The Bayh–Dole Act or Patent and Trademark Law Amendments Act (Pub. L. 96–517, December 12, 1980)).

62 Cook-Deegan and Heaney, *supra* note 52.

63 The authors may be referring specifically to non-government funded research here.

64 Lee, *supra* note 61, p. 36.

political realm continue to underwhelm,[65] the ethical licensing efforts of the likes of Broad/Editas is not to be dismissed. Such voluntary initiatives, as well as the aforementioned cases of ethical licencing, highlight the potential for the commercial setting to act, and propose to act, in ethically sound ways. However, some examples such as these do not represent every commercial entity and it would be wilfully ignorant to have viewed the commercial setting as one with a greater history of social justice rather than the cause of social injustice. It would be naïve to expect such voluntary, and noble, instances of moral actions to simply become the dominant form of action in an unregulated commercial context in the future.[66]

6 Conclusion

Farrelly's justification of patents is problematic on a number of levels. If he, as he seems to, advocates patents 'as is', it is not evident that the incentive argument will apply for some very significant, and broad/foundational, developments, such as CRISPR-Cas9 and other emerging genome editing techniques. In fact, if we also invoke his positive appraisal of the Bayh-Dole Act, his approach might actually be counter-productive. In other words, the very fact of Bayh-Dole patents (including their contribution to promoting wasteful inter-university competition) may be the very thing raising the costs and subsequent inequalities, not reducing them.

Socially, just patents would be those that would speed up the arrival of safe and effective interventions (for all/least advantaged) or, at least, not contribute to slowing them down (or making them more expensive). Alternatively, if we take the spirit of Farrelly's argument, perhaps it can be used to re-assess such assumptions within a non-ideal social justice frame with a focus on giving a workable guide in policy terms (not ideal theory).

Farrelly's rationale may not justify the forms of patent protection that he envisioned but it may offer some framework — combined with Sen's modest approach — to assessing the level of moral justifiability of different patenting approaches and licencing strategies that are realistic.[67] For instance, non-exclusive licencing within relatively narrow patent scopes would seem more

65 Nordberg et al., *supra* note 11.

66 Feeney et al., *supra* note 23.

67 While a more comprehensive examination is beyond the scope of this chapter it should be noted that this social justice-political philosophical framework is not the only framework that can be taken regarding 'patents in the real world' (legal theory, for instance, may take a different approach).

promising than exclusive licencing and broad patents to this end. Whatever the approach, it would also be necessary to keep in mind how legal changes may affect norms over time, considering Cohen-Boyer's non-exclusive, collaborative, public mission approach to Bayh-Dole and to ongoing developments and trends arising from the legacy of the recent infamous CRISPR-Cas9 patent dispute.

Acknowledgements

The idea for this chapter initially arose from discussions during a research visit with Prof. Sigrid Sterckx and Dr Julian Cockbain at the Bioethics Institute Ghent. I wish to thank them for fostering my research in this area, and, in particular, to thank Dr Cockbain and Dr Ana Nordberg for their very helpful comments on a previous version of this chapter. This work is supported by the Hans Gottschalk-Stiftung.

Balancing Innovation, '*Ordre Public*' and Morality in Human Germline Editing: A Call for More Nuanced Approaches in Patent Law

Duncan Matthews | ORCID: 0000-0002-8585-0711
Queen Mary Intellectual Property Research Institute (QMIPRI), Queen Mary University of London, 67–69 Lincoln's Inn Fields, London WC2A 3JB, UK
Corresponding author, e-mail: d.n.matthews@qmul.ac.uk

Timo Minssen | ORCID: 0000-0002-3286-4888
Centre for Advanced Studies in Biomedical Innovation Law (CeBIL), University of Copenhagen, Karen Blixens Plads 16, DK-2300 Copenhagen S, Denmark
timo.minssen@jur.ku.dk

Ana Nordberg | ORCID: 0000-0002-3009-1033
Faculty of Law, Lund University, Lilla Gråbrödersgatan 4–6, Lund, Sweden
ana.nordberg@jur.lu.se

Abstract

This chapter analyses the role that '*ordre public*' and morality exceptions can play in the granting of patents on inventions in the field of human germline editing and the consequences of this policy option. In order to provide the context for such an analysis, the chapter will, first, provide an overview of the current patent landscape for relevant genome editing technologies, drawing attention to recent patent disputes and, second, examine '*ordre public*' and morality exceptions under patent law in international, national and regional law, and the implications for innovation and access to novel treatments. The chapter argues that patent exceptions should not be used as a blunt policy instrument, nor interpreted in a way that is contrary to the patent system's overall objectives. The '*ordre public*' and morality based exceptions in the context of human germline editing should not be interpreted and applied in a way which results in outcomes counterproductive to the goal of balancing innovation with the protection of societal higher normative values. Instead, the application of the exception should be based on a sound understanding of both the underlying science as well as the broader ethical, social, and legal implications, thus enabling case-by-case decisions that provide the basis for patent claim amendments and nuanced purpose-bound protection.

 | DOI:10.1163/9789004526136_013

Further analysis and debate as to the role that such flexibilities can play in the context of genome editing technologies is therefore both necessary and desirable, and can be facilitated in the ways set out in this chapter.

Keywords

patent law – morality exception – genome editing – genome editing governance – law and ethics – CRISPR

1 Introduction

Genome editing technologies hold great potential for scientific research and society. Compared with previous technologies, they provide fast, efficient, precise, and relatively inexpensive tools to modify the cells of any living organism. Using genome editing techniques, cells of the body (somatic cells) can be modified, treating or potentially curing patients of chronic, lifelong illnesses. Editing the genome of human embryos can also repair the germline of human beings, eradicating hereditary diseases in new-born babies such as Duchenne muscular dystrophy, Huntington's Disease, beta thalassaemia and cystic fibrosis and creating resistance to life-threatening conditions for future generations.[1]

Genome editing offers bio-scientists a relatively simple tool to change any organism's deoxyribonucleic acid (DNA). This allows genetic material to be added, removed, or altered in particular locations in the genome. Several clinical trials have or are being conducted around the globe offering great hope for patients so far having very limited treatment options.[2]

---

1 For Duchenne muscular dystrophy see E.N. Olson, 'Toward the correction of muscular dystrophy by gene editing', *Proceedings of the National Academy of Sciences of the United States of America* 118 (22) (2021) e2004840117, https://doi.org/10.1073/pnas.2004840117; for cystic fybrosis, see G. Maule, D. Arosio and A. Cereseto, 'Gene Therapy for Cystic Fibrosis: Progress and Challenges of Genome Editing', *International Journal of Molecular Science* 21 (11) (2020) 3903, https://doi:10.3390/ijms21113903; for Huntington's Disease see T. Biswas, 'CRISPR in Huntington's Disease: Progress and Possibilities for Future Cure', *Synthego* (13 May 2021), available online at https://www.synthego.com/blog/crispr-in-huntingtons-disease.

2 For some examples of clinical trials see: H. Henderson, *CRISPR Clinical Trials: A 2021 Update* (3 March 2021), available online at https://innovativegenomics.org/news/crispr-clinical-trials-2021/.

The most commonly used genome editing techniques are zinc finger nucleases (ZFNs), transcription activator-like effector nucleases (TALENs) and Clustered Regularly Interspaced Short Palindromic Repeats (CRISPR). Each represents a type of engineered nuclease that can be used to recognise, bind, and cleave a specific sequence in the genome. In order to do so, ZFNs and TALENs require the creation of a custom protein for each targeted DNA sequence. Whereas ZFNs and TALENs are entirely protein based, CRISPR has both protein and ribonucleic acid (RNA) components, making it a simpler and less time-consuming process than ZFNs and TALENs CRISPR because the process requires only a short RNA sequence. More recently, new promising technologies, such as Rerotron Library Recombineering (RLR) have also emerged.[3]

Since 2012, CRISPR has been used in combination with Cas9 (CRISPR associated protein number 9, which plays a vital role in the natural immunological defence system of the body) to guide and cut DNA, and therefore editing a cell's genome. The CRISPR-Cas9 techniques, as well as follow-on technologies such as CRISPR-Cas 12a and CRIPR-Cas13, have provided a faster, cheaper, more accurate and more efficient method than other previously known genome editing techniques.[4] Yet, safety risks, ethical concerns and IP battles regarding the commercial control over the technology have also emerged due to the far-reaching implications and applications of the technology. Hence, genome editing also raises new challenges in terms of how governance systems regulate technologies.

This chapter argues that international organisations, policy makers and legislators need to pay greater consideration to the interface between patent policy, ethics, regulation and the governance of genome editing. Such consideration is crucial since the regulation of genome editing involves the critical public policy imperatives of avoiding unnecessary collective or individual risks, taking into account human rights, managing public expectations, ensuring fair and equitable access to the benefits of these new technologies' use, and acting in the public interest with regard to these potentially transformational healthcare technologies.

---

3 M.G. Schubert, D.B. Goodman, T.M. Wannier, D. Kaur, F. Farzadfard, T.K. Lu, S.L. Shipman and G.M. Church, 'High-throughput functional variant screens via in vivo production of single-stranded DNA', *Proceedings of the National Academy of Sciences of the United States of America* 118 (18) (2021) e2018181118, https://doi.org/10.1073/pnas.2018181118.

4 See also National Institutes of Health (NIH), *US. National Library of Medicine, 'Your Guide to Understanding Genetic Conditions: What Are Genome Editing and CRISPR-Cas9?'*, available online at https://ghr.nlm.nih.gov/primer/genomicresearch/genomeediting (accessed 30 March 2022).

On 12 July 2021 the World Health Organization (WHO) Expert Advisory Committee on Developing Global Standards for Governance and Oversight of Human Genome Editing published a set of reports entitled *Human Genome Editing: A Framework for Governance and Recommendations*.[5] The Expert Advisory Committee's *A Framework for Governance* highlights explicitly the role that patents and licences may play as an avenue for a form of governance of human genome editing. However, absent from the WHO Expert Advisory Committee's reports was either substantive discussion or recommendations on the role that morality exceptions can play in the granting of patents on certain inventions and the consequences of this policy option.

In collaboration with an international group of renowned patent law scholars, we published a response to the WHO Expert Advisory Committee's findings on 30 July 2021 and made explicit our recommendation, inter alia, that further consideration of the extent to which '*ordre public*' and morality exceptions in patent law impact on the sector.[6] In our research group's response, we have already highlighted the need for public debate and stated that it is a particularly important consideration for countries considering introducing or developing further guidance on the use of '*ordre public*' and morality exceptions to patentability in the area of genome editing. In this chapter we build on our previous response to the WHO Expert Advisory Committee's reports, undertaken with our colleagues, and propose a pragmatic way forward by way of our new and original contribution to the policy debate.

While it should be acknowledged that many of the issues considered in this chapter apply equally to somatic therapeutic uses (the cells of the body that are not involved in reproduction) and to agricultural or fisheries food production, human germline applications will remain the chapter's primary focus. We focus primarily on '*ordre public*' and morality issues concerning human germline editing, since in our view this specific application of genome editing technologies accords most closely and immediately with concerns about the patent policy implications in terms of the impacts on society outlined above.

Based on the premise that the patent system is an integral part of how governance systems regulate technologies, we believe that patent policy needs to

5 WHO Expert Advisory Committee on Developing Global Standards for Governance and Oversight of Human Genome Editing, *Human Genome Editing: A Framework for Governance* (2021), available online at www.who.int/publications/i/item/9789240030060, iii (accessed 23 July 2021).

6 D. Matthews, A. Brown, E. Gambini, T. Minssen, A. Nordberg, J.S. Sherkow, J. Wested, E. van Zimmeren and A. McMahon, 'The Role of Patents and Licensing in the Governance of Human Genome Editing: A White Paper', *Queen Mary Law Research Paper No. 364/2021* (30 July 2021), available online at SSRN: https://ssrn.com/abstract=3896308.

be considered carefully whenever regulation of genome editing is being scrutinised. In essence, governance through patents contains three major discussions: first, whether patents should be granted to certain inventions; second, how to guarantee ethical exploitation of patent rights; and, third, the interface between the enjoyment of patent rights to reward innovation and a fair and equitable access to technologies.

This chapter focuses on the first of these discussions, and in particular the role that morality exceptions can play in the granting of patents on certain inventions and the consequences of this policy option. In order to provide the context for such an analysis, the chapter will, first, provide a contextualising overview of the current patent landscape for relevant genome editing technologies, and highlight recent patent disputes. Then, we examine the extent of '*ordre public*' and morality exceptions under the TRIPS Agreement and national/regional patent law, and the implications for innovation and access to novel treatments. It is followed by a discussion of the actual and potential impact of such provisions on the governance of genome edition technologies. We will also carve out potential avenues of how to deal with these dynamics in the future. This will allow us to draw policy conclusions.

2 The Current Patent Landscape for CRISPR Gene Editing Technologies

Right holders may assert their patent rights, i.e. negative exclusionary rights, in different ways and in accordance with applicable regulations and standards. Their strategy will depend on a range of factors, such as the ambitions and goals of rights holders, the nature and applications of the patented technology, the competitive environment, as well as the scope, significance and validity of relevant exclusivities.[7] So far, hundreds of patents, directed to genome editing technologies, have been granted by patent offices across the world, with many more applications still under examination.[8]

Moreover, many pending patent litigations and disputes over different aspects of genome editing technologies are currently unresolved, which has resulted in considerable legal uncertainty. In addition, it is important to note

7 Note that exclusivities may be protected and enforced through other forms of IP which may affect patent strategies.

8 See D. Kwon, *A Brief Guide to the Current CRISPR Landscape*, available online at www.the-scientist.com/news-opinion/a-brief-guide-to-the-current-crispr-landscape-66128 (accessed 27 July 2021).

that patents are also sought for other genome editing technologies, including meganucleases, ZFNs, TALENs, and fundamental gene editing tools, such as genome editing vectors.[9] This complexity resulted in a rich diversity of patents and models of technology transfer, but it has also resulted in competitive struggles over the control of the technologies at both the pre-grant and post-grant level.[10]

Against this background, any discussion regarding the role of patents in genome editing governance must carefully consider the rapidly evolving patent landscape, including information of the prevalent forms of patents claims, licensing models, patentees and regional differences around the globe. It is therefore important to continuously monitor the outcome of patent litigations and regulatory developments.

Several landscaping studies have been conducted in the area, mostly focusing on patents and revealing substantial global differences across the genome editing technology landscape.[11] A common finding appears to be that the number of patents and patent applications, the procedures for patent prosecution, as well as the question of patent ownership and the licensing of gene editing technologies, such as CRISPR, varies considerably in various patent systems. Accordingly, what can be claimed as patentable and on which terms — if at all — human genome editing technologies are licensed can differ across regions.[12]

Concerning the situation in the US, studies of patent data highlight fierce competition not only in CRISPR-related science, but also in the race to the patent office between the main academic rivals, i.e., the Broad Institute (of Harvard University and the Massachusetts Institute of Technology — MIT), which is the home institution of Feng Zhang et al., and the University of

9 For more details and a good overview of these technologies, see G.D. Graff and J.S. Sherkow, 'Models of Technology Transfer for Genome-Editing Technologies', *Annual Review of Genomics and Human Genetics* 21 (1) (2020) 509–534.

10 *Ibid.*

11 See, e.g., '2020 CRISPR Patent Landscape — Where Do We Stand?', *IPStudies*, available online at www.ipstudies.ch/2020/10/2020-crispr-patent-landscape-where-do-we-stand/ (accessed 27 July 2021); P. Ghosh, 'Patent Landscape of CRISPR/Cas', in: A. Bhattacharya, V. Parkhi and B. Char (eds.), *CRISPR/Cas Genome Editing. Concepts and Strategies in Plant Sciences* (Berlin: Springer, 2020), pp. 213–220; J. Martin-Laffon, M. Kuntz and A.E. Ricroch, 'Worldwide CRISPR Patent Landscape Shows Strong Geographical Biases', *Nature Biotechnology* 37 (6) (2019) 613–620; J.S. Sherkow, 'The CRISPR Patent Landscape: Past, Present, and Future', *CRISPR Journal* 1 (1) (2018) 5–9; see WIPO, 'Patent Landscape Reports by Other Organizations', available online at www.wipo.int/patentscope/en/programs/patent_landscapes/plrdb_search.jsp?territory_code=CH (accessed 27 July 2021).

12 *Ibid.*, '2020 CRISPR Patent Landscape — Where Do We Stand?'.

California, which employs Jennifer Doudna.[13] Furthermore, the datasets confirm that "both license their core CRISPR technology IP to a number of large industrial players, such as DuPont in agricultural applications, as well as to a set of pioneering CRISPR spin-offs primarily heading for therapeutic applications, namely Editas Medicine out from the Broad Institute, CRISPR Therapeutics initially founded by Emmanuelle Charpentier, and Intellia Therapeutics out from the University of California."[14]

3 Patent Battles in the US and Europe

Genome editing technologies have been subject to considerable and ongoing patent litigation concerning the ownership of such technologies. As a result, a highly contested global patent landscape has emerged, characterized by a considerable lack of legal certainty. The main dispute in this context in the United States (US) and Europe, relates to patent claims over CRISPR Cas-9 technologies asserted by University of California (UC) Berkeley (where Prof Doudna's team worked, and in collaboration with Prof Charpentier, now at Max Planck), and Broad Institute MIT and Harvard (involving a research team led by Prof Feng Zhang). While the ongoing patent battles over claims directed to CRISPR-Cas9 technology within the European and US patent system have probably attracted most attention, disputes over these patents are also raging in other countries and regions such as Asia and South America.[15] Many of these disputes have evolved around the issues of priority[16] and the novelty requirements. These proceedings are often inter-related and they are monitored carefully around the globe, since decisions on priority claims in e.g. the US or European patent systems, often have a significant effect on the outcomes in pending litigations in other countries.[17] In our previous paper, written with colleagues in response to the WHO Expert Advisory Committee on Developing

13 *Ibid.*

14 *Ibid.* For a discussion of the problems related to this complex licensing landscape see V.M. de Grandpré and F. Lozon, 'Making Sense of the Battle for the CRISPR-Cas9 Patent Rights', *Osler* (15 March 2021), available online at www.osler.com/en/resources/critical-situations/2021/making-sense-of-the-battle-for-the-crispr-cas9-patent-rights (accessed 27 July 2021).

15 See, e.g., J.A. Tessensohn, 'Japanese CRISPR Patent and Biotech Developments in the Early Reiwa Era' *Biotechnology Law Report* 40 (3) (2021) 242–273.

16 For further explanation see V. Lin, 'What Is a Patent Priority Claim?', *Patent Trademark Blog/IP Q&A*, available online at www.patenttrademarkblog.com/patent-priority-claim/ (accessed 27 July 2021).

17 See de Grandpré and Lozon, *supra* note 14.

Global Standards for Governance and Oversight of Human Genome Editing, we describe these recent developments in patent litigation in some detail. This trend for litigation continues, most recently in the dispute at the United States Patent and Trademark Office (USPTO) Patent Trial and Appeal Board (PTAB) over who invented the guide RNA molecule.[18]

4 Patent Governance through '*Ordre Public*' and Morality Exceptions

Patent rights create an exclusivity over the commercial exploitation of a given invention, but they also directly and indirectly dictate the direction of research efforts and activities. Patent laws of all countries include both some form of pre-grant limitations on what may be protected by a patent and post-grant limits to the free exercise of the rights conferred by a patent. Legal terminology may vary depending on local legal traditions, but most commonly these are enunciated in statutes, case-law and legal literature as either exclusions, exceptions or limitations.[19] Collectively these are known in legal circles as TRIPS flexibilities and allow national patent laws to contain mechanisms of public governance over technological innovation.

Pre-grant limitations can be an effective instrument for public governance, e.g., by delimiting the object, also known as subject-matter, of a patent. Pre-grant limitations also can intervene by excluding certain subject-matter from the concept of patentable invention (exclusions from patent subject-matter) or by determining that certain types of inventions cannot obtain patent protection (exceptions to the general rule of availability of patents to inventions in all fields of technology).

Post-grant measures may limit the rights conferred by a patent, by exempting certain activities (e.g., research exemptions) or persons from the scope of patent protection (e.g. liability exemptions for medical practitioners) or restricting the patent owner's contractual freedom concerning the patent as an object of property (e.g. compulsory licenses).

Post-grant limitations may exist in patent laws, but also in laws that regulate the introduction and use of a given technology in the market. Since the grant of a patent does not guarantee the possibility of commercialization, some substances may not succeed in meeting the necessary efficiency and

18 J. Cohen, New CRISPR Patent Hearing continues high-stakes legal battle, *Science* (4 February 2022), available online at https://www.science.org/content/article/new-crispr-patent-hearing-continues-high-stakes-legal-battle#.YgMGWwkTd2M.twitter.

19 When providing national or regional examples, the original terminology will be employed.

safety standards in clinical trials. Products originally approved as medicines may later in clinical practice be found to have long term side effects or provoke rare severe adverse reactions, and in such cases the market authorizations are withdrawn. Historically, some substances initially developed as medicines were later classified as illegal drugs, its sale completely prohibited or severely restricted.

Regulations in the medical and pharmaceutical sector offer several other examples of post-grant limitations to the rights conferred by a patent in order to protect public health. Most medicines can only be sold by licensed operators — pharmacies or dispensaries, and in many jurisdictions retailers are not always free to set the prices, since these are pre-negotiated between pharmaceutical companies that produced them and health authorities or insurance providers; most medicines also cannot be freely sold to customers, as a medical prescription is required. Professional standards, treatment protocols and medical deontological norms may further determine how and when drugs are prescribed (e.g. conservation rules for antibiotics).

In this chapter we focus on a specific type of pre-grant patent limitation mechanism known as the '*ordre public*' and morality exception to patentability, which may include directly or indirectly a specific prohibition of patentability of methods for human germline modification. Such pre-grant patent limitation can be found in Europe and some jurisdictions around the globe and is most relevant in the context of governance through patent law of genome editing technologies.

4.1 *Patentability Exceptions and the TRIPS Agreement*

The World Trade Organization (WTO) Agreement on Trade-Related Aspects of Intellectual Property Rights (the TRIPS Agreement) explicitly allows WTO Members, in Article 27(2) and 27(3), to exclude certain inventions from patentability if justified by, in essence, overriding societal interest.[20] These overriding societal interests include 'to protect human, animal or plant life or health or to avoid serious prejudice to the environment'.[21] Specifically, Article 27(2) permits WTO members to "exclude from patentability inventions, the prevention within their territory of the commercial exploitation of which is necessary to

20 See also UNCTAD-ICTSD Project on IPRs and Sustainable Development, *Resource Book on TRIPS and Development* (Cambridge: Cambridge University Press, 2005) 378.

21 Article 27(2) of the, World Trade Organization, Agreement on Trade-Related Aspects of Intellectual Property Rights (as amended on 23 January 2017), Annex 1C of the Marrakesh Agreement Establishing the World Trade Organization, signed in Marrakesh, Morocco on 15 April 1994 (TRIPS Agreement), available online at www.wto.org/english/docs_e/legal_e/31bis_trips_01_e.htm (accessed 27 July 2021).

protect '*ordre public*' and morality, including to protect human, animal or plant life or health or to avoid serious prejudice to the environment, provided that such exclusion is not made merely because the exploitation is prohibited by their law."

Although TRIPS does not provide for a definition of '*ordre public*' and morality, it expressly includes within this the concept the protection of life and health. In WTO Dispute Settlement Panel Report in *Canada — Patent Protection of Pharmaceutical Products*, the Panel confirmed that Article 8(1) of the TRIPS Agreement in the context of the prohibition on discrimination as to the field of technology contained in Article 27(1) of TRIPS "does not limit the ability to target certain products in dealing with certain of the important national policies referred to (in Article 8(2)). It would appear therefore, that there exists considerable scope for WTO Members to include in national legislation exclusions based on the measures necessary to protect public health ... and to promote the public interest ..." under Article 27(2) of TRIPS.[22]

However, whether such tools are the most effective remedy to specific challenges to promote good governance of a given type of technology depends on a complex array of economic and social factors. For this reason, it can be observed that some countries have a very narrow approach to some of these flexibilities, and even abstain from enacting general '*ordre public*' and morality clauses. It is a question for each member state to decide if and how to legislate in this matter, and whether to enact or develop via case-law '*ordre public*' and morality exceptions to patentability. Article 8(1) and 27(2) of the TRIPS Agreement do not impose patentability exceptions. It merely provides member states with options or flexibilities concerning patentability to be used as legislative tools to promote public policy goals and ethical regulation of technology.

Exceptions from patentability on the ground of commercial exploitation being contrary to '*ordre public*' and morality are included in some regional patent treaties. Such clauses are either directly applicable or constitute grounds for national harmonization of national patent laws of the member states of the respective regional Patent Organizations,[23] these include the protocol on Patents and Industrial Designs within the framework of the African Regional Intellectual

---

22 WTO, *Canada — Patent Protection of Pharmaceutical Products, Report of the Panel, WT/DS114/R* (17 March 2000), available online at www.wto.org/english/tratop_e/dispu_e/7428d.pdf, para. 7.92 (accessed 27 July 2021).

23 These implement and, in some cases, supplement the TRIPS Agreement including for example making use of the flexibilities allowed by Article 8 and further developed in Articles 27, 30 and 31 concerning patent exclusions, exceptions and limitations. World Trade Organization, TRIPS Agreement (as amended on 23 January 2017), Annex 1C of the Marrakesh Agreement Establishing the World Trade Organization, signed in Marrakesh,

Property Organization (ARIPO),[24] Patent Regulations under the Eurasian Patent Convention adopted by the Administrative Council of the Eurasian Patent Organization (EAPO)[25] and the European Patent Convention administered by the European Patent Organization and European Patent Office.[26]

In parallel with these harmonization efforts, the national law of a large number of WTO members (see Table 1) also contains specific '*ordre public*' and morality provisions, conceptualized in the context of local legal traditions. However, it should be emphasized that not all WTO members have implemented in their respective national patent laws' '*ordre public*' and morality exceptions, and among those that have, application and enforcement practises may vary considerably.[27] Namely, some member states specifically preclude the patentability of human germline modification (Table 2), while others do not even contain general '*ordre public*' and morality clauses.[28] Furthermore, among the large number of countries that have '*ordre public*' and morality based patentability exceptions or exclusions, many do not necessarily enforce

---

Morocco on 15 April 1994, available online at www.wto.org/english/docs_e/legal_e/31bis_trips_01_e.htm (accessed 27 July 2021).

24 Section 3, Article 10 (j), Protocol on Patents and Industrial Designs within the framework of the African Regional Intellectual Property Organization (ARIPO), adopted on 10 December 1982, at Harare (Zimbabwe), and amended by the Administrative Council of ARIPO on 11 December 1987, 27 April 1994, 28 November 1997, 26 May 1998, 26 November 1999, 30 November 2001, 21 November 2003, 24 November 2006, 25 November 2013, 17 November 2015, 5 December 2016, 22 November 2017, 23 November 2018 and 20 November 2019, available online at www.aripo.org/wp-content/uploads/2020/01/Harare-Protocol-2020-Edition-1.pdf (accessed 27 July 2021).

25 Rule 3(4), Patent Regulations under the Eurasian Patent Convention Adopted by the Administrative Council of the Eurasian Patent Organization (EAPO AC) at its second (1st ordinary) session on 1 December 1995, with the amendments and addenda adopted by EAPO AC up to its thirty-sixth (27th ordinary) session on 10–11 September 2020 (non-official English translation), available online at www.eapo.org/en/documents/norm/instr2020_eng.pdf (accessed 27 July 2021).

26 Article 53(a), Convention on the Grant of European Patents (European Patent Convention — EPC) of 5 October 1973 as revised by the Act Revising Article 63 EPC of 17 December 1991 and the Act revising the EPC of 29 November 2000.

27 T. Minssen, 'Patenting Human Genes in Europe — and How It Compares to the US and Australia', in: D. Matthews and H. Zech (eds.), *Research Handbook on Intellectual Property and the Life Sciences* (Cheltenham: Edward Elgar, 2017), Chapter 3, p. 26. See A. Nordberg and T. Minssen, 'A 'Ray of Hope' for European Stem Cell Patents or 'Out of the Smog into the Fog'?: An Analysis of Recent European Case Law and How It Compares to the US', *International Review of Intellectual Property and Competition Law* 47 (2) (2016), 138–177, DOI: 10.1007/s40319-016-0449-x.

28 WTO Standing Committee on the Law of Patents, Twelfth Session, Geneva, June 23 to 27, 2008, *Annex II of Report on the International Patent System (document SCP/12/3 Rev.2)* (status as of October 2021), available online at https://www.wipo.int/export/sites/www/scp/en/national_laws/exclusions.pdf.

them, since local patent offices do not conduct *ex oficio* substantive examinations, and thus such rules are only enforced through judicial activity.[29]

TABLE 1 Countries with national laws providing exceptions from patentability on the ground of commercial exploitation being contrary to *ordre public* or morality include:

Albania, Algeria, Andorra, Argentina, Armenia, Austria, Azerbaijan, Bahrain, Barbados, Belarus, Belgium, Belize, Bhutan, Bolivia, Bosnia and Herzegovina, Brazil, Bulgaria, Chile, the People's Republic of China, Hong Kong China, Colombia, Costa Rica, Côte d'Ivoire, Croatia, Cyprus, Czech Republic, Denmark, Dominica, Dominican Republic, Ecuador, Egypt, El Salvador, Estonia, Ethiopia, Finland, France, Georgia, Germany, Ghana, Greece, Guatemala, Hungary, Iceland, India, Indonesia, Ireland, Italy, Japan, Jordan, Kazakhstan, Kenya, Kyrgyz Republic, Latvia, Liechtenstein, Lithuania, Luxembourg, Madagascar, Malaysia, Malta, Mauritius, Mexico, Moldova, Morocco, Mozambique, Netherlands, New Zealand, Nicaragua, Nigeria, Norway, Republic of North Macedonia, Oman, Pakistan, Panama, Papua New Guinea, Paraguay, Peru, Philippines, Poland, Portugal, Republic of Korea, Romania, Russian Federation, Serbia, Singapore, Slovak Republic, Slovenia, South Africa, Spain, Sri Lanka, Sweden, Switzerland, Syrian Arab Republic, Tajikistan, Thailand, Trinidad and Tobago, Tunisia, Turkey, United Kingdom, Uruguay, Uzbekistan, Zambia.

SOURCE: WIPO STANDING COMMITTEE OF THE LAW OF PATENTS (SCP), APRIL 2020 AND DIRECT LEGAL SOURCES

TABLE 2 Countries with national laws providing specific exceptions from patentability on processes for modifying germ line identity of human beings include:

Albania, Armenia, Bosnia and Herzegovina, Croatia, Czech Republic, Denmark, Ecuador, Estonia, Finland, France, Germany, Hungary, Italy, Mexico, Moldova, Norway, New Zealand, Portugal, Russian Federation, Serbia, Slovak Republic, Spain, Sweden, Switzerland, Turkey, United Kingdom.

SOURCE: WIPO STANDING COMMITTEE OF THE LAW OF PATENTS (SCP), APRIL 2020 AND DIRECT LEGAL SOURCES

29 In general, patent offices' search and examination practices can be categorized into three types of policy options: (i) formality examination only; (ii) formality examination and prior art search; and (iii) formality examination, prior art search and substantive examination.

In the following sections we analyze patent laws in the USA and Europe as examples of two divergent patent policy options that directly affect genome editing.

4.2 *Jurisdictions without Statutory Exceptions from Patentability: Developments in the US*

As mentioned, there are several jurisdictions without explicit '*ordre public*' and morality exceptions from patentability in their laws and statutes, including the notable example of the US. Such an approach does not always mean that corresponding issues are not addressed by these patent systems. Although morality issues have been considered in the context of the US utility doctrine and claims directed to, or encompassing, human organisms are categorically excluded from patentability,[30] there are no enforceable statutory provisions in US Law directly corresponding to '*ordre public*' and morality exceptions to patentability.[31] Conversely, most jurisprudential activity concerns the determination of the boundaries of subject-matter eligibility and corresponds, in EPC terminology, to an exclusion from patentability concerning natural laws, products, phenomena or abstract ideas.[32] The US Supreme Court decision in *Diamond v. Chakrabarty* (1980)[33] clarified that whether an invention embraces living matter is irrelevant to the issue of patent eligibility, with the seminal conclusion that statutory subject matter under section 101 includes "anything under the sun that is made by man."

More recent decisions have introduced a stricter approach to patent eligibility. In *Bilski v. Kappos* (2010)[34] the Supreme Court ruled on the contested topic of the general patent eligibility of method patents. Section 101 of the US Patent Act lists the types of claims allowed in patent applications: "process, machine, manufacture, or composition of matter."[35] The Court rejected a categorical exclusion from patent eligibility of business methods (such as the

30 See: Minssen and Nordberg, *supra* note 27.

31 The HR 1249 (the so-called "America Invents Act") introduced an immediately effective ban on patents covering tax strategies and/or claims "directed to or encompassing" human organisms (see section 33). These will apply to all pending applications.

32 Historical authors refer to this approach as the "moral utility" doctrine. See M.A. Bagley, 'Patent First, Ask Questions Later: Morality and Biotechnology in Patent Law', *William and Mary Law Review* 45 (2) (2003) 469–547.

33 *Diamond v. Chakrabarty* 447 US 303 (1980); 206 USPQ 193 (The Supreme Court of the United States).

34 *Bilski v Kappos* 130 s. Ct. 3218; 177 L.Ed.2d 792 (2010).

35 35 U.S.C. para. 101, available online at https://uscode.house.gov/view.xhtml?path=/prelim@title35/part2/chapter10&edition=prelim (accessed 27 July 2021).

ones existing in Article 52 of the EPC), while also rejecting the machine-or-transformation test.

In *Mayo v. Prometheus* (2012), the US Supreme Court focused again on Section 101 and its implicit exception that excludes patents on laws of nature, natural phenomena, and abstract ideas, here concerning the question of patent eligibility of a '*medical method*'.[36] The matter was again raised in *Association for Molecular Pathology v. Myriad Genetics* (2013), concerning the controversial patents on the BRCA1 and BRCA2 genes.[37] Here the US Supreme Court decided on the patent eligibility of isolated genes concluding that a naturally occurring DNA segment was a product of nature and not patent eligible under 35 U.S.C. para. 101 merely because it was isolated, but cDNA was patent eligible because it was not naturally occurring. In *Alice Corp. v. CLS Bank International* (2014),[38] although in this case concerned a software patent,[39] the deliberations of the Supreme Court are also instructive to the patent eligibility of the pharma sector because the court discussed the boundaries between non-patentable abstract ideas and patent eligibility of implementations of ideas.

As of today, patent rules in the US do not specifically prevent the patentability of genome editing technology nor restrict patentability of modification of germ line identity of human beings. However, the abovementioned case-law illustrates how a patent system may choose to address many of the public policy concerns in a general and systematic manner through the application of patent eligibility standards. In contrast, jurisdictions such as most European

36 *Mayo Collaborative Servs. v. Prometheus Labs, Inc.*, 132 S. Ct. 1289 (2012). See Timo Minssen and David Nilsson, 'The US Supreme Court in Mayo v. Prometheus — Taking the Fire from or to Biotechnology and Personalized Medicine?', *Queen Mary Journal of Intellectual Property* 2 (4) (2012) 376–388.

37 *Association for Molecular Pathology, et al. v. Myriad Genetics, Inc.* 569 US 576, 133 S. Ct. 2107 (2013). An account of the developments leading to the Myriad decision is provided by R.M. Schwartz and T. Minssen, 'Life after Myriad: The Uncertain Future of Patenting Biomedical Innovation & Personalized Medicine in an International Context', *Intellectual Property Quarterly* 3 (2015) 189–241; E. van Zimmeren, D. Nicol and R. Gold, 'The BRCA Patent Controversies: An International Review of Patent Disputes' in S. Gibbon, G. Joseph, J. Mozersky, A. zur Nieden and S. Palfner (eds.) *Breast Cancer Gene Research and Medical Practices: Transnational Perspectives in the Time of BRCA* (London: Routledge, 2014), 151. For a discussion of the ethical issues and gene patentability in this context see A. McMahon, "Gene Patents and the Marginalisation of Ethical Issues', *European Intellectual Property Review* 41(10) (2019) 608–620.

38 *Alice Corp. v. CLS Bank International*, 573 US 208 (2014).

39 Regarding the impact of the *Alice* decision on biotechnology patents, see M. Aboy, K. Liddell, C. Crespo, I.G. Cohen, J. Liddicoat, S. Gerke and T. Minssen, 'How Does Emerging Patent Case Law in the US and Europe Affect Precision Medicine?', *Nature Biotechnology* 37 (10) (2019) 1118–1125.

countries address such concerns through rules based on the exceptions from patentability allowed under Article 27(2) of the TRIPS Agreement.

4.3 *Jurisdictions with Statutory 'Ordre Public' and Morality Exceptions: Developments in Europe*

Patentability prohibitions based on '*ordre public*' and morality have a long tradition in European national laws and already existed in several jurisdictions in the nineteenth century.[40] Thus, historically these provisions' origin pre-dates both the TRIPS Agreement, and regional treaties such as the EPC. Currently, the general '*ordre public*' and morality clause is prescribed in Article 53 (a) of the EPC in terms very close to those of Article 27 (2) the TRIPS Agreement.[41] Similar clauses are also observed in the respective national patent codes or laws of at least each of the 38 countries that are full members of the European Patent Organisation.

The EPC does not provide a direct statutory definition of '*ordre public*' and morality, however the implementing regulations to the EPC[42] exemplify categories of inventions that will fall under the scope of the provision. These regulations incorporate both the jurisprudence of the EPO Boards of Appeal and European Union (EU) rules contained in the Biotechnology Directive.[43] The inclusion of the Biotechnology Directive patent substantive provisions and related Court of Justice of the European Union (CJEU) jurisprudence in the implementing regulations indirectly extends their scope of territorial application to those member states of the EPO which are not part of the EU. Although the EPO, is an international organization based on an international treaty — the European Patent Convention (EPC) — and is independent from and not subject to the treaties and legislation of the EU, the EPO Administrative

40 See L. Bently, B. Sherman, D. Borges Barbosa, S. Basheer, C. Visser and R. Gold, 'Exclusions from Patentability and Exceptions and Limitations to Patentees' Rights', *WIPO Standing Committee on the Law of Patents SCP/15/3 Annex I* (2010), available online at https://www.wipo.int/edocs/mdocs/scp/en/scp_15/scp_15_3-annex1.pdf.

41 Article 53(a) EPC 2000 *supra* note 26, reads as follows: 'European patent shall not be granted in respect of: (a) inventions the commercial exploitation of which would be contrary to '*ordre public*' or morality; such exploitation shall not be deemed to be so contrary merely because it is prohibited by law or regulation in some or all of the Contracting States.'

42 Implementing Regulations to the Convention on the Grant of European Patents of 5 October 1973 as adopted by decision of the Administrative Council of the European Patent Organisation of 7 December 2006 and as last amended by decision of the Administrative Council of the European Patent Organisation of 15 December 2020.

43 Directive 98/44/EC of the European Parliament and of the Council of 6 July 1998 on the legal protection of biotechnological inventions [1998] OJ L213/13 (Biotechnology Directive).

Council policy has been to incorporate EU patent law and policy into its own legal order via the implementing rules to the EPC.[44]

The Biotechnology Directive, enacted by the EU in 1998 after a decade-long legislative process, was an attempt to improve legal certainty regarding both patent eligibility and patentability exclusions and exceptions applicable to the, then emerging, biotechnology field. It contains rules that distinguish patentable inventions from non-patentable discoveries, as well as examples of what inventions might not fall under the scope of the '*ordre public*' and morality exception.

Article 5 of the Biotechnology Directive focusing on patent subject-matter, clarifies that the human body which, at various stages of its formation and development, and the simple discovery of one of its elements, including the sequence or partial sequence of a gene, cannot constitute patentable inventions since these are considered a mere discovery of a naturally occurring element. Nevertheless, Article 5 of the Biotechnology Directive also declares that an element isolated from the human body or otherwise produced by means of a technical process, including the sequence or partial sequence of a gene, may constitute a patentable invention, even if the structure of that element is identical to a natural element, provided that the industrial application of a sequence or a partial sequence of a gene is disclosed in the patent application.

Regarding exceptions from patentability, Article 6(2) of the Biotechnology Directive sets out a non-exhaustive list of examples of biotechnological inventions that are excluded from patentability on '*ordre public*' and morality grounds, including: (a) "processes for cloning human beings"; (b) "processes for modifying the germ line genetic identity of human beings"; and (c) "uses of human embryos for industrial or commercial purposes."

It is important to again emphasize that the EPO is not an institution of the European Union and not all of its members are EU member states. Therefore, EU directives and CJEU decisions are not legally binding for the EPO. Even if such rules and jurisprudence can be invoked during proceedings and the BoA may decide to find the arguments substantively persuasive. It has also been part of the EPO institutional practice to incorporate CJEU patent jurisprudence in the guidelines for examination. These are two parallel systems that although interlinked, are not always completely equivalent. Regarding '*ordre*

44 The key articles 5 and 6 of the Biotechnology Directive are included in Rules 28 and 29 of the Implementing Regulations to the Convention on the Grant of European Patents. Administrative Council Decision, OJ EPO 7/1999, 437.

public' and morality exception both the EPO BoA and the CJEU have established interpretative guidance through a number of high-profile cases.

The EPO BoA, through the *OncoMouse* case[45] developed a balancing test weighing animal suffering against the therapeutic value of the invention under consideration.[46] In *Relaxin*,[47] it was instead suggested that the main criterion for morality assessment rested on whether the invention is so abhorrent to the public that it would seem inconceivable.[48] While in *Plant cells*,[49] it was stated that 'the concept of "*ordre public*" covers the protection of public security and the physical integrity of individuals as part of society',[50] and that the concept of morality is related to the accepted norms which are deeply rooted in the culture inherent in European society and civilisation.[51]

The specific criteria and acceptable sources of evidence that can be taken into consideration for determining the actual substantive content of what constitutes an accepted norm that is deeply rooted in European society remains mostly undetermined. In *Transgenic Animal* (a decision issued after the adoption of the EU Biotechnology Directive) it was stated that no single definition of morality based on, for instance, economic or religious principles, represents the content of an accepted standard in European culture.[52] In *WARF*, the EPO found that the legislature had made morality part of the EPC[53] in the context of innovation linked ultimately with embryos and declined to grant patents.[54]

Currently, any genome editing invention that implies at some point in time the destruction of an embryo, even if such destruction, is absent from the patent application (namely in either the claims or description), is not patentable. An invention that uses human embryonic stem cells (hESCs) is only patentable

---

45 T 19/90 Harvard/*Onco-mouse* [3 October 1990] OJ EPO 1990, 476.

46 *Ibid.*, reasons 5.

47 Decision of the EPO Opposition Division, Howard Florey Institute/*Relaxin* [8 December 1994] OJ EPO 1995, 388 and T 272/95 Howard Florey Institute/*Relaxin* [23 October 2002] unpublished.

48 Howard Florey Institute/*Relaxin, supra* note 47, reasons 6.2.1.

49 T 356/93 Plant Genetic Systems/*Plant cells* [21 February 1995] OJ EPO 1995, 545.

50 *Ibid.*, reasons 5.

51 *Ibid.*

52 T 315/03 HARVARD/*Transgenic Animal* [6 July 2004] OJ EPO 2005, 246.

53 See A. Warren-Jones, 'Finding a "Common Morality Codex" for Biotech — a Question of Substance', *International Review of Intellectual Property and Competition Law* 39 (6) (2008) 638–661.

54 WARF/*Embryonic Stem Cells* [2009] EPOR 15, 143 para 41, and A. Plomer, K.S. Taymor and C.T. Scott, 'Challenges to Human Embryonic Stem Cell Patents', *Cell Stem Cell* 2 (1) (2008) 13–17.

if stem cell lines were obtained from parthenotes.[55] According to the CJEU in *Brüstle*, this limitation even applies if the destruction occurred at an undetermined historical moment and does not form part of the core of the invention, as described in the claims.[56] The CJEU[57] focused on establishing the meaning of embryo within the Directive and did not engage with wider questions of human dignity and morality, despite the opinion of the Advocate General in this case.[58] The *Brüstle* jurisprudence, later also adopted by the EPO, contrasts with the restrictive approach to patenting regarding genetic innovation in earlier EPO BoA decisions, including the balancing test adopted concerning animals in *Harvard/Onco-mouse*[59] where the BoA balanced the negative impact (on the animals) with the longer term expected benefit for humans.

Modifying the germline genetic identity of human beings is currently specifically covered by the morality patentability exception under the EU Biotechnology Directive and adopted by the EPO under the corresponding Rule 28(1)(b) in the EPC Implementing Regulations. This specific exception to patentability follows prohibitions of germline modifications outside patent laws, such as those contained in the in UN UNESCO Declarations,[60] The Council of Europe Bioethics Convention (Oviedo Convention).[61] Germline interventions are prohibited also in several national jurisdiction and heavily

55 C-364/13, *International Stem Cells Corporation v Comptroller General of Patents, Designs and Trade Marks* ECLI:EU:C:2014:2451.

56 Minssen and Nordberg, *supra* note 27.

57 Case C-34/10 *Oliver Brüstle v Greenpeace e.V* [2011] OJ C 362/5 Judgment of the Court (Grand Chamber) of 18th of October 2011.

58 Opinion of Advocate General Bot of 10 March 2011, Case C-34/10 *Oliver Brüstle v Greenpeace e.V.*

59 *Supra* note 45, 476; D. Beyleveld and R. Brownsword, *Mice, Morality and Patents: the Oncomouse Application and Article 53a of the European Patent Convention* (Intellectual Property Institute 1993), also considered in Warren-Jones, *supra* note 53; A. Bonfanti, 'Environmental Risk in Biotech Patent Disputes', *European Journal of Risk Regulation* 3 (1) (2012) 47, 49–56.

60 Universal Declaration on the Human Genome and Human Rights, adopted by the UNESCO General Conference on Nov. 11, 1997 and endorsed by the United Nations General Assembly, 53rd session, resolution AIRES/53/152, 9 December; International Declaration on Human Genetic Data, adopted by the UNESCO General Conference on 16 October 2003; Universal Declaration on Bioethics and Human Rights, adopted by the UNESCO General Conference, 19 October 2005.

61 Council of Europe Convention for the Protection of Human Rights and Dignity of the Human Being with regard to the Application of Biology and Medicine: Convention on Human Rights and Biomedicine, signed in Oviedo, 4 April 1997, European Treaty Series No. 164.

regulated in others.[62] Rule 28(1)(b) explicitly includes in the morality exception 'processes for modifying the germ line genetic identity of human beings'. Because the wording of the exception expressly refers to *'processes'*, product claims have to be considered on a case-by-case basis under the general '*ordre public*' and morality exception, making EPO decisions on the morality of the invention to some extent depend on the type of claim.[63]

The text of the Biotechnology directive contains several relatively vague and undetermined autonomous concepts of EU law, these have been a source of legal discussion and require clarification. Under a literal interpretation, all genome editing interventions resulting in modifications of the germline will be excluded from patentability, including also therapeutic interventions with well-defined curative purposes and not in any way connected with eugenic purposes or elective interventions. EU law and thus the biotechnology directive, is traditionally not intended to be interpreted merely following its literal meaning, but rather using a teleological interpretation method.[64] Therefore, it has been argued that concerning therapeutic interventions a less strict

62 Concerning Europe, see, for example, the restriction imposed by Article 13, Council of Europe Convention for the Protection of Human Rights and Dignity of the Human Being with regard to the Application of Biology and Medicine: Convention on Human Rights and Biomedicine (CETS no. 164). Only 28 countries have ratified, those who did not ratify include the EU as an institution and the following EPO member states: Ireland, Italy, The Netherlands, Poland, Sweden and the UK. For an account of both European and non-European jurisdictions, see F. Baylis, M. Darnovsky, K. Hasson and T.M. Krahn, 'Human Germline and Heritable Genome Editing: The Global Policy Landscape', *The CRISPR Journal* 3 (2020) 365–377, http://doi.org/10.1089/crispr.2020.0082. For comparative discussion, see also C. Romano, J. Almqvist (Eds.), *Human Germline Genome Modification and the Right to Science: A Comparative Study of National Laws and Policies* (Cambridge: Cambridge University Press, 2020); S. Slokenberga, K. Siemaszko, Z. Warso and H.C. Howard, 'SIENNA D2.2 Analysis of the legal and human rights requirements for genomics in and outside the EU (V2.0)', *Zenodo* (2019), available online at https://zenodo.org/record/4066659#.YjBN3Y_MI2w; A. Nordberg, 'Report: Genome Editing in Humans: A Survey of Law, Regulation and Governance Principles', Panel for the Future of Science and Technology (STOA), *European Parliament* (forthcoming, 2022).

63 A. Nordberg, 'Patents, Morality and Biomedical Innovation in Europe: Historical Overview, Current Debates on Stem Cells, Gene Editing and AI, and de Lege Ferenda Reflections' in D.J. Gervais (ed.), *Fairness, Morality and Ordre Public in Intellectual Property* (Cheltenham: Edward Elgar, 2020), pp. 243–267.

64 Concerning legal interpretation and construction of international patent law, see also with further references, A. Nordberg, 'Legal Method and Legal Interpretation in International Intellectual Property Law: Pluralism or Systemic Coherence' in S. Frankel (ed.), *Is Intellectual Property Pluralism Functional?* (Cheltenham: Edgar Elgar, 2019), Chapter 4, p. 96.

interpretation would be reasonable as a contextual interpretation would allow patents on in vitro methods.[65]

This line of argumentation is supported by recital 42 of the EU Biotechnology Directive, which has interpretative value. This recital states that the germline exception from patentability is not intended to be applicable to claims for 'inventions for therapeutic or diagnostic purposes which are applied to the human embryo and are useful to it'. The EU patent law concept of embryo is broad extending to any fertilized ova capable of developing into a human being, as defined under the doctrine of the CJEU in *Brüstle* and *ISCC*. This broad interpretation of the legal concept of embryo entails that a therapeutic intervention at the blastocyst stage is considered a therapeutic intervention in an embryo. Therefore, it can be argued that germline editing for a therapeutic purpose is patentable.[66] Likewise, following such reasoning but now *a contrario*, methods for germline editing would be patentable as long as not able to result in modifications to a human being, meaning for example processes to be applied for research purposes in parthenotes which are not considered by the jurisprudence of the CJEU as capable of developing into a human being, since the prohibition in Article 6(2) of the Biotechnology Directive/Rule 28(1)(b) EPC only applies to modifying human beings.

Although there are currently no BoA decisions concerning the application of exceptions in the field of genome editing, patent applications procedural history shows that the EPO actively makes use of the '*ordre public*' and morality exceptions as governance tools to assess and manage what types of inventions should be excluded from patentability on grounds that they are, broadly speaking, socially undesirable and/or violate human dignity. Rather than relying only on adversarial procedures (refusals and appeals) EPO administrative procedural rules and praxis on patent processing and examination allow the EPO examining division to regularly invite applicants to voluntarily introduce amendments to claims — known as disclaimers — explicitly excluding from the claims the use of a process for modifying the germline genetic identity of human beings.[67]

65 A. Nordberg, T. Minssen, S. Holm, M. Horst, K. Mortensen and B. Lindberg Møller, 'Cutting Edges and Weaving Threads in the Gene Editing (Я)evolution: Reconciling Scientific Progress with Legal, Ethical, and Social Concerns', *Journal of Law and the Biosciences* 5 (1) (2018) 35–83; A. Nordberg, T. Minssen, O. Feeney, I. de Miguel Beriain, L. Galvagni and K. Wartiovaara, 'Regulating Germline Editing in Assisted Reproductive Technology: An EU Cross-Disciplinary Perspective', *Bioethics* 34 (1) (2020) 16–32, with further references.

66 Nordberg, *supra* note 63, p. 243.

67 I. Schneider, 'Patent Governance, Ethics and Democracy: How Transparency and Accountability Norms Are Challenged by Patents on Stem Cells, Gametes and Genome

Disclaimers have routinely been added to genome editing-related patent applications introducing claim limiting expressions such as "non-human," "human germline not modified" or "wherein the cells are not germ cells."[68] European patent claims have also been allowed to the "composition" or "vector system."[69] These procedural aspects of the patent examination process are particularly important and attest to the relevance of the governance role assumed by the '*ordre public*' and morality exceptions. Moreover, they were relevant for the European Academies Statement on Patent-Related Aspects of CRISPR-Cas Technology[70] issued in 2016, which concluded that the patent granting practice of the EPO is fit for purpose and flexible enough to take account of future regulatory developments related to genome editing technology.

5 The Impact of '*Ordre Public*' and Morality Patent Exceptions on Human Germline Editing

Applying '*ordre public*' and morality exceptions provisions has for long been a source of controversy and academic debate.[71] Enforcing such clauses during patent examination procedures, involves determining what is contrary to '*ordre public*' and morality and thus involves ethical normative decisions being made by administrative institutions (the EPO or national patent offices).

Editing', in: T.C. Berg, R. Cholij and S. Ravenscroft (eds.), *Patents on Life: Religious, Moral and Social Justice Aspects of Biotechnology and Intellectual Property* (Cambridge: Cambridge University Press, 2019), 263–288.

68 *Ibid.*

69 Examples include the European Patents EP 2800811 (UC Berkeley) and EP 2771468 (Broad Institute) with similar amended claim language, i.e. "provided that said method is not a method of modifying the germline genetic identity of a human being" (in the case of the Broad '468 EP, this wording being upheld during Oral Proceedings at the EPO, 5–7 February 2020, even if the patent was ultimately revoked on other grounds, as explained in Section 2 above).

70 ALLEA, *Statement on Patent Related Aspects of CRISPR-Cas Technology* (18 July 2016), available online at https://allea.org/allea-releases-statement-patent-related-aspects-crispr-cas-technology/ (accessed 27 July 2021).

71 For some background see: Nordberg, *supra* note 63, p. 243; EU Commission Expert Group on the development and implications of patent law in the field of biotechnology and genetic engineering, 'Report on patents in the field of human stem cells of the Expert Group on the development implications of patent law in the field of biotechnology and genetic engineering' (2016), available online at https://ec.europa.eu/growth/industry/policy/intellectual-property/patents/biotechnological-inventions_en (accessed 27 July 202)1; S. Sterckx and J. Cockbain, *Exclusions from Patentability: How Far Has the European Patent Office Eroded Boundaries* (Cambridge: Cambridge University Press, 2012), p. 75.

Commentators argue that patent offices lack the structure, technical expertise, institutional culture of transparency and accountability, or indeed the democratic mandate to make such determinations.[72] Likewise, even the role of the CJEU and national courts in determining standards of morality for patent law purposes has been questioned.[73]

Arguments linked to the nature of patents, as negative exclusionary rights, and its function as guarantee to economic incentive to innovation speak against the efficiency of such provisions as a governance tool. After all, granting a patent does not mean that the patent proprietor would be allowed to use the invention in any possible way. The use of the patented technology would still have to comply with the applicable regulations. On the contrary, denying patentability puts an invention in the public domain, and does not mean its commercialization and use will be restricted. It could further be argued that logic would dictate that such use would increase and become less controllable in the absence of patents. A patent right holder could be theoretically obliged to (a) exclude certain unwanted uses from the claim language thereby restricting the scope of protection to morality-accepted purposes or (b) follow regulatory obligations to deny licenses on unwanted uses of the patented invention. This would help to monitor, control and govern the uses of such technologies.

In that way, patentability exceptions can also have an indirect governance and symbolic effect precisely from the economic incentive mechanism. The enforcement of exceptions from patentability effectively diminishes the availability of the economic incentive provided by patent rights to the target inventions or technologies and thus commercial actors in the pharmaceutical sector are comparatively more reluctant to invest large sums in research and product development, adapting manufacturing capabilities, distribution channels, professional training and marketing of products that are not covered by a market exclusivity. Furthermore, because the exception generally signals society, economic actors and consumers that such technology is unethical, commercial entities will think carefully before associating their 'brand' with such technologies.

The '*ordre public*' and morality exception applicable to a given type of inventions also functions as a chilling effect on academic research, not only due to the stigma of working with technology that is classified by an administrative authority as 'immoral' but also because patents are to some extent included in

72 See, e.g., J. Pila, 'Adapting the *Ordre Public* and Morality Exclusion of European Patent Law to Accommodate Emerging Technologies', *Nature Biotechnology* 38 (2020) 555–557; Nordberg, *supra* note 63, p. 243.

73 See with further references, Nordberg *supra* note 64, p. 96.

academic portfolios used for assessment of career progression. Research funding agencies and private foundations also tend to be cautious about providing grants to technologies falling under the '*ordre public*' and morality exception. Ultimately, however, it should be acknowledged that perhaps this cannot be attributed solely to an indirect pedagogic effect of patentability norms, but is instead more likely to be the cumulative result of a variety of regulatory and governance considerations. Still the result is that alternative incentives such as grants, prizes and academic awards will typically also be severely reduced and that lack of incentive will extend beyond a specific unethical application of the technology and affect the entire field. A cautionary example is stem cell research in Europe after the Brüstle decision, discussed above.[74]

Moving forward, and as the technology further develops and specific therapeutic applications are developed, it is essential that interpretation issues are clarified. In particular two essential concepts in the text of the exception should be carefully considered: (a) 'modifying the germ line'; and (b) 'genetic identity of human beings'.

Regarding interpreting what standard should be used to determine when a claim for a process should be excluded on grounds of 'modifying the germ line', it should first be considered that there is considerable diversity and variation in any given species' genetic pool — including humans. Interventions that erase such diversity in order to select, introduce or remove certain traits might modify the genetic identity of the individual subject to the intervention. However, treatments that merely remove mutations known to be responsible for severe diseases are no different to surgically removing a tumour, and by analogy it is as such that these genome editing therapies should be considered, even if such intervention also passes on and is also curing descendants. Meaning that in such cases, there is not in a strict sense a modification of the germline (in the sense of introducing something ad novum) but rather a therapeutic genetic surgery repairing a damaged germline. The concept of modification of the germ line should be narrowly constructed in cases where patent claims are directed to genetic treatments to improve health, prevent diseases, and promote wellbeing. Such claims should be allowed[75] in light of the abovementioned Recital 42 of the Biotechnology Directive which clarifies for interpretative purposes that the germline 'exclusion does not affect inventions for

74 See also A. Odell-West, 'Invention and the Human Embryo', *Intellectual Property Quarterly* 1 (2020) 1–19, p. 19, who argues that the dignitarian perspective adopted in the case fails to adequately consider the balance between investor and society interests.

75 Provided that these are in vitro treatments that do not fall under the exception for medical methods under Article 53 (c) EPC.

therapeutic or diagnostic purposes which are applied to the human embryo and are useful to it'.

The patent exception preventing the patentability of 'processes for modifying the germ line genetic identity of human beings' is based on the understanding that eugenic practices are an offense to '*ordre public*' and morality. In fact, such practices are largely unanimously understood as offensive to human dignity.[76] Unlike the dystopic scenario of eugenics programs where a large number of individuals are created as a result of in vitro fertilization and genetic editing, therapeutic interventions to repair damaged DNA will only result in curing individuals and preventing disease from passing down a family line. This means that the exception should not be interpreted as applicable to individual therapeutic intervention to correct genetic mutations or irregularities affecting a given family. Under a narrow interpretation of the exception, only those modifications that affect the global identity of humanity would be considered an offense to human dignity and a danger to the human genome, as the collective heritage of humanity. Individual therapeutic interventions will not have a global impact on the collective human genome and as such also here a narrow construction would not interpret such therapeutic treatments as processes that modify the genetic identity of human beings, since these only restore or treat a DNA abnormality of specific individuals and not the collective human identity.

Although challenges remain and the search for balance runs throughout patent law, it has been argued that pursuing limitations and disclaimers, or refusal to grant, may start a chain reaction leading to an overall reduction of incentives to innovate and invest in controversial areas for R&D.[77] However, given that most technologies have dual or multiple types of uses — including some ethically objectionable and some highly desirable — the problem remains as to how to reduce incentives to the first and still incentivise the latter.

Finally, the implementation of the European model as a type of public technology governance tool is highly dependable on the existence of a

---

76 See, for example, J. Habermas, *The Future of Human Nature* (Cambridge: Polity Press, 2003), 27; F. Fukuyama, 'How to Regulate Science', *The Public Interest* (2002) 3–22; E. Fenton, 'Liberal Eugenics & Human Nature: Against Habermas', *The Hastings Center Report* 36(6) (2006) 35–42. Views to the contrary have also been expressed, e.g., J. Harris, 'Enhancements are an obligation', in: J. Savulescu and N. Bostrom (eds.), *Human Enhancement* (Oxford: Oxford University Press, 2013) pp. 131–154.

77 See S. Harmon, G. Laurie and A. Courtney, 'Dignity, Plurality and Patentability: The Unfinished Story of Brüstle v Greenpeace (Case Comment)', *European Law Review* 38 (1) (2012) 92–106; Nordberg et al., *supra* note 65, 35.

fully-functioning patent examination system and cannot be adopted in countries with a mere patent recognition system.

Patent exceptions should not be used as a blunt policy instrument, nor interpreted in a way that is contrary to the patent system's overall objective.[78] Namely, the morality-based exception concerning germline editing should not be applied in a way which results in outcomes counterproductive to this objective. The application of the morality exception should be based on a good understanding of the science and should enable case-by-case decisions that provide the basis for claim amendments and nuanced purpose bound protection.

Above all, we would caution against outcomes whereby patent law would regard certain germline editing inventions as falling within the scope of the '*ordre public*' and morality exceptions, whereas at the same time research regulation can enable scientists to conduct research on such inventions in many settings. Such a paradox would lead to a situation, as happened in the Brüstle decision,[79] whereby scientists operating on the basis that conducting legally compliant research by following all research guidelines might be constrained in the commercial exploitation of their inventions by a contrary position in patent law.

6 Conclusions

Our analysis has illustrated how legal systems can set limits on the patentability of human genome editing as an instrument of governance, including the exceptions from patentability on grounds that the commercialization of certain inventions is contrary to '*ordre public*' and morality. Some patent systems have already incorporated this exception and that there is variety in the

78 Trevor Cook expresses similar views in T. Cook, *Pharmaceuticals Biotechnology and the Law*, 3rd edn. (New York, NY: LexisNexis, 2016), p. 238, in which he emphasises that the function of patents has traditionally been to prevent others from the use of a particular technology, not to serve as a tool to regulate the creation and distribution of technology.

79 Considering the wide variety of regulations and national perceptions pertaining to research involving genome editing (https://www.frontiersin.org/articles/10.3389/fpos.2021.793134/full (on diverse genome editing landscape, published 27 January 2022)) or germline editing (https://www.liebertpub.com/doi/10.1089/crispr.2020.0082 (on diversity in germline editing landscape)), there is a plausible risk for such outcomes. See also Romano and Almqvist, *supra* note 62; Slokenberga et al., *supra* note 62; and A. Nordberg, 'Genome editing in Humans: a survey of Law, regulation and governance principles' (report, forthcoming, April 2022).

application of patent law by courts and patent offices in the way this provision has been interpreted.

Such '*ordre public*' and morality exceptions can have a considerable impact on the patentability and hence most likely on the developments and availability of novel therapies that would involve modification to the germ line. Balancing the great risk for potential misuses on the one hand, and the risk that novel and potentially life-saving therapies are not being developed on the other hand, as we state with colleagues in our response to the WHO Expert Advisory Committee's reports, there is consequently a need for greater understanding and more inclusive public debate on the role of patents and the broader legal system considerations in countries considering introducing or developing further guidance on the use of '*ordre public*' and morality exceptions to patentability in the area of genome editing.

In our view, we need to pursue more nuanced approaches to the application of '*ordre public*' and morality exceptions in patent law in order to allow for a case-by-case application. As we pointed out previously, the assessment of risks and benefits of patent exceptions need to be research-based, taking into account inputs from all relevant stakeholders as well as those engaged directly in patent and innovation law and policy.

While recent social science landscaping studies are welcome, we believe that a more comprehensive comparative legal analysis is required. Such an approach should take into account the complexities of patent law and procedure in order to better inform the policy debate. In addition to identifying which countries currently have '*ordre public*' and morality exceptions, there is also a need to examine in more detail how the law is applied in practice when it is subject to decisions by patent offices and by the courts.

An additional step would be defining clear guidelines for examination and application of the '*ordre public*' and morality exceptions, with special emphasis on the exception for 'processes for modifying the germ line identity of human beings'.

Such a debate on patent exceptions needs to acknowledge that imposing a complete ban on patentability of inventions concerning germ line modifications may in fact reduce incentives to the prevention and treatment of serious genetic diseases.

Above all, patent exceptions should not be used as a blunt policy instrument, nor interpreted in a way that is contrary to the patent system's overall objective to promote innovation for the benefit of mankind and society. In particular, the '*ordre public*' and morality based exceptions in the context of human germline editing should not be interpreted and applied in a way which results in outcomes counterproductive to the goal of balancing innovation with the protection of societal higher normative values. Instead, the application of the exception should be based on a sound understanding of both the underlying science as well as the broader ethical, social, and legal implications, thus enabling case-by-case decisions that provide the basis for patent claim amendments and nuanced purpose-bound protection. Further analysis and debate as to the role that such flexibilities can play in the context of genome editing technologies is therefore both necessary and desirable, and can be facilitated in the ways set out in this chapter.

Acknowledgements

Timo Minssen's research for this contribution was supported by a Novo Nordisk Foundation for a scientifically independent Collaborative Research Programme in Biomedical Innovation Law (Grant agreement number NNF17SA0027784). With special thanks to Maciej Padamczyk for research assistance.

The Application of EU Competition Law to the Exploitation of Human Genome Editing Technology

Vladimir Bastidas Venegas | ORCID: 0000-0002-8257-6542
Department of Law, Faculty of Law, Uppsala University, Box 256, 751 05 Uppsala, Sweden
vladimir.bastidas@jur.uu.se

Abstract

This chapter explores the application of EU Competition Law to the exploitation of human genome editing technology. Holders of key patents in the sector have applied different methods for disseminating the technology, such as different forms of licensing agreement and patent pools. It is found that that the competition rules are ill-suited to assess some of the licensing arrangements applied, which give rise to legal uncertainty. Accordingly, holders of patents on human genome editing technology may be discouraged to apply efficient methods for disseminating the technology. This may delay or obstruct some of the benefits the technology is supposed to deliver to the market, maker actors and consumers.

Keywords

competition law – human genome editing technology – patent pool – ethical license – exclusive license – technology transfer

1 Introduction

This chapter discusses potential competition law issues that may emerge as regards the exploitation of human genome editing technology. Ever since human genome editing technology was developed in the end of the past century, it has been a rapid developing technology. The technology has been described a bearing great potential for developing cures to diseases as the

DOI:10.1163/9789004526136_014

technology permits the modifying of cells in the human body. In particular, it is expected that human genome editing may be used to cure and treat diseases which so far have not been possible to treat effectively. While the technology promises great benefits to society, it is apparent that such technology raises a number of interesting legal issues related to ethics, public policy, ownership, dissemination and governance. Access to the technology and its exploitation, may under certain conditions raise competition law issues. In particular, human genome editing technology are protected by patent rights, meaning that access and use to the technology is controlled and "regulated" by those private parties that hold the relevant patents. As these entities enter into different forms of licensing arrangemwyents, as e.g. patent pools, such collaborations may collide with different provisions in competition law. In addition, when discussing ground-breaking and valuable technology, there is always a risk that the holders of such technology may find themselves in a position of significant market power, which potentially opens up for compulsory licensing in individual cases under competition law. These competition law issues are discussed in this chapter.

Importantly, the readers of this chapter are expected to be mainly non-competition lawyers, but also to a limited extent competition lawyers that are interested in the application of the competition rules to the exploitation of human genome editing technology. For this reason, some basic elements that may be self-evident for most competition lawyers may deserve some additional explanation in this chapter. At the same time, some elements of human genome editing technology, which are fascinating and may be important for the regulation of the sector with regards to concerns of ethical nature, public policy, public health and patent law, are not discussed in this chapter. The focus of this chapter is on the narrow and specific field of *competition law* and not general *competition policy* and regulation of the sector. Consequently, this chapter does not focus on the general benefits and detriments of the technology as such, but rather on specific actions taken by companies within the sector that may fall within the scope of the competition rules. To a great extent, as will be explained below, the general benefits of the technology are unlikely to affect the competition law analysis and *may* only indirectly have an impact on the legality of what companies do in terms of regulating, granting and refusing access to technology on human genome technology. The main contribution of this chapter is the discussion on how competition law may limit the behavior of holders of patent rights within this particular field of technology. Naturally, such limitations may have an impact on the dissemination of this important technology and its benefit to society.

A brief introduction to some key elements in the exploitation of the technology, which are relevant for competition law are presented in Section 2. In Section 3, an inventory of the potential competition law issues is carried out. Finally in Section 4, some preliminary conclusions are drawn.

2 The Exploitation of Human Genome Editing Technology

Although technology for editing genes and the human genome has existed at least since the 1990s, it was first with the breakthrough of the new editing tool CRISPR (Clustered Regularly Interspaced Short Palindromic Repeats) that it was made possible to edit genomes in a more precise and effective way.[1] In addition, with the use of the Cas9-protein, it has created an enormous potential for the use of this technology (CRISPR-Cas9), as it is possible to make cuts at specific DNA sequences permitting the addition, removal or altering of DNA in the genome. For instance, a cell that is infected with HIV could potentially be altered as to remove parts of the genome that would reproduce the virus and in the long-term avoid that the infection develops into a full-scale AIDS. As the technology can be used to alter the genome in all living organisms, it also means that it may be used to alter genomes in plants or animals, e.g., by introducing parts in the genome that would make it resistant to a particular type of disease.[2] Obviously, the technology as such has great potential, in particular for the development of more effective treatment to human diseases and the promotion of public health, but also for improvements and the protection of other living organisms such as crops and animals used for human consumption.

While the technology and its potential uses is a fascinating topic in itself, it is not so interesting from a competition law perspective. The interesting part from a competition law perspective is the competitive situation as regards access to the technology in question, as well as the exploitation of that technology in markets for products and services. As the technology is held by private parties or state actors (like some universities) acting as private actors (by e.g. transferring the patent rights to a company under their control), access to

1 O. Feeney, J. Cockbain and S. Sterckx, 'Ethics, Patents and Genome Editing: A Critical Assessment of Three Options of Technology Governance', *Frontiers in Political Science* 3 (2021) 731505, p. 3.

2 Feeney et al., *supra* note 1, p. 4; L. Grobler, E. Sulemanb, D.B. Thimiri and G. Raja, 'Patents and technology transfer in CRISPR technology' in: V. Singh (ed.), *Reprogramming the Genome: Applications of CRISPR-Cas in Non-mammalian Systems Part B* (San Diego, CA: Academic Press, 2021), Chapter 7.

the technology is mainly governed by the holders of the technology. Naturally, there are other bodies of rules that may affect access to the technology or its use. Regulation on what kind of research that is permitted or not within a particular jurisdiction will affect the further development of technology (follow-on innovation), which is a particular kind of competition between market actors. Regulation on legal and illegal therapeutic uses will impact to what an extent there will be a market for a particular application of the technology. Moreover, the rules in patent law, which may be different in between different jurisdictions, may prohibit the patenting of certain technologies or stipulate exemptions to the exclusive right for particular uses of the technology. For instance, in certain jurisdictions there may be a wider research exemption which permits researchers to further develop the technology without permission from the owner of a patent. Importantly, an analysis under the competition rules will take the legal framework provided by other bodies of rules as granted and as part of the market conditions in a specific case. However, it must also be noted that just because a particular behavior is tolerated by other bodies of rules, it does not mean that the behavior is immune from the application of competition law.[3]

From what may be read out from the literature at the moment, there are few elements regarding the competitive situation related to the technology itself as well as to the access to the technology that are of particular interest from a competition law perspective. Firstly, like in many other markets which are driven by R&D there is a presence of some key patent rights on the basic technology as well as hundreds of patent rights which constitute different developments of the basic technology. Importantly, the necessity to receive licenses under certain patent rights to use the basic technology means that a few patent holders may be in a position of so-called market power as the exclusive right grants them a legal monopoly to use the technology. This may trigger the application of competition law as discussed more specifically below (Section 3.5).

Moreover, as in many other fields where different actors are racing for patenting new technology, several actors have been involved in patent disputes regarding the CRISPR-Cas9 technology.[4] Although the details of these disputes

3 See, e.g., Case C-457/10 P AstraZeneca AB and AstraZeneca plc v European Commission, EU:C:2012:770.

4 D. Matthews, A. Brown, E. Gambini, A. McMahon, T. Minssen, A. Nordberg, J.S. Sherkow, J. Wested and E. van Zimmeren, 'The Role of Patents and Licensing in the Governance of Human Genome Editing: A White Paper' (2021), *Queen Mary Law Research Paper no. 364/2021*, pp. 14–23; D. Mathews, 'Access to CRISPR Genome Editing Technologies: Patents, Human Rights and the Public Interest' (2020), *Queen Mary University of London, School of Law Legal Studies Research Paper No. 332/2020*, pp. 12–17.

are irrelevant for the purpose of this chapter it follows that the litigation has created uncertainty about issue of ownership, which also has repercussion for those companies that would like to access and use the technology. As patent rights to both the basic technology as well as to more specific developments of that technology are held by different market actors, there may be a need for several patent holders to collaborate through agreements either for the purpose of using the technology or licensing the technology to interested third parties. Such collaborations, depending on the design of the relevant agreements, may also trigger competition law as they may reduce competition between the parties or between the patent holders and third parties. For instance, one such type of collaboration that has been discussed is patent pools, whereby several patent holders pool their technologies to license to third parties. The MPEG-LA launched an initiative in 2020 to create a patent pool consisting of CRISPR-Cas9, even though not all key actors have joined in this initiative.[5]

Furthermore, there are also some few details concerning existing and planned collaborations as regards the CRISPR-Cas9 technology that are interesting from a competition law perspective. To begin with, it seems as some universities use a licensing arrangement referred to as surrogate licensing. With surrogate licensing it is meant that the commercialization and licensing is outsourced to a private party (surrogate licensor).[6] For instance, one the technology holders of the patents of CRISPR-Cas9 (University of California) has licensed the technology to a third party that both develops and licenses the technology to others. In other words, the institute has completely given up control of the technology to its licensee. Such licensing arrangements seem primarily to have been concluded in order to avoid certain obligations imposed on universities, which is not necessarily a relevant factor for the competition law analysis.[7] However, as discussed below in Section 3.3, the use of surrogate licenses may have an impact on which specific rules that apply under EU Competition law, which makes the use of this type of licensing interesting.

Additionally, it has been mentioned above that the CRISPR-Cas9 system could have a variety of different uses. Technology holders may therefore limit the use of the technology for particular purposes, through so-called field-of-use restrictions.[8] For instance, one of the patent holders on CRISPR-Cas9 (the Broad institute) has retained the licensing for non-commercial non-human

5 Grobler et al., *supra* note 2, p. 168; P. Neville, 'MPEG LA's Use of a Patent Pool to Solve the CRISPR Industry's Licensing Problems', *Utah Law Review* 2 (2020) 535–567.

6 J.S. Sherkow, 'Patent Protection for CRISPR: an ELSI Review', *Journal of Law and the Biosciences* 4 (2017) 565–576; Matthews et al., *supra* note 4, p. 42.

7 Grobler et al., *supra* note 2, p. 167.

8 *Ibid.*

therapy uses, while a surrogate licensor licenses the technology for commercial use. The surrogate licensor has in turn subsequently granted a specific license for the use of the technology in plants. Field-of-use limitations are typical license restrictions. They may be used in order to protect certain markets where either the licensor or other licensees are active. Technology holders may have legitimate reasons for protecting their own commercial activities or those of other licensees in order to create incentives to invest in the development of the technology within a particular field-of-use. A field-of-use can also be seen as reflecting the specialization of a firm's commercial activities. However, field-of-use restrictions may also be used to divide markets between market actors, meaning that each actor may face none or very little competition from other market actors within a specific product market, which make such restrictions interesting for a competition law assessment.[9]

Importantly, in the context of CRISPR-Cas9, there is also a discussion on so-called ethical licenses. The meaning of an ethical license is that the licensee is prohibited to use the licensed technology for specific purposes that are deemed as unethical.[10] The (potential) use of ethical licenses are interesting because they constitute a way for technology holders to introduce conditions that would not otherwise follow from national legislation where a licensee is active. For instance, if national legislation would not prohibit the use of CRISPR-Cas9 in research to manipulate the genome in human embryos, the technology holders could impose such limitations (under the condition that they have patent protection in the country where the technology is used). Accordingly, a group of technology holders could use ethical licenses as a form of self-regulation within specific markets or for certain types of research. Under competition law, limitations through ethical licenses constitute or are comparable to a field-of-use restriction, which make them interesting to discuss below.

Finally, it is also necessary to mention that licenses may be exclusive or non-exclusive. This is a typical feature of licensing agreements in general and seems also to apply in licensing of genome editing technology.[11] As a licensee may have to invest heavily into the further development of the used technology, it is not uncommon that a licensee may request and will be granted an exclusive license in order to have sufficient incentives to develop the technology. Importantly,

9 See, e.g., Communication from the Commission, Guidelines on the application of Article 101 of the Treaty on the Functioning of the European Union to technology transfer agreements, OJ [2014] C 89/3 (TT Guidelines), paras 208–215.

10 Matthews et al., *supra* note 4, p. 46.

11 Matthews et al., *supra* note 4, p. 42.

without exclusivity, some market actors may not be willing to risk heavy investments into the further development or commercialization of new technology. Exclusivity may concern either particular fields-of-use or territories. As mentioned above, certain surrogate licensees have received an exclusive license for a particular purpose, such as the commercial use of CRISPR-Cas9 technology. From a competition law perspective, exclusive licenses may be problematic if they result in that only one company will be able to compete in a particular market. The licensing of several exclusive licenses may also be used to prevent competition in between licensees and thus the division of markets. Accordingly, exclusivity is also an interesting feature that is relevant to discuss.

3 Potential Competition Law Issues

There are several unknows about the governance and the dissemination of the human genome editing technology that makes a more specific discussion of the potential competition law issues somewhat speculative. Accordingly, this section purports to make an inventory of possible issues under competition law, rather than giving straightforward answers about the legality of particular governance arrangements. In such a way, possible weaknesses with the current competition law regime may be identified. Considering that the competition law regime for R&D cooperation agreements is up for review by the Commission,[12] and that a review of the rules on technology transfer (patent and know-how licensing for the purposes of producing particular products or services) is likely to occur in the coming years, the inventory below may raise interesting issues for further discussion.

As mentioned above, it seems as the dissemination of human genome editing technology at the moment is being carried out through a variety of private governance methods, including patent pools or ordinary licensing agreements. It seems as licensing to other research institutes and for non-profit purposes is being done through non-exclusive licenses. Some of the commercial exploitation, including further research, is being carried out through exclusive licenses. In addition, there is a discussion about the use of licensing agreements for ethical uses. Even though ethical licenses are probably not very problematic according to competition law, they will be briefly touched upon below. Moreover, under competition law there is a possibility to force

12 An overview of the review may be found at https://ec.europa.eu/competition-policy/public-consultations/2019-hbers_en.

access to patented protected technology to prevent patent holders to monopolize existing and potential markets for product and services. This is also addressed below.

Importantly, the analysis below is based on accounts of licensing arrangements given by other academics. These accounts are naturally too superficial to give a good factual basis for a competition law analysis. The arrangements discussed below should therefore be seen as *examples* of possible licensing arrangements.

3.1 *An Overview of the Relevant Competition Rules*

Although somewhat simplified, it could be said that competition law mainly deals with problems related to *market power*. With market power it is meant that a market actor or a group of market actors to a certain extent may determine market conditions, such as price and output, for particular products or services. By contrast, under conditions of effective competition undertakings would normally have to adapt themselves to market conditions in order to survive on the market, being so-called price takers. A position of market power, in various degrees, may be reached through cooperation between market actors, in particular through agreements between competitors, but also between non-competitors, which may limit competition to the extent that the cooperating parties may influence market conditions in terms of price, quality and innovation. A position of market power for individual market actors may also emerge as natural development in the market. However, such market power may be exploited to restrict competition from other market actors, but also to impose unfair conditions on customer and consumers. Competition law purports to hinder the emergence and exploitation of market power through cooperation as well as prevent exploitation of market power unilaterally by individual market actors. In addition, in EU Competition Law there is the additional goal of promoting the internal market. This affects the application of competition law to both cooperation and unilateral conduct that may reduce or obstruct trade between Member States, as this is viewed as contravening the goal of integrating Member States' national markets into one internal market.

The main provisions in EU Competition Law that apply to the actions and behaviors of private parties are Articles 101 and 102 TFEU. Article 101 TFEU prohibits anti-competitive agreements that restrict competition and affect trade between Member States under the prohibition under Article 101(1) TFEU and which do not meet the requirements for the exemption under Article 101(3) TFEU. The provision aims in particular to capture agreements that result in increased prices, the limitation of output, the sharing of markets and the hindrance of competition through R&D and the exploitation of technology.

Article 101(3) TFEU exempts agreements that result in an economic benefit, consumer benefit through restrictions of competition that are indispensable for the beneficial effects of the agreement while not eliminating competition for a substantial part of the product/services in question. As there is not much case law on the application on Article 101(3) TFEU, which is still surrounded by uncertainty and vagueness, the so-called block exemptions regulations adopted by the Commission are of utmost importance. Block exemptions refer to those regulations that pinpoints more specific requirements for particular categories of agreements, such as vertical distribution agreements, R&D agreements and technology transfer agreements, and that are exempted on 'block'. The block exemptions therefore constitute an expression of the application of the requirements in Article 101(3) TFEU to specific categories of agreements.

In addition, the Commission also adopt soft law instruments, such as guidelines and notices, that accompany particular block exemptions by explaining the rules in those regulations. Moreover, they give a general account of how the Commission views and analyzes specific category of agreements and contract clauses under Article 101(1) and (3) TFEU. While the Commission's guidelines constitute soft law, meaning that those rules are not binding on the Union Courts, national courts and the national competition authorities, they may be binding upon the Commission. In practice, the Commission's soft law provide with much valuable guidance by providing an accurate account of competition law as it stands, in particular regarding areas where the case law is scarce, as e.g. technology transfer agreements. In the sections below there are several references to both block exemptions and the Commission guidelines.

Article 102 TFEU deals with unilateral conduct. The provision prohibits the abusive behavior by a company with a certain degree of market power, dominance, that allows it to a certain extent behave independently from its competitors, its customers and ultimately the end-consumers. In a competitive market each undertaking has to a adapt itself to market conditions such as price, quality of the products or sales methods in order to remain on the market. However, a dominant undertaking will have the power to influence or set market conditions to a certain extent. The problems that may emerge with a dominant undertaking is that it may engage in three types of abusive behavior that may be detrimental to the market. First, it may exploit its market power by extracting benefits from customers that it could probably not extract in the absence of market power, e.g. by imposing a supra-competitive price. Secondly, it may also use its market power to exclude competitors (exclusionary abuse) in an effort to strengthen or maintain its market position or to expand its market power to related markets. Thirdly, it may use its market power to harm integration in the single market, normally with the purpose of protecting itself from parallel trade or to extract higher profit margins in different Member States. Finally, while Article 102 TFEU does not include a rule that gives possibilities for exemption, it follows from the Court's case law that is possible to justify prima facie abusive behavior with so called objective justifications or by demonstrating that the abusive conduct results in efficiencies that outweigh the negative effects on competition.

3.2 *The Applicable Block Exemptions in EU Competition Law*

One important but tricky issue in the competition law regime is the application of the block exemption regulations to different licensing agreements. Even though Article 101(1) and (3) TFEU may always be applied, there is a considerable uncertainty in the interpretation and application of these rules as case law is relatively scarce and the Commission's soft law is not sector specific. For a company to be on the safe side it is best, if possible, to adapt licensing and cooperation agreements as to make them comply with the block exemption regulations. Naturally, as the design of licensing agreements usually have to consider idiosyncrasies of a particular sector, the particular technology that is subject to license, and the risks with collaboration caused by e.g. free riding or uncertainties, this is not always possible to do. The benefits with being block exempted is that even if an agreement would ultimately be found problematic in an individual case, exemption under one of the block exemptions regulations would afford protection from sanctions under competition law until the Commission withdraws the block exemption from the specific agreement.

It seems as the owners of the CRISPR-Cas9 technology are engaged in licensing for both further R&D and the commercial application the technology. Importantly, both the block exemptions on R&D cooperation and technology transfer may *prima facie* be applied to licensing agreements. Regulation 316/2014 on the application of Article 101(3) TFEU (TTBER) applies to so-called technology transfer agreements. Technology transfer is defined as the licensing of technology rights for the production of the contract products.[13] Regulation 1217/2010 on the application of Article 101(3) TFEU to R&D agreements (RBER),[14] also applies to licensing of technology rights if they

13 Commission Regulation (EU) No 316/2014 of 21 March 2014 on the application of Article 101(3) of the Treaty on the Functioning of the European Union to categories of technology transfer agreements Text with EEA relevance OJ [2014] L 93/17 (TTBER).

14 Commission Regulation (EU) No 1217/2010 of 14 December 2010 on the application of Article 101(3) of the Treaty on the Functioning of the European Union to certain categories of research and development agreements OJ [2010] L 335/36 (RBER).

occur within the context of a R&D collaboration. R&D agreements under the RBER includes, *inter alia*, the licensing of technology rights shared for the purpose of conducting new joint research and exploitation,[15] and the licensing of technology as a form of exploitation if the licensing is pursuant to R&D conducted by the parties under the agreement or pursuant to a previous R&D agreement.[16]

The distinction between the scope of one block exemption and the other is not always easy to make. The crucial element in the definition of technology transfer in the TTBER is that the licensing is made for the manufacture and sales of the contract products on the market. With other words, the focus of the block exemption is the licensing of products/services that are supposed to be *manufactured* and *placed on the market* by the licensee. There may be some R&D activity related to such an agreement, as e.g. the development of a manufacturing process for the contracted products (which are protected by the licensed technology rights). However, if the primary purpose of the license is to conduct R&D, the agreement will fall outside the scope of the TTBER. According to the Commission Guidelines on Technology Transfer (TT Guidelines), it is required that the contract products have been identified for the TTBER to apply.[17] As regards licensing agreements with the purpose of manufacturing and selling the contract products, they may in theory fall both under the RBER and the TTBER. Such a licensing agreement falls, *prima facie*, under the scope of the TTBER. However, if the licensing agreement concerns technology rights that are the output of an R&D collaboration between the parties (e.g. through a previous R&D agreement), the RBER applies.[18] Importantly, the TTBER does not apply to agreements which are covered by the RBER.[19]

The distinction between the TTBER and RBER is important as the latter has more generous rules. In particular, when the research agreement is concluded between non-competitors, the RBER exempts the agreement between the parties during the research development phase and up to seven years in the exploitation phase from that the contracts products are placed in the

15 Article 1(1)(a)(iii)–(iv) and (vi) RBER, *supra* note 14; Article 2 RBER, *supra* note 14.

16 Article 1(1)(a)(i)–(ii) and (v) RBER, *supra* note 14.

17 Communication from the Commission, Guidelines on the application of Article 101 of the Treaty on the Functioning of the European Union to technology transfer agreements, OJ [2014] C 89/3 (TT Guidelines).

18 Communication from the Commission, Guidelines on the applicability of Article 101 of the Treaty on the Functioning of the European Union to horizontal co-operation agreements Text with EEA relevance OJ [2011] C 11/1 (Horizontal Guidelines).

19 *Ibid.* para. 70; Recital 7 TTBER, *supra* note 13.

market.[20] Importantly, as long as the parties are non-competitors, there is no market share ceiling during this time. After the seven years period, the agreement is exempted as long as the parties cumulative do not exceed a market share ceiling of 25%.[21] By contrast, under the TTBER, licensing between non-competitors is exempted when the parties do not exceed market shares of 30% in their respective markets.[22] In addition, also the other requirements under the block exemptions are more generous under the RBER than the rules in the TTBER. For instance, the RBER permits non-competition clauses (meaning that the parties to the agreement may be prohibited from selling competing products or technology) during the time the parties jointly exploit the results.[23] By contrast, the TTBER exclude such clauses from the block exemption and require an individual assessment under Article 101 TFEU, while the rest of the agreement may still be block exempted under the TTBER.[24] Also as regards cooperation between competitors, the RBER is more generous than the rules in the TTBER. The RBER applies a 25% market share threshold, while the TTBER applies a market share threshold of 20%.[25] The RBER also permits some restrictions between the competing parties that would not be exempted under the TTBER. For instance, as the RBER permits the joint exploitation of the results of R&D, such as the licensing of the researched technology to third parties, a uniform royalty can be charged for such licenses.[26] Any coordination on prices would however be excluded under the TTBER.[27]

It follows that RBER is more beneficial than the rules in the TTBER. It is also likely that at an early stage licensing regarding CRISPR-Cas9 technology would primarily concern agreements for the purpose of the further R&D, rather than the manufacturing of specific products and services. The more lenient treatment of licenses for the purpose of R&D follows the logic in competition law that the farther away from sales of specific products and services on the market, the less problematic an agreement is likely to be for competition. For licensing that occurs "closer" to a market, like a technology transfer agreement, where the contracts products that are going to be manufactured and sold by the licensee are already determined, the conditions for block exempting such agreements become stricter. The lenient treatment of licensing at an

20 Article 4(1) RBER, *supra* note 14.

21 *Ibid.*, Article 14(3).

22 Article 3(2) TTBER, *supra* note 13.

23 Article 5(b)(iv) RBER, *supra* note 14.

24 Article 5(2) TTBER, *supra* note 13.

25 Article 4(2) RBER, *supra* note 14 and Article 3(1) TTBER, *supra* note 13.

26 Article 5(c) RBER, *supra* note 14.

27 Article 4(1)(a) TTBER, *supra* note 13.

early research stage under the RBER may be important in the development of CRISPR-Cas9 technology. It is likely that there may be market actors that will hold key patents and perhaps even the only patents within a specific field-of use. The RBER will still apply as long as licensing does not occur with competitors, which somewhat simplified refers to licensees that are in hold of competing technology.

It should also be noted that where the RBER and TTBER overlap, the legal regime has a more favorable view on long-term R&D cooperation between two parties. Parties that have engaged in a previous R&D agreement (that falls within the RBER) can also benefit from the more lenient rules in the RBER (instead of the TTBER) at a later stage when the technology can be exploited for sales of specific products and services.

Obviously, the main issue with both the RBER (for licensing between competitors) and the TTBER is the application of market share thresholds. As stated above, with the development of new technology there is a risk that market shares may be high for certain actors that have key patents on CRISPR-Cas9 technology. Accordingly, there may always exist a risk that certain technology holders will not be covered by the block exemptions when licensing to other market actors. However, from a competition law perspective it is inevitable that an individual assessment must be made of agreements when there is market power. As discussed below, the main problem with the current legal regime is probably not an overly strict assessment of licensing agreements under the RBER or the TTBER because of market share thresholds, but rather other issues related to the scope of the block exemption regulations.

3.3 *Surrogate, Exclusive and Ethical Licenses under EU Competition Law*

As stated above, some owners of the key patents in the CRISPR-Cas9 technology have concluded surrogate licenses with partners (surrogate licensors), which in turn have concluded exclusive licenses limited to a certain field-of-use with third parties (third-party license). In addition, in the context of CRISPR-Cas9 technology there is also a discussion on the use of *ethical licenses* with the aim to prevent that licensees engage in research or application of the technology that raise problems with ethical concerns.

Importantly, as concerns surrogate licenses, it is first interesting to discuss the relation between the academic institutions and those partners that have been granted an exclusive license for the exploitation of the CRISPR-Cas9 technology. Importantly, if the academic institutions are shareholders or owners of the partner that has received a surrogate license, such arrangement may fall outside of Article 101(1) TFEU. According to the doctrine of an economic unit, agreements with undertakings that are controlled by the licensor are not viewed as agreements *between* undertakings. Accordingly, Article 101(1) TFEU would not capture such arrangements irrespectively of the conditions in such licenses.[28]

If surrogate licenses are concluded with independent undertakings, or if licenses are concluded between the surrogate licensor and independent third parties (third-party licensees), such arrangements could fall within Article 101(1) TFEU. Exactly which legal regime that would regulate such licenses, depends on the purpose of the license. As discussed above, if the surrogate licensor only exploits the technology by further R&D (including the use of a research tool), it could fall within the scope of the RBER. However, it is important to note that an arrangement whereby only one party would conduct R&D does not fall within the RBER. The RBER only captures "joint" R&D where there is a collaboration between two parties.[29] Granting a license for the purpose of R&D to another undertaking is not necessarily captured by the definitions of joint R&D. While the RBER covers paid-for research, defined as R&D carried out by one party and financed by another,[30] the task imposed on a licensee to license to third parties is not covered by the term R&D. In addition, the RBER also requires that the parties have full access to the results and may also require access to pre-existing know-how that the parties have "brought into" the R&D collaboration.[31] These requirements are too technical and complex to elaborate further on here, but it may be said that it seems unlikely that the current licensing arrangements on CRISPR-Cas9 technology would necessarily meet these requirements. Accordingly, licensing agreements where one party is merely given the permission to exploit patent rights to conduct research without involving any elaborated cooperation between the parties are likely to fail the preconditions for being covered by the RBER. In addition, such licenses with the purpose of R&D would also fall outside the TTBER. As regards R&D that is carried out by the surrogate licensor independently and that is not financed by the other party would also probably fall outside both the RBER and TTBER.[32] If the license however is used to manufacture and sell specific contract products, it falls under TTBER.

It follows that rules in the RBER are complex and may give rise to uncertainty of the coverage of R&D licensing agreements. This is also a theme that has been

28 Case C-73/95 P Viho Europe BV v Commission of the European Communities (EU:C:1996:405) (*Viho*), paras 16–17.

29 Article 1(1)(m) RBER, *supra* note 14.

30 *Ibid.*, Article 1(1)(a)(vi).

31 *Ibid.*, Article 3(2)–(3).

32 *Ibid.*, Article 1(1)(p).

raised in the Commission's review of the RBER and the Horizontal Guidelines. However, that discussion has mainly concerned the requirements of granting all parties to an R&D agreement full access to the results as well as pre-existing know-how.[33] The review does not seem to focus on the requirement of "joint" research which may also be problematic for surrogate license arrangements, including third-party licenses. Naturally, the current legal regime under the RBER and TTBER may raise problems of legal certainty as regards the licensing agreements that are concluded on CRISPR-Cas9 technology. In the worst case scenario, an ordinary licensing agreement for the purpose of R&D that does not entail any actual collaboration between the parties (like R&D conducted by a joint research team) may have to be assessed directly under Article 101 TFEU. On the other hand, if the license between an academic institution and surrogate licensor are non-competitors, which would seem likely considering that academic institutions are involved, it is unlikely that such a license would raise any competition concerns. An academic institution would in such cases not be involved in licensing to third parties of any technology in competition with the technology licensed by the surrogate licensor. Even if the surrogate licensor has a high market share, the license would probably be unproblematic as no competition is restricted between the parties. However, if the academic institution would continuously license technology exclusively to the surrogate licensor, which reinforces or maintains a position of market power of the latter, it could infringe Article 102 TFEU.[34]

The assessment may be more difficult as regards licenses between the surrogate licensor and licensees. As mentioned in the literature on CRISPR-Cas9 technology, it seems as surrogate licensors may engage in both further R&D of the technology as well as exploitation by licensing to third parties. In such cases, there is a greater likelihood that the surrogate licensor may constitute a competitor to the licensee (at the time of licensing or later), which can make the assessment under Article 101(1) TFEU more difficult, as agreements between competitors more easily can restrict competition. In addition, as it seems as surrogate licensors may grant exclusive licenses limited to particular fields-of use (see above, section 2), a network of such licenses may be seen as dividing market between licensees, where each licensee is granted exclusivity within a particular market. If those licensees could potentially be active in each other's

33 See, e.g., Commission Staff Working Document Evaluation of the Horizontal Block Exemption Regulations, 6.5.2021 SWD (2021) 103 final. See also the Inception impact assessment, available online at https://ec.europa.eu/competition-policy/public-consultations/2019-hbers_en.

34 Case T-51/89 Tetra Pak Rausing SA v. European Commission (EU:T:1990:41) (*Tetra Pak I*).

exclusive field-of use (and thereby compete), an assessment outside the block exemption regulations could be problematic under competition law.

In situations where a surrogate license or a third party-license fall within the RBER, the rules are fairly generous for granting exclusive licenses. Importantly, EU block exemptions are obsessively focused on territorial exclusivity. This is motivated by the protection of the single market (see above, Section 3.1) and the fact that territorial protection has the very purpose to restrict trade. However, the little information on the forms of governance of CRISPR-Cas9 technology indicates that exclusivity normally refers to field-of-use restrictions, for instance that a license is limited to the use for producing a particular variant of a plant. To begin with, the RBER recognizes this type of licensing restriction as form of specialization which falls under the RBER as long as the R&D collaboration is classified as joint R&D under the regulation.[35] Such licenses may also be exempted as they are not classified as hardcore restrictions,[36] as long as the license respect the market share thresholds discussed above (see above, Section 3.2).

In case a license (probably a third-party license) falls under the TTBER, the rules are more or less the same. In agreement between competitors, a field-of-use restriction is permitted under the condition that no field of use is imposed on the licensor and that the market share threshold of 20% is not exceeded.[37] In agreements between non-competitors, field of use restrictions imposed on both licensor and licensee are tolerated under the market share threshold of 30%.[38]

It is also pertinent to address the issue of so-called ethical licenses. It is discussed in the literature that ethical licenses may be used in order for patent holder to control the use of the technology by the licensee. Importantly, ethical licenses could be used by key patent holders to impose a form of self-regulation in the sector with the purpose of promoting ethical or other societal goals which are not directly connected to the economic aspects of exploiting the technology. Naturally, ethical licenses can be designed in different ways and with different restrictions which may or may not be problematic from EU Competition Law perspective. For instance, ethical licensing may include the obligation on the licensee to grant farmers rights to save and resew seeds for the next coming year.[39] One form of ethical licensing that is interesting for

35 Article 1(1)(m)(iii) and Article (1)(1)(n)–(o) RBER, *supra* note 14.
36 *Ibid.*, Article 5(b)(iii).
37 Article (4)(1)(c) TTBER, *supra* note 13; TT Guidelines, *supra* note 17, para 113.
38 Article 4(2) TTBER, *supra* note 13.
39 Sherkow 2017, *supra* note 6, pp.572–573.

competition law are licenses that prevent the use human genome editing technology, like CRISPR-Cas9, for certain uses that may raise ethical concerns,[40] such as the extreme example of Lulu and Nana, the genome-edited twins.[41] The key aspect from a competition law perspective is that such licenses permit companies to use the technology for particular uses while excluding the same companies from entering a particular market. Obviously, in theory, such licensing can be used for allocating markets between different parties, which restrict competition. Although it is not completely certain, such an "ethical" restriction imposed through a license would amount to a technical field-of-use restriction.[42] Currently, it seems likely that an ethical license would primarily be used in a R&D collaboration as the restriction is aimed at preventing a certain type of research rather than the application of already existing technology. Accordingly, such ethical licenses would be assessed in the same manner as the field-of-use restrictions discussed above.

As discussed above, a potential problem with field-of-use restrictions is that they can be used to divide up markets between different licensees, which could restrict competition. In particular, if such licenses would not fall under the block exemption regulations and involve a larger network of licensees which are granted a particular exclusive product market, they could potentially be struck down under the competition rules. However, it seems unlikely that the imposition of ethical restrictions through field-of-use restrictions could result in such a division of market. If the licensor genuinely prevents all licensees for applying the technology for some unethical uses, they would not result in carving out particular markets where only one licensee would be active. If the patent holder is consistent by excluding all licensees from a certain field-of-use, there should not be any problem under competition law.

Would an ethical license nonetheless be found to restrict competition, it should be noted that it may be difficult to justify such a restriction on ethical grounds. The exemption under Article 101(3) TFEU does not give much room for "soft" goals unconnected to the improvement of efficiency (by reducing costs or increasing quality of the product and services affected by the agreements entered into by the parties). And while there is case-law that supports that private parties may enter agreements that constitutes a form of self-regulation, such as setting rules of conduct for lawyers by a bar association or rules of the game in sports, it seems unlikely that this would apply to a self-regulation on

40 Feeney et al., *supra* note 1, p. 4.

41 Matthews et al., *supra* note 4, pp. 11–12.

42 TT Guidelines, *supra* note 17, para. 208.

the use of CRISPR-Cas9 technology.[43] Importantly, those cases have concerned the regulation of particular activities and professions, where the state has left the regulation of those activities to the sector itself. A self-regulation regarding CRISPR-Cas9 technology would firstly concern a much broader area as technology can be used for multitude of activities and markets. Moreover, several aspects of the technology are already directly or indirectly regulated by patent law, pharmaceutical law etc. At first glance, it appears therefore as it would be difficult to justify ethical field-of-use restrictions once a restriction of competition has been established in an individual case.

3.4 *Patent Pooling of CRISPR-Cas9 Technologies*

As mentioned above, some of the key patents protecting CRISPR-Cas9 technologies have been gathered in a patent pool run by the MPEG-LA.[44] It is initially important to underline that patent pools may be both good and bad from a competition law perspective. In the past, patent pools were controversial for their similarity to the most serious type of agreements restricting competition, so called cartel agreements. A cartel agreement exists when competitors agree to stop competing with each other, e.g., by setting a uniform price for their products or dividing up markets by categories of products or by territory. The pooling of patent rights covering competing technology which is sold to a uniform price does not differ from a cartel agreement. In addition, the pooling of all technology necessary for the production of particular products or services can also grant market power to the collective of patent holders that are members of a patent pool. Such patent holders could therefore impose unfair conditions or restrict competition when entering into agreements with users of the technology. Patent pools may however also be highly beneficial. By accumulating all necessary technology, it reduces the costs for users that only need to turn to one "seller" instead of having to negotiate several licensing agreements, which may create a "bottleneck" if a particular patent holder would be unwilling to license. If the patent pool has on beforehand set a royalty (or the price) that users have to pay for a license, there is also no risk that a licensee may be "blackmailed" to pay exorbitant royalties. Patent pools may also reduce costs for patent holders to supervise potential infringers of their patent rights as well as costs of enforcement. Patent pools that license the pooled technology to all

43 Case C-309/99 J.C.J. Wouters, J.W. Savelbergh and Price Waterhouse Belastingadviseurs BV v Algemene Raad van de Nederlandse Orde van Advocaten, intervener: Raad van de Balies van de Europese Gemeenschap, EU:C:2002:98; Case C-519/04 P David Meca-Medina and Igor Majcen v Commission of the European Communities, EU:C:2006:492.

44 Grobler et al., *supra* note 2, p. 168, Neville, *supra* note 5.

interested parties, without discrimination, may be an efficient way of disseminating technology.

Importantly, patent pools, including licenses from the patent pool to third party users, do not fall within the RBER or the TTBER. A patent pool is defined as an arrangement whereby two or more owners of patent rights (patent pool members) pool their patents for the purpose of licensing in between the patent pool members and/or to third parties (third-party users).[45] The patent pool as such can be organized in different ways. Patents may be licensed to a third party that in turn licenses to third-party users, or the patents are licensed to one of the patent pool members, which licenses to third-party users. The focus of the RBER lies on the R&D cooperation between two or more undertakings. Licensing of technology that constitutes the output of such collaboration, so-called exploitation of the results, falls within the RBER. The mere gathering together of a package of technology for the sole purpose of licensing to third parties thus falls outside the scope of the RBER.

As regards the TTBER, the focus lies on the licensing of technology for manufacturing and sales, which at first blush may give the impression of covering patent pools as the pooled technologies are licenses for the purpose of manufacture and sales of contract products. However, the agreements that encompasses a sharing of technology between the owners of the technology included in the patent pool do not have the purpose of manufacturing and sales.[46] In case the patent pool is created by the licensing to a third party that in turn licenses to third-party users, such an arrangement would also not have the purpose of manufacturing and sales. By contrast, a third-party license from the patent pool to interested users may have the purpose of manufacturing and sales. In such cases, the enabling regulation that gives the power to the Commission to adopt the TTBER limits the exemption of such licenses to be concluded between two parties.[47] A third party license is seen as involving not only the pool, but also its owners. Thus, even patent pools with only two members, would be classified as an agreement between at least three parties.[48] Accordingly, patent pool arrangements will always fall outside both the RBER and TTBER.

While patent pools and third-party licenses of the pooled technology do not benefit from the legal certainty of the RBER and TTBER, the TT Guidelines

45 TT Guidelines, *supra* note 17, para 244.

46 *Ibid.*, para 247.

47 Regulation No 19/65/EEC of 2 March of the Council on application of Article 85 (3) of the Treaty to certain categories of agreements and concerted practices, OJ [1965] 36/533, Article 1(1)(b).

48 TT Guidelines, *supra* note 17, para 247.

provide a 'safe harbor'. With a safe harbor it is meant that when pools meet the conditions stated in the TT Guidelines, they are presumed to fall outside Article 101(1) TFEU, irrespective of the parties' market positions.[49] Patent pools are deemed to fall within the safe harbor when the following conditions are met: participation is open to all interested technology right owners; there are sufficient safeguards to only include essential patents in the pool; there are safeguards to limit exchange of sensitive information to what is necessary for the creation and the operation of the pool; the patent pool has non-exclusive licenses on the essential patents; licenses are given on FRAND (Fair, Reasonable and Non-Discriminatory terms) to interested users; parties are free to challenge the validity and the essentiality of the pooled patents; patent pool member and third-party users are free to develop competing products and technology.[50]

The TT Guidelines state that there is no inherent link between patent pools and standardization.[51] Nonetheless, it seems as the safe harbor in the TT Guidelines has been designed in the light of arrangements concerning technical standards, which are typically applied in the sectors of telecom and electronics. This is illustrated, in particular, by the distinction between essential and non-essential patents, which is one relatively easy to make in technical standards as these are to some extent defined by the technology protected by the patent rights. The situation seems to be somewhat different in the biotech industry where standards cannot be "created" in the same fashion as in areas such as telecommunications.[52] Moreover, a patent pool on CRISPR-Cas9 technology may include technology for a variety of uses, which are therefore not "essential." Patent pools could also be used to resolve patent litigation issues by including those patent rights that are subject to litigation. Such an approach may facilitate for users that will not have to run the risk of infringing the patent of a third party even though they have already licensed the "necessary" technology from a patent holder which is involved in patent litigation. The reasons for creating a patent pool on CRISPR-Cas9 technologies may simply be different from the rationale behind patent pools that are connected to standardization. The problem is that such patent pools may fall afoul of the competition rules. It has been argued that a problem with pools including non-essential patent results is that they will not resolve the bottleneck issues that pools are

49 TT Guidelines, *supra* note 17, para 261.

50 *Ibid.*, para 261.

51 *Ibid.*, para 245.

52 Neville, *supra* note 5, p. 545.

supposed to resolve.[53] Accordingly, such patent pools may be seen as more "suspicious" by competition authorities. From a practical perspective, a pool that includes non-essential patents may not benefit from the safe harbor described above.[54] As a consequence, because of the uncertain status of patent pools under the competition rules, key patent holders may be discouraged from entering such arrangements. Importantly, as patent pools can be an efficient way of managing and disseminating key technology to a large group of potential users and for a variety of uses, competition law may delay or obstruct dissemination of technology that would be good for the market, market actors and ultimately the consumers.

3.5 *Refusal to License*

While the discussion above has concerned Article 101(1) TFEU and licensing, Article 102 TFEU may also be relevant for owners of the CRISPR-Cas9 technology. It has been reported that owners of technology have used exclusive licenses to certain undertakings for the commercial use of CRISPR-Cas9 technology. These licensees are in charge of either developing the technologies and/or sublicensing to third parties. The licensees have replaced the academic institutes with the task to commercially exploit the technology through the so-called *surrogate licensing*.[55] These licensees have subsequently licensed the technology to third parties for either therapeutic use or use in plant technology. It has also been identified as potential problem that the licensees, which are involved in both further developing and applying the technology, as well as licensing, may not have an incentive to license to certain third parties, as they may constitute a competitive threat. Considering that the technology is fairly new and that there may not be viable substitutes, there is a risk that the holder of such technology may be, at least temporarily be in a dominant position. Accordingly, if such a holder of key technology refuses to license to third parties, this may raise the issue of whether such a refusal constitutes an abuse under Article 102 TFEU. Although the assessment of whether a company is in a dominant position is crucial, it may be difficult with the limited amount of information available to make a determination of dominance at the moment. Below, the discussion will therefore be limited to the issue of abuse assuming that a holder of technology is found to be dominant.

Under Article 102 TFEU, refusal to supply goods and services may be found abusive in particular when such a refusal may result in that the dominant

53 Neville, *supra* note 5, p. 553.

54 TT Guidelines, *supra* note 17, paras 261(b) and 262.

55 Sherkow, *supra* note 6, p. 571.

undertaking eliminates competition on an adjacent market. Refusal to license intellectual property rights (IPRS) constitutes a 'branch' of the case law on refusal to supply. Because of the importance of IPRS for competition (through innovative activities) the Court has held a somewhat high threshold to find abuse in cases regarding refusal to license.

Refusal to license was first established as abuse in *Magill*.[56] The case concerned the refusal to license copyrights from three TV-broadcasters to a company that wanted to put together TV-listings of programs into a weekly magazine. Oddly, although those listings were hardly an expression of original and creative work, which is the protected subject-matter under copyright, those listings were protected under national copyright law. The Court held that the refusal to license constituted an abuse. It found that the refusal had prevented the emergence of new product; reserved an adjacent market to the dominant company by eliminating competition in the market; there were no objective justifications for the refusal.[57] In *Bronner*, the Court held that all refusal to supply cases also require the demonstration that the input product/services must be indispensable before an abuse can be established.[58] The confirmation of the indispensability requirement in refusal to licenses case follows from *IMS Health*.[59] Accordingly, a license must be considered as indispensable to enter the adjacent market for the product or service that incorporates the licensed technology.

The refusal to license cases, in essence, make a balance between the interest of maintaining competition and the protection of the interests under IPRS. Importantly, IPRS permit right holders to deny access to the use of an invention, artistic works, trademark, etc. The possibility to refuse a license constitute the very essence of IPRS. While it follows from *Magill*, *IMS Health* and *Microsoft* that under exceptional circumstances the interests of competition will triumph the protection afforded under IPRS, the threshold set by the case law is supposed to be relatively high.

In particular, the indispensability requirement normally sets a high threshold for finding an abuse in refusal to supply cases, although this may be

56 Joined cases C-241/91 P and C-242/91 P Radio Telefis Eireann (RTE) and Independent Television Publications Ltd (ITP) v Commission of the European Communities (EU:C:1995:98) (*Magill*).

57 *Ibid.*, paras 54–56.

58 Case C-7/97 Oscar Bronner GmbH & Co. KG v Mediaprint Zeitungs- und Zeitschriftenverlag GmbH & Co. KG, Mediaprint Zeitungsvertriebsgesellschaft mbH & Co. KG and Mediaprint Anzeigengesellschaft mbH & Co. KG (EU:C:1998:569) (*Bronner*), para 41.

59 Case C-418/01 IMS Health GmbH & Co. OHG v NDC Health GmbH & Co. KG (EU:C:2004:257) (*IMS Health*), para 38.

different for IPR protected inputs as discussed below. With indispensability it is meant that the company requiring access must show that it would not be possible to enter the (adjacent) market without a license from dominant undertaking. The requesting company must not to be able to get supplies from other undertakings and should not be able to produce the input on its own. It is not sufficient that without a license it would become less economically viable for the requesting company to offer the goods/services in the adjacent market. The fact that it would be less economically viable for the requesting company to produce the input because it is an undertaking with less turnover than the dominant undertaking does not amount to indispensability.[60] Thus, indispensability requires that a company which is comparable the dominant undertaking would not be able to reproduce the requested input.

In *Commercial Solvents* the Court found that alternative methods of production which could have afforded the requesting company an alternative source of supply could not be pursued in an industrial scale.[61] By contrast, in *Bronner*, the Court hinted that there were no barriers, legal or technical, for the requesting company to establish its distribution network (of magazines), even though the establishment and operating of such a network could have been more costly than getting access to the network of the dominant undertaking.[62]

As regards indispensability and IPRs, it follows that the license in *Magill* was *de facto* indispensable. Obviously, if the content of the TV-listings were protected by copyright, it would not be possible to produce an alternative input as the requesting company needed an exact copy of copyrighted materials. However, the situation in *Magill* could be viewed as an extreme case. It would be unusual that a piece of text would constitute an input that could not be substituted with something else. However, *IMS Health* also concerned the request for copyright related rights. The case concerned the use of a database structure which had been created by the company NDC Health. The database structure had been developed together with the dominant undertaking's customers. Some employees left NDC Health and created a competing service based on a database structure, which was more or less the same as the one offered by NDC Health and probably infringed the IPR protection on database structure. The case triggered litigation between the parties regarding the potential infringement of IPRs as well as competition law issues. Ultimately, the competition

60 *Bronner, supra* note 58, para 45.

61 Joined cases 6 and 7/73 Istituto Chemioterapico Italiano S.p.A. and Commercial Solvents Corporation v Commission of the European Communities (EU:C:1974:18) (*Commercial Solvents*), para 16.

62 *Bronner, supra* note 58, paras 44–45.

law case reached the Court through a preliminary ruling procedure. Assuming that there was a breach of NDC Health's IPRS, the Court found that the license was indispensable. As the database structure had been developed in cooperation with the customers, it was not really possible to offer services to those customers based on a system built on different structure.[63] Finally, in *Microsoft* the General Court (then the Court of First Instance) also found that a refusal to license so-called application interface protocols (API) constituted an abuse under Article 102 TFEU.[64] The APIS were also found to be indispensable as it was not possible to otherwise make programs (network server operating system) interoperable with Microsoft operating system (Windows). As Windows was found in approximately 90% of personal computers (PCS), a competitor on the network server market could not compete effectively without making their products with Windows. The APIS were probably covered by both copyright and patents. Arguably, the situation in *Microsoft* was somewhat different in comparison with the situations in *Magill* and *IMS Health*. In theory, there were alternative ways of achieving interoperability and it could also be discussed whether interoperability with Windows was necessary for companies to be active in the network server operating systems market.

What follows from cases on IPRS and indispensability is that the threshold may not be perceived as so high as when compared to other refusal to supply cases. The very purpose of an IPR is to grant a legal monopoly that permits its holder to prohibit the use of the protected subject-matter. If that subject matter is a necessary input, and it is not possible to compete on the market without such input, the indispensability requirement is met. Arguably, the situation may be somewhat different between different IPRS. It is unlikely that access to a trademark is deemed as indispensable. By contrast, a copyrighted artistic work which has a technical function may easier meet the requirement of indispensability.

As regards patents (which is more interesting for the purpose of this chapter), it is not unusual that there may be competing technologies that are protected by different patents. In addition, the distinction between different types of patents, process or product patents, may also affect the assessment under the indispensability requirement. If a particular product is covered by a patent, which constitutes its own market, the indispensability requirement will be met. As regards process patents, the situation is different as it is likely that there may several alternative processes that may be used to manufacture

63 *IMS Health*, *supra* note 59, para 29.

64 Case T-201/04 Microsoft Corp. v Commission of the European Communities (EU:T:2007:289) (*Microsoft*).

a certain product. That process patents may grant less protection, is evident from antitrust cases on pay-for-delay where pharma companies have obviously attempted to protect their products with agreements as process patents have been possible to circumvent.[65] In addition, as regards technology that is essential to a standard (standard essential patent — SEP), it follows that users cannot substitute the protected technology, unless there are other competing standards that could be used to enter the market.[66] Accordingly, it is more likely that an SEP will be deemed as indispensable when compared with other types of patents.

Another essential requirement in refusal to license cases concerns the prevention of the marketing of a new product. Importantly, if the case law on refusal to license is compared to case on refusal to supply, this requirement is what provides or should provide IPRs with extra protection.[67] It could however be discussed to what extent this requirement actually provide protection in cases concerning patent as discussed below.

The criterion of the prevention of a new product was established in *Magill*. As explained above, in that case the refusal to license copyright protected lists directly prevented the compiling of those lists into a weekly TV-magazine. The idea behind the requirement of the prevention of new products could be seen as an expression that in the balance between the competition and IPRs, the consumer's interest in innovation ultimately takes precedence over the interest protected by IPRs. In *Magill*, in particular the judgment by the Court of First Instance, the discussion of possible objective justifications did not indicate that the interests to protect by the copyright in question would be under threat.[68] Thus, *Magill* and the following case law should not be interpreted as that competitive harm to innovation will always triumph the interests of the IPR holder. A balance must be made. On one hand is necessary to establish that new products and services are prevented, while on the other hand it must be assessed that the IPR holder cannot objectively justify its refusal. In particular, an objective justification may be raised on the grounds that the interests protected by the IPR may be undermined. While this may sound like a fair balancing exercise, it is not certain that the balancing is so fair after the Court's judgment in *IMS Health*. As explained above, the rival company that requested

65 Case C-307/18 Generics (UK) Ltd and Others v Competition and Markets Authority (EU:C:2020:52).

66 Case C-170/13 Huawei Technologies Co. Ltd v ZTE Corp. and ZTE Deutschland GmbH (EU:C:2015:477) (*Huawei*), paras 49–50.

67 As the requirement does not apply to ordinary refusal to supply cases. *Microsoft*, *supra* note 64, para 334.

68 Case T-76/89 Independent Television Publications Ltd v Commission of the European Communities, EU:T:1991:41, paras 57–59.

a license had basically used the same structure for its own database that it offered for sale. While the Court probably did not intend to depart from its approach in *Magill*, it could be discussed whether the Court's statement *de facto* lowered the requirement of a new product. The requirement would be met as long as the requesting company's product would not essentially duplicate the product/service supplied by the dominant undertaking.[69] The statement by the Court could be interpreted as meaning that a small added functionality in the rival's product could meet the requirement. In *Microsoft*, the Court of First Instance definitely lowered the bar, as it declared that the new product requirement was not an absolute requirement.[70] In practice, the refusal in the case prevented the marketing of already existing products, namely the network server operating system that were present on the market until Microsoft had stopped providing the APIs. It has been suggested that *Microsoft* gives an expression for the view that the prevention of the sales of "old products" *potentially* would hinder a form of follow-innovation by preventing the development of products competing with Microsoft's own network server operating system. Arguably, the judgment seems to give a very broad view of innovation. Reading *IMS Health* and *Microsoft*, it could be debated how strong protection the case law on refusal to license actually grants to IPRs. This may be problematic, in particular, when it comes down to the protection of patent rights. Most innovation builds upon previous technology and incremental follow-on innovation may simply encompass relatively small changes to inventions covered by previous patents.

Discussing the case law on refusal to license in relation to situation in human genome editing technology two observations should be made. Firstly, as concerns the requirement of indispensability, it should be noted that although the key technology related to the CRISPR-Cas9 system has been described as revolutionizing, there are previous systems that have been used for genome editing. Zinc-finger nucleases (ZFN) and transcription activator-like effector nucleases (TALEN) are two systems that may be used for genome editing.[71] From a competition law perspective, the issue arises whether the potential refusal to license could amount to an abuse in the presence of less efficient substitutes. Naturally, there is too little information to make a full-scale assessment here, meaning that the following discussion is somewhat speculative. To what an extent alternative technology actually constitutes a substitute in an individual case depends partly on the purpose the technology is used for. The

69 *IMS Health*, *supra* note 59, para. 49.

70 *Microsoft*, *supra* note 64, para. 647.

71 Feeney et al., *supra* note 1.

CRISPR-Cas9 has been described as being potentially useful for a number of different therapeutic uses as well as use in plant technology. Arguably, the use of the CRISPR-Cas9 can be divided up in a number of different field-of-use which according to competition law probably constitute different and separate product markets. Competition in each one of those markets defined by a field-of-use is dependent on the access to genome editing technology in each respective market. Accordingly, it should be possible to capture a refusal to license only within one field-of-use. Thus, whether previous technology like ZFN and TALEN constitute substitutable technology in the sense of the Court's statement in *Bronner*, depends on the specific quality of those technologies for the application within the specific field-of-use. In addition, the facts that CRISPR-Cas9 is a more efficient technology does not necessarily mean that it is indispensable. Rather, the assessment must be made objectively by determining if an efficient competitor would be able to use the alternative technology to enter and compete on the market. Only in the case that the use of the alternative technology would be costly to the extent that efficient competitor would not be able to be active on the market, the CRISPR-Cas9 technology would be classified as indispensable *within that specific field of use.*

Secondly, it is also interesting to address the requirement of a new product. It should initially be noted that there has not been a 'hard' case on refusal to license putting the interest of protecting patent rights and innovation on the one hand, and competition through innovation on the other. While such a discussion was touched upon in *Microsoft*, the General Court found that the parties requesting the APIs would hardly have the capability (nor the interest) to clone Microsoft's operating system.[72] Thus, similar to *Magill*, it could not be established that a refusal to license would *de facto* threaten the incentives to create of the dominant undertaking. Arguably, the situation would be quite different in the biotech sector, in particular regarding the CRISPR-Cas9 technology. It could be argued that a party requesting a license to CRISPR-Cas9 technology could in many cases claim that the refusal to license would prevent the emergence of new product (as follows from *Magill* and *IMS Health*) or follow-on innovation (as implied by *Microsoft*). The problem with such a reasoning is that a compulsory license would probably also threaten the patent holder's incentives to invent. A full protection of patent rights should encompass the social value of the patent. The social value includes the value created for society as a whole and would include the potential uses of the technology that its holder have not developed. It could be argued that the very purpose of a patent is to give the patent holder control of the development of the patented

72 *Microsoft, supra* note 59, para 700.

technology. If the patent holder could not realize the social value of the patent, there is a risk that the initial incentives to R&D of the protected invention are not sufficiently protected, which would decrease more generally the incentives to innovate. Naturally, it could be counterargued that even a 'compulsory license' under EU Competition Law would encompass royalties for the patent holder. However, the literature on compulsory licensing does not express a positive view on state actors determining royalties, as these have a tendency to undervalue the patent holder's technology. It is also important to make a distinction between *Microsoft* and the situation described above. Importantly, the request for a license in that case concerned the possibility for interoperability between the requesting undertaking's products and Microsoft's operating system, while the situation above would explicitly concern the application or the further development of the patented invention(s) on CRISPR-Cas9 technology. Arguably, the threat to incentives to innovate should be seen as more severe.

4 Conclusions

Importantly, competition law may affect the exploitation of human genome editing technology particularly by limiting and to some extent regulating the methods that holders of key patents on human genome editing technology may apply when collaborating with other market actors. In addition, EU Competition Law may theoretically also be used, in very exceptional circumstances, to get access to such key technology which would otherwise be held by a *de facto* monopolist. Accordingly, competition law may mainly affect the *dissemination* of human genome editing technology.

It follows from the discussion above that competition law may in some instances discourage dissemination because of problems of legal certainty. There is particularly an uncertainty about if and which block exemption that may apply to agreements that are part of surrogate licensing scheme. As falling outside a block exemption creates a serious situation of uncertainty about the legality of the agreements in question, considering that the application of the exemption rule in Article 101(3) TFEU is complex and difficult, it is important for technology holders to make sure that their licenses fall within one of the block exemptions. However, the scope of the block exemption regarding research (RBER) is particularly difficult to assess in relation to agreements licensing the technology to a surrogate licensor, as well as licenses between the surrogate licensor and licensees. As these agreements do not necessarily relate to research activities that are genuinely carried out *jointly*, they may simply not be covered by the RBER. At the same time, as such agreements may be entered into at a relative early stage of research and development, they are not likely to be covered by the block exemption regulation that applies to technology transfer (TTBER). The uncertainty regarding surrogate licensing arrangements may potentially trigger two responses. Either technology holders may apply such licensing arrangements running the risk to be struck down by competition law at a later stage or they can adapt their licensing arrangements to make them "fit" with the current block exemption regulations. Arguably, there is nothing that indicates that technology holders could not apply other form of methods of dissemination than surrogate licensing that may satisfy their needs and that will result in a widespread dissemination of human genome editing technology. On the other hand, it may also be that surrogate licensing schemes are the most *efficient* way for technology holders to arrange licensing to potential users of the technology and to diversify the follow-on research and the use of the technology amongst several users that in turn are specialized in particular branch of the technology. Surrogate licensing may also permit the technology holders to keep sufficient control over certain parts of the technology, while granting access to other fields-of-use to other market actors. It would be counterproductive for competition law to discourage an efficient form of disseminating the technology and it may also complicate arrangements that would promote further follow-on innovation or the further development of the commercial applications of human genome editing technology. From a wider perspective, competition law *could potentially* delay or obstruct the spread of technology and thereby some of the benefits to public health that the technology is supposed to deliver.

Another type of collaboration discussed above which give rise to issues of uncertainties under EU Competition Law is the potential use patent pools for disseminating key technology. While patent pools have always been controversial in EU competition law, it cannot be denied that this form of IPR management is an effective way of opening access to may potential users, which may lead to a widespread use of the technology that can lead to more competition in particular branches of human genome editing technology as well as faster development of commercialization of applications of the technology that may reach end-consumers. The current state of the competition rules on patent pools seems particularly be adapted to the needs of the telecom and electronics industries. While patent pools do not enjoy that same legal certainty as other licensing agreements by block exemptions, the Commission has at least provided a so-called safe harbor for patent pool arrangements that fulfil certain conditions. However, it is doubtful whether those conditions can be easily met by a patent pool in the biotech sector, in particular as concerns the requirement that the pooled technology should be limited to essential patent rights. If this preliminary conclusion is correct, no safe harbor for patent pools may be available for the management of key patent rights on human genome editing technology. This may, potentially, close the door for an efficient method of disseminating the technology in question. Importantly, the importance of patent pools should not be overstated, as it is uncertain whether this type of licensing arrangements ultimately will be widespread. At the moment, there is only one patent pool on human genome editing technology, and there have been doubts expressed about its future success.[73]

What the discussion above demonstrates is that there is unclarity about the application of competition law to different methods of disseminating technology that seem to be important in this particular sector. While it has not been argued above that the application of competition law will necessarily strike down these forms of dissemination, the legal uncertainty is problematic as such. This may call for a calibration of the current rules in competition law, in particular the scope of the RBER. However, the revision of the RBER is currently at a late stage and the discussion so far does not seem to have been focused on the particular needs in the biotech industry. However, there is a possibility for the Commission to also make revisions in its soft law that accompany the RBER. It may be good idea for the Commission to anticipate issues in the biotech industry, like licensing arrangements related to R&D cooperation regarding human genome editing technology, which are likely to raise competition law issues in the coming ten years.

Finally, it should also be noted that competition law may open up, although in very exceptional circumstances, for the possibility demanding a compulsory license from a patent holder that refuses to license key technology that is indispensable for the production of certain novel goods or services that will satisfy demand for end-consumers. This application of competition law may hinder IPR holder to monopolize (existing or potential) markets for products and services that do not merely reproduce what the IPR holder already offers, but which provides an added value to consumers for which there is demand. Arguably, this line of case law within competition law could potentially be relevant for human genome editing technology, as the key patents for CRISPR-Cas9 technology, can be used for a wide set of potential uses, some of which have not been developed yet. Additionally, it is unlikely that patent holders of such technology could exploit on their own the technology for all possible uses. Accordingly, competition law could be used to force licensing in order to promote competition and to hinder a patent holder from becoming a gatekeeper. From a societal perspective, such an application of competition

73 Neville, *supra* note 5, p. 566.

law could speed up dissemination that could ultimately benefit consumers by e.g. allowing the development of treatments or plant varieties, activities which the patent holder would either not have engaged in or monopolized. However, to grant compulsory licenses may also have a negative effect on patent holders' incentives to engage in R&D of innovations such as the CRISPR-Cas9 technology. Arguably, there is no "hard" case under competition law where the granting of a compulsory license would truly negatively affect the incentives for developing a patent protected technology. In this author's view, the possibility to force licensing with the help of competition law should be used restrictively to technology such as CRISPR-Cas9, as it may otherwise open up for abuse from those that may want to get access to the technology. A patent holder should as a starting point legitimately be able to hold on to the exclusivity granted under a patent right and to be able to control the further development and application of the technology. If a compulsory license is to be granted under competition law, it should be established that such a license will truly bring benefits to consumers by the introduction of something novel (for instance, by hindering a particular new treatment to a disease or the development of a new plant that is more resistant to certain diseases), when the reward for developing the patent protected technology is genuinely at risk. Such a view would probably require a stricter assessment of certain conditions for finding an abusive refusal to license and a more lenient approach as regards the possibilities to justify such a refusal under the current case law.

Index of Subjects

Index of Legal Sources

Index of Judicial Cases

Court of Justice of the European Union

National Decisions

www.ingramcontent.com/pod-product-compliance
Lightning Source LLC
Chambersburg PA
CBHW050521240926
51846CB00003B/650
* 9 7 8 9 0 0 4 5 2 6 0 8 2 *